Assessment for Instructional Planning in Special Education

Assessment for Instructional Planning in Special Education

Naomi Zigmond
University of Pittsburgh

Ada Vallecorsa
University of North Carolina at Greensboro

Rita Silverman
Rutgers University

Prentice-Hall, Inc.
ENGLEWOOD CLIFFS, NEW JERSEY 07632

Library of Congress Cataloging in Publication Data

ZIGMOND, NAOMI, *(date)*
    Assessment for instructional planning in special
education.

    Bibliography: p.
    Includes index.
    1. Educational tests and measurements.   2. Ability testing.   3. Exceptional children—Education.
I. Vallecorsa, Ada, *(date)*.   II. Silverman, Rita, *(date)*.   III. Title.
LB3051.Z54   1983   371.9   82-14995
ISBN 0-13-049643-X

Editorial/production supervision and
    interior design by Tom Aloisi
Page layout by Meryl Poweski and Diane Koromhas
Manufacturing buyer: Ron Chapman

Printed in the United States of America

10 9 8 7 6 5 4 3 2 1

ISBN 0-13-049643-X

Prentice-Hall International, Inc., *London*
Prentice-Hall of Australia Pty. Limited, *Sydney*
Editora Prentice-Hall do Brasil, Ltda., *Rio de Janeiro*
Prentice-Hall of Canada, Inc., *Toronto*
Prentice-Hall of India Private Limited, *New Delhi*
Prentice-Hall of Japan, Inc., *Tokyo*
Prentice-Hall of Southeast Asia Pte. Ltd., *Singapore*
Whitehall Books Limited, *Wellington, New Zealand*

Contents

The figures listed in the Table of Contents will be particularly useful in implementing the *Assessment for Instructional Planning*. They may be reprinted or reproduced for personal use.

5 Assessment of Written Expression   127
(Vallecorsa, Silverman, and Zigmond)

6 Assessment of Mathematics   203
(Silverman and Zigmond)

7 **Assessment of Learning Style, Interest, and Motivators   269**
(Silverman and Zigmond)

PART III
PUTTING IT ALL TOGETHER

8 **Organizing and Managing the Assessment Process   307**
(Vallecorsa and Zigmond)

9 **Concluding Comments   341**
(Zigmond)

Preface

Over the past few years, many educators have come to realize the essential role that assessment plays in educational practice. Information gathered in an assessment contributes to educational decision-making in a variety of ways: assessment for screening purposes leads to an initial identification of deviant behavior; assessment for classification leads to labeling and educational placement; assessment for evaluation of pupil progress leads to information on how effective an educational program has been; assessment for instructional planning leads to decisions regarding what and how to teach. It is this last type of assessment which is the focus of this text.

Assessment for Instructional Planning offers the reader a strategy for planning and implementing the assessment. It provides clear and systematic procedures for where and how to begin, guidelines for selecting or developing assessment instruments, techniques for interpreting assessment findings, and methods for organizing and managing the assessment procedure within the day-to-day realities of elementary and secondary schools. Our emphasis is on the use of informal, teacher-made tests for obtaining instructional planning information. We do not review formal published tests; there are several texts on assessment available which provide excellent reviews of the content and technical adequacy of published tests. In our discussion of test development and test selection, however, we do refer the reader to published tests as alternative sources of assessment data. In all such cases, we are recommending these published tests for gathering *performance data* only. We do not recommend utilizing the *scores* themselves, since, in many instances, reliability information is either inadequate or totally absent. Of necessity, we have limited our text to assessment of reading, written expression, and mathematics, certain dimensions of learning style, and interest and responsiveness to motivators. In a book of this size, we felt we could not also deal with several other topics which may have relevance for instructional planning, such as assessment of setting or curriculum demands, knowledge of content, vocational aptitude or social skill competence. Nevertheless, we believe that we have provided a discussion of the most critical areas of assessment for teachers of children and adolescents with special needs. And although the numerous case studies found throughout the text concentrate on assessment of handicapped students who may be in programs for the learning disabled, emotionally disturbed, or mentally retarded, and on underachieving students in remedial or compensatory education, it is our hope that this book will be useful to *any* educator, clinician, diagnostician or consultant who is responsible for creating and implementing individualized educational programs.

The text is organized into three parts. **Part I** provides the theoretical foundation for the assessment strategy. In Chapter 1 we introduce the principles which underlie our approach to assessment for instructional planning. Chapter 2 is devoted to a discussion of the characteristics of good tests, and techniques for interpreting test results. Chapter 3 presents our twelve-step assessment strategy. **Part II** of the text puts theory into practice. The strategy described in Chapter 3 is applied to the major skill areas, with case studies to illustrate the approach. A substantial portion of Part II is devoted to assessment of *what* to teach. Chapter 4 demonstrates the use of the strategy in assessing reading. Chapter 5 demonstrates the strategy in assessing written language. Chapter 6 applies the strategy to assessment of mathematics. Techniques for determining *how* to teach are presented in Chapter 7. **Part III** of the text addresses the problems of organizing and managing the assessment strategy with a classroom. Chapter 8 provides the reader with guidelines for how to get the assessment underway in a self-contained class or resource room. Chapter 9 offers a review of the major principles underlying the approach and some concluding comments on the assessment process.

Found throughout the text are sample recordkeeping forms. We have designed them to be particularly useful to a teacher in implementing the assessment for instructional planning. We have highlighted these figures by listing them in the Table of Contents. These figures may be reproduced or reprinted for personal use. Some of the teacher-made tests which are introduced in the text are reprinted in Appendix F. These may also be reproduced for personal use.

This book is the product of a long-term collaboration among the three of us. We each contributed to the initial conceptualization of the text and to the development of the strategy for assessment described in it. One of us then had responsibility for developing the first drafts of each chapter: Naomi Zigmond— Chapters 1 and 9; Ada Vallecorsa—Chapters 3, 5(part) and 8; Rita Silverman— Chapters 2, 4, 5(part), 6 and 7. Subsequently, we worked together on the entire manuscript so that the final text represents a truly collaborative work.

Many people provided invaluable assistance and encouragement to us during the preparation of this book. We wish to thank Warren Crown, Mary W. Moore, Jan Sansone, and Sharon Stanek for reading early versions of the manuscript and for their helpful comments and criticisms. We are also grateful to the administrators, teachers and students in the Division for Exceptional Children, Pittsburgh Public Schools, in whose classrooms we developed and refined our assessment procedures. We thank Pat Graw for typing the manuscript and Nancy Blatnica for preparing all the figures and tables. And we acknowledge with deep appreciation the support of our families and friends throughout the months that we have been preoccupied.

N.Z., A.V., and R.S.

Assessment for Instructional Planning in Special Education

1

Assessing Students' Skills: An Introduction

This book has been designed to help teachers to teach well. What is "good teaching"? Good teaching is systematic teaching with carefully planned instructional sequences. Good teaching is interesting lessons that motivate the student to learn. Good teaching requires that the teacher understand what needs to be taught to each individual student and design instructional programs which meet that need. Good teaching requires assessment.

Assessment is a process of collecting information about students and interpreting the likely meaning of that information for educational decision-making. Over the last few years many educators have come to realize the essential role that assessment can play in educational practice. Assessment of newborns, infants, and young children can lead to early identification of serious physical and cognitive disorders and to early initiation of treatment programs. Assessment of students as they enter school can lead to recognition of high-risk learners for whom preventive or compensatory educational programs might be provided. Assessment for classification of students as exceptional can permit some students access to special education and related services and to more appropriate educational programs and placement. Assessment for evaluation of pupil progress can provide information on how effective an educational program has been. Assessment for instructional planning can help the teacher to decide what and how to teach.

Each of these types of assessment has a different goal. Each utilizes different sets of instruments and different sets of activities. Each poses different questions. Our focus in this book is on *assessment for instructional planning*. It is this assessment that is carried out by the teacher after the student has been assigned to a remedial program. It does not tell the teacher how the student came to be assigned or what may have caused the learning problems, but it does tell the teacher what to do and, as such, is an essential ingredient in the remedial process.

BASIC ASSUMPTIONS

Before we begin to describe the specific approach advocated in this text, there are several issues to be addressed. First, this is a noncategorical, or cross-categorical, assessment book. It is designed for teachers of underachieving students. These students may be in classes for the learning disabled, the emotionally disturbed, or the mentally retarded, or they may be in remedial or compensatory education classes. In our view the need for thoughtful and thorough assessment practices applies regardless of the label attached to the student or the funding sources for the class. This book reflects our concern that all underachieving students be taught well. It does not deal extensively with the known and/or hypothesized characteristics of these students themselves. It may be that there are real differences among these special populations, but our experience has shown that the decisions on how to teach underachieving students are made on the basis of individual profiles and not on the basis of label. We will try in this book to describe techniques and procedures that are equally appropriate to any student who is experiencing difficulty in learning basic skills.

Second, we make no claims that the idea of assessment for instructional plannning is new. There is general agreement among educators that one of the hallmarks of good teaching is careful assessment. And, without adequate assessment, selection of a teaching plan for any student or set of students is haphazard, if not impossible. Many teachers assess their students. They gather information from daily work using worksheets, questions, or quizzes. They administer standardized achievement tests, diagnostic tests, or curriculum mastery tests. They collect samples of student performance. They keep anecdotal records on student behavior. But teachers are not always systematic about this data collection. They do not always know what is especially useful information to collect. Furthermore, not all teachers know what to do with the information once it is collected or what are appropriate educational program decisions to make for the student on the basis of this information. Although most teachers accept the premise that assessment is important, and implement some assessment activities, they are not always able to carry out assessments that are actually useful in their day-to-day planning. This book is designed for in-service teachers who want to make their assessment activities more useful and for preservice teachers who will use these assessment techniques to become effective teachers.

Third, the Individualized Educational Program (IEP) requirement written into Public Law 94–142 has formalized the special educator's commitment to a diagnostic-prescriptive model of instructional programming. The IEP requirement has forced many teachers to look more carefully at their assessment findings and to try to glean from them the information that must be written on the IEP. Teachers who never engaged in assessment practices before have begun to do so in order to complete the IEP. But the IEP is only a recordkeeping tool which describes the link between assessment findings and instructional goals. Generating information for the IEP is not the reason for doing assessment for instructional planning. We did not write this book to help teachers write IEPs, although the information contained will certainly be helpful in that regard. Were there no federal or state mandate to write IEPs, we would still be addressing the issue of assessment for instructional planning. We firmly believe that without an assessment that leads to specific instructional goals for students, teachers of underachieving students cannot teach well.

Finally, while we are clearly committed to having teachers carry out an assessment before planning instruction, and are devoting an entire book to detailing how this is done, we must emphasize at the outset that the most important activity for teachers to engage in is not assessment but teaching. Teachers have an awesome responsibility. Teachers must help students resistant to instruction to learn skills they will need in order to manage their lives successfully. They must help students to learn what they cannot learn on their own and what others have failed to teach them. And there is no time to waste, not in the elementary school or in the high school. There is already precious little time in which to get this important job done. Assessment for instructional planning can help to make the teaching more targeted, more precise, more efficient, and more likely to succeed. Without such an assessment, we believe that the remedial teaching is unlikely to be as effective as possible. But it is the teaching that is critical. Therefore, assessment, as important as it is, cannot take too much time. It must be quick, efficient, and easily interpreted. It must lead the teacher to immediate and sensible instructional decisions. To do this kind of assessment takes more than knowledge about available tests. It requires that the teacher have a plan, a strategy for deciding what information needs to be collected and how to collect, record, and interpret that information. The purpose of this book is to help teachers to develop this assessment strategy.

PRINCIPLES WHICH GUIDE THE ASSESSMENT FOR INSTRUCTIONAL PLANNING

Several principles have guided us in the formulation of the specific procedures suggested in this book. All will be described in some detail because they are the basis for our approach.

1. *The teacher has the flexibility to make choices in terms of what to teach and how to teach each student.*

Some teachers of underachieving students find that they are working with a prescribed curriculum, a required textbook, and even a time schedule for covering the content they are expected to teach. When teachers are locked into such a prescribed routine, the kind of assessment that we are describing in this text will not apply as well. These teachers will find that many of the ideas suggested in this book can be adapted to fit into their instructional regimen, but it will take some ingenuity. However, when teachers are permitted some flexibility, when they can choose to teach basic skills instead of subjects like English literature, science, or social studies; when they can choose which basic skills each student will be taught; when they can choose the materials with which to teach those skills; and when they can choose the motivators used for keeping students interested and on-task, then this book on assessment procedures will be invaluable. It will show the teacher how to make the best use of the choices to be made.

2. *The initial assessment will not be exhaustive.*

An assessment for instructional planning is not expected to tell a teacher everything there is to know about a student. It will not provide an exhaustive listing of what each student does and does not know. Instead, the assessment for instructional planning will be done quickly; it will tell the teacher where to get started. The assessment for instructional planning will be an ongoing process, with additional information on what each student does and does not know forthcoming in the course of teaching.

Our strategy of assessment for instructional planning is different from the assessment models implied by the IEP mandate and by the typical diagnostic-prescriptive teaching cycle. These models suggest an exhaustive initial assessment that would permit the writing of an extensive plan for instruction. These models suggest a one-year cycle of test-teach-test. Ours does not. Ours utilizes a very short test-teach-test cycle, an almost daily updating of assessment and planning information on the part of the teacher. We do not expect the teacher to write a year-long, specific IEP on the basis of the initial assessment. It may be possible to record a general projection of what needs to be taught, but only that. We also believe that continuous and specific assessments imbedded in teaching are more efficient and, in the long run, more useful than long and exhaustive assessments each fall designed to provide a year's worth of short-term and long-term objectives. Figure 1-A reflects our approach. This approach emphasizes the importance of teaching. It suggests that a

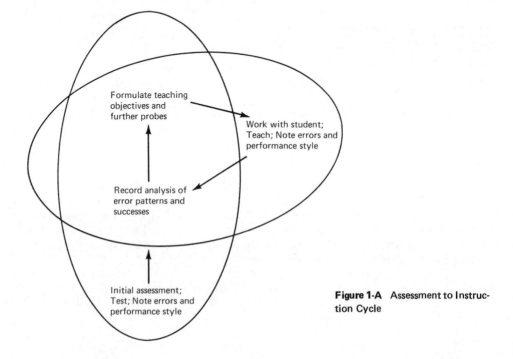

Formulate teaching
objectives and
further probes

Work with student;
Teach; Note errors and
performance style

Record analysis of
error patterns and
successes

Initial assessment;
Test; Note errors and
performance style

Figure 1-A Assessment to Instruction Cycle

significant part of teaching is the recording of student error patterns, the analysis of student behaviors, and the specification of new teaching objectives. We call this response-contingent instruction. Figure 1-A illustrates a quick turnaround of the test-teach-test cycle. It puts the initial assessment for instructional planning into perspective.

3. *The assessment plan will proceed from survey level assessment to probes.*

For the assessment to be efficient in terms of teacher and student time and effort, it must yield usable information quickly. Therefore, our strategy calls for beginning with *survey level assessments*. The purpose of the survey is to obtain a broad sample of the student's behavior across the range of the abilities of interest to the teacher. The behavior sample may be derived from having the student take a test, complete a teacher-made task, or carry out a class assignment. The survey provides an overview of the skills the student seems to have mastered and those which seem to be lacking. The student's performance on the survey allows the teacher to begin to see where the problems may lie. It is a first look—a chance for the student to show what he/she can and cannot do. The survey quickly generates global information.

Once the survey sample has been obtained, the teacher's attention is focused on the student's incorrect responses. Assumed causes for the errors are generated by either an analysis of the errors themselves or an analysis of the stimuli which elicited the errors. The survey is then followed up by *probes*, or in-depth analyses, designed to verify the presence of errors, to investigate the assumed causes of the errors, and/or to obtain more specific information. The probes provide a level of detail that permits the teacher to pinpoint the deficiencies and, in so doing, to generate a remediation plan.

A survey can be thought of as a test which provides a very general sample of the student's ability to perform in a particular area, while a probe may be viewed as a much more specific and precise measure of performance. For example, a survey of math computation might include a few addition, subtraction, multiplication, and division problems using whole numbers as well as fractions and decimals. Figure 1-B illustrates what such a survey might look like. After administering this survey to a fifth-grade student, the teacher might find that the student performed well on some of the problems, made errors on the subtraction and the division items, and failed to complete all items involving fractions. Having obtained this profile on the survey, the teacher would speculate that some math skills are known and some are not known. He/she would then probe to verify this speculation and to determine more precisely what must be taught and where instruction should begin.

The teacher's selection of one or more probes would follow a logical plan. First, the probes would be used to verify that there is a problem in basic skill performance. To do this, the teacher would select probes which test the same skills as those tested on the survey, but they would be tested in a different way. That is, the first probe might change the manner in which the problems are presented or the way in which the student is expected to respond. A math survey consisting of printed numbers might be followed by a probe of math problems presented orally, or with real objects that could be manipulated to demonstrate the problem. Here the probes have varied the presentation (stimulus) mode of the survey. A probe could also alter the student's response mode. A survey which required the student to write his/her answers could be followed with a probe in which responses were to be given aloud,

1. 46
    +23

2. 67
    +44

3. 571
    +869

4. 186
    37
    20
    +462

5. 87
    -42

6. 51
    -38

7. 506
    - 69

8. 834
    -597

9. 43
    x2

10. 76
     x8

11. 57
     x63

12. 478
     x243

13. $7\overline{)84}$

14. $6\overline{)925}$

15. $9\overline{)2747}$

16. $27\overline{)5844}$

17. 4.52 + 6.38 =

18. 43.8 - 3.82 =

19. 2.93
     x 4.2

20. $1.4\overline{)1.88}$

21. $7\overline{)93.2}$

22. $.21\overline{)109}$

23. $\frac{4}{8}$
     $+\frac{1}{8}$

24. $\frac{3}{6}$
     $+\frac{2}{5}$

25. $\frac{9}{12}$
     $-\frac{3}{12}$

26. $\frac{7}{8}$
     $-\frac{2}{3}$

27. $\frac{4}{7} \times \frac{1}{3} =$

28. $\frac{1}{2} \div \frac{1}{3} =$

Figure 1-B Math Skills Survey

drawn, constructed, or selected from an array. These first sets of probes, which systematically vary the stimulus and/or response characteristics of the survey, help the teacher to determine if there are testing conditions under which the student *can* perform a skill.

If it is clear from the survey or an initial probe that the student cannot perform the skill, a different set of probes would be administered. These provide detailed information as to which specific subskills or prerequisite skills the student

1. 8 - 3 = _____	2. 9 - 6 = _____	3. 6 - 5 = _____

4. 13	5. 12	6. 17	7. 11	8. 10
- 4	- 5	- 8	- 3	- 2

9. 27	10. 38	11. 96	12. 82
- 5	- 4	-25	-30

13. 748	14. 694	15. 355	16. 35
- 26	-524	-120	- 8

17. 72	18. 91	19. 84	20. 457
- 5	-39	-77	- 28

21. 756	22. 585	23. 712	24. 607
- 92	-288	-164	-429

25. 300	26. 5678	27. 3001
-126	-2981	-1234

Figure 1-C Subtraction Probe

has mastered and which need to be taught. If that fifth-grade student was unable to perform subtraction problems presented under stimulus and response conditions different from those of the survey in Figure 1-B, a subtraction probe like the one presented in Figure 1-C might be administered. It includes sums which measure the student's ability to solve problems involving subtraction of single digit, two-digit, and three-digit numbers; sums calling for regrouping; and sums involving complex subtraction. Clearly, the teacher would have a better picture of a student's instructional needs with respect to subtraction after administering such a probe. But it would not have been an efficient use of time to administer this detailed probe right from the start, given the student's facility with some aspects of the survey.

The "survey to probe" principle is summarized in Figure 1-D. Assessments which are guided by this principle save time, help the teacher to be logical about collecting assessment data, and provide information that leads easily to the development of intervention strategies.

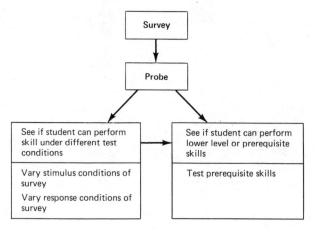

Figure 1-D Survey to Probe

4. For efficiency, the assessment for instructional planning will proceed from the top down, i.e., teachers will "test down" hierarchies of behavior rather than "test up" them.

Before initiating the assessment, the teacher thinks about each skill-domain of interest as consisting of a hierarchical set of behaviors ranging from the lowest level, or easiest form, of that skill to the highest level, or hardest form, of that skill. For example, the reading domain may be thought of as ranging from recognizing letter shapes and sounds in words to reading continuous text fluently. The writing domain may be conceptualized as ranging from copying letter forms to writing an essay or short story. Then, in initiating the assessment, the teacher begins with a survey of skill performance at the *highest level* that seems appropriate for the particular student. In other words, in order to save time and to evaluate efficiently, the teacher estimates the limit of a student's skill competence and begins testing at that point. If the student can perform the complex tasks on the survey, the teacher will presume that the student can perform less complex ones. If the student cannot perform the complex tasks, the teacher will use probes to verify that finding and/or to "test down" the skill hierarchy to determine the level of complexity at which the student *can* perform. For instance, if a student appears capable of reading continuous text with some degree of fluency, it would be most efficient to begin with an assessment survey which requires the student to read sentences or paragraphs rather than one which assesses the student's competence on a phonics test or a word list. By analyzing the student's overall performance on the paragraph reading task, the teacher can draw some conclusions about the student's ability to perform individual prerequisite skills such as blending sounds or decoding phonetically regular, irregular, or multisyllabic words. The teacher would only probe these specific component skills (i.e., "test down" the reading skill hierarchy) if there were some evidence in the survey to suggest a problem in a particular area.

Similarly, if a student was known to be capable of writing sentences, it would be most efficient to begin an assessment of written language skills by having the student generate a story. This would survey the student's ability to demonstrate the component skills of handwriting, spelling, grammar, and generation of ideas in a complex writing task. Each of the components of written language, and the subskills involved in them, would be probed only if the student had difficulty performing this higher level written language task.

The alternative to "testing down" is "testing up," a procedure that is typically used on standardized achievement tests. In the "test up" paradigm the teacher, or the test developer, begins with easy items and moves the student *up* the skill hierarchy until the student is no longer capable of performing. That is, the test stops when the student has made more than an acceptable number of errors. In our view, the "test up" paradigm wastes precious time by measuring lower level skills which could be assumed to be known if the student demonstrated appropriate performance at a higher level. Furthermore, the "test up" paradigm leaves the student in a failure state; the test is terminated when the student can no longer perform. The "test down" paradigm, on the other hand, leaves the student in a success state; the test is terminated when the student demonstrates that he/she *can* perform a skill.

Our use of the "test down" principle will be obvious not only in the testing of skill hierarchies, but also in the design of probes which systematically vary the response requirements of a task. In Figure 1-E we present a response hierarchy which we use to develop probes. At the highest level of the hierarchy—the total recall level—the student is required to produce an answer from memory without the assistance of prompts or cues. Having a student write spelling words from dictation is an example of a total recall production task which requires a student to generate the correct spelling of words from memory without cues. At the next level of the response hierarchy, the task permits aided recall or recall with the use of prompts or cues. A dictated spelling test of this type might require the student to fill in missing syllables on a response sheet on which the spelling words are partially written out. The partial spellings provide an aid for the student in filling in the blanks. The next level down is recognition. At this level, the answer is embedded in the test item, and the student has only to choose the correct answer from an array. A multiple choice spelling test in which the student has to pick the correctly spelled word from a series of four words, only one of which is spelled correctly, would be an example of a test of spelling at the recognition response level. The lowest level in the response hierarchy involves matching or copying. Now the correct answer is available to the student, and no choice needs to be made. When students are asked to copy spelling words from one page to another, or to copy words from the blackboard, the task requires a spelling response at the matching or copying level.

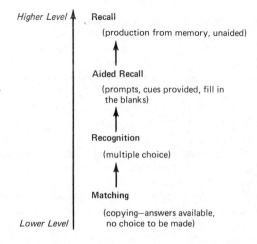

Higher Level   Recall
(production from memory, unaided)

Aided Recall
(prompts, cues provided, fill in the blanks)

Recognition
(multiple choice)

Matching
(copying—answers available, no choice to be made)

Figure 1-E Response Hierarchy   *Lower Level*

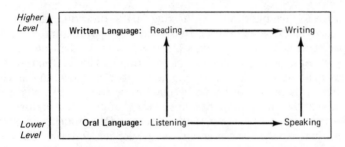

Figure 1-F The Elements of Language: A Developmental Hierarchy

The principle of "test down" using this response hierarchy is applied in the assessment strategy in the following manner. The teacher designs survey tests which require the student to perform at the recall/production level of response. If the student cannot perform at this level, probes would measure aided recall, then recognition, then matching levels of performance. One can think of the response hierarchy as a measurement of how well or how expertly the student can perform the skill, rather than as a measurement of whether or not the student can perform the skill at all. A student who can recognize a correctly spelled word does not have as firm a grasp of its spelling as the student who can spell the word correctly from memory, but such a student does have some knowledge of the spelling of the word. It is helpful to the teacher in planning instruction to identify the level on the response hierarchy at which the student can perform, if performance at the recall/production level is not possible.

Another way in which the "test down" principle is evident in our thinking is in our use of a language hierarchy (Figure 1-F) in our evaluations of reading and written language. We propose procedures which assume that if students can read and understand what they have read, they can probably understand material presented orally at that same level. If a student cannot understand information presented in print, then probes would "test down" the language hierarchy to determine whether or not the information could be understood if presented in oral form. In the same way, if students can express ideas adequately in written form, then we would assume that they can express this same level and quality of ideas in spoken form. If a student cannot express ideas in written form, the teacher would probe the student's capability in the oral mode, utilizing a "test down" paradigm.

5. *Try to guarantee that the student's best level of performance is being elicited.*

Assessment is more than the teacher administering questions from a book or handing a student a test booklet or a worksheet to complete. Assessment requires that the teacher interact with the student; and the quality of that interaction can influence the outcome of the assessment and the usefulness of the information derived from it. The student who is to be tested may be scared or angry or both. In all likelihood, the student has not been very successful in school, has a history of not performing well on academic tasks, is nervous about the questions that the teacher will ask, and is wondering why he/she has to take yet another set of tests. At best, the testing situation can be anxiety-producing for the student. At worst, it can be devastating.

The purpose of the assessment for instructional planning is not to place the student in a failure situation. It is to find out what he/she knows well, what he/she knows uncertainly, and on what it would be useful for the teacher and the student to spend their time. Therefore, the teacher is principally interested in observing and recording the student's *best* performance. To elicit best performance the teacher will have to take several precautions to insure that the testing situation runs smoothly and that it is not a long and frustrating experience for the student. The teacher will want to obtain valid results while creating an environment which will be conducive to further teacher/learner interactions.

Therefore, the first thing the teacher should do is arrange the environment so that it is comfortable for the student. Physical discomforts are distracting and tend to invalidate test performance. A comfortable setting includes furniture (chair and desk or table) that is the correct size and height for the student being tested, and a well-lit work area which is neither too hot nor too cold.

Second, the teacher should take the time to establish open, honest, and empathetic communication with the student before beginning the assessment process, and that rapport should be maintained throughout the testing. Establishing rapport with the student will reduce his/her state of anxiety or hostility and will help to elicit best performance. To begin to establish this kind of open communication, the teacher should explain to the student why he/she is being tested, ask the student what he/she thinks will happen as a result of the tests, and clarify any misconceptions about the use to which the test information will be put. The student should understand what the teacher is trying to find out as a result of the testing and how it will help the teacher and the student to plan an instructional program. Establishing rapport is especially important with older students who have a long history of school/test failure and so tend to approach the testing situation with more anxiety and hostility, and who also tend to give up on tasks that seem difficult. Such students often have a defeatist attitude. The teacher must assure the student that he/she can accomplish the tasks that are being presented in the assessment and that it is worthwhile to put forth maximum effort.

Third, in order to insure a high level of performance, the teacher may have to utilize a "motivated" assessment strategy. To do this, a teacher might pair a reward with working hard on the assessment tasks or even with responding to each test item. The reward will reduce tension or anxiety that is associated with responding and increase the likelihood that the student will respond at his/her best level. Rewards may be tangible items like checkmarks or stars that can be accumulated and traded in later. The only caution in developing a motivated assessment strategy is to be certain that the rewarding stimuli are not so powerful as to distract the student from the test itself.

Fourth, the teacher must be prepared for the testing situation. Materials such as pencils, paper, tape recorders, tapes, batteries, extension cords, manuals, and record forms, which will be needed in the testing situation, should be at hand. The teacher should know the procedures that will be followed in the administration of tests and the recording of responses so as to make certain that the testing runs smoothly and calmly.

Attention to these four considerations—the student's physical comfort, rapport with the examiner, motivation to perform, and the teacher's preparedness for the testing situation—will make it more likely that the teacher will elicit a student's best performance. If a student performs poorly on an assessment task, the teacher can be assured that the poor performance occurred in spite of attention to these considerations. When the testing conditions have been designed to insure maximum student performance, the teacher can proceed with testing and interpreting the findings with a measure of confidence.

6. *Select the appropriate vehicles for obtaining assessment information.*

There are a variety of ways for a teacher to obtain information that is useful in instructional planning. In order to make the assessment as efficient and effective as possible, the teacher must use the vehicle that is particularly appropriate for the assessment question being posed. As used in this book, the term assessment refers to all activities that the teacher engages in to obtain information about students' instructional needs. These activities include administering, scoring, and interpreting both formal and informal tests; using direct observation of students in everyday school situations; and interviewing students and teachers. At one time or another the teacher will employ each of these activities to assess the student thoroughly. But certain activities will be more useful than others for finding out certain kinds of information. We will review each of these assessment activities—testing, observing, and interviewing—in order to help the teacher to understand the advantages and disadvantages of each, and the use to which each can be put in an assessment for instructional planning.

a. Testing.   Tests are predetermined collections of questions or tasks to which predetermined types of responses are sought (Salvia and Ysseldyke, 1981). Tests are especially useful in an assessment for instructional planning to determine what skills to teach each student. Tests fall into two general categories: *norm-referenced* and *criterion-referenced.*

Norm-referenced tests are those which compare a student's performance to the performance of a peer group on which the test was standardized. The usefulness of norm-referenced tests with underachieving students is often limited because norm-referenced instruments should only be used with students who closely resemble the group which was used to norm the test. Norm-referenced measures are created so that the answers are objective; there is only one predetermined answer for each question. Administration, scoring, and interpretation of norm-referenced tests are well delineated. Every attempt is made to eliminate the possibility of examiner bias affecting a score. Norm-referenced tests may be administered to groups or individuals. Achievement tests, diagnostic tests, and intelligence tests are the most frequently used norm-referenced assessment instruments. Achievement tests generally cover broad content in several school subjects and yield grade-equivalent scores. Diagnostic tests survey a narrower range of skills and include items which assess specific skill components or prerequisite skills. While the results from diagnostic tests lead to comparisons among children, they are designed primarily to pinpoint specific areas of skill deficit and to provide detailed information to the tester.

Intelligence tests sample behaviors according to the test author's conception of "intelligence." Some tests sample behaviors across a wide range (e.g., the Wechsler Intelligence Scale for Children), while others sample only a single behavior (e.g., The Peabody Picture Vocabulary Test). As with all norm-referenced tests, the result of an intelligence test is expressed as a quantitative score that can be used to compare one student's performance to that of a normative group.

Like norm-referenced tests, criterion-referenced tests have explicit directions for administration and scoring. But criterion-referenced tests are not designed to compare performances or to determine a student's relative standing in a group. Criterion-referenced tests measure whether or not a student has mastered a skill. Rather than answering the question "How well does Roger do in addition?", a criterion-referenced test permits an analysis of whether Roger can add three-digit numbers by regrouping in the ones and tens columns. Unlike norm-referenced tests, criterion-referenced tests do not require a standardization group. Results from these tests are not transformed into grade scores, percentiles, and stanines. The student is not compared to a norm but to a relative level of mastery.

Criterion-referenced tests are based on objectives which are stated in observable behaviors. These objectives are translated into performances which the examiner can assess and compare to the predetermined criterion for success. In criterion-referenced tests, the emphasis is on assessing specific and relevant behaviors rather than on deriving a score. Criterion-referenced tests offer several advantages over norm-referenced tests for teachers who are trying to determine what to teach. Students are judged according to their own abilities rather than being compared with others. Items on criterion-referenced tests are often linked to instructional objectives, thereby facilitating the writing of teaching plans. Test items often sample sequential skills, enabling the teacher to specify the beginning point for instruction.

Like norm-referenced tests, criterion-referenced tests are available in the commercial market. There are several reasons for choosing a published criterion-referenced test over one that the teacher designs. First, in a commercially available test, technical information—the design and development characteristics of the test—will probably be available from the publisher. Reading this information may reassure the teacher of the appropriateness of the measure. Second, using a published test may save the teacher considerable time and effort.

However, there are many advantages to criterion-referenced tests that are teacher-made. First, the teacher can choose to test only those areas which are of particular interest. The teacher can develop a test specific to the student's needs and measure exactly what has to be measured. According to Hammill and Bartel (1978), an informal teacher-made assessment yields information that is very directly usable in planning remediation activities. Of course, there are some drawbacks to teacher-made tests. Such tests will only be as good as the teachers who create them. Many teachers lack experience with a task-analytic approach to instruction, and their tests may reflect that inexperience. Moreover, teacher-made tests take time to create. But when tests are to be administered for the purpose of helping the teacher plan what to teach, teacher-made criterion-referenced tests are recommended.

b. Observing.   To develop instructional plans, teachers need to know not only *what* to teach but *how* to teach the student. They need to understand each student's performance style, learning style, and work habits in order to design appropriate, successful lessons. Observations can provide accurate, detailed, and verifiable information about the student's performance that can be used by the teacher in deciding *how* to teach. The two most common types of observation are systematic and nonsystematic observation (Salvia and Ysseldyke, 1981). Systematic observation requires that the observer determine in advance which observable behaviors are to be noted and then measure those behaviors. This is usually done by counting behaviors for a predetermined period of time using a predetermined number of observations. For example, if Ms. Smith suspected that one of her students, Roger, was spending a lot of reading time off-task, she might set about designing a systematic observation schedule to measure Roger's off-task behavior during reading. She might decide to do three observations during her daily fifteen-minute independent reading period, one at the beginning of the third, eighth, and thirteenth minutes of the period. At each observation she would simply note whether or not Roger was off-task. She would observe for two weeks. At the end of two weeks she would have made thirty observations of Roger's off-task behavior and would be able to state how many of those thirty times Roger was off task. These data would help to verify her suspicions.

While the data gathered through this kind of systematic observation are very specific and clearly usable, the drawbacks to this kind of observation strategy are

Student _____ Teacher _____

Behavior	Date Observed							
Remains in seat								
Seeks help appropriately								
Stays on task								
Does not disturb others								
Follows directions								
Works independently								
Completes task								
Follows clean-up procedures								
Knows what to do when task is completed								
Follows daily routine								
Finishes seatwork								
Finishes homework								
Other:								

Key:
√ - exhibits behavior consistently
0 - exhibits behavior intermittently
X - does not exhibit behavior

Figure 1-G Checklist of Seatwork Behaviors

obvious. The method demands a great deal of time and organization from the teacher and may even require somebody trained in systematic observation to produce meaningful information. The alternative is nonsystematic observation which will produce less specific and accurate data, but which can be done by a teacher without a great expenditure of time. Nonsystematic observation requires that the teacher simply watch an individual in his/her environment and take note of the behaviors, characteristics, and personal interactions that seem most significant. Nonsystematic observation yields anecdotal and subjective information which can be useful in understanding how a student responds in an instructional situation.

Checklists and rating scales may be combined with nonsystematic observations to help the teacher organize his/her findings. They will be most useful if they contain only items that are appropriate to the behavior being measured, items that are observable and listed in the order in which they are likely to occur, and items that require only a simple notation process. Figure 1-G is an example of a checklist which meets the above requirements. Checklists should not be scored as such, but used instead as a record of the teacher's observation of the behavior that occurred during a learning activity.

c. Interviewing.   Interviews and questionnaires may also be used to gather information for instructional planning. Although information on *what* to teach can be gathered in this way, for the purposes of this text, interviews and questionnaires will be suggested primarily for gathering information on *how* to teach. The results of interviews and questionnaires are descriptive data, the quality of which depends heavily on the knowledge of the person being interviewed and the skill of the interviewer. The ease of interpretation of the information generally depends upon the clarity of the purpose for gathering the information and the degree of structure supplied. The greatest advantage of interviews and questionnaires is that they can provide information about students' interests and motivations, information not always available to the teacher through tests or observation.

Although each technique of obtaining assessment information—testing, observing, and interviewing—can be used by the teacher to generate the needed data for instructional planning, we urge teachers to choose carefully the method that will help to make the assessment process as efficient as possible. Throughout the text, we will rely heavily on the use of formal and informal *tests* for information on *what* to teach, and *observation* and *interview* for information on *how* to teach.

7. When information is gathered by testing, the assessment instruments should be technically sound.

Although our emphasis is on the use of informal or teacher-made tests to obtain the data needed for instructional planning, we recognize that many teachers will opt to use formal, published tests as they apply our strategy of assessment for instructional planning. Often, time constraints preclude the creation of teacher-made tests.

If formal tests are chosen, they should be used for the analysis of student performance rather than for the scores that they produce. As such, we prefer diagnostic measures rather than broad ranging achievement tests. But we emphasize that whenever a formal test is selected, the teacher has a responsibility to assure that it is a technically sound test. In Chapter 2, we present information on how to judge the soundness of a published test. We believe that it is an important chapter to review, because time will be wasted if inappropriate or inaccurate assessment devices are used and inappropriate or inaccurate conclusions are drawn. And time is a critical factor in teaching underachieving students.

2

Assessment Tools

Assessment of *what to teach* relies heavily on testing as the primary source of data. While we prefer to have teachers make up their own tests so that they are sure to measure exactly what they want to measure in precisely the way in which they want to measure it, we know from experience that many classroom teachers prefer to use commercially available tests rather than their own informal tests. Commercially prepared tests require less time than teacher-created measures. Moreover, teachers seem to have more faith in published materials than in materials designed by themselves. Teachers often believe that if a test is copyrighted, packaged, and published, it must be valid, reliable, appropriate, and good. Of course, this is not always the case. There are many technically unsound tests on the educational assessment market, and teachers will have to select assessment instruments carefully. To do this, the teacher will have to look beyond the title of the test to appraise its technical adequacy.

The purpose of this chapter is to remind teachers what to look for in selecting a commerically available test.

The most important factor in the selection of a test is its *validity*, i.e., the degree to which the test measures what it claims to measure. But there are also other characteristics that are salient in the search for a good test: the reliability of the instrument, that is, the extent to which the results of the test are stable and can be trusted; the appropriateness of the sample on which the test was standardized; and the time, expense, and effort required of students and teachers in using the test.

VALIDITY

A test is valid to the extent that it provides information relevant to the questions being raised (Chase, 1978). A test is not simply valid or invalid; validity is a matter of degree. If two tests measure reading comprehension skills, and the teacher finds that test A gives a more complete student protocol on various levels of reading comprehension than test B, the teacher cannot say that test A is valid and test B is invalid. The teacher can only say that, for the purposes of profiling reading comprehension skills, test A is more valid than test B.

We will discuss three kinds of validity: content validity, criterion-related validity, and construct validity.

Content validity may be defined as the extent to which the test measures the skills and information that it purports to measure. Content validity is not statistically determined. Rather, it requires that the person administering the measure examine the test content critically. First, the test should be reviewed for the appropriateness of the items included. The teacher should have a clear idea in mind of what is to be measured. Then he or she should examine the test items to determine if they are really measuring the domain in question. Second, the test should be examined for the completeness of the item sample. The validity of a test could be called into question if it does not contain a sufficient number of items to be truly representative of the topics that are supposed to be measured. If it is apparent that there are not enough items on a test to measure a skill effectively, the test would probably not yield a valid score. The third factor to consider in establishing content validity is the way in which the test items assess content, i.e., the stimulus and response requirements of the tasks. A test will be more valid for a particular teacher if it measures the content in a manner that is desired by the teacher.

In establishing content validity, it is not sufficient to question only the title of the test. Its actual content must be carefully reviewed to determine whether the items on the test and the manner in which they are presented are appropriate for the teacher's purposes.

Criterion-related validity compares the scores obtained on the test in question with those of another test, task, or observation which is understood to be related to it.

To establish criterion-related validity, scores on the test in question are compared with results from a test or activity that is known to measure the same skills. If the two measures of student performance are taken at the same time, the comparison is referred to as *concurrent validity*. If the scores on the test in question are related to a performance in the future, the comparison is referred to as *predictive validity*. For example, a teacher might administer a pencil and paper test which he/she believes will assess spatial reasoning. The teacher could then have the children read a map and could rate their actual skill performance in spatial reasoning. If the pencil and paper test were valid, the students' results on the test would be similar to the results obtained from the map reading task. The teacher would have demonstrated the concurrent validity of the pencil and paper task. Or, if students were given a new reading readiness test at the end of kindergarten and, at the end of the following school year, their scores on a reading task were compared with their earlier scores, the comparison would yield a measure of the predictive validity of the readiness test.

The statistical procedure used to determine the extent of the relationship between two measures is called a correlation. The number derived from the calculation shows the intensity of the relationship and is called a correlation coefficient, symbolized by r. The relationship between the two tests is indicated by a number which falls in the range between −1.00 to +1.00. Correlation coefficients that are close to 0.00 indicate a random relationship between the two measures, that is, performance on one measure is virtually unrelated to performance on the second measure. A positive correlation coefficient would indicate that a person with a high score on one measure tends to have a high score on the other measure and that a person with a low score on one measure tends to have a low score on the other measure. A coefficient of +1.00 would show that the students' scores on the two measures have an identical rank. A correlation coefficient close to −1.00 would show that the higher the score on one measure the lower the score on the other, and vice versa. A perfect correlation coefficient of −1.00 would indicate a perfect negative relationship between two measures, i.e., the highest score on one measure was the lowest on the other.

According to Chase (1978), typical validity coefficients range between 0.40 and 0.60. A validity coefficient within this range would indicate that as the scores on one measure increase, so do the scores on the second measure, although the correspondence between the two scores is somewhat less than perfect.

The question of what constitutes an adequate validity coefficient cannot be answered easily; different authors suggest different guidelines. Chase recommmends that in situations where the tester is trying to make a judgment about an individual student's educational program, the validity coefficient must be higher than 0.70. Turnbull, Strickland, and Brantley (1978) recommend that the validity coefficient be at least 0.80. And Howell, Kaplan, and O'Connell (1979) state that, as a rule, correlations should be higher than 0.90 if the test results are to be used to guide the instruction of the individual student.

All would agree that the higher the validity coefficient, the less likely it is that erroneous judgments will be made on the basis of the test results.

Construct validity assesses whether the test in question measures the theoretical construct it purports to measure. Constructs are psychological ideas, or concepts. They cannot be seen or physically identified, but we presume that they exist because we can see their manifestations. Intelligence, generosity, and self-concept are all examples of constructs. Construct validity is usually demonstrated by correlation studies using other measures assumed to tap the same theoretical construct.

In selecting tests for an assessment for instructional planning, the teacher may not be as concerned about construct validity as about other forms of validity, since he/she will be more interested in measuring behavior—reading, written language, math—than in measuring psychological constructs. However, teachers will often come across tests in which some subtests measure behaviors and others measure psychological constructs. The teacher should exercise caution when considering those subtests which measure constructs. As well, the teacher will not be very interested in predictive validity, since the main focus of an assessment for instructional planning is on students' present performance and not on their performance in the future. The kinds of validity that will be of greatest interest are content validity and concurrent validity, because both indicate the extent to which the current measure of behavior is appropriate for the teacher's purposes.

RELIABILITY

Validity is certainly the most important technical characteristic of a test. If a test does not measure what the teacher wants to measure, or measures it in a way in which the teacher is not interested, the test should not be used. But once validity has been established to the teacher's satisfaction, the reliability of the test should be considered. The term *reliability* is used to mean the consistency of the scores derived from a particular test. A reliable test is one that can be counted on to give stable, consistent results. That is, if that test were to be given several times to the same individual, the test results would not fluctuate randomly. In our strategy for an assessment for instructional planning, reliability is usually established by verifying a student's errors. In the "survey to probe" paradigm, when a student has demonstrated an error on a survey test, the teacher administers a probe to verify the error and to determine the consistency of the student's performance. If the student makes the same mistake again, the teacher can conclude with some certainty that the student cannot perform the task or skill. If the student performs correctly on the probe, the teacher can conclude that the survey provided unreliable information. As long as the teacher verifies student *performance* with probes, he/she need not be overly concerned with the reliability of the student's *score* on the survey test. Sometimes, however, teachers want to use the survey or probe results for a dual purpose. They plan to use the test results to analyze error patterns for instructional planning and to derive a *score* that can be recorded on the student's IEP or reported to the student's parents or teachers. Now the issue of the reliability of the test score becomes more critical, because the teacher must understand how stable and consistent are the scores that they intend to report. Before they report the data to someone else, they should consider how likely it is that the student would obtain a like score if reexamined on the same test.

With formal tests, statistical analyses are usually reported to indicate the level of confidence one might have regarding the reliability of a particular measure. The statistical procedures are derived from correlating two sets of scores, and the results are reported as reliability coefficients. Typically there are two methods for determining the reliability of a test.

1. Students' performance on two test administrations are compared to yield a *test-retest* or *equivalent forms* reliability coefficient.
2. Students' performance on a single administration of a test is studied to yield a *split-half* or *internal consistency* reliability coefficient.

Table 2-1 summarizes these methods.

Test-retest is the simplest way to obtain reliability data. The same test is given to the same group of students, usually with an interval of no less than one and no more than two weeks. The two sets of scores are then correlated to yield a reliability coefficient. Because the element of practice may influence the second score in a test-retest procedure, an alternative method for determining reliability is the *equivalent forms* procedure.

This procedure requires that two tests be designed, each sampling the same content or domain, but with no identical questions. The two tests are then administered to the same group of students, and the two sets of scores are correlated to determine how well the two measures correspond. The problem of practice is eliminated by this method, but the question of equivalence needs to be studied carefully.

Table 2-1   Methods of Establishing Test Reliability*

Method	Procedure	What It Reveals
Test-retest	Same test given to same students on two separate occasions; first scores correlated with second scores.	Consistency of scores over a time lapse.
Equivalent forms	Build two tests to assess a common behavior domain, give both tests to the same students, correlate the two scores.	Comparability of two assessments of the same skill or trait.
Split-half method	Give a test to a group of students, score the odd-numbered items, score the even-numbered items, correlate odd score with even score (note use of correction for test length).	Since two scores are samples of content of same test, split-half indicates extent to which one part of test measures same way as another part of same test.
Internal consistency	Compare performance of students from item to item.	Extent to which each individual item is producing similar results.

*Chase, C., *Measurement for Educational Evaluation,* © 1978. Addison-Wesley, Reading, MA., p. 80. Reprinted with permission.

It must be clear that the two tests actually measure equivalent items and that one does not contain items that may be more difficult than the other.

Split-half reliability differs from test-retest and equivalent forms in that the test has to be administered only once. The scores from the full test are split in half, either by assigning all the even numbered items to one half and the odd numbered items to the other half, or by randomly assigning items to one half of the test or the other. Then the scores on the two halves of the test are correlated. For example, if a test developer administers a 50-item test to a group of students, he/she treats the test as if it were two 25-item tests. The developer correlates the scores from one of the 25-item tests with the scores from the other 25-item test and obtains a split-half reliability coefficient. The drawback to the split-half is that two shorter tests are probably a less adequate sample of the skills or behaviors being tested than the one longer test, and the size and adequacy of the item pool affects the reliability score. There are, however, statistical formulas which may be applied to correct this problem.

Internal consistency refers to the consistency of one test item with all other test items. Test makers determine internal consistency if test items are presumed to measure a single common trait. The procedure for computing internal consistency was developed by Richardson and Kuder (1939).

All reliability coefficients indicate the amount of variability in a set of scores. Reliability coefficients range from 1.00 (indicating perfect reliability) to 0.00 (indicating total unreliability). Reliability coefficients are usually provided in the technical manuals of formal tests.

Any teacher who intends to use a student's *score* on a test must ask, "Is the reliability coefficient of this test high enough for me to trust the score I get and to report that score on an IEP or in my discussions with teachers?" Although there are no universally agreed upon guidelines for what is adequate reliability, we subscribe to the standards proposed by Salvia and Ysseldyke (1981). If the test has been administered for screening purposes and further testing will occur (as in the case of a survey test), a reliability of 0.80 should be standard. If the results of the test will lead to significant educational decisions about a student (e.g., classification or declassification for special services), then the minimum reliability of the test should be 0.90.

Another very useful way for a teacher to judge the consistency of scores on a given test is to look at the *standard error of measurement* (SEM) reported in the technical manual of the test. The standard error of measurement is an indication of just how variant scores would be if the same test were given to the same student an infinite number of times. Since a test is typically given only once (and this is the reason we are interested in the reliability of the test score), the teacher can use the standard error of measurement to estimate the range of scores that could reasonably be expected from the student just by chance alone. For example, if the test maker of a 100-item math test reports a SEM of 4 raw score points, that means that the raw score obtained by students on the test will vary ± 4 points 68% of the time. A raw score of 38 achieved by a student on that test could fall between ± 1 SEM or between scores of 34 and 42 on 68% of test administrations given to that student. If that same student were to take that same math test 100 times, the score would not be 38 each time; rather the score would fall somewhere between 30 and 46 (± 2 SEMs) 95% of the time and between 26 and 50 (± 3 SEMs) 99% of the time, just by chance alone. Of course, the student will not be given the same test 100 times, but, using the standard error of measurement, the teacher must conclude that, with 99% certainty, the score of 38 could just as easily have been a score of anywhere between 26 and 50.

The standard error of measurement provides information about the certainty with which a score can be reported. If the standard error of measurement is relatively large, the uncertainty is large; the teacher cannot report the student's score with any degree of confidence. The student's score could have been very different from the one obtained by chance alone. If the standard error of measurement is relatively small, the uncertainty is small; the teacher can be more confident that the score is a true estimate of the student's level of functioning, and the teacher can report the score with confidence. As a general rule, we recommend that the teacher construct a 95% confidence interval using the standard error of measurement reported in the test manual. To do this, the teacher would search the technical manual for the standard error of measurement and double that figure, and the range that would be established would reflect the possible true score variation 95% of the time. The teacher could then be assured that scores within the range ± 2 standard errors of measurement are all virtually the "same score." This concept is especially important for teachers who are trying to judge changes in student scores over a period of time. Again, let's use our example of the math test which reports a standard error of measurement of 4. If a student gets a score of 38 on that test in the fall, and a 43 on that same test in the spring, the teacher can conclude that, given the standard error of measurement of 4 points, the spring score of 43 is virtually the same as the fall score of 38 (38 ± 8 is the 95% confidence interval). The teacher must presume that no significant growth has taken place.

Once a teacher begins to consider the reliability of test scores and the standard errors of measurement of tests, he/she should be very cautious about placing special significance on any student's actual score and about making significant educational decisions on the basis of any one score.

INTERPRETING TEST SCORES

If the teacher is planning to report the scores from the assessment for instructional planning in addition to analyzing error patterns, then issues of the reliability of the score and standard error of measurement of the test are extremely important. The teacher should also be aware of how to interpret raw scores on tests so that they can be reported in the most accurate and meaningful way. If a teacher has given the same test to a group of students, perhaps to a whole class, then he/she can look at the whole set of scores in order to put the score of any one student into perspective.

First the teacher could list the scores from lowest to highest—that is, distribute the scores—and inspect the results. If Ms. Smith gave a group of 11 children a 40-item survey of irregular spelling words, the fact that Roger scored 28 and Ian scored 19 may not be meaningful. But by distributing the scores, Ms. Smith would be able to see where the boys' scores fell in relation to the group (Table 2-2). Ms. Smith could also do a frequency distribution which would display how many students achieved each score (Table 2-3).

Another way of looking at the group of scores is to calculate the mean, the median, and the modal scores, that is, to look at *measures of central tendency* for the group of scores. The *mean* is the arithmetic average of all the scores, derived simply by totaling the scores and dividing by the number of scores. To determine the mean for Ms. Smith's spelling test, we would add the scores found in Table 2-2 (34 + 34 + 30 + 29 . . . + 17) and divide by 11, the total number of scores. The mean for this set of scores would be 26.3. Now we know that Roger's score of 28 was slightly above the mean of the group and Ian's score of 19 was well below.

Table 2-2   Distribution of Scores on Ms. Smith's Spelling Test

Name	Score	Name	Score
Bob	34	Beth	24
Daniel	34	Julie	24
Lisa	30	Michael	24
Gary	29	Ian	19
Roger	28	Ruth	17
Adam	26		

Table 2-3   Frequency Distribution of Scores on Ms. Smith's Spelling Test

Score	Number of Scores	Score	Number of Scores
34	2	25	0
33	0	24	3
32	0	23	0
31	0	22	0
30	1	21	0
29	1	20	0
28	1	19	1
27	0	18	0
26	1	17	1

The *median* is the point at which one-half of the scores fall above and one-half below. In the case of the scores found in Table 2-2, the median is the point at which 5 scores are higher and 5 are lower. By counting down to the sixth score we can determine that the median is 26. Again we find that Roger's score is slightly above the median and Ian's score is below. The most frequently occurring score is called the *mode*. In our example the modal score is 24; that score occurred three times (Table 2-3).

Measures of central tendency give the teacher information about typical performance but they do not indicate how scores for the whole group are spread out. For this the teacher needs a *measure of dispersion*. A quick indication of dispersion is *range*, reported either as the lowest to the highest score (in Ms. Smith's class the range of scores is 17 to 34) or calculated by subtracting the lowest score from the highest and adding 1 (in Ms. Smith's class the scores ranged over 18 points [34 − 17 + 1]).

Another useful indication of dispersion is the *standard deviation*, represented by the Greek letter σ [sigma]. The standard deviation represents the distribution of a set of scores around the mean. The standard deviation is computed by calculating the mean and then following the next five steps:

1. Subtract the mean from each score to determine the deviations from the mean.
2. Square each of the deviations.
3. Sum the squares.
4. Divide the sum of the squares by the number of scores.
5. Take the square root of that figure.

The standard deviation is a unit of measurement, and, with normal distributions, scores can be expressed in terms of standard deviation units from the mean. As can be seen in Figure 2-A, over 68% of scores fall between ± 1 standard deviation; over 95% fall between ± 2 standard deviations; and over 99% fall between ± 3 standard deviations. In Table 2-4 the standard deviation calculation is done for the scores for Ms. Smith's class. As we can see, the sum of the squared deviations is 298.15. When that sum is divided by the total number of scores (11) the result is 27.10. The square root of 27.10 is 5.206. That figure is the standard deviation of

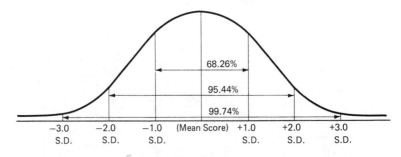

Figure 2-A The Normal Curve Divided into Standard Deviation Units

Table 2-4 Calculations of Standard Deviation for Scores on
Ms. Smith's Spelling Test

Score	−	Mean	=	Deviation	Deviation Squared
34		26.27		7.73	59.75
34		26.27		7.73	59.75
30		26.27		3.73	13.91
29		26.27		2.73	7.45
28		26.27		1.73	2.99
26		26.27		− .27	.07
24		26.27		−2.27	5.15
24		26.27		−2.27	5.15
24		26.27		−2.27	5.15
19		26.27		−7.27	52.85
17		26.27		−9.27	85.93
					298.15

Sum of the squares
Number of scores

$$\frac{298.15}{11} = 27.10$$

$$\sqrt{27.10} = 5.206$$

Standard deviation = 5.206

scores for Ms. Smith's class on the spelling test. That standard deviation allows her to determine the relative position of any one score among the group of scores.

NORMATIVE SCORES

Often, the teacher does not intend to give one test to the whole class and will not be able to use classmates' scores to interpret an individual student's test performance. Then the teacher may turn to the technical manual for information on the test performance of a group of subjects known as the normative sample or the norm group. Two kinds of comparisons with the norm group are possible: reporting in terms of scores of relative standing (percentiles, standard scores, stanines) or reporting in terms of developmental scores (age or grade score conversions).

Scores of Relative Standing. *Percentile ranks* permit the teacher to report a given student's score by the percent of people in the norm group who had scores at or below that score. Percentile ranks range from 0 to 99. It is impossible to score in the 100th percentile since, by definition, a percentile rank identifies the percent of people scoring at or *below* a certain score. (Percentile ranks are not to be confused with the percentage of correct answers. It is possible for someone to be the highest ranking person in the group and to receive a high percentile ranking but to answer only 50% of the test items correctly.) Percentile ranks cannot be added or subtracted because the various ranks do not represent equal units at all points along the scale.

The teacher should never calculate arithmetically the average percentile rank of a group of students' scores.

Standard scores transform raw scores into a set of scores that always have the same mean and standard deviation. A *z* score is defined as a standard score with a mean of 0 and a standard deviation of 1. A *t* score is a standard score with a mean of 50 and a standard deviation of 10. Deviation IQs are standard scores with a mean of 100 and a standard deviation of 15, 16 or greater, depending on the test. Standard scores permit the teacher to translate a given student's raw score into the number of standard deviation units below or above the mean of the normative comparison group.

Stanines are also a form of standard scores that are based on a distribution of the raw scores into nine equal parts. If a student receives a stanine score of 5 he/she is located exactly in the center of the distribution. A stanine of 9 means that the student is in the upper extreme of the distribution; a stanine of 1 is in the lower extreme. Like all standard score conversions, and unlike percentile scores, the intervals between various points on a stanine scale are equal. Furthermore, stanines and standard scores may be used in arithmetic computations.

Developmental Scores.   *Grade equivalents* translate raw scores into a number representing a school year and month. The school year is divided into tenths; a grade equivalent of 3.2 is what one would expect from a typical student who had completed 2/10 of the third grade. A grade equivalent of 7.5 represents the work of a typical student midway through the seventh grade.

A caution to be applied in using grade equivalents is that these numbers are not absolute. Two students can take the same test, receive the same raw score translated into the same grade equivalent, and miss different items. Two sixth-grade students, each with a grade equivalent score in reading of 4.5, may have very different patterns of strengths and weaknesses on their profiles. Moreover, different tests may define typical grade performance based on dissimilar criteria.

Age norms are similar to grade norms but are based upon the average score obtained by students of different ages. An age equivalent means that a student's raw score is the average—the mean or median—performance for that age group. Age equivalents are expressed in years and months; a hyphen is used in age scores (i.e., 7 years, 6 months is 7–6). The same limitations on the interpretation of grade scores may be imposed on age scores. The child who earns an age equivalent of 7–2 years has merely answered as many questions correctly as the average child of 7 years 2 months in the normative sample. He/she has not necessarily performed *like* a 7–2 year old in the sense that he/she may have missed a different array of problems or have attacked the task differently from many 7–2 year old children.

Whether the teacher is converting raw scores to scores of relative standing or to developmental scores, the derived scores are only useful if the normative group on which the test was standardized is clearly representative of the characteristics of the students taking the test. Some of the differences among students can be traced to differences in the parents' socioeconomic status, geographic location, and/or size of the community in which the students live, or to the race, sex, age, or grade of the students. Test users are cautioned to read the technical manuals of the standardized instruments carefully to determine if the students about whom they are seeking information are represented in the normative population of the test. If students like the ones being tested were not part of the norm group, the derived scores will not be appropriate and should not be reported.

A PERSPECTIVE ON TESTS

In this text we will place heavy emphasis on student *performance* on individual test items and little emphasis on the tally of right and wrong responses which leads to a *score*. Therefore, we will not be very concerned with issues of test score reliability, standard errors of measurement, or reporting derived scores. We have provided some discussion on these issues because, from our experience, many teachers will assess a student's *performance* to gather information to be used in instructional planning *and also* to derive a score to be reported on an IEP, to parents, or to other teachers. It is imperative that if *scores* are obtained and reported, issues of reliability and test norms be considered. Teachers should choose only a test which reports reliability coefficients of at least 0.80, preferably 0.90, and a relatively small standard error of measurement. The population on whom the test was normed should include students like the ones who are to be tested.

Throughout the remainder of the text, although we will not be concerned with test *scores*, we will be concerned with selecting and designing tests that serve very particular purposes. For this we will continue to raise the issue of test validity. Tests should measure what the teacher wants to measure, in the way the teacher wants to measure it. Validity is an issue which is central to carrying out an efficient and effective assessment for instructional planning.

3

The Assessment Strategy

To carry out an assessment for instructional planning, the teacher must do more than put the student at ease, gain a broad knowledge of available tests, select technically sound instruments, and administer a battery of tests to each student. The teacher must have a plan. He/she must have a systematic strategy for gathering and interpreting the assessment data, or the findings will not lead easily and quickly to instructional decisions. In this chapter we will present such a plan. The plan is procedural in nature. It describes a sequence of steps for the teacher to follow. It is, in effect, a roadmap for the assessment process. In subsequent chapters we will show how this plan can be applied to the assessment of reading, written expression, mathematics, interest, motivators, and learning style. But first, we will describe in some detail each step of the plan.

Step 1: Decide What to Assess

The first thing the teacher must do in any assessment for instructional planning is to decide what subject areas, skill areas, or personality characteristics will be assessed for each student. To do this the teacher must determine which skills will fall within his/her instructional responsibilities and what non-academic information about the student would be helpful in instructional planning. For example, if a teacher works only in the area of reading, then the decision will be to assess only

Students	What To Teach			How To Teach		
	Reading	Written Language	Math	Learning Style	Interest	Motivators

Code: ◻ To be assessed   ⊠ Assessment completed   ▦ Not to be assessed

Figure 3-A What to Assess

reading skills. If the teacher is responsible for all basic academic skills, then the teacher will probably decide that reading, written expression, and arithmetic will all be areas in which assessment must take place. If the teacher is responsible for teaching different academic skills to different students, then individual decisions will have to be made for each student. Figure 3-A is a recordkeeping form on which the teacher can note what will be assessed for each student. Given across the top are the possible areas of concern: reading, written language, and math, as well as learning style, interest, and motivators. Down the left side are listed the names of the students to be assessed.

| Students | What To Teach | | | How To Teach | | |
	Reading	Written Language	Math	Learning Style	Interest	Motivators
Lynn	/	/	/	/	/	/
Vicky	/	/	▓	/	/	/
Gerry	▓	▓	/	/	/	/
Alice	▓	▓	/	X	X	X
Todd	/	/	▓	X	X	X
Jimmy	▓	▓	/	/	/	/
Frank	/	/	/	/	/	/
Ray	/	/	/	/	/	/

Code: ⧄ To be assessed   ⊠ Assessment completed   ▓ Not to be assessed

Figure 3-B What to Assess: Example

In Figure 3-B, we have shown what this form would be like for a class of eight special education students. The teacher marks a diagonal (/) in a box to indicate that an assessment should be undertaken, and an X when assessment information is in hand. If an area will not be assessed, it is blackened out. Two of the students (Alice and Todd) were assigned to this teacher last year, and the teacher is confident that she needs no new information on learning style, interest, and motivators. These boxes are marked with X's. Some students (Vicky and Todd) are assigned to mainstream teachers for math, so the special education teacher does not plan to assess their math competency. Three other students (Gerry, Alice, and

Jimmy) are out of the room for reading and language arts, so they will not be assessed in these areas. Three students (Lynn, Frank, and Ray) remain with the special education teacher for developmental reading, math, and language arts. This chart provides the teacher with a diagram of what information needs to be collected on each student, and a way to record that the initial assessment for each student has been completed.

Step 2: Select or Develop a Skill Hierarchy for Each Basic Skill Area To Be Assessed

Once the teacher has decided what will be assessed for each student, he/she must find or develop a *skill hierarchy* for each area to be assessed. This skill hierarchy needs to be in written form and arranged so that it can serve as a guide for both the assessment itself and the summary sheet of assessment findings. This means that the skill hierarchy needs to be detailed enough for the specific elements comprising each instructional area to be clearly identified—yet not so detailed as to overwhelm the teacher. Depending on the needs of the teacher, the degree of specificity of skill hierarchies can vary considerably. If one teacher is following a particular curriculum for reading instruction (e.g., the Ginn Reading 720 basal reading series), his/her reading skill hierarchy would reflect the scope and sequence of that curriculum. It might look like the one in Table 3-1. A skill hierarchy constructed in this way would enable the teacher to determine which reading skills should have been mastered by a student who is placed at a particular level of the basal series, or which skills are considered prerequisite to adequate functioning at a particular level.

In another instance, the skill hierarchy will reflect the teacher's own task analysis of a basic skill area, and build on the variety of curriculum guides, teachers'

Table 3-1 Curriculum-Specific Skill Hierarchy*

9. Contractions:	'll, n't, 's
8. Plural:	s
7. Consonant blends:	st, gr, fr, sm, nd, nt, tr
6. Consonant digraphs:	th, ch, sh, wh, qu
5. Long vowels:	e-marker pattern (C$\overline{\text{V}}$Ce) ay, ee, ea CVVC pattern (ee/ea)
4. Short vowels:	CVC pattern (i) CVC pattern (e) CVC pattern (a) CVCC pattern (i, e, a)
3. Medial consonants:	l m n
2. Final consonants:	b p t d ck k g m n l s v x f
1. Initial consonants:	b l r h j k f y n d g t v m s w p z

*Adapted from Ginn Reading Program 720, Ginn & Company. The skill hierarchy reflects decoding skills taught in the first five levels of the curriculum.

Table 3-2 Word Recognition Hierarchy

7. **Reading Continuous Text**
   a. stories
   b. passages
   c. paragraphs

6. **Reading Single Sentences**

5. **Reading Words**
   a. multisyllable, phonetically irregular
   b. multisyllable, predictable
   c. root with affix
   d. single syllable, phonetically irregular
   e. single syllable, predictable
   f. high frequency words (basic sight words)

Higher Level

4. **Reading Word Parts**

   — Affixes
   a. prefixes
   b. suffixes

   — Irregular phonograms

   — Vowels
   a. diphthongs
   b. digraphs
   c. r-controlled
   d. pairs

   — Consonants
   a. unsounded
   b. digraphs
   c. blends

Lower Level

3. **Reading Single Letters**

   — Vowels
   a. schwa
   b. short
   c. long

   — Consonants
   a. multisound (blends)
   b. single-sound

2. **Hearing Sounds in Words (Auditory Analysis)**

1. **Recognizing Letter Shapes (Visual Analysis)**

manuals, and scope and sequence charts available to that teacher. The skill hierarchy in Table 3-2 is a hierarchy of word recognition skills that combines information from several sources into a single listing. This kind of skill hierarchy would be particularly useful to a teacher who creates individualized reading curricula for each student in the class. Sometimes a teacher will find a published skill hierarchy (perhaps part of a criterion-referenced test) that can be utilized, like the one shown in Table 3-3, taken from Alexander (1979). Any skill hierarchy fulfills the require-

Table 3-3 Skill Hierarchy for Early Decoding Skills*

Structural Analysis

Words in context

Common prefixes:	un	in,im
	re	ex
	dis	en,em
	post	be
	pre	con,com,col

Common suffixes:	s,es	tion,sion
	ed	ry,ty,ity
	ing	ble,able,ible
	er,or,ist	ment
		ful

Identification of root words

Compound words

Applied Phonics

Syllabication

Common phonograms:	-all,-ight,-and,-ay -tion,-ing
Vowel diphthongs:	oy,oi,ow,ou others
Vowel digraphs:	oa,ee,ay,ai,ea,ai aw,au,oo,ew
Vowels controlled by r:	ar,or,er,ir,ur
Consonant blends:	bl,cl,fl,pl br,cr,pr,tr sm,st,scr,spr others
Consonant digraphs:	ch,th,sh,wh ph,gh,ng,nk others
Long vowels:	CV pattern CVe pattern (e-marker)
Short vowels:	CVC pattern
Consonants:	(simple) b,d,g,h,m,n, hard c and g (more difficult) z,r,j, soft c and g g,v,l,x and voiced s

*The source of information for this table is from J. Alexander (Ed.), *Teaching Reading.* Boston: Little Brown & Company, 1979.

ments of Step 2, as long as it identifies the skills encompassed within the area being assessed and the order in which these skills are learned. For convenience, we have arranged each skill hierarchy so that it reads from the top of the page to the bottom, from the highest level of skill performance to the lowest.

Not all teachers will need to develop or select a skill hierarchy that extends across all developmental levels of the skill, that is, from kindergarten through eighth grade. While some teachers teach across the whole spectrum of ability, most do not. The skill hierarchy selected in Step 2 should reflect the curriculum range for the students in each teacher's class. If a teacher routinely works with students on fractions, decimals, and percentages in math, these skills would all be included in the math skills hierarchy. On the other hand, if the teacher seldom works with students beyond simple computation of whole numbers, then including fractions and decimals on the math skill hierarchy would seem unnecessary. Similarly, a teacher who works with beginning readers may need to include a variety of readiness skills on the skill hierarchy for reading. Including these skills would not be particularly useful to a teacher who deals primarily with more skilled readers.

Since experts frequently disagree on the arrangement of skills within a curriculum-domain, the teacher can expect to have different skill hierarchies, depending on the source of information used. Regardless of the source, the goal of Step 2 is for the teacher to have an outline of the component skills and subskills within each curriculum area of interest.

Step 3: Decide Where to Begin

Once the teacher has determined which areas will be assessed and has found or developed skill hierarchies for those areas, he/she must decide where to begin with each student. This is not a simple decision: in a "test down" paradigm the teacher cannot just start at the beginning of the hierarchy and test until the student fails. The teacher's goal is to choose a starting point at which the student will make enough errors for the teacher to analyze the error patterns, but not so many as to frustrate the student. Therefore, the teacher must ask, "What do I know about this student, with respect to the skills outlined on my skills hierarchy, that would help me decide how high up the hierarchy I can initiate the assessment process?" To answer this question the teacher must look at any data that are already available.

The teacher could begin the search by examining the student's permanent school record. Such a record generally indicates how well a student has performed on academic tasks in the past. It might also contain computer printouts profiling the student's performance on a recently administered group achievement test. Sometimes, the school psychologist and/or educational diagnostician has administered some achievement and aptitude tests as part of a placement evaluation. Useful information may be available in the psychological or child study team report. Information can also be gained from teachers who taught the child previously. Often they can describe the skills that the child had mastered and those which seemed to be lacking. A final source of data might be the most recent IEP. All of this information should be reviewed to help the teacher decide the level and complexity of the tasks to be given in the initial stages of the assessment.

As the teacher reviews the available data, he/she has several options for deciding where to begin. These options are summarized in Table 3-4. In Situation 1,

Table 3-4   Guidelines for Deciding Where to Begin

Situation	Descriptions	Decisions
1. Data sources yield consistent information	All information places student's functioning level within same level ±1 year	Choose survey at highest point of functioning
2. Data sources yield no usable information	Information is out of date or nonexistent	Administer quick placement test
3. Data sources yield inconsistent information	Information shows fluctuation in functioning level > 1 year	a) Administer quick placement test b) Split the difference c) Choose most reliable source

the data sources yield consistent information, allowing the teacher to make a best guess as to where to begin. For example, when Jimmy's teacher needed to choose a starting point for Jimmy's math assessment, he reviewed several sources of data. Jimmy's IEP stated that his math functioning was at a 2.5 grade level. Jimmy's math score on the Metropolitan Achievement Test administered the previous spring was at the 2.8 grade level. Jimmy's previous teacher had reported that Jimmy had finished the second-grade math book. Given the consistency of this information, the teacher decided to survey Jimmy using materials appropriate for students beginning third grade.

If the search for information leads to Situation 2, in which the information is unavailable or useless, the teacher would have to administer a quick assessment. Vicky was a transfer student from another school. Her most recent test scores were two years old and there was no current IEP in her file. To establish a starting point for Vicky's reading assessment, the teacher administered a graded word list (such as the one from the Spache Diagnostic Reading Scales) which took only five minutes and gave an estimate of Vicky's reading level.

In Situation 3, the information is inconsistent and requires that the teacher use his/her judgment about how to interpret the available data. The information search on Frank yielded math scores which ranged from 1.5 grade level on the Metropolitan Achievement Test to 3.4 grade level on the Key Math Arithmetic Diagnostic Test, both administered the previous spring. Frank's report card indicated that in third grade he had received D and F grades in math. The teacher had three options:

1. He/she could administer a quick assessment such as the arithmetic subtest of the Wide Range Achievement Test to obtain a computational level.
2. He/she could assume that Frank's skills fell somewhere between mid-first and mid-third grade and "split the difference" by designing a survey at the mid-second-grade level.
3. He/she could trust that the Key Math score was more reliable—because it was derived from an individually administered test—and choose or create a survey which contains third-grade items.

Because in all three situations the decision about where to begin relies heavily on teacher judgment, the teacher should keep in mind that this initial decision is, at best, an "educated guess." It may have to be revised once the initial assessment data are collected. But if the teacher has established rapport with the student prior to initial testing and has presented the assessment task as an opportunity to help the student rather than as a "pass/fail" situation, then revising the starting point should not have a negative impact on the student. In our experience we have found that teachers become better at deciding where to begin the assessment after they have used the assessment plan several times. This means that inexperienced teachers should adopt a "learn as you go" attitude and accept the fact that there are no simple rules.

Step 4: Select or Develop Survey Instrument

The assessment will proceed from a broad survey of competence to a more in-depth probe of errors and weaknesses in a particular instructional area. Therefore, the next step is to select or develop a *survey instrument* to measure skill competence at the approximate level decided upon in Step 3. The purpose of the survey is to get a sample of the student's behavior in one or more of the following areas: reading word recognition, reading comprehension, written expression, mathematical concepts and computation, mathematical problem solving and application, learning style, interest, and motivators. And although it is important for the teacher to test efficiently and try to get a lot of information as quickly as possible, it is also important that the teacher not try to accomplish too much with any single survey test. A general rule is to find or develop measures that assess only one of these instructional areas at a time. Each survey will contain items or tasks for the student to perform at the level selected in Step 3, and each survey will provide an overview of what the student can and cannot do. It may be necessary to select or develop as many as eight survey measures for some students.

In selecting or developing a survey, the teacher needs to consider the complexity level of the skills to be assessed, and some characteristics of the student who is being tested. There are thousands of paragraphs available for surveying oral reading competence at approximately the fifth-grade level. The choice of paragraph should be dictated by the interests and experiences of the student. This will make it more likely that the student will be familiar with the vocabulary in the passage, and be motivated to read as well as he/she can.

Step 5: Get Ready to Test

After the teacher has selected or developed the survey instruments, and before testing can actually get underway, the teacher needs to answer some questions. Is this survey to be administered one-to-one, or is this a test the student can do independently? If it is to be an independent work assignment, will the student be working alone at a desk with pencil and paper, or will the student need special equipment—a tape recorder, typewriter, or card reader—in order to carry out the test? Does the student know how to use the equipment, or will instruction be needed? Has the teacher provided a quiet, comfortable place for the student to work? Will the other students be assigned work which keeps the noise level low enough for the student to remain undistracted? If this is to be a teacher-administered test, does the teacher have a copy of the test for him/herself as well as one for the student, and a form on which to record student responses? If equipment will be needed in the teacher-administered test, is it available? What will the other students in the class be doing while the teacher is administering the test? Being prepared, thinking ahead, and testing in an organized, well-managed environment does much to put the student at ease and elicit his/her best performance.

Step 6: Administer the Survey

Since it is not the *score* that is important in survey testing, but the details of the student's *performance* that will give the teacher usable assessment data, the teacher needs to capture both how the student responds and how he/she arrives at the responses. Therefore, students doing a math survey should be encouraged to write out all their computations. Students given writing assignments should be asked to avoid erasing, and to cross out unwanted responses. Students providing oral responses should be tape-recorded. During the administration of the survey, the teacher should also be prepared to introduce reinforcers to students reluctant to respond and to alter the test directions for students unable to understand the test requirements. But teachers should always note these alterations in the test conditions, because they will influence the interpretation of test results.

Step 7: Note Errors and Performance Style

While the student is performing the tasks of the survey, the teacher should record the conditions under which the test was administered and the performance style of the student. If the test is administered one-to-one, the teacher is in an excellent position to observe student performance and note important patterns in behavior. For example, does the student consistently approach unknown words in a particular way? Does the student use inappropriate phrasing while reading? Does the student count on his/her fingers while solving computation problems in math? As well, the teacher can cue the student during individually administered tests to determine if performance improves when some support is given. Such cues for eliciting responses must be noted, so that correct interpretation of the survey results can be made. Nonacademic behaviors can also be observed during the survey. The teacher should be able to figure out how long the student can remain on-task, if he/she can work independently, and if the support or reinforcement sought from the teacher is task-related or merely attention-seeking.

While the test is going on, or after the test has been completed, the survey must be scored and errors identified. The scored copy of the survey, together with the teacher's notes on errors and performance style, form the basis for the analysis and summary of findings in Step 8.

Step 8: Analyze Findings and Summarize Outcomes

Once the survey has been scored and the individual errors have been identified, the teacher must analyze the findings and summarize them in a meaningful way. The importance of this step in the assessment process cannot be overemphasized. It is at this point that the teacher interprets and summarizes the data in a way that can lead to hypotheses about student needs. These hypotheses form the basis for generating *probes* and initiating instructional plans. Therefore, the teacher cannot simply convert the raw score the student achieved on the survey into a grade score, percentile rank, or age score, nor can the teacher simply make some judgments about which grade level book the student should be working with. Rather, on the basis of the student's performance on the survey, it should be possible for the teacher to specify where probing needs to be done and where teaching might begin.

To accomplish Step 8, the teacher looks at the survey results to determine *patterns of errors* (that is, classes of skills that seem to be deficient) and *single persistent errors* (that is, specific mistakes made every time the task was presented). For example, the teacher may find that a student misread several words, all of which contain blends, or that the student misspelled all words with double consonants. The teacher does not focus on each blend or misspelled word, but notes the *pattern*, or class, of errors that has been uncovered on the survey. Another teacher may find that a student read most blends well but missed every word beginning with "bl," or misspelled words with "tion." These are single persistent errors.

In analyzing the survey for patterns of errors or single persistent errors, it is just as important to consider the items performed correctly as those performed incorrectly. If the teacher focuses only on the missed items, he/she may fail to recognize instances where that same skill may have been demonstrated appropriately. For example, while a student may have missed several items on an oral reading test involving a particular vowel digraph, further analysis may indicate numerous instances where words containing that digraph were read correctly. Such a pattern of performance suggests that the skill *has* been learned, though perhaps not mastered totally. This finding would lead the teacher to provide the student with additional opportunities to practice the skill of reading digraphs, but would save the teacher from having to plan introductory lessons on that skill. When the student has made many similar errors on the survey, and further analysis indicates correct performance on few items with the same pattern, it may be appropriate to re-survey at a less difficult level. The student needs to be given the opportunity to demonstrate the skills he/she has mastered, those which are deficient, and those which the student consistently cannot demonstrate.

In Step 8, then, the teacher reviews all the errors the student has made and all the items the student performed correctly. The teacher searches for patterns of errors in skill performance and tries to determine whether the student demonstrates deficits on a consistent or inconsistent basis. The teacher uses a recordkeeping form to note the particular skills that seem to be demonstrated adequately, those which appear deficient, and those ·which were not tapped by the survey. At this stage, the use of the skill hierarchy as a guide to the recordkeeping form allows the teacher to begin to organize his/her analysis of the assessment data. It cues the teacher about what to look for in the survey results, so that he/she can determine which skills must be judged before further assessment and/or teaching decisions can be made.

Figure 3-C is an example of a form on which survey data collected in reading might be summarized. It is derived from the skill hierarchy given in Table 3-2. At this point in the assessment for instructional planning, the teacher would complete the Survey line of the form. Probe lines would be completed after probe results have been analyzed.

Student _____   School _____   Teacher _____

Reading Level—Initial Survey / ASSESSMENT TASKS	Reading continuous text (a,b,c)*	Reading sentences	Reading words (a,b,c,d,e)*	Reading word parts—affixes (a,b)*	Reading word parts—irregular phonograms	Reading word parts—vowels (a,b,c,d)*	Reading word parts—consonants (a,b,c)*	Reading single letters—vowels (a,b,c)*	Reading single letters—consonants (a,b,)*	Hearing sounds in words	Recognizing letter shapes	High frequency words—phonetically predictable	High frequency words—phonetically irregular	System for attacking unknown words
Survey														
Initial Probe														
Further Probe														
Further Probe														
Further Probe														
UPDATE														

*Refer to skill hierarchy presented in Table 4-1.

Code—Survey and Probe

1—Skill known	3—Need more information	5—Not assessed
2—Skill known at lower level	4—Skill not known	

Figure 3-C Assessment to Instruction Data Sheet (Word Recognition)

Figure 3-D shows the form as it might look after the teacher had analyzed a survey. The teacher can see, at a glance, the reading skills that were not tapped by the survey (reading continuous text, reading word parts, etc.), those which the student performed competently (reading sentences), and those which the students performed inconsistently or not at all (reading multisyllable phonetically irregular words and attacking unknown multisyllable phonetically irregular words).

Student _____   School _____   Teacher _____

Reading Level— Initial Survey **3.5** / ASSESSMENT TASKS	Reading continuous text (a,b,c)*	Reading sentences	Reading words (a,b,c,d,e)*	Reading word parts—affixes (a,b)*	Reading word parts—irregular phonograms	Reading word parts—vowels (a,b,c,d)*	Reading word parts—consonants (a,b,c)*	Reading single letters—vowels (a,b,c)*	Reading single letters—consonants (a,b.)*	Hearing sounds in words	Recognizing letter shapes	High frequency words—phonetically predictable	High frequency words—phonetically irregular	System for attacking unknown words
Survey	5	1	3	5	5	5	5	5	5	5	5	3	3	4
Initial Probe														
Further Probe														
Further Probe														
Further Probe														
UPDATE														

*Refer to skill hierarchy presented in Table 4-1.

Code—Survey and Probe

1—Skill known   3—Need more information   5—Not assessed

2—Skill known at lower level   4—Skill not known

Figure 3-D Assessment to Instruction Data Sheet (Word Recognition)

Step 9: Hypothesize Reasons for Errors and Determine Areas to Probe

Once the teacher has completed a summary of the student's error patterns on the survey, it is time to hypothesize the reasons for the errors and determine what testing or probing needs to be planned. First, the teacher must eliminate the possibility that the errors on the survey resulted from a student's disinterest in performing the task. The teacher must re-think whether or not this survey result was indeed a measure of the student's *best* performance. If the results of the survey can be attributed to a student's lack of comfort, interest, or motivation, then the teacher must re-design the testing environment and re-survey, discarding, for the moment, the results of the initial survey. If, however, the teacher can reassure him/herself that the survey results represent a student's motivated performance, then the teacher can proceed with hypothesizing the causes for the errors.

Two hypotheses are possible: either the errors were made because the skill is known but could not be performed under those particular test conditions, or the errors were made because the skill is not known. If the teacher hypothesizes that the student could demonstrate the skill under different circumstances, the teacher must have some evidence that it was the task requirements which led to the errors. For example, while writing a paragraph, a student's use of capital letters and periods was erratic. Because the task of writing demanded a variety of skills (i.e., generating ideas, representing the ideas graphically, spelling words, and using conventions of print), it is logical for the teacher to hypothesize that the student's erratic performance was the result of trying to think of too many things at once. The teacher would then choose to probe capitalization and punctuation skills, using a less complex writing task.

However, if a student never used capital letters in a story that was one run-on sentence with no punctuation, the teacher might hypothesize that the student does not know these skills. In that case, the teacher would probe knowledge of capitalization and punctuation at a lower level, perhaps using "fill in the blanks" or recognition tasks.

Hypothesizing the causes for errors on the survey test helps the teacher to clarify what further information is needed about the student, what skills need to be tested, and under what conditions. Table 3-5 summarizes possible causes for errors and the next step for each.

Table 3-5 Hypothesizing Causes for Errors

Hypothesized Cause	Next Step	EXAMPLE	
		Survey Required	Probe Should Require
Task too complex	Probe with less complex task	Reading paragraphs	Reading words
Response mode inappropriate	Probe with different response mode	Writing	Speaking
Response level too difficult	Probe at lower response level	Recall responses	Recognition responses
Student required cues/prompts	Probe 1:1 with teacher prompts	No teacher help	Teacher to offer cues
Skill not known	Probe prerequisite skills	Reading words	Giving letter sounds

Step 10: Probe (Select or Develop Probes/ Administer Probes/Analyze Errors)

With a clear picture in mind of what further information is needed on each student, the teacher must select or generate probes. Very often probes can be found in subtests of commercially available tests or in unit tests or workbook pages that are part of curricular materials. Sometimes probes must be created by the teacher. The teacher must take special care that the probe selected accurately reflects the skill to be tested and the manner in which the teacher wishes to test the skill.

Then the teacher would administer the probe and, following the same procedures as in Step 8, analyze errors and summarize findings.

Step 11: Complete Recordkeeping Forms and Generate Teaching Objectives

Perhaps the most essential part of assessment for instructional planning is the recordkeeping. The skill hierarchies generated in Step 2 are converted into a recordkeeping form, which is utilized in Steps 8 and 10 for summarizing error patterns from the surveys and probes. These recordkeeping forms guide the teacher in identifying further assessment needs. It is also from these recordkeeping forms that the teacher can generate instructional plans. The forms summarize information in three areas: skills known, skills not known, and skills for which further information must be gathered or for which information is not yet complete. The teacher should be able to glance at his/her recordkeeping forms for each student and determine areas that need not be taught (skills known), areas in which to begin teaching (skills not known), and areas in which more information must be gathered as teaching progresses (incomplete information). Using this information, the teacher can generate a list of teaching objectives for each student, beginning with the easiest skill on the hierarchy in which the student demonstrated poor performance.

Step 12: Start Teaching/Update Assessment Information

As the teacher utilizes assessment information and begins instruction, additional information will quickly emerge. Information on skills that were not measured initially with the survey or probes will become available. Student responses during teaching will provide information with which the teacher can regularly update the recordkeeping forms. As new information comes to light in the course of teaching, and the recordkeeping forms are filled in, new skill needs may be identified. New instructional objectives can be written from this new information on a regular basis, and the response-contingent instruction cycle continues (see Figure 1-A).

SUMMARY

This 12-step procedure for conducting an assessment for instructional planning (summarized in Table 3-6) is a systematic approach for gathering and interpreting assessment data. The strategy provides a way for assessment information to become part of instructional planning. While the strategy is utilized most easily in the assess-

Table 3-6 Steps in the Assessment Process

1. Decide what to assess.

2. Select or develop a skill hierarchy.

3. Decide where to begin.

4. Select or develop survey instrument.

5. Get ready to test.

6. Administer the survey.

7. Note errors and performance style.

8. Analyze findings and summarize outcomes.

9. Hypothesize reasons for errors and determine areas to probe.

10. Probe.

11. Complete recordkeeping forms and generate teaching objectives.

12. Start teaching; update assessment information.

ment of *what* to teach (reading, written expression, and math), we also advocate use of the strategy in the assessment of interest, motivators, and learning style—factors which help teachers determine *how* to teach.

In the next four chapters we will move through this strategy in a step-by-step sequence, in order to illustrate its use in assessing reading, written expression, mathematics, learning style, interest, and motivators. In each chapter the discussion will begin at Step 2 since we will assume that the decision to test each area has already been made. At the beginning of learning to do an assessment for instructional planning, we suggest that teachers move through each of the steps without cutting corners. As a teacher becomes more familiar with the strategy, understanding of the goal of each step, and experienced in implementing the plan, it will be possible to skip steps, to condense steps, or to modify this assessment sequence to suit the teacher's own style and approach with children. We see learning to approach assessment systematically much like learning to cook. When starting out, it is important to follow each directive of the cookbook precisely, and to perform each function exactly as the cookbook suggests. As one achieves some success and some experience in cooking, one begins to learn where it is possible to change the sequence of steps, where it is possible to adapt the recipe, and where it is possible to add a style or flair of the cook's own without jeopardizing the recipe. The same is true in becoming an expert at assessment for instructional planning. No step should be skipped until the teacher is confident that the end result of the assessment will be information derived in a systematic and thoughtful way to provide the basis for instructional planning.

4

Assessment of Reading Skills

Learning to read is basic to all academic functioning. Reading can be defined as word calling (the ability to translate the letter code into the words the letters represent), decoding (deciphering the code by knowing and blending the parts), or comprehension (matching oral and written words and understanding their meanings). However it is defined, reading is a complex and demanding task that should be mastered during the school-age years. Since many students seem to have difficulty learning to read well, remedial programs often focus on the teaching of reading skills. Most teachers will find that in Step 1 of the assessment sequence they have determined that an assessment of reading skills is of critical importance for many of their students.

Before an assessment of reading can begin, we must decide which skills will be considered part of the reading domain. There have been hundreds of books and articles on reading in the last decade, and little agreement on what constitutes the field. For example, Howards (1980) discusses reading in terms of word recognition, meanings, and study skills. Fry (1977) includes four areas as basic to reading: phonics, word analysis, vocabulary, and comprehension. Ingram (1980) suggests reading assessment be done in the areas of readiness, sight words and vocabulary, word analysis skills, and higher competencies (e.g., reference materials). Wallace and Larsen (1978) separate the reading task into word analysis and reading comprehension.

In this chapter we will consider the reading domain as consisting of two broad areas: *word recognition* (which includes both instant recognition of high frequency words and decoding skills) and *comprehension*. Our assessment for instructional planning will evaluate student performance in these two broad areas separately—although, of course, interrelatedly.

We have divided reading this way because our experience has shown that these two areas of reading develop in a parallel, not hierarchical fashion, and because students often do not show equal growth in these two areas. We have seen children who are adept at word recognition but who demonstrate serious deficiencies in comprehension tasks; they do not understand what they read. Other students, with inadequate decoding skills for their age and/or capacity, have shown comprehension skills that are commensurate with their decoding skills; they understand everything they are capable of reading. A third group of students understands material at a level well beyond the test-derived competency level of their decoding skills; they can read and understand material exceeding what we know to be their decoding capacity. Yet another group of students demonstrates age- or capacity-appropriate comprehension of reading material if the material is presented orally, although they cannot decode the reading material; they can understand the meaning of the printed text but they cannot read it. Our observations of students in each of these four groups lead us to believe that it is useful to organize the reading assessment into the broad areas of word recognition and comprehension and to assess these two components of reading separately.

In applying the strategy of assessment for instructional planning, steps 2 through 12 are carried out first for the assessment of word recognition skills, then for the assessment of reading comprehension skills.

ASSESSMENT OF WORD RECOGNITION SKILLS

Step 2: Select or Develop a Skill Hierarchy (Word Recognition)

Word recognition is defined as the ability to identify words automatically and to demonstrate a system for decoding new or unknown words. An operational definition for word recognition is: *The student can read the words that are presented to him/her.*

There are a variety of sources for establishing a skill hierarchy in word recognition. These include the scope and sequence charts from basal reading series and the hierarchies, or skill lists, presented in any textbook on teaching reading. The hierarchy shown in Table 4-1 was created from a combination of these sources. We have constructed the hierarchy so that it includes both skill complexity (Levels 7 and 6) and skill development (Levels 5–1). This is in keeping with our "test down" philosophy of assessment.

The highest level of performance in the word recognition hierarchy is reading continuous text (stories, passages of several pages in length, or several continuous paragraphs). In this kind of textual reading, the student confronts a large quantity of print and uses strategies of word attack, as well as context cues, to read the material.

One step down the hierarchy, the amount of print is reduced, and the stu-

Table 4-1 Word Recognition Hierarchy

7. Reading Continuous Text
  a. stories
  b. passages
  c. paragraphs
	— Vowels
	  a. diphthongs
	  b. digraphs
	  c. r-controlled
	  d. pairs

6. Reading Single Sentences	— Consonants
	  a. unsounded
	  b. digraphs
	  c. blends

5. Reading Words
  a. multisyllable, phonetically irregular
  b. multisyllable, predictable
  c. root with affix
  d. single syllable, phonetically irregular
  e. single syllable, predictable
  f. high frequency words (basic sight words)
	3. Reading Single Letters
	— Vowels
	  a. schwa
	  b. short
	  c. long
	— Consonants
	  a. multisound (blends)
	  b. single-sound

4. Reading Word Parts
— Affixes
  a. prefixes
  b. suffixes
— Irregular phonograms
	2. Hearing Sounds in Words (Auditory Analysis)
	
	1. Recognizing Letter Shapes (Visual Analysis)

dent reads single sentences. The possibility of using context cues to read difficult words is maintained in sentence reading.

Level 5 on the hierarchy reduces the amount of print confronting the student even more. Here the student reads lists of single words, either as sight words or as words to sound out. At this level the use of context as a way of figuring out a word is eliminated. Within the single word level are words of varying difficulty—from phonetically irregular multisyllable words to single syllable phonetically regular or predictable words.

One step down from reading words is reading word parts—combinations of letters. Word parts include vowel-letter combinations, consonant-letter combinations, and affixes.

Below the reading of word parts is decoding of single letters. Here the student would provide sounds for individual vowel or consonant letters.

Levels 2 and 1 of the hierarchy deal with important readiness skills: hearing sounds in words, and recognizing and discriminating letter shapes.

Step 3: Decide Where to Begin (Word Recognition)

Based on information available, the teacher needs to make a gross distinction: is this student a functional reader (skills at the level of grade 2.5 or better) or a beginning reader (skills below grade 2.5)? If the student is a functional reader, the student's word recognition skills will be surveyed at the highest level of the hierarchy: reading continuous text (Level 7). If the student is a beginning reader, the survey will begin at the level of reading words (Level 5).

In order to classify readers as functional or beginning, the teacher would review the student's record to find the student's most recent reading scores on a

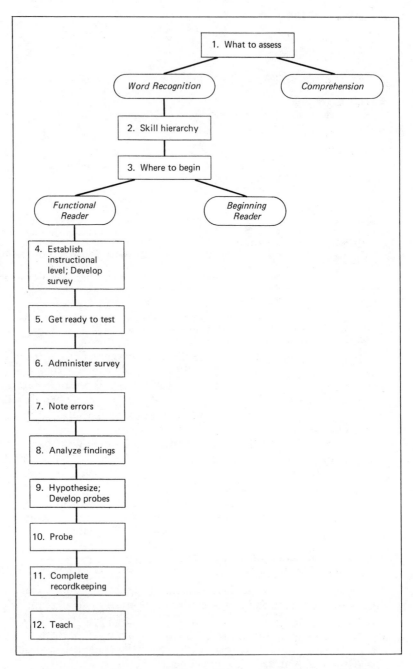

Figure 4-A Organization of Reading Chapter: Assessment Model Thus Far

group-administered achievement test (such as the California Achievement Test, the Iowa Test of Basic Skills, or the Metropolitan Achievement Test) or on an individually administered diagnostic test (such as the Woodcock Reading Mastery Test). Or, the teacher could base the decision on the reading level of the basal series in which the student is working. If none of these sources is available or none provides useful information, the teacher could determine a reading level quickly by administering either a graded word list or the reading recognition subtest of a standardized test such as the Wide Range Achievement Test, the Peabody Individual Achievement Test, or the Woodcock Reading Mastery Test. (Complete references for these and other tests can be found in Appendix A). The teacher should remember that the only purpose of this testing is to determine whether the student should be categorized as a functional reader (at or above grade 2.5) or a beginning reader (below grade 2.5). Therefore, the teacher should not do any lengthy or elaborate testing at this point—only enough to establish this distinction.

Because the reading assessment for functional and beginning readers begins at different steps in the hierarchy, and uses a different selection of assessment instruments (though both follow the 12-step procedure), the remaining discussion on assessment of word recognition skills will describe Steps 4 through 12 for functional readers first. Then we will retrace Steps 4–12 for assessment of beginning readers. Figure 4-A illustrates how the decision-making, thus far, has influenced the organization of material for this chapter.

ASSESSMENT OF WORD RECOGNITION: FUNCTIONAL READERS

Step 4: Select or Develop Survey Instrument
(Word Recognition / Functional Readers)

The assessment of word recognition skills for the functional reader will begin at Level 7, by having the student read textual material aloud. The first decision the teacher makes is what material will be read. In making this decision, the teacher must consider the level, content, and length of the material.

The level of material is determined by establishing the child's instructional reading level. (Frustration and independent levels may also be established at this time, although these will be less important in determining the material for the survey instrument.)

According to Smith and Robinson (1980), the instructional level is established if the student can read 95% of the words on a graded informal reading inventory (IRI) or word list. Betts (1950) suggests that instructional level is determined at a level of 90% accuracy on word recognition. We believe that the Betts criterion is adequate when the purpose in establishing instructional level is to help the teacher determine the appropriate level of survey test materials.

Most reading texts suggest using an informal reading inventory to determine instructional reading level. A sampling of published inventories which are appropriate for gathering this information can be found in Table 4-2. If the teacher does not have access to a published IRI, it is possible to create one. Smith and Robinson (1980) and Betts (1950) offer guidelines for teachers who wish to create their own IRIs.

Table 4-2 Published Reading Inventories

Name	Publisher	Aspects
Advanced Reading Inventory, J. L. Johns, 1981	Wm. C. Brown	*Grade 7—College* Includes graded word lists, graded passages and cloze tests Comprehensive for older students
Analytical Reading Inventory, (2nd ed.), M. L. Woods and A. Moe, 1981	Chas. E. Merrill	*Pre-reading—9th grade* Includes 7 graded word lists, and 10 graded passages Has three forms Comprehensive for elementary students
Informal Reading Diagnosis, (2nd ed.), G. Rae and T. C. Potter, 1981	Prentice-Hall	*Pre-reading—8th grade* Spanish and English word lists and paragraphs Includes graded word lists, paragraphs, and cloze test More comprehensive than IRI
On the Spot Reading Diagnosis File, including San Diego Quick Assessment, M. H. LePray, 1978	The Center for Applied Research in Education	*Primary—11th grade* Reproducible tests Graded word lists and paragraphs More than IRI
Sucher-Allred Reading Placement Inventory, F. Sucher and R. A. Allred, 1973	Economy	*Primer—Grade 9* Graded word lists and paragraphs Individual student booklets
Classroom Reading Inventory, N. J. Silvaroli, 1976	Wm. C. Brown	*Grade 1—8* Inventory Graded word lists and paragraphs Graded spelling lists
Individual Reading Placement Inventory, E. H. Smith and W. G. Bradtmueller, 1969	Follett	*Middle School—Adult* Graded word recognition and paragraphs

Our interest in establishing the instructional level of a functional reader is to enable the teacher to choose oral reading materials that are difficult enough so that the student will make sufficient errors for an analysis to be done, but not so difficult that the student will be unable to read any of the material correctly. Our rule is to select survey materials that are 1/2 to 1 grade level above the student's instructional level.

Table 4-3 Published IRIs and Reading Tests:
Sources for Reading Survey Materials

Name of Test	Publisher
Advanced Reading Inventory	Wm. C. Brown
Analytical Reading Inventory	Chas. E. Merrill
Botel Reading Inventory	Follett
Brigance Diagnostic Inventory of Basic Skills	Curriculum Associates
Brigance Inventory of Essential Skills	Curriculum Associates
Diagnostic Reading Scales	CTB/McGraw-Hill
Durrell Analysis of Reading Difficulty	Harcourt Brace Jovanovich
Gates-McKillop Reading Diagnostic Tests	Teachers College Press
Gilmore Oral Reading Test	Harcourt Brace Jovanovich
Gray Oral Reading Test	Bobbs-Merrill
Informal Reading Diagnosis	Prentice-Hall
Mann-Suiter Developmental Reading Diagnosis	Allyn & Bacon
On the Spot Reading Diagnosis File	The Center for Applied Research in Education
Reading Miscue Inventory	Macmillan
Stanford Diagnostic Reading Test	Harcourt Brace Jovanovich

The instructional level is also used to determine the length of the material to be read. All students should be asked to read at least 100 words. However, for students whose instructional reading level is better than grade 2.5 but less than 4.0, a shorter passage—no more than 400 words—is suggested. For students whose instructional reading level appears to exceed grade 4.0, a longer passage is recommended.

The content of the material should be selected to match the student's interest area. There are two reasons for this. First, the more interesting the material, the more likely it is that the student will stay with the task. Second, and of more importance, if the material is of interest to the student, he/she will probably have some familiarity with the language being used. If this is the case, the examiner will be able to gather information on the student's use of context clues, word substitutions, and reading for meaning, as well as word attack and vocabulary skills.

Once the teacher has established the level, the length, and the content of the survey materials, the text for the survey can be chosen from a variety of sources. Basal readers and high interest-low vocabulary materials are prepared at graded reading levels and are good sources for survey materials. Published IRIs and reading tests often contain useful texts for oral reading assessment (Table 4-3). Popular magazines, tabloid newspapers, or library books could also capture the interest of the student. The readability level of any materials that are not already graded can be determined by a simple formula. One such procedure, developed by Fry (1977), is given in Appendix B.

Step 5: Get Ready to Test (Word Recognition/Functional Readers)

The survey will require that the functional reader read aloud. The reading survey should be tape-recorded to guarantee greater accuracy in scoring. It will also free the teacher to listen to the survey without having to mark the errors, and this should help the student's performance. Often, when the examiner marks down errors as the student reads aloud, the student will interrupt to ask, "Was that wrong?" or "What did you write down?" Taping allows the student to concentrate on the task and the examiner to mark errors later, when the student is not present.

Before administering the survey, then, the teacher must secure a tape recorder (and extension cord, if necessary), a microphone, and a blank tape, making sure that the equipment is set up near an electrical outlet. The teacher should record the student's name and the date onto the tape. The teacher should also have one copy of the reading material for the student and one copy for him/herself, for following along. Before the testing begins, the teacher should identify and underline all high frequency or basic sight words on this second copy, using a single underscoring to identify highly predictable words, and a double underscoring to identify less predictable (phonetically irregular) words. This marked teacher's copy of the passage will be used later for scoring the student's performance; the marks under high frequency predictable and phonetically irregular words will help the teacher to identify error patterns. (Appendix C lists high frequency words commonly found on basic sight word lists. The words are divided into predictable and phonetically irregular words. This appendix can be used as a reference in marking the teacher's copy of the text).

Next, the teacher has to decide whether the student and teacher should work one-to-one in the oral reading survey, or whether the student would perform just as well, or better, reading the passage into a tape recorder in a quiet corner, alone. In an attempt to use teacher time efficiently, it would, of course, be useful to have the student read the survey into a tape recorder independently, while the teacher works with other students. However, we suggest that the teacher remain with the student, unless it is clear that the student would function more effectively alone.

Whether or not the student works alone, the teacher should provide a quiet, comfortable environment and some motivation to the student to remain on-task and to complete the survey to the best of his/her ability.

Step 6: Administer the Survey (Word Recognition/Functional Readers)

The teacher should be certain to explain to the student the purpose of the oral reading survey and the reasons for the taping. The student should be told clearly where to begin reading and how much to read, what to do when he/she encounters an unfamiliar word, whether or not to expect help from the teacher, what kind of notes, if any, the teacher will be taking, and what will be done with the tape and the teacher's notes.

Once the student begins reading, the teacher should follow along in the second copy of the text. The teacher should be prepared to halt the survey if the student becomes extremely frustrated or fatigued. The teacher should also keep mental notes on the student's posture, anxiety level, and attitude during the reading task. Such information will be recorded on a checklist of reading behaviors (Figure 4-B, Sec-

Student _____ Date _____ Reading Level of Passage _____

I. READING STYLE

CHECKLIST OF BEHAVIORS	Always	Sometimes	Seldom
Reads with expression			
Reads clearly			
Reads word by word			
Observes punctuation			
Reads for meaning (tries to make sense of material)			
Skips or refuses unfamiliar words			
Substitutes linguistically appropriate words			
Perseveres with task			
Is easily frustrated			
Knows beginning sound/unit			
Knows medial sound/unit			
Knows ending sound/unit			

Has method of attack for unknown words—

____ Depends on letter sounds   ____ Tries various methods

____ Depends on syllables   ____ Gives up quickly

Figure 4-B Score Sheet for Error Analysis (Word Recognition)

II. HIGH FREQUENCY WORDS

Phonetically Predictable Words		Phonetically Irregular Words	
Word	Student's error response	Word	Student's error response
Examples of Non-Errors		Examples of Non-Errors	

Total predictable words _____

Number of words known by student _____

Total phonetically irregular words _____

Number of words known by student _____

Figure 4-B Score Sheet for Error Analysis (Word Recognition)—**Continued**

Single Syllable Phonetically Predictable	
Word	Student's error response
Similar words read correctly	

Single Syllable Phonetically Irregular	
Word	Student's error response
Similar words read correctly	

Root with Affix	
Word	Student's error response
Similar words read correctly	

Multisyllable Phonetically Predictable	
Word	Student's error response
Similar words read correctly	

Multisyllable Phonetically Irregular	
Word	Student's error response
Similar words read correctly	

Figure 4-B Score Sheet for Error Analysis (Word Recognition)—Continued

tion I) immediately following the survey and will be useful in interpreting the test results.

The teacher should also be prepared to introduce incentives for completing the reading task, should they become necessary. These might include a token or candy at the end of each paragraph or page of text, and/or a reward for completing the entire reading survey satisfactorily.

Step 7: Note Errors and Performance Style (Word Recognition/Functional Readers)

To "score" the oral reading survey, the teacher first marks the items on Section I of Figure 4-B. Then the teacher listens to the recording of the student's reading and marks the errors on the teacher's underscored copy of the text. Table 4-4 presents a list of errors that should be marked and a set of optional notations for marking them. There are a wide variety of marking systems offered in the literature. They range from very simple to complex. The teacher should use any system with which he/she is comfortable.

We do not think it is necessary for the teacher to mark hesitations, repetitions, or corrections; if a student takes his/her time to decode words, the teacher need only mark if the word is finally decoded incorrectly. When a student initially reads a word incorrectly and then goes back and corrects it, that performance style should be noted by the teacher in Section I, but we see no reason to mark the original reading error.

After listening to the tape and noting the errors, the teacher analyzes the student's reading style. At this point the teacher would add to his/her notes in Section I of Figure 4-B. The teacher tries to answer the question "What global information do I now have about this student vis-à-vis his/her reading of continuous text?"

Step 8: Analyze Findings and Summarize Outcomes (Word Recognition/Functional Readers)

To analyze the findings from the oral reading survey, the teacher would now complete Sections II and III of the score sheet in Figure 4-B, by recording the student's high frequency word errors and decoding word errors. Because the teacher's copy of the passage has already been marked for high frequency words, part of this recording task is simplified. The score sheet has sufficient space to record all incorrectly read words for each error type. Because the teacher groups the errors as he/she records them, it should be possible to see, at a glance, any error pattern(s) that stand out for a particular student.

The next step in the analysis is to go back over the passage to find examples of non-errors (correct reading) in the various categories. In Section II, non-errors are instances of the student reading the same high frequency word correctly. On Section III, non-errors are instances of the student reading similar words, with similar phonetic elements, correctly. These are also noted on Sections II and III of the score sheet.

Next, the teacher counts the number of words in the reading passage that were underscored once or twice and records that number, along with the number of each type read incorrectly, at the bottom of Section II. This tally provides a perspective on the severity of the problem in reading high frequency words.

Table 4-4   Errors to be Recorded on Word Recognition Survey

Type of Error	Suggested Teacher Notation(s)
1. Omission	1. Cross out
2. Addition/insertion	2. Write in with caret is
3. Mispronunciations/substitutions	3. Write student's response above word
4. Teacher-given	4. T above word
5. Ignored punctuation	5. Circle punctuation mark
6. Started word and gave up	6. Write student's attempt followed by ellipses (. . .)
7. Inverted word order	7. Draw an elongated line between inverted words

Examples

1.   She did ~~not~~ like the cakes.

2.   Please ^go^ help me ^with^ carry the table.

3.   Everyone ^goes^ ~~went~~ to the movies.

4.   He came to the ⊤ front ⊤ door.

5.   He went shopping ⊙ Jan bought a new sweater.

6.   The goldfish are in the th... tank.

7.   Sam was⌐not very kind.

Finally, the teacher needs to make note of what system the student is using to attack unknown words. To do this, the teacher examines the misread words, reviews his/her notes on performance style, and tries to answer the following questions: What does the student do when he/she finds words that are unfamiliar? Does the student substitute other words randomly, and if so, are the substitutions linguistically appropriate (e.g., noun for noun)? Are the substitutions contextually correct?

Student _____   School _____   Teacher _____

Reading Level— Initial Survey / ASSESSMENT TASKS	Reading continuous text (a,b,c)*	Reading sentences	Reading words (a,b,c,d,e)*	Reading word parts— affixes (a,b)*	Reading word parts— irregular phonograms	Reading word parts— vowels (a,b,c,d)*	Reading word parts— consonants (a,b,c)*	Reading single letters— vowels (a,b,c)*	Reading single letters— consonants (a,b,)*	Hearing sounds in words	Recognizing letter shapes	High frequency words— phonetically predictable	High frequency words— phonetically irregular	System for attacking unknown words
Survey														
Initial Probe														
Further Probe														
Further Probe														
Further Probe														
UPDATE														

*Refer to skill hierarchy presented in Table 4-1.

Code—Survey and Probe

1—Skill known   3—Need more information   5—Not assessed

2—Skill known at lower level   4—Skill not known

Figure 4-C Assessment to Instruction Data Sheet (Word Recognition)

Does the student rely on beginning letters, smaller units within words, or other phonetic cues? The answers are added to Section I of Figure 4-B.

Now the teacher reviews the survey data and summarizes it on the Assessment to Instruction Data Sheet (Figure 4-C). The form allows the teacher to keep track of ongoing assessment and instructional decisions. The form is designed to give the teacher information in three areas: skills known, skills not known, and skills for which information has not yet been gathered or is not yet complete. The teacher completes the Survey line of the form based on the information gathered thus far, using the code printed at the bottom of the form. The form is organized to match the word recognition hierarchy (Table 4-1) in order to keep the form simple for the teacher and, therefore, easier to use. The lower case letters, (e.g., a, b, c) in the area of "reading continuous text," refer to subcategories of skills as listed in the word recognition skills hierarchy. The teacher can note which of the specific skills within each area were tapped by the survey by circling the appropriate letters.

If the survey was at Level 7, reading continuous text, and the student made errors, the teacher would mark a *3* in the first three columns, because problems in textual reading may involve text, sentences, or words. If there were high frequency words in the text, the teacher would mark the high frequency columns as well. In the final column the teacher would code the student's performance in word attack. For functional readers, the teacher would not survey word parts, but would place a *5* in the columns indicating Levels 4, 3, 2, and 1 of the skill hierarchy.

Step 9: Hypothesize Reasons for Errors and Determine Areas to Probe (Word Recognition/Functional Readers)

Next, the teacher reviews the score sheet which summarizes the errors made on the reading survey and the Assessment to Instruction Data Sheet, and he/she considers one of three hypotheses (summarized in Table 4-5). First, is it possible that these errors were made because the survey material was at too high a grade level and, therefore, frustrating? If the student was unable to read more than three out of ten words in the first three sentences, the teacher should consider the survey material to have been too difficult. The teacher's next step would be to re-survey with material at a lower reading level.

A second possibility is that, although the grade level of the material was appropriate, the content of the material was not. This could occur if the language level or subject matter were inappropriate for the student being tested. Often, stu-

Table 4-5 Summary of Options (Hypothesizing Errors)

Type of Error	Hypothesis	Next Step
More than 3/10 errors in first 3 sentences	Reading level of material too high	Re-survey at lower reading level
Many errors with sight words related to content	Language and/or interest level inappropriate	Re-survey at same reading level using different content
Consistent decoding errors	Task too complex	Probe at same reading level with simpler task

dents are asked to read material containing words which are not in their own vocabularies. If they have reading deficiencies, they are likely to have problems decoding or recognizing words for which they do not have oral language referents. For example, a story about American Indians may contain vocabulary (names of tribes, Indian words) that is unfamiliar to a child who expressed an interest in "cowboys and Indians." If the teacher hypothesizes that this is so, the next step would be to administer another survey using different materials.

A third hypothesis to consider is that the errors represent problems the student has in performing tasks that high on the word recognition hierarchy. If the teacher believes that this hypothesis explains the errors, then the teacher would design or select probes to "test down" the skill hierarchy. If a functional reader has been surveyed at the highest level, i.e., reading continuous text, the teacher should choose one level down the hierarchy for the first probe. This means that the first probe might be to have the student read several single sentences (see Table 4-1).

Step 10: Probe (Word Recognition/ Functional Readers)

If the next step is to probe down the skill hierarchy, the teacher should isolate, from the survey text, sentences in which the student made several errors, and present those sentences, one at a time, to the student. If the student can read more words correctly at the sentence level, the teacher has learned some important things. First, the teacher knows that it is not the words themselves that give the student trouble, but the words embedded in an abundance—perhaps an overwhelming abundance—of text. The teaching task for a student who can read sentences, but not paragraphs, is very different from the teaching task for a student who cannot read the words. Second, the teacher has information on words that were missed on the probe. This information can be compared to the survey results as a measure of the student's consistency and reliability in performing. By using the score sheet from the survey (Figure 4-B) and adding the errors made on the probe, the teacher can validate some initial impressions about word recognition error patterns. Now the teacher might develop a second probe made up of single words which represent these error types, and perhaps a third probe measuring reading of word parts. By continuing to probe down the skill hierarchy, the teacher can identify two things: what skills in the word recognition hierarchy require direct instruction, and how complex this student's reading material should be.

For probes down the skill hierarchy, the teacher can use teacher-made tests or subtests selected from the diagnostic tests listed in Table 4-3. For convenience, we have prepared Table 4-6—a cross-reference of the skills listed on the word recognition hierarchy of Table 4-1 and the diagnostic instruments of Table 4-3. Several tests without oral reading passages have been added. They can be used for other kinds of probes.

Step 11: Complete Recordkeeping Forms and Generate Teaching Objectives (Word Recognition/Functional Readers)

Once the teacher has the results of some probes, those data are added to the Assessment to Instruction Data Sheet. Then, using the data on this form, the teacher can determine in what areas not to teach (skills known), in what areas to begin teaching (skills not known), and in what areas more information must be gathered as

Table 4-6   Reference from Skill Hierarchy to Diagnostic Tests

	7. Reading Continuous Text	6. Reading Single Sentences	5. Reading Words	5. Reading Words (High Frequency)	4. Reading Word Parts	3. Reading Single Letters	2. Hearing Sounds in Words	1. Recognizing Letter Shapes
Advanced Reading Inventory	X		X					
Analytical Reading Inventory	X		X					
Botel Reading Inventory			X			X		
Brigance Diagnostic Inventory of Basic Skills	X		X	X	X	X	X	
Brigance Inventory of Essential Skills	X		X	X	X	X	X	
Diagnostic Reading Scales	X		X		X	X	X	
Dolch Basic Word List				X				
Doren Diagnostic Reading Test			X			X		
Durrell Analysis of Reading Difficulty	X		X		X	X	X	X
Gates-McKillop Reading Diagnostic Test	X		X		X	X	X	X
Informal Reading Diagnosis	X		X					
Informal Reading Placement Inventory	X		X			X	X	
McCullough Word-Analysis Tests			X		X	X	X	X
On the Spot Reading Diagnosis File	X	X	X		X	X	X	X
Stanford Diagnostic Reading Test	X		X			X	X	
Woodcock Reading Mastery Tests			X					X
Wisconsin Tests of Reading Skill Development			X			X		

teaching progresses. Teaching areas and teaching objectives will be generated directly from the recordkeeping form.

Each mark of *4* (survey or probe completed, skill not known) or *2* (skill known at lower level) would become a teaching objective. Each *3* (survey or probe completed, need more information) would alert the teacher that more information should be gathered as the teaching of reading progresses. Each *1* would indicate that the skill does not need to be taught.

Step 12: Start Teaching/Update Assessment Information (Word Recognition/Functional Readers)

Most reading tasks require students to demonstrate a variety of skills. During the course of reading instruction, the student will often be confronted with tasks requiring those skills for which more assessment information is needed. An alert teacher will keep in mind the skills that are in the "more information needed" category and update the recordkeeping form when the information becomes available. If the new assessment information moves a skill to the "skill not known" category, then a new teaching objective would be generated.

ILLUSTRATION: SHAWN

To illustrate the word recognition assessment sequence for functional readers, we will move through Steps 3–12 for Shawn, a fifth-grader who has just been placed in a classroom for learning-disabled students. We begin at Step 3 because Steps 1 and 2 have already been completed. We have decided to assess word recognition skills (Step 1—What to Assess) and will use the hierarchy of skills presented in Table 4-1 (Step 2—Select or Develop Skill Hierarchy).

Step 3: Decide Where to Begin (Shawn)

The teacher found the following information about Shawn's reading performance on Shawn's cumulative record.

Peabody Individual Achievement Test:
  Reading recognition—grade 2.6
  Reading comprehension—grade 2.3
Last basal reader completed—2–1 level

The teacher decided to assess Shawn as a functional reader.

Step 4: Select or Develop Survey Instrument (Shawn)

The teacher administered the Analytical Reading Inventory to Shawn and got the following results:

Independent level: 2.5
Instructional level: 2.7
Frustration level: 3.0

Sudana was sick. Something was wrong inside those four tons of flesh and bone. The big African elephant was leaning against the steel bars of her cage in the Elephant House. Her huge ears were folded back against her neck and shoulders. Not once did she flap them. Her usually restless tail hung straight down not twitching at all.

"What's the matter, old girl?" the zoo doctor asked. He reached through the bars to lay a hand on the elephant's trunk. He felt it in several places. He slipped his hand under her ear, down the length of her rough leg, and back along her body. It was like rubbing warm cement. Sudana had a fever, and a high one.

As he stepped back over the guardrail, the doctor spoke to Bob, her keeper. "Did you give her anything to drink today?"

"Yes," said the keeper. "I filled her water trough twice. She begged for more, but I didn't think she should drink so much."

The doctor nodded. "Don't give her any more," he said. "We've got to get some medicine into her, and she isn't going to like it. Maybe if she's thirsty enough, she'll take some sulfa in her drinking water."

The doctor sat on the guardrail and watched her. He wonder how to handle his heavy patient. The sulfa would have to be weighed out; sixty grams of sulfa were used for every thousand pounds of elephant.

The zoo had no scale big enough to weigh Sudana, so he would have to guess at her weight. The doctor made a guess. About eight thousand pounds was what Sudana must weigh. At sixty grams of sulfa for every thousand pounds of elephant, it would take 480 grams of sulfa. How would the doctor ever get all of that medicine into Sudana?

Figure 4-D Zoo Doctor*

In a conversation with Shawn, the teacher learned that he likes animals and is particularly interested in learning more about zoo animals. The teacher decided to find a survey at the 3.5 grade level, of approximately two pages in length, on the topic of animals. She selected a two-page passage from the story "Zoo Doctor," taken from the Goodman-Burke Reading Miscue Inventory. The passage had a readability level of approximately grade 3.5. The passage is reprinted in Figure 4-D.

Step 5: Get Ready to Test (Shawn)

The teacher found a tape recorder, blank tape, extension cord, and microphone, and set up the testing table. She made an extra copy for herself of the "Zoo Doctor" passage, and drew one line under all the high frequency predictable words, and two lines under all high frequency, phonetically irregular words. The teacher decided to stay with Shawn while he was reading the passage, and to reward him with five minutes of free time if he read through to the end.

Step 6: Administer the Survey (Shawn)

The teacher explained to Shawn the purpose for the testing and the tape recording. She let him try out the tape recorder and microphone to see how they work, then told him about the reward he would get for completing the oral reading task. Then the teacher turned on the tape recorder and had Shawn begin reading the passage. As he read, the teacher began to make mental notes on his reading style to record later on Section I of the score sheet. When he was frustrated by a word, she told him the word, and noted the fact on her copy of the test.

Step 7: Note Errors (Shawn)

First the teacher noted Shawn's reading style, and then she listened to the tape. Figure 4-E shows the teacher's copy of the passage after she had listened to the tape and marked the errors. Single underlined words are the high frequency predictable words and double underlined words are high frequency, phonetically irregular words which were marked by the teacher in advance. The code for the teacher's scoring is the same as the one found in Table 4-4.

Step 8: Analyze Findings and Summarize Outcomes (Shawn)

Next, the teacher recorded the errors on Sections II and III of the score sheet. Figure 4-F is the teacher's record of Shawn's survey, including Section I, which was marked immediately following the taping. Looking over the errors, the teacher drew the following tentative conclusions:

1. Shawn has a good high frequency vocabulary.
2. Shawn stayed with the task and tried to make sense of the story.
3. Shawn remembered some words the teacher told him (e.g., *sulfa* and *medicine*).
4. Shawn's weaknesses lie primarily in the following areas:
    -affixes (particularly suffixes)
    -recognition of phonetically irregular words
    -lack of system to decode unknown words.

Based on these conclusions, she completed the Survey line of the Assessment to Instruction Data Sheet (Figure 4-G). She marked a *3* in the first three columns to indicate the problems he had on the reading passage. She marked a *1* in the high frequency word columns, because performance there had been relatively good. She marked a *4* to indicate lack of competence in word attack skills, and a *5* to indicate that there had been no testing of word parts or single letter-sound correspondences.

Step 9: Hypothesize Reasons for Errors and Determine Areas to Probe (Shawn)

Based on Shawn's performance on the survey, the teacher felt certain that she had used an oral reading passage of the correct length, the correct level of difficulty, and the correct content. She decided that the next step would be to probe down the skill hierarchy, that is, to present Shawn with sentences containing some of the words he missed.

Step 10: Probe (Shawn)

Because Shawn was able to read words structurally similar to one he had missed (he knew 8 words with affixes and misread 16), the teacher decided to create three sentences containing words Shawn had missed. Figure 4-H is the first probe

[handwritten: Susan]
Sudana was sick. Something was wrong inside those four tons *[handwritten: went in / tiny]*
of flesh and bone. The big African elephant was leaning against *[handwritten: fish / lean / hug]*
the steel bars of her cage in the Elephant House. Her huge ears
were folded back against her neck and shoulders. Not once did *[handwritten: fold / shirt / only / usual resting]*
she flap them. Her usually restless tail hung ~~straight~~ down not *[handwritten: turning / tail]*
twitching at all.

"What's the matter, old girl?" the zoo doctor asked. He
reached through the bars to lay a hand on the elephant's trunk. *[handwritten: reach / slip / tail]*
He felt it in several places. He slipped his hand under her ear,
down the length of her ~~rough~~ leg, and back along her body. It *[handwritten: long]*
was like rubbing warm cement. Sudana had a fever, and a high one. *[handwritten: rubber / Susan]*

As he stepped back over the guardrail, the doctor spoke to

Bob, her keeper. "Did you give her anything to drink today?" *[handwritten: fill / tank t...]*

"Yes," said the keeper. "I filled her water trough twice. *[handwritten: fill / fill]*
She begged for more, but I didn't think she should drink so much." *[handwritten: beg / many]*

Figure 4-E Zoo Doctor: Sample*

[handwritten: nod]
The doctor nodded. "Don't give her any more," he said.

"We've got to get some medicine into her, and she isn't going

to like it. Maybe if she's thirsty enough, she'll take some *[handwritten: drink]*
sulfa in her drinking water."

The doctor sat on the guardrail and watched her. He *[handwritten: gate / watch]*
wondered how to handle his ~~heavy~~ patient. The sulfa would have *[handwritten: wonder]*
to be weighed out; sixty grams of sulfa were used for every thousand *[handwritten: six g...]*
pounds of elephant.

The zoo had no scale big enough to weigh Sudana, so he would *[handwritten: walk Susan]*
have to guess at her weight. The doctor made a guess. About eight
thousand pounds was what Sudana must weigh. At sixty grams of sulfa *[handwritten: six / Susan]*
for every thousand pounds of elephant, it would take 480 grams of
sulfa. How would the doctor ever get all of that medicine into *[handwritten: Susan]*
Sudana?

Student ___Shawn K.___   Date ___9/15___   Reading Level of Passage ___3.5___

I. READING STYLE

CHECKLIST OF BEHAVIORS	Always	Sometimes	Seldom
Reads with expression	✓		
Reads clearly	✓		
Reads word by word		✓	
Observes punctuation	✓		
Reads for meaning (tries to make sense of material)		✓	
Skips or refuses unfamiliar words		✓	
Substitutes linguistically appropriate words		✓	
Perseveres with task	✓		
Is easily frustrated			✓
Knows beginning sound/unit	✓		
Knows medial sound/unit		✓	
Knows ending sound/unit			✓

Has method of attack for unknown words—

__✓__ Depends on letter sounds   ____ Tries various methods

____ Depends on syllables   __✓__ Gives up quickly

Figure 4-F Score Sheet for Error Analysis (Word Recognition)

II. HIGH FREQUENCY WORDS

Phonetically Predictable Words		Phonetically Irregular Words	
Word	Student's error response	Word	Student's error response
of	*omitted*	*once*	*only*
much	*many*		
didn't	*did*		
Examples of Non-Errors		Examples of Non-Errors	
of (read correctly 7 times)			

Total predictable words __*170*__

Number of words known by student __*167*__

Total phonetically irregular words __*30*__

Number of words known by student __*29*__

Figure 4-F Score Sheet for Error Analysis (Word Recognition)—**Continued**

Multisyllable Phonetically Irregular

Word	Student's error response
shoulders	shirt
guardrail	(refused)
medicine	(refused)
guardrail	gate
patient	(refused)

Similar words read correctly
elephant
body
enough
medicine
(read correctly 1 time)

Multisyllable Phonetically Predictable

Word	Student's error response
Sudana	Susan
inside	in
African	(refused)
twitching	turning
several	(refused)
sulfa	(refused)

Similar words read correctly
matter
doctor
fewer
handle
thousand
fever
sulfa
(read correctly 3 times)

Root with Affix

Word	Student's error response
tons	tiny
leaning	lean
folded	fold
usually	usual
restless	resting
twitching	turning
reached	reach
slipped	slip
rubbing	rubber
filled	fill
begged	beg
nodded	nod
drinking	drink
watched	watch
wondered	wonder
sixty	six
weighed	(refused)

Similar words read correctly
keeper
bars
asked
places
stepped
thirsty
pounds
ears

Single Syllable Phonetically Irregular

Word	Student's error response
wrong	went
tons	tiny
straight	(omitted)
rough	(omitted)
trough	tank
weigh	walk
weight	(refused)

Similar words read correctly
body
high

Single Syllable Phonetically Predictable

Word	Student's error response
flesh	fish
huge	hug
truck	tail
length	long
twice	t . . .
grams	g . . .

Similar words read correctly
still   tail
spoke   hung
scale   lay
flap   felt
sick   leg
bone
neck
grams
(read correctly 2 times)

Figure 4-F Score Sheet for Error Analysis (Word Recognition)—Continued

Student _Shawn K._____   School _Miller_____   Teacher _Browne_____

Reading Level—Initial Survey **3.5** / ASSESSMENT TASKS	Reading continuous text (a,ⓑ,c)*	Reading sentences	Reading words (ⓐ,ⓑ,ⓒ,ⓓ,ⓔ)*	Reading word parts—affixes (a,b)*	Reading word parts—irregular phonograms	Reading word parts—vowels (a,b,c,d)*	Reading word parts—consonants (a,b,c)*	Reading single letters—vowels (a,b,c)*	Reading single letters—consonants (a,b,)*	Hearing sounds in words	Recognizing letter shapes	High frequency words—phonetically predictable	High frequency words—phonetically irregular	System for attacking unknown words
Survey	3	3	3	5	5	5	5	5	5	5	5	1	1	4
Initial Probe														
Further Probe														
Further Probe														
Further Probe														
UPDATE														

*Refer to skill hierarchy presented in Table 4-1.

Code—Survey and Probe

1—Skill known   3—Need more information   5—Not assessed

2—Skill known at lower level   4—Skill not known

Figure 4-G Assessment to Instruction Data Sheet (Word Recognition)

Sentence	Shawn's Version
1. The boy's shoulders twitched as he reached straight down.	1. The boy's shirt twisted as he reach straight down.
2. The guard refused to admit the rough talking students.	2. The gun refer to add the red talking students.
3. In Africa, patients begged for tons of drinking water.	3. In Africa, parrots beg for tons (rhymed with dons) of drink water.

Figure 4-H   First Probe (Shawn)

administered to Shawn. The teacher presented the sentences, one at a time, and recorded Shawn's errors.

Based on the information from her first probe, the teacher concluded that Shawn could read some unfamiliar words—*straight, talking, Africa*—in sentences that he could not read in a long passage. But he was still misreading words and omitting endings. So, the teacher created a second, third, and fourth probe.

The second probe contained twelve phonetically predictable words Shawn had missed. (These were taken from the words recorded in Section III, Figure 4-E.) The teacher printed these words onto index cards so that she could present them to Shawn, one at a time. The purpose of this probe was to determine if Shawn could sound out the words. On this probe, the teacher discovered that Shawn knew all the letter sounds but that he had no system for decoding. Yet, with the teacher guiding him, he was able to sound out 90% of the words he had previously missed.

The third probe consisted of the phonetically irregular words Shawn had missed (also selected from Section III, Figure 4-E). These were printed on index cards as well. Shawn was able to read only two of the words: straight and once.

The fourth probe was for affixes. The teacher wrote the words, separating the root word from the affix, and Shawn read each part and then blended them. Shawn was able to complete this probe at 95% accuracy.

Step 11: Complete Recordkeeping Forms and Generate Teaching Objectives (Shawn)

With the information from the four probes, the teacher continued to complete the Assessment to Instruction Data Sheet shown in Figure 4-G. She marked a *1* to indicate that the initial probe had tested reading of sentences and that Shawn seemed able to do that. The *3* in the reading words column indicated a need for more information at the word level. The results of the second probe were coded as adequate knowledge of word parts (*1s*), competence at reading phonetically predictable words with teacher assistance (*2 b, e*), and poor word attack skills (*4*). The third probe indicated lack of competence in phonetically irregular words (*4*). The final probe showed knowledge of affixes in isolation (*1*) and capacity to read affix words with teacher assistance (*4*). Her completed Assessment to Instruction Data Sheet is shown in Figure 4-I.

Student _Shawn K._   School _Miller_   Teacher _Browne_

Reading Level— Initial Survey **3.5** / ASSESSMENT TASKS	Reading continuous text (a,ⓑ,c)*	Reading sentences	Reading words (ⓐ,ⓑ,ⓒ,ⓓ,ⓔ)*	Reading word parts— affixes (a,b)*	Reading word parts— irregular phonograms	Reading word parts— vowels (a,b,c,d)*	Reading word parts— consonants (a,b,c)*	Reading single letters— vowels (a,b,c)*	Reading single letters— consonants (a,b,)*	Hearing sounds in words	Recognizing letter shapes	High frequency words— phonetically predictable	High frequency words— phonetically irregular	System for attacking unknown words
Survey	3	3	3	5	5	5	5	5	5	5	5	1	1	4
Initial Probe		1	3											
Further Probe			2 (b, e)	1	1	1	1							4
Further Probe			4 (a, d)											
Further Probe			2 (c)	1										
UPDATE														

*Refer to skill hierarchy presented in Table 4-1.

Code—Survey and Probe

1—Skill known   3—Need more information   5—Not assessed

2—Skill known at lower level   4—Skill not known

Figure 4-I Assessment to Instruction Data Sheet (Word Recognition)

Now Shawn's teacher was ready to create a teaching plan based on the assessment information. The objectives for Shawn were to:

1. Instantly recognize phonetically irregular words that are not high frequency words at 90% accuracy. The initial words to be taught are generated from the survey and probes. As those words are learned, additional words will be added.
2. Learn and apply a system for decoding unknown phonetically regular words with 95% accuracy.
3. Learn and apply a system in order to read words with affixes at 95% accuracy.

Shawn's reading instruction would begin with short passages, and the teacher would gradually increase their length.

Step 12: Start Teaching/Update Assessment Information (Shawn)

Shawn and his teacher will begin working on these objectives. The teacher will take each opportunity to note skills that Shawn masters and new areas in which he appears to be deficient. In this way, new objectives will be identified as the initial teaching objectives for Shawn are mastered.

Now that we have gone through the steps-of-the-assessment model in word recognition for a functional reader, we will follow the same format for a beginning reader.

ASSESSMENT OF WORD RECOGNITION: BEGINNING READERS

If the information obtained in Step 3 indicates that the student is a beginning reader, the teacher executes Steps 4 through 12 of the assessment of word recognition skills in a slightly different manner. The assessment will begin at Level 5 of the skill hierarchy (Table 4-1): reading single words. The teacher will find it easier to assess high frequency words and decoding skills separately. Figure 4-J is an update of Figure 4-A, showing that the next section of our discussion on assessment of word recognition skills in beginning readers will cover assessment of high frequency words and decoding skills, from Steps 4 through 10. Finally, data on both high frequency words and decoding skills are recorded onto a recordkeeping form, and Steps 11 and 12 are completed for beginning readers.

As can be seen in Figure 4-J, the same skill hierarchy applies for the assessment of word recognition skills in both functional and beginning readers. Therefore, our discussion begins at Step 4.

Step 4: Select or Develop Survey Instrument (Word Recognition/Beginning Readers/High Frequency Words)

All beginning readers should be given an assessment of high frequency words by having to read a word list. The length of the list presented to the student should be determined by the student's reading level—the lower the reading level, the shorter the list.

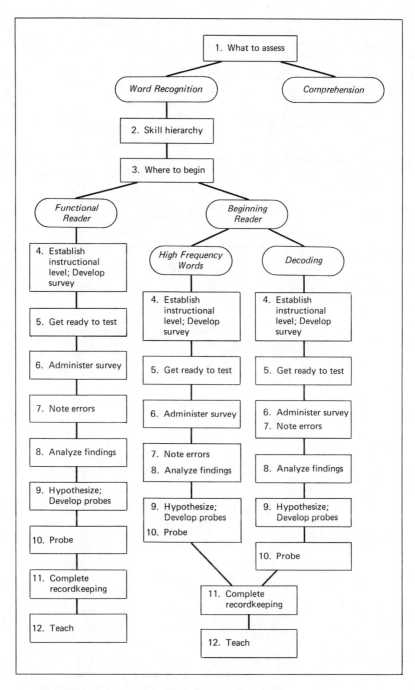

Figure 4-J Organization of Reading Chapter: Assessment Model Thus Far

High frequency word lists can be taken from four sources: published word lists (see Table 4-7 and Appendix C); basal reading texts; graded word lists on reading tests (see Table 4-6); and teacher-made lists of words related to a student's interest area. For elementary age students, any of the first three sources would be appropriate for developing a survey. For secondary age students, we suggest includ-

Table 4-7 Sight Word Lists

Name	Publisher
The Dolch Basic Sight Word List	Garrard Publishing Company, Champaign, Illinois
Fry Instant Word List	In Fry, E., *Reading Instruction for Classroom and Clinic,* (New York: McGraw-Hill, 1972).
The Kucera-Francis Word List	In Kucera, H., and Nelson, F., *Computational Analysis of Present-Day American English,* Providence, R.I.: Brown University Press, 1967).
The Corrective Reading System Basic Sight Word List (Ekwall)	Psychotechnics, Inc., Glenview, Illinois

Table 4-8 Sight Word Survey (Interest Area)

Basketball	Cars	Food
basket	accelerator	apple pie
buzzer	brake	banana
center	cam	cheese
dribble	carburetor	chocolate
forward	clutch	French fries
foul	Corvette	hamburger
foul line	engine	hoagie
game	fender	hot dog
guard	gallon	ice cream
jump shot	gas	MacDonald's
lay up	hood	milk
playoff	hubcaps	orange juice
points	miles	pizza
quarter	muffler	popcorn
rim	piston	scrambled eggs
score	shift	soda
shoot	speed	spaghetti
shot	tires	toast
time out	wheels	tuna fish
tip	whitewalls	Wheaties

ing words from the student's interest area. Older students who are beginning readers (reading at lower than grade 2.5) are more likely to be willing to read and learn interest words that they do not know. Therefore, assessing these words should be useful to the teacher in understanding where teaching might begin. Table 4-8 is a list of words used as a survey for three junior high school students whose reading grade levels ranged from 1.6–2.2 and whose expressed interests were basketball, automobiles, and food.

Step 5: Get Ready to Test (Word Recognition/Beginning Readers/High Frequency Words)

The survey of high frequency words should be administered one-to-one, with the student reading the words aloud to the teacher. Words to be read by the student should be printed on cards or typed on a page. If a page is used, and if the teacher is planning to administer several levels of a word list, each level should be prepared on a separate page. The teacher should have a score sheet that corresponds to the order in which the student will read the words. It is helpful for later scoring to indicate the phonetically irregular, high frequency words on the teacher's score sheet. This sheet should have three columns for marking responses: known, almost known, and not known. Table 4-9 is an example of one such score sheet, using a list of words found in Table 4-8. Finally, the teacher should choose a quiet, comfortable place to administer the survey.

Step 6: Administer the Survey (Word Recognition/Beginning Readers/High Frequency Words)

The student reads the words, one at a time, and the teacher records the responses by placing a checkmark in one of the three columns. A word is scored as *known* if the student reads the word correctly within 2 seconds. A word is scored as *unknown* if the student reads the word incorrectly or refuses to read it. Typically, these are the two categories used for scoring word lists. We suggest a third category, *almost known*, to identify those words the student can read by sounding them out. Since most people define sight vocabulary as those words which the student should recognize instantly, either because they cannot be decoded (words such as *the* or *although*) or because of their high frequency, an examiner would usually mark a sight word over which the student stumbled, or which was decoded slowly, as *not known*. We believe this leads to a misinterpretation of the findings. Suppose, for example, that the student is presented with the word "small." The student looks at the word and subvocalizes "all ..., sm ..., sm-all," and then, triumphantly, says "small." He/she has, in fact, read the word correctly, even though instant recognition of the word was not demonstrated. If we had marked that word *unknown*, we would have ignored the fact that the student did finally work it out. Therefore, we would consider that word to be *almost known*, and mark the middle column to designate the student's hesitation.

The teacher should stop the survey when the student becomes visibly frustrated with the task or when 10 to 20 *not known* or *almost known* words have been checked. The stopping point depends on the student's age and frustration tolerance.

Table 4-9   Score Sheet for Sight Vocabulary Survey

	P-I*	Known	Almost Known	Not Known
basket				
buzzer				
center				
dribble				
forward				
foul				
foul line				
game				
guard				
jump shot				
lay up				
playoff				
points				
quarter				
rim				
score				
shoot				
shot				
time out				
tip				

*Check indicates phonetically irregular word.

Step 7: Note Errors and Performance Style
(Word Recognition/Beginning Readers/
High Frequency Words) and Step 8: Analyze
Findings and Summarize Outcomes (Word
Recognition/Beginning Readers/High
Frequency Words)

Because errors are noted directly onto the score sheet as the survey is being administered, the teacher has already completed most of Steps 7 and 8 in the course of completing Step 6. After reviewing the student's errors, the teacher codes the final three columns of the Assessment to Instruction Data Sheet (Figure 4-C) on the Survey line.

Step 9: Hypothesize Reasons for Errors and
Determine Areas to Probe (Word
Recognition/Beginning Readers/High
Frequency Words) and Step 10: Probe (Word
Recognition/Beginning Readers/High
Frequency Words)

These next two steps in the assessment strategy can be eliminated when assessing sight vocabulary. The survey should generate sufficient *unknown* or *almost known* words for the teacher to know what sight vocabulary words to begin teaching the student.

To complete the word recognition assessment in the beginning reader, the teacher now returns to Step 4 to assess decoding skills. Figure 4-J should help the teacher to see where we are in our discussion of reading assessment.

Step 4: Select or Develop Survey Instrument
(Word Recognition/Beginning Readers/
Decoding)

Like the assessment of high frequency words in beginning readers, assessment of decoding skills begins at the single word level. We suggest beginning with a word list of 10 to 20 words either drawn from the published tests found in Tables 4-3 or 4-6, or designed by the teacher. A teacher-made list, like the one presented in Table 4-10, can be designed to include words containing the various elements found in Level 5 of the word recognition hierarchy.

Some tests survey decoding skills by presenting the student with nonsense words. This is done to eliminate the possibility of the student already knowing the word and to allow the examiner the opportunity to analyze the student's system(s) for decoding. The major drawback to this method is that some students attempt to generate a "real" word, despite admonitions from the examiner not to. Thus, a student will read "cuz" as "cause," or "lig" as "leg," in an attempt to produce a familiar word. A second drawback to the use of nonsense words is that the examiner is prevented from determining if the student knows the difference between real and nonsense words. Often, poor readers "create" words which are nonsensical and they do not seem to understand that the words they say do not exist. Using real words affords the examiner the opportunity to gather assessment information about the student's vocabulary and judgment, as well as data on his/her reading skill.

Table 4-10 Word Lists Based on Reading Hierarchy

Multisyllable	Root with Affix	Single Syllable	
(phonetically irregular)		(phonetically irregular)	
minute	morning	light	
certain	walking	bear	
believe	acted	shoe	
science	reuse	through	
bicycle	inside	eight	
women	unhappy	calm	
	defend	aunt	
	bigger	rough	
	fastest	watch	
	quietly		
(phonetically irregular)		(phonetically regular)	
birthday		fish	shun
animal		like	pin
empty		train	feel
squirrel		ride	white
garden		tag	
excitement		stop	
middle		race	
several		roof	
realize		branch	
winter		leg	

Step 5: Get Ready to Test (Word Recognition/Beginning Readers/ Decoding)

Published tests are prepared with a student booklet, or equivalent, and an administrator's score sheet. These can be used as specified in the test manual or adapted as the teacher sees fit. If the teacher uses a self-made survey, the words to be used must be prepared for the student, with another copy of the word list for the teacher. As with other surveys of word recognition skills, testing should occur one-to-one, in a quiet, comfortable environment.

Step 6: Administer the Survey (Word Recognition/Beginning Readers/Decoding) and Step 7: Note Errors and Performance Style (Word Recognition/Beginning Readers/ Decoding)

After the teacher has explained the purposes of the test, the student should be instructed to begin reading the list of words. The teacher should note the student's responses on his/her copy of the word list as the student reads.

Step 8: Analyze Findings and Summarize Outcomes (Word Recognition/Beginning Readers/Decoding)

Using the same score sheet as the one used for summarizing high frequency word errors for functional readers (Figure 4-B), the teacher can record errors within the appropriate categories on Section III. The teacher could also complete Section I by using information gathered in the high frequency word survey, combined with the information from the decoding survey. When the score sheet has been completed, the teacher should have, at a glance, a useful summary of errors and the data necessary to begin to detect consistent error patterns. Results of the decoding survey should be added to the Survey line of the Assessment to Instruction Data Sheet, in the appropriate columns.

Step 9: Hypothesize Reasons for Errors and Determine Areas to Probe (Word Recognition/ Beginning Readers/Decoding)

If the student read fewer than 70% of the survey words correctly, the teacher should begin to probe down the hierarchy, testing less difficult kinds of words, word parts, or letter sounds. If the student met the 70% accuracy criterion, the teacher should look for consistent patterns of errors to try to understand the reasons behind them.

Typically, students cannot read words for one of two reasons: either the word was unfamiliar to the student or the word was of a type too high up the skill hierarchy. The way the student read the word will usually offer the teacher a clue to one of these two reasons. As an example, let's use the word "elegant." If the student read the word as "e-leg-ant," stressing the second syllable, it seems likely that the student could sound out the word but that it was unfamiliar, and so he/she pronounced it incorrectly. If this were the case, the teacher would design a probe of the student's comprehension of the meaning of words read incorrectly. However, if the student read the word "elegant" as "elevator," "every," "engine," or some unrelated nonsense word, it is likely that the problem was in the complexity of the word relative to the skill hierarchy. If the latter were the case, the teacher would design probes which "test down" the hierarchy.

Step 10: Probe (Word Recognition/ Beginning Readers/Decoding)

If the teacher hypothesized that the problem is based in the student's oral language capacity, the teacher could ask the student to either use the incorrectly read words in a sentence or tell what the words mean. If the teacher hypothesized that the problem is with knowledge of word parts, the teacher could design probes which have the student read word parts in isolation, then blend them together. The words in Table 4-11 are appropriate for a student who was unable to read root words with affixes. The teacher could create a probe in which the student is asked first to read the root words and the affixes separately, and then to blend them. If the hypothesis is that the student does not know letter sounds, the teacher might use a probe of letter-sound associations in single syllable words (Table 4-12).

The student's responses to any of these probes will lead either to further probes in blending or to more specific probes in vowel or consonant word parts or

Table 4-11   Probe for Root Words with Affixes

1. try	ing	trying
2. un	bend	unbend
3. con	found	confound
4. dress	es	dresses
5. pre	heat	prevent
6. end	less	endless
7. de	fend	defend
8. light	ly	lightly
9. re	use	reuse
10. high	est	highest

Table 4-12   Probe of Word Parts

Beginning	Medial	Ending	Word
s	u	n	sun
f	a	t	fat
gr	a	b	grab
tr	i	m	trim
b	ai	t	bait
m		ade	made
sh	i	n	shin
ch	ea	p	cheap
l	e	ft	left
cr		ow	crow
ch	ur	ch	church

single letters. The goal of this probing is to determine at what point in the skill hierarchy the student's reading skill breaks down.

Step 11: Complete Recordkeeping Forms and Generate Teaching Objectives (Word Recognition/Beginning Readers)

The information gathered on the probes is now added to the Assessment to Instruction Data Sheet. The teacher knows that the initial assessment for word recognition skills is complete when he/she has identified specific word recognition skills that are *unknown*. These will have been noted on the recordkeeping form as *2, 3,* or *4*. Teaching would begin with these skills.

Step 12: Teach/Update Assessment Information (Word Recognition/Beginning Readers)

As with assessment of word recognition skills for functional readers, it is not necessary for the teacher to have surveyed or probed every skill in the hierarchy for teaching to begin. Ongoing assessment is an integral part of teaching, and the teacher will continually update assessment information based on observations made during directed teaching and practice activities.

ILLUSTRATION: KAREN

To illustrate the procedures for assessment of word recognition skills in a beginning reader, we will now move through Steps 3 to 12 for Karen, who, midway through third grade, reads in the first level of the basal reading series. As before, we begin at Step 3 because we have already determined what to assess (Step 1) and what we will use to guide our assessment (the skill hierarchy introduced at the beginning of this chapter—Step 2).

Step 3: Decide Where to Begin (Karen)

Looking back through Karen's cumulative record file, her teacher found the following information:

> Metropolitan Achievement Test (administered at the end of second grade): 1.7 grade level; 11th percentile
>
> Basal reader completed in second grade: 1–1 level

The teacher decides to assess Karen as a beginning reader. He would, therefore, assess high frequency words and decoding skills separately. Then he would combine the two sets of information in Step 11 to complete the recordkeeping form.

Step 4: Select or Develop Survey Instrument (High Frequency Words) (Karen)

The teacher selected the Ekwall Corrective Reading System word list and picked 25 words from each level, beginning with the primer list. He decided that he would continue until Karen had missed 25 words.

Step 5: Get Ready to Test (High Frequency Words) (Karen)

The teacher printed each word selected from the Ekwall list (up through level 3) onto an index card and prepared a typed score sheet for himself. The teacher's score sheet contained three levels of the list on each page, an indication of the phonetically irregular words, and columns for marking the words *known, almost known,* and *unknown*.

Student __Karen__   Date __1/26/81__   Teacher __Gibson__

P	d	Known	Almost known	Not known
1. came		✓		
2. blue		✓		
3. saw		✓		
4. help		✓		
5. she		✓		
6. is		✓		
7. wants		✓		
8. very				✓
9. could	X			✓
10. as		✓		
11. ride		✓		
12. day		✓		
13. back		✓		
14. green		✓		
15. there	X			✓
16. now		✓		
17. way		✓		
18. from		✓		
19. after		✓		
20. ran		✓		
21. had		✓		
22. jump		✓		
23. would	X	✓		
24. was	X	✓		
25. give	X	✓		

1	d	Known	Almost known	Not known
1. side		✓		
2. four	X	✓		
3. long				✓
4. ask		✓		
5. new		✓		
6. sleep		✓		
7. stand				✓
8. think		✓		
9. just				✓
10. girl		✓		
11. fast		✓		
12. black		✓		
13. ball		✓		
14. again	X			✓
15. began		✓		
16. if		✓		
17. high	X	✓		
18. new		✓		
19. must		✓		
20. name		✓		
21. rabbit				✓
22. well		✓		
23. white		✓		
24. at		✓		
25. thought	X			✓

2	d	Known	Almost known	Not known
1. best	X			✓
2. enough				✓
3. ten		✓		
4. gave		✓		
5. each		✓		
6. told				✓
7. started				✓
8. round				✓
9. once	X			✓
10. hand				✓
11. both		✓		
12. open				✓
13. hold		✓		
14. keep				✓
15. together				✓
16. every				✓
17. next				✓
18. should	X			✓
19. home				✓
20. place				✓
21. still		✓		
22. right	X	✓		
23. last		✓		
24. wait				✓
25. warm	X			✓

Figure 4-K High Frequency Words Survey

***Step 6: Administer the Survey (High
Frequency Words) (Karen) and Step 7: Note
Errors (High Frequency Words) (Karen) and
Step 8: Analyze Findings (High Frequency
Words) (Karen)***

The teacher had Karen read the words one at a time, continuing until she had missed a total of 25 words. Karen got to the end of list 2-A. For each word read, the teacher put a mark in the appropriate column.

Figure 4-K is the result of the sight vocabulary survey.

The teacher made a note on Section I of the word recognition score sheet that Karen never attempted to sound out a word she did not know. He also completed part of the Survey line on an Assessment to Instruction Data Sheet indicating problems with phonetically irregular, high frequency words (*4*) and only very low level knowledge of predictable high frequency words (*2*).

Because Steps 9 and 10 are omitted in the sight vocabulary assessment of a beginning reader, the teacher returned to Step 4 to begin assessment of decoding skills.

***Step 4: Select or Develop Survey Instrument
(Decoding) (Karen)***

Based on the information from the high frequency word survey and the teacher's preliminary observations of Karen during reading class, the teacher decided to survey decoding using a 15-item word list of one- and two-syllable, phonetically regular words that were probably unfamiliar to Karen. The teacher made up a list.

***Step 5: Get Ready to Test (Decoding)
(Karen)***

The teacher printed the words on index cards and prepared a word list for himself on which to record errors.

***Step 6: Administer Survey (Decoding)
(Karen) and Step 7: Note Errors (Decoding)
(Karen)***

The teacher asked Karen to begin reading the cards. When Karen refused to read a word, the teacher urged her to "sound it out" and noted on the survey which words required prompts. Figure 4-L shows the results of the decoding survey.

Word List	Student's Response	Word List	Student's Response	Word List	Student's Response
side	some	tag	tag	branch	bank*
lace	lake	leg	let	train	train
feel	fight	shun	should*	garden	garbage*
moat	more	sin	sit	winter	winter*
cute	come	plop	pop	empty	unbrella*

*indicates a prompt from the teacher

Figure 4-L Decoding Survey

Student _Karen_ _____   Date _2/4/81_   Reading Level of Passage _Single words_

I. READING STYLE

CHECKLIST OF BEHAVIORS	Always	Sometimes	Seldom
Reads with expression			
Reads clearly			
Reads word by word			
Observes punctuation			
Reads for meaning (tries to make sense of material)			
Skips or refuses unfamiliar words	✓		
Substitutes linguistically appropriate words		✓	
Perseveres with task		✓	
Is easily frustrated			✓
Knows beginning sound/unit	✓		
Knows medial sound/unit		✓	
Knows ending sound/unit			✓

Has method of attack for unknown words—

_✓_ Depends on letter sounds   ___ Tries various methods

___ Depends on syllables   _✓_ Gives up quickly

Figure 4-M Score Sheet for Error Analysis (Word Recognition)

II. HIGH FREQUENCY WORDS

Phonetically Predictable Words	
Word	Student's error response
very	vase
long	like
stand	stay
just	jump
rabbit	(refused)
best	big
(Refused the remainder of missed words, very frustrated)	
told	
started	
round	
hand	
open	
together	
every	
next	
home	
place	
wait	
Examples of Non-Errors	

Phonetically Irregular Words	
Word	Student's error response
could	comes
there	three
again	against
thought	(refused)
enough	(refused)
once	old
should	(refused)
warm	(refused)
Examples of Non-Errors	

Total predictable words __61__

Number of words known by student __44__

Total phonetically irregular words __14__

Number of words known by student __6__

Figure 4-M Score Sheet for Error Analysis (Word Recognition)—**Continued**

III. DECODING WORDS

Multisyllable Phonetically Irregular		
Word	Student's error response	
Similar words read correctly		

Multisyllable Phonetically Predictable		
Word	Student's error response	
garden	garbage	
empty	umbrella	
Similar words read correctly		

Root with Affix		
Word	Student's error response	
Similar words read correctly		

Single Syllable Phonetically Irregular		
Word	Student's error response	
Similar words read correctly		

Single Syllable Phonetically Predictable		
Word	Student's error response	
side	same	
lace	lake	
feel	fight	
moat	more	
cute	come	
leg	let	
shun	should	
pin	sit	
plop	pop	
branch	bank	
Similar words read correctly		

Figure 4-M Score Sheet for Error Analysis (Word Recognition)—Continued

Step 8: Analyze Findings (Decoding) (Karen)

The teacher categorized Karen's errors using the word recognition score sheet. He incorporated his findings from the sight vocabulary survey onto the score sheet as well, to have all the information in one place. The completed word recognition score sheet is given in Figure 4-M (see pages 84−86). The Teacher then completed the Survey line of the Assessment to Instruction Data Sheet, coding a *3* under reading words and a *3* in system for word attacks.

Step 9: Hypothesize Reasons for Errors
and Determine Areas to Probe
(Decoding) (Karen)

Since Karen read only two of the fifteen survey words correctly (not nearly 70% of them), the teacher decided that the first probe must be down the skill hierarchy (Table 4-1) from Level 5 (reading single words) to Level 4 (reading word parts).

Step 10: Probe (Decoding) (Karen)

From the Gates-McKillop Reading Diagnostic Tests, the teacher chose two probes for Karen: recognizing and blending common word parts, and final letters. Figures 4-N and 4-O are the results of those probes. The teacher also probed vowel sounds by showing Karen a card with each vowel printed on it and asking her if she knew the long sound, and then the short sound, for each vowel. Karen was able to produce all 10 vowel sounds correctly.

Step 11: Complete Recordkeeping and
Generate Teaching Objectives (Karen)

Using information obtained on the follow-up decoding probes, the teacher completed the Assessment to Instruction Data Sheet for word recognition. Looking over his results (Figure 4-P, page 90), the teacher was able to draw the following conclusions:

1. Karen's sight vocabulary is consistent with her reading level, but there is a list of high frequency words that can be taught to her.
2. Karen knows single-sound consonants but needs to learn consonant blends and digraphs, and vowel pairs and digraphs.
3. Karen has no system for decoding unknown words. She needs to be taught how to blend sounds together to form words.

Consulting the Assessment to Instruction Data Sheet, the teacher established the following initial learning objectives for Karen:

1. To read all unknown consonant blends and digraphs with 100% accuracy.
2. To read vowel pairs and digraphs with 100% accuracy.
3. To instantly recognize 20 high frequency words with 90% accuracy.
4. To blend known word parts to form words with 100% accuracy.
5. To learn and consistently apply a strategy for decoding unknown words.

V. KNOWLEDGE OF WORD PARTS: WORD ATTACK

V-1. Recognizing and blending common word parts

(Page 7 of Test Materials)

To examiner: Give only one trial. Stop after five consecutive errors in column 1.

Ex.	spack	___	sp ___	ack X	spack X
1.	sked X	sk ___	ed ___	sked ___
2.	whickle X	wh ___	ickle X	whickle X
3.	glemp X	gl X	emp X	glemp X
4.	slome X	sl ___	ome ___	slome X
5.	bleen X	bl ___	een ___	bleen X
6.	dwer ___	dw X	er ___	dwer X
7.	twasp ___	tw ___	asp X	twasp ___
8.	plew ___	pl ___	ew X	plew ___
9.	shable ___	sh X	able ___	shable ___
10.	trock ___	tr X	ock X	trock ___
11.	crell ___	cr X	ell ___	crell ___
12.	drack ___	dr ___	ack X	drack ___
13.	wrick ___	wr X	ick X	wrick ___
14.	smow ___	sm ___	ow X	smow ___
15.	proy ___	pr ___	oy X	proy ___
16.	fring ___	fr ___	ing ___	fring ___
17.	clidge ___	cl X	idge X	clidge ___
18.	chible ___	ch X	ible X	chible ___
19.	gright ___	gr X	ight X	gright ___
20.	thate ___	th X	ate ___	thate ___
21.	stind ___	st ___	ind ___	stind ___
22.	swite ___	sw X	ite ___	swite ___
23.	flark ___	fl ___	ark X	flark ___

Number correct
Fraction: ___ ___ ___ ___
Number attempted

Form II   X- Not Known

Figure 4-N Probe (Karen)*

VI-3. Final Letters

To examiner: Say each word twice only. Words are in manual, page 10. Have child circle his choices on this sheet.

1. s (f) t j v

2. v n k (l) t

3. (p) d b t r

4. (t) l k h q

5. g n t m (c)

6. k (g) c t s

7. f w n v (m)

8. v l s (r) t

9. x j f (z) y

10. k (d) v b h

11. d (k) t g b

12. (n) w b t m

13. j t g r (s)

14. p c d r (b)

Raw score (number correct) _14_

Interpretation _____

Form II

Figure 4-O Probe (Karen)*

The teacher also noted that Karen should read continuous text at her instructional reading level while the decoding skills are being taught.

Step 12: Start Teaching/Update Assessment Information (Karen)

The teacher will begin to teach Karen knowing that, in the course of teaching, new information will come to light about skills known and not known. The Assessment to Instruction Data Sheet will be updated as the teacher records his new findings.

---

*Reprinted by permission of the publisher from the Pupil Record Booklet, Form 2 of Arthur I. Gates and Anne S. McKillop, Gates-McKillop *Reading Diagnostic Tests.* (New York: Teachers College Press, copyright © 1962 by Arthur I. Gates and Anne S. McKillop), pp. 9 and 12.

Student _Karen_   School _Lincoln_   Teacher _Gibson_

Reading Level—Initial Survey < 2.5 / ASSESSMENT TASKS	Reading continuous text (a,b,c)*	Reading sentences	Reading words (a,ⓑ,c,d,ⓔ)*	Reading word parts—affixes (a,b)*	Reading word parts—irregular phonograms	Reading word parts—vowels (a,ⓑ,ⓒ,ⓓ)*	Reading word parts—consonants (a,ⓑ,ⓒ)*	Reading single letters—vowels (a,ⓑ,ⓒ)*	Reading single letters—consonants (a,b,)*	Hearing sounds in words	Recognizing letter shapes	High frequency words—phonetically predictable	High frequency words—phonetically irregular	System for attacking unknown words
Survey	5	5	3	5	5	5	5	5	5	5	5	2	4	3
Initial Probe				4		4 (b, d)	4 (b, c)							4
Further Probe											1			
Further Probe								1						
Further Probe														
UPDATE														

*Refer to skill hierarchy presented in Table 4-1.

Code—Survey and Probe

1—Skill known   3—Need more information   5—Not assessed

2—Skill known at lower level   4—Skill not known

Figure 4-P Assessment to Instruction Data Sheet (Word Recognition)

ASSESSMENT OF
COMPREHENSION SKILLS

Once assessment of word recognition skills has been completed, the teacher should begin an assessment of reading comprehension skills. Wilson (1977) defines comprehension as "the ability to bring meaning and understanding to words and groups of words and their interrelationships". We think of comprehension simply as *understanding what one reads*. Because we have already decided what to assess, i.e., reading comprehension, we start the assessment at Step 2.

Step 2: Select or Develop a Skill Hierarchy
(Comprehension)

Most reading tests which include a comprehension subtest will survey skills in the areas of facts and details, main idea, sequence, drawing conclusions, and making inferences. Seldom are these skills listed as a hierarchy. Often, students are asked to answer one each of several different types of comprehension questions based on their reading of a single paragraph or short passage. (Questions are derived from a taxonomy of reading comprehension skills like the one presented in Table 4-13.)

In developing a skill hierarchy for reading comprehension, we have tried to consider two dimensions: the length of the material being read by the student and the types of comprehension skills being assessed. In the first dimension, students might read continuous text (stories or passages of more than two pages, or one or more paragraphs of up to two pages), single sentences (not organized in paragraphs or connected thematically) or single words (not connected into sentences). In the second dimension, students might be asked for different aspects of understanding: literal, inferential, and evaluative. Each requires a different kind of meaning to be drawn from the reading material. *Literal comprehension* requires the student to understand information that is explicitly stated in the reading material. Literal comprehension does not require that the reader interpret the material presented, only that he/she remember the information or locate it in the text. *Inferential comprehension* requires the student to use the information presented in the text to go beyond what is explicitly stated and draw conclusions about what is only implied. *Evaluative comprehension* requires the student to judge the text and read the information in a critical fashion. The student needs to draw on his/her own experiences and knowledge to extend both the explicit and implicit meanings he/she has gathered from the text.

The hierarchy presented in Table 4-14 combines these two dimensions. It will be used to guide our assessment of reading comprehension. At the highest level of the hierarchy, a student would be able to read continuous text and answer a variety of comprehension questions. At the fourth level, the student would read one or more connected paragraphs and answer a variety of comprehension questions. At the third level, the student would read single sentences. At this level, only questions dealing with literal comprehension are appropriate. At the second level, the student would be given single words and asked their literal meaning. At the lowest level of the reading comprehension hierarchy, the student does not read the text material. Rather, he/she is asked comprehension questions based on words read to him/her.

Table 4-13 A Taxonomy of Skills in Comprehension*

I. Literal Comprehension

1.0 Recognition/Identification of:
1.1 Main ideas
1.2 Supporting ideas
1.3 Details
1.4 Vocabulary meanings
1.5 Cause and effect relationships
1.6 Similarities and comparability of language, plot, and structure
1.7 Figurative language
1.8 Direct statements of opinions
1.9 Character traits, sequence, setting, and mood

2.0 Recall of:
2.1 Main ideas
2.2 Sequence
2.3 Details of plot and information
2.4 Character traits, setting, and mood
2.5 Vocabulary meaning
2.6 Cause and effect relationships

3.0 Analysis and Reorganization by:
3.1 Summarizing
3.2 Synthesizing, reducing, and capsulizing ideas
3.3 Transfer and restatement
3.4 Outlining
3.5 Classifying
3.6 Response to questions that analyze organization or organize differentially

II. Inferential Comprehension

4.0 Interpretive
4.1 Interpreting themes, overall purposes, or moral lessons not directly stated

II. Inferential Comprehension (cont.)
4.2 Interpreting character
4.3 Interpreting meaning of plot and mood
4.4 Interpreting figurative language
4.5 Identifying multiple meanings and symbolism

5.0 General Inferential
5.1 Visualizing unstated supporting details
5.2 Inferring character traits
5.3 Identifying character types
5.4 Describing sequence not specifically stated
5.5 Inferring events and information not specifically described
5.6 Identifying missing elements
5.7 Inferring details
5.8 Inferring cause and effect relationships
5.9 Inferring reality base and moral philosophy

6.0 Predictive
6.1 Predicting character development
6.2 Predicting sequence outcomes and results
6.3 Predicting language use and vocabulary patterns
6.4 Predicting philosophy, moral interpretation, and presence or absence of a lesson
6.5 Predicting style

III. Evaluational Comprehension

7.0 Judgmental
7.1 Philosophical judgments indicating basic agreement or disagreement with author
7.2 Reality judgments of degree of possibility or impossibility (realism or fantasy)

III. Evaluational Comprehension (cont.)
7.3 Judgments of evidence, reasonableness, experience to substantiate (fact versus opinion)
7.4 Relational judgments of appropriateness (determination of relevance or fit of reading selection to a problem or issue)
7.5 Judgments of completeness (adequacy)
7.6 Judgments of worth and weight (validity, strength, and importance)
7.7 Judgments of agreement or acceptability

8.0 Appreciative
8.1 Emotional reactions to content or subjects
8.2 Extension of emotional and attitudinal aspects of concepts
8.3 Emotional response to story line movements (plot)
8.4 "Draw" and sensory feel of setting
8.5 Identification with and feeling of knowing and understanding characters
8.6 Response to descriptive power of author
8.7 Internalization of emotion and mood
8.8 Appeal of author's use of language patterns
8.9 Response to specific selection of words

9.0 Critical
9.1 Questioning of opinions, information, format, and presentation
9.2 Development of definite ideas of dissatisfaction or satisfaction
9.3 Identification of specific flaws either of the whole or of parts
9.4 Taking exception to particular ideas
9.5 Questioning authenticity and authority
9.6 Comparison of style, language, and substance of different writers and reading sections
9.7 Formulation of contrary opinions to those of the author

*From Thomas N. Turner, "Comprehension: Reading for Meaning," in J. Estill Alexander, General Editor, *Teaching Reading.* Copyright © 1979 by Little, Brown and Company (Inc.). Reprinted by permission.

Table 4-14   Hierarchy of Comprehension Skills

5. Continuous Text
   A. Evaluative questions
   B. Inferential questions
   C. Literal questions

4. Paragraph(s)
   A. Evaluative questions
   B. Inferential questions
   C. Literal questions

3. Sentence(s)
   A. Literal questions

2. Words
   A. Vocabulary meaning

1. Oral vocabulary

Step 3:   Decide Where to Begin
(Comprehension)

As with assessment of word recognition, the assessment of comprehension skills proceeds differently for functional readers and for beginning readers. This gross distinction between functional and beginning readers should be made in the same way as was done for assessment of word recognition—by using information on hand in the cumulative record or by giving a quick word recognition test. The comprehension assessment for functional readers will begin at Level 5 or 4 of the skill hierarchy, depending on the competence level of the student. Comprehension assessment of a beginning reader will begin at Level 4-C, or below, on the skill hierarchy.

For the remainder of this chapter we will describe Steps 4 through 12, first for functional readers, then for beginning readers.

Figure 4-Q completes the picture of our strategy for assessment of reading.

ASSESSMENT OF COMPREHENSION: FUNCTIONAL READERS

Step 4: Select or Develop Survey Instrument
(Comprehension/Functional Readers)

Before the teacher can select or develop a comprehension survey for a functional reader, he/she must establish the reading level, the length, and the content of the survey. Before making a decision about the level, the teacher should consider the

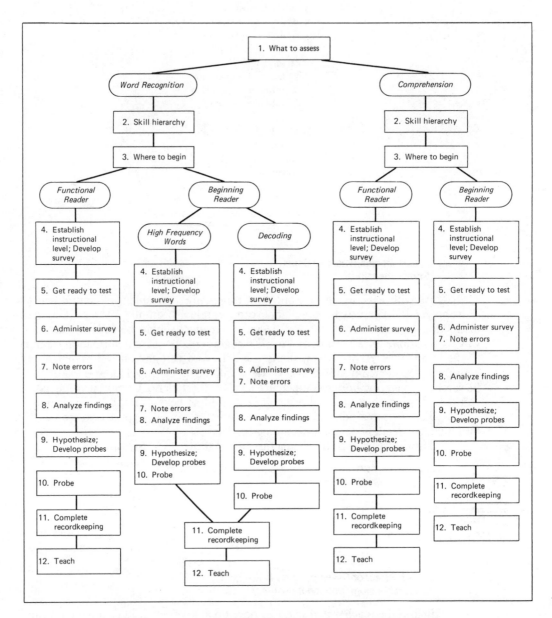

Figure 4-Q Organization of Reading Chapter: Assessment Model Thus Far

Perfetti and Hogaboam study (1975) of the relationship between decoding and comprehension skills. Their findings indicated that students who were more skilled at comprehension tasks were also better decoders than students less skilled at reading comprehension. It would appear that the effort poor decoders put into reading words detracts from their ability to bring meaning to what they have read.

Based on this and other research studies, and on our clinical experience, we advocate assessing comprehension at the level where the student is competent with decoding (that is, at his/her *independent reading level*), so that the assessment information gathered is not confounded by problems with decoding. Therefore, to determine the reading level for the survey material, the teacher must establish the student's independent reading level. This can be done using an IRI. (It may have already been done as part of the determination of instructional level in Step 4 of word recognition for the functional reader.) Howards (1980) suggests that the independent level is lower than the instructional level, that it is the level of graded reading material at which at least 95% of words are read correctly.

The length of the comprehension survey will also be determined by the student's independent reading level. For students whose independent reading level is less than grade 5.0, we recommend using one or more passages, each no more than 3 pages long. Several comprehension questions of each type should be generated from each passage. For students whose independent reading level is greater than grade 5.0, we suggest using continuous text of up to 5 pages in length. Questions generated from this text should encompass all three levels of comprehension and may be presented at the end of the 5 pages or at intervals within the text.

It is also important that the material used be of interest to the student. For the reasons given in the section on selecting word recognition surveys, material which is interesting to the student is likely to provide the examiner with more comprehensive information.

Material that is at the appropriate reading level and of the appropriate length and content can be chosen from a variety of sources. Passages from published tests, such as those found in Tables 4-2 and 4-3, are often used to assess reading comprehension. Many of these materials include comprehension questions. The teacher may use the prepared questions, or create his/her own questions that tap the various types of comprehension. Passages can also be drawn from the stories in basal readers and from high-interest materials which are graded (such as the Pal Paperbacks, Point-31 or RD 2000). Other choices for materials include newspaper articles or editorials (which are particularly appropriate for critical questions), magazines, and books of short stories. Mystery stories are an excellent source for both literal and inferential questions. If the teacher chooses to develop his/her own survey, he/she should check the readability of passages chosen using the Fry Formula (see Appendix B) and develop comprehension questions that are appropriate.

Figure 4-R is an example of a teacher-developed survey for a student whose independent reading level is grade 3.5. It consists of text followed by a set of twelve comprehension questions that include some literal, some inferential, and some evaluative questions. Figure 4-S is a survey appropriate for a student with an independent reading level of grade 6.0. Note that it is divided into three sections. Literal questions were developed based on the first section read. Inferential questions were based on the next section, and evaluative questions on the final section.

Funny Hat*

There was a fire and his face was burned. Not his arms, not his legs, but his face, where it would show most.

After that he stayed in his room. He slept a lot. And when he was not sleeping, he walked around in circles. He didn't even come down to dinner.

His father and mother ate alone in the kitchen, which was right below his room. As they ate, they heard him walking above them.

"Those burns aren't so bad," his father said.

"You tell him that, and I tell him that," said his mother. "But he thinks his friends will laugh at him."

He would not go to school, because he didn't want anyone to see him. Two times a week a teacher came to him. On those mornings, he sat in a dark corner. He made the teacher sit across the room.

As the months passed, he began to feel closer to the teacher. He found himself sitting beside her during his lessons. He did well. He liked to learn.

The first time she asked him if he wanted to go for a walk, he became afraid. It was all he could do to keep from shaking. He told her he did not want to go outside. From then on, she asked him once a week. He always said, "No." But he was no longer afraid to be asked.

One day--it was winter now--she came in with a hat for him. He put it on. The hat had a big brim, which hid his face in its shadow. Then she wrapped a scarf around his neck. That way no one would see his face.

They went for a walk in the middle of the day, when all his friends were at school. The people he saw laughed at his hat. But his hat was not his face. They could not see his face. And none of them knew who he was.

As spring came closer, he and his teacher went for longer walks. Sometimes they stopped for sodas in a place with mirrors on the walls. In a way, the place made him feel good. Everywhere he looked he saw himself in his hat and scarf. But nowhere could he see his face.

The same girl waited on them every day. She was his age and he liked to talk to her. After a while, she started to call him "Funny Hat."

"What will it be today, Funny Hat?"

"You know, Funny Hat, I think you keep coming here because you like me."

Once he went to the place alone. He wanted to tell her it was true. He did like her.

"Did you come to see me again, Funny Hat?"

Before, he had always laughed with her. Today he couldn't laugh. If he said yes, she would expect him to ask her out. And if he took her out, she would see his face.

"Just a soda," he said.

"Oh. Playing hard to get?"

Figure 4-R Reading Comprehension Survey: Independent Level Approximately 3.5*

*Reprinted by permission of Scholastic Inc. from *Action Unit Book 2 & 3.*
Copyright © 1977 by Scholastic Inc.

He could not think of a smart answer. Two more times he went back alone.
Neither time could he make himself say what he wanted to say.

"I guess you just want a soda," she said.

"Yes," he said. "I guess that is all I want."

As he was leaving, he felt a tug on his scarf. It was his teacher,
"I brought you here so you could meet my daughter," she said. "I know
she likes you, but she thinks you do not like her."

For a moment he just stood there. Then he went back into the store.
He went over to the girl and said, "Will you go out with me?"

"Before I go out with you, I have to see what you look like," she said.

He took a deep breath. Then he took off his hat and looked down at
the floor, waiting for her to say something.

He waited for what seemed like a long time. Finally he looked up.
She was not even looking at him. She was behind the counter, leaning over
something.

"What are you doing?" he said.

She smiled. "Just putting this funny hat away. I don't think you will
need it anymore."

He smiled back at her. "I think you are right," he said. As he left
the soda shop with her, he looked at himself in the mirror. He didn't look
bad at all, he thought. He looked better than he had in that funny hat.

Comprehension Questions

1. Why didn't the boy go to school?

2. What did he wear when he went out with the teacher?

3. What did the girl behind the counter call him?

4. Who was the girl's mother?

5. What would be a good name for the story?

6. Why did the teacher take him to a particular place for a soda?

7. How bad do you think the burns made the boy look? Why?

8. What do you think will happen next? Why?

9. What did the boy think would happen if he went out? Do you
    think he was right?

10. What do you think the author of the story wanted the reader
    to understand?

11. How do you know that the girl liked the boy?

12. Is it true that people laugh at other people if they look funny?
    Do you think the boy in this story would have been laughed at?

Figure 4-R Reading Comprehension Survey: Independent Level Approximately 3.5—**Continued**

Never Jam Today*

PART I

Maddy Franklin was only seventeen years old in 1917--not old enough to vote even if women were to be granted that right. Yet Maddy believed in the cause enough to go to jail for it.

The picket line Maddy joined that November day was to be the longest one in the now nearly year-long history of White House demonstrating. It was to be the National Woman's Party's protest against the persecution of their leader, Alice Paul, and the delay in passing the federal suffrage amendment. Whatever their sentiments--for or against suffrage, for or against militant tactics--most people who came to see the line could not help but admire the courage of the women who came and were arrested.

Many of the pickets carried bags containing toilet necessities for the ordeal ahead. The suffragists had learned that coming to picket often meant not having time to go home and pack.

There were many New Yorkers among the first wave of pickets that dark afternoon. Maddy and Mrs. Armbruster were with them. They were both arrested, and were tried two days later for obstructing traffic. Mrs. Armbruster was sent to Occoquan with the majority of the prisoners, but for some reason, Maddy's sentence was for thirty days in the District Jail, apparently because Occoquan was crowded with political prisoners.

Comprehension Questions

1. How old was Maddy Franklin?

2. Why was Maddy arrested?

3. Put the events in order:

    a) Maddy was sentenced to 30 days in jail.
    b) The women came to picket the persecution of Alice Paul.
    c) Maddy was arrested.

4. What was a suffragist?

PART II

Maddy was upset at being separated from her friend. For one thing, she did not know any of the women at the District Jail, and for another, she felt that, brave as she was, Mrs. Armbruster was too frail to be left without someone to look after her. However, there was nothing Maddy could do about it, except face enclosure herself in the row of airtight cells with as much equanimity as she could muster. Secretly she had the distinct impression that she had been buried alive.

Trying to hold back her trembling that first horrible night, Maddy gazed through the bars of her steel cell. Down along the lower tier she

Figure 4-S Reading Comprehension Survey: Independent Level 6.0*

*Adapted from Carole Bolton, *Never Jam Today.* Copyright © 1971 by Carole Bolton (New York: Atheneum, 1971). Used with the permission of Atheneum Publishers.

saw a face peering out from a similar set of bars. The face seemed familiar.
It was the pale, drawn countenance of Alice Paul, who had not eaten--volun-
tarily--for over a month. A whole month! How could she hold out for six more?

That evening they brought Maddy a dinner that consisted of skim milk, a
strange inedible corn bread and raw salt pork. Since she could not eat the
food anyway, it was easy to join the hunger strike immediately.

Easy, at first. But although Maddy had missed a meal occasionally in her
life, she had never really been hungry. After one day of sitting bored in her
cell, all she could think of was food: the stuffed turkey her family would be
eating this Thanksgiving, cranberry sauce, steak, mashed potatoes, cold orange
juice, even hot oatmeal swimming in rich milk.

She hated herself for dwelling on food, and after such a short time, too.
Think of anything else, she told herself firmly.

But there was nothing else to think of. She had no newspapers to read,
no magazines or books. Fortunately, however, the women in the District Jail,
unlike those at Occoquan could talk from cell to cell. There was no one in
the cell to the right of Maddy, but she soon got to know the woman on the
other side of her, a Mrs. Gordon from Baltimore.

"How do you feel?" Mrs. Gordon asked her on the third day.

"Rather weak, I guess," said Maddy. "How about you?"

"Do you know, I can't even reach up to brush my hair!"

"How long since you ate?" Maddy asked.

"About as long as you."

"I wonder how Miss Paul is."

"The jailor said they have her in the psychiatric ward."

"Why?"

"I guess they're trying to hint that she's out of her mind."

Later in the day Maddy heard a terrible gagging noise. "What was
that?" she asked.

"They're force feeding Rose Winslow."

"Try to shut your ears to it," the older woman suggested. Then she
laughed. Maddy knew she was doing it as a distraction. "Do you know this
cell is alive with roaches?"

"Mine is too."

"Odd they'd come here. There's nothing for them to eat."

Comprehension Questions

    5. What would be a good title for this passage?

    6. What was the worst part about being in jail?

Figure 4-S Reading Comprehension Survey: Independent Level 6.0—**Continued**

7. Why would it be bad for the suffragists if Alice Paul were in the psychiatric ward?

8. Will this experience turn Maddy against the suffrage movement? Why/why not?

PART III

As the days passed Maddy's bones began to ache as if she had the flu, but then she felt better. Perhaps, she thought, a person could get used to going without food. Therefore, she couldn't understand at all why she fainted.

But after that they took her to the office and questioned her.

"Will you eat now?" asked the Commissioner, or whoever he was--Maddy didn't much care.

"Will you promise to treat us as political prisoners?"

"You women are rioters, not political prisoners."

"Then I don't eat."

"We'll have to feed you by force," he warned.

Maddy was silent for a minute. "I can't help that," she said finally.

His voice became kind, solicitous. "Why do you keep this up? Don't you know that you're the only one who hasn't given in? The others are eating. Why don't you? You're suffering for nothing."

"All right," said the man. "You can starve." He motioned to the matron. "Take her away."

Maddy was glad to go back to her cell. She felt weak and wanted to lie down. At the moment even the thought of food was not as strong as her longing for her cot. She walked down the hall slowly and carefully, so she would not weave like a drunkard or let the matron see that her knees were about to buckle. How long had she been without food? She could not keep track.

They were bringing in another prisoner and putting her in an empty cell. Maddy smiled as cheerfully as she could at the woman, who somehow looked like someone she knew. The woman, about to enter the cell, gasped when she saw Maddy, and Maddy, startled, gazed back at her.

She opened her mouth, but words would not come for a few seconds. Then, "Mama!" she said in a strangled voice.

"Oh, my baby!" Mrs. Franklin cried, and she would have run to clasp her daughter in her arms if the jailor had not held her back.

Maddy was shoved into her cell. From somewhere in the distance she could hear a receding voice crying, "Maddy! Maddy! Are you all right? Say something." She tried to hear the voice, to hold onto its sound consciously, but a dreadful clamminess was coming over her. Muscles in her mouth tightened with nausea, and she gagged dryly. Then a familiar wave of blackness poured over her, and she fainted again.

The next thing she knew she was in bed, and the matron was mopping her forehead with a cold wet rag, and once more she heard her mother's voice calling.

Figure 4-S Reading Comprehension Survey: Independent Level 6.0—**Continued**

"Hello, Mama," she managed to call. "I'm all right. I'm fine."

The matron straightened up and looked down at her. She didn't say anything. Then she went out and locked the door, and Maddy heard her tell her mother, "If she's your daughter, see if you can get her to eat something."

"Maddy, she's right," said Mrs. Franklin. "You've got to eat."

Comprehension Questions

9. Is the author of the story for or against the suffrage movement? How can you tell?

10. The Commissioner said that Maddy was a rioter. Was she? How do you know?

Figure 4-S Reading Comprehension Survey: Independent Level 6.0—**Continued**

Step 5: Get Ready to Test (Comprehension/ Functional Readers)

The student should read the survey material silently. We subscribe to the idea that, when assessing for reading comprehension, the important thing is not how accurately the student reads the material, but how well he/she derives meaning from it. If the student is required to read aloud, he/she may be more interested in reading words correctly (because the examiner is listening) than in reading for meaning. By having the student read the material silently, the examiner maximizes the possibilities of getting a true picture of reading comprehension abilities.

Although the student will read the passage silently, there are still two choices to be made regarding the questions to be asked. First is the choice of the response level to be used. Will the questions be at the recall level (that is, the student will not have the passage to refer back to) or at the recognition level (where the student can go back to the text to locate the answers)? Following the "test down" rule, we suggest that the questions initially be asked at the recall level. If the student is not successful, the examiner can probe by using the same material but, this time, permitting the student to refer back to the text to find the answers.

The second choice to be made is the language mode of the questions and responses. The mode can be either written or oral. Written questions are appropriate if the reading level of the questions is no higher than the reading level of the passage. Written answers should be used only if the examiner is sure that the student has achieved a satisfactory level of written language skills. The examiner has more flexibility in gathering information if the questions are answered orally. Figure 4-T shows a reading comprehension score sheet that outlines these choices. If both the questions and answers are presented to the student in written form, the comprehension survey can be completed as an independent seatwork activity. If the teacher will ask the questions and/or the student will respond orally, the comprehension survey will need to be administered one-to-one.

Once decisions about mode of questioning have been made, the teacher must, as always, organize the testing area by gathering together the materials that he/she and the students will require. The teacher must also consider what motivation might be needed to ensure maximum performance on the test.

Student _____ Date _____ Teacher _____

COMPREHENSION SKILLS	Complexity of Task				Conditions		
	Continuous text	Para-graphs	Sentences	Words	Response level	Mode of questions	Mode of responses
Literal							
Main Idea							
Sequence							
Details							
Vocabulary							
Cause-effect							
Inferential							
Interpretive							
General inferential							
Predictive							
Evaluative							
Judgmental							
Appreciative							
Critical							

Code—Task
1 - Skill known @ 75% accuracy
2 - Skill not demonstrated to criterion
√ - Skill tapped and known
X - Skill tapped and not known
— - Skill not tapped

Code—Conditions
RC - Recall response
RG - Recognition response
W - Written questions and responses
O - Oral questions and responses

Figure 4-T Reading Comprehension Survey: Score Sheet

Step 6: Administer the Survey
(Comprehension/Functional Readers)

If the survey is to be completed as a seatwork activity, the teacher should find a quiet, comfortable place for the student to perform the task and explain to the student how the task is to be completed and what time constraints will be involved. Then the teacher should leave the student to work independently. If the teacher will administer the survey one-to-one, the teacher must remind the student that once he/she has completed reading the text, he/she should alert the teacher, so that the teacher can administer the questions. The teacher will have to arrange the time so that the student can be asked the questions immediately after he/she completes the text.

If the answers to comprehension questions will be given orally, the teacher should be prepared to take down the student's responses, rather than to note them as correct or incorrect.

Step 7: Note Errors and Performance Style
(Comprehension/Functional Readers)

If the student wrote out answers to the comprehension questions, those answers should now be scored. The teacher should ignore spelling, sentence structure, and punctuation, and be concerned only with the essence of the response in judging it correct or incorrect.

If the student responded orally, the teacher's notes should be reviewed when the teacher is free. The scoring for each question should be checked, and the total number of correct and incorrect responses for each type of comprehension question should be noted.

Step 8: Analyze Findings and Summarize
Outcomes (Comprehension/Functional
Readers)

Using the survey data, the teacher would complete the Reading Comprehension Survey Score Sheet (Figure 4-T). This should provide a clear picture of what kinds of comprehension skills were tested, and at what level on the skill hierarchy they occurred. The teacher would treat as a unit each set of comprehension questions that measures one of the three types of comprehension. Using the judgment of 75% accuracy as a criterion for successful completion of the set of questions, the teacher would mark a *1* for each portion of the score sheet passed and a *2* for each portion failed. The teacher would indicate the kinds of comprehension questions that were tapped by the survey.

Now the teacher summarizes the survey data onto the Survey line of the Assessment to Instruction Data Sheet (Figure 4-U). The format of this sheet is consistent with the recordkeeping form for word recognition and is the same format that will be followed throughout the text. The teacher notes which levels of comprehension were tested on the survey, the conditions under which the tests were administered, and the conclusions to be drawn from the results.

Student _____ School _____ Teacher _____

ASSESSMENT TASKS	Continuous text—evaluational	Continuous text—inferential	Continuous text—literal	Paragraphs—evaluational	Paragraphs—inferential	Paragraphs—literal	Sentences—literal	Words—vocabulary	Oral vocabulary	CONDITIONS		
										Response level	Questions—mode	Responses—mode
Survey												
Initial Probe												
Further Probe												
Further Probe												
Further Probe												
UPDATE												

Code—Survey and Probe
1 - Skill known
2 - Skill known at lower level
3 - Need more information
4 - Skill not known
5 - Not assessed

Code—Conditions
RC - Recall response
RG - Recognition response
O - Oral questions and responses
W - Written questions and responses

Figure 4-U Assessment to Instruction Data Sheet (Word Recognition)

Step 9: Hypothesize Reasons for Errors and Determine Areas to Probe (Comprehension/ Functional Readers)

If the student failed to meet the 75% correct criterion for a particular set of comprehension questions, the teacher should question whether the survey materials were inappropriate in some way (level, length, content). Perhaps the student's background and experience were not sufficient or appropriate for the material used in the survey. For example, let us assume that a student who had indicated to the teacher an interest in women's issues was given the survey in Figure 4-S. The teacher had chosen that passage because the content seemed appropriate and the student's independent reading level had measured about mid-sixth grade.

But what if the student knew nothing about the history of the women's movement, and was only familiar with current topics. She might not know the name Alice Paul, or the word "suffrage," or the concept of civil disobedience. The teacher

Table 4-15 Responses to Comprehension Questions Based on *Never Jam Today*

Questions	Student's Answers
1. How old was Maddy Franklin?	13
2. Why was Maddy arrested?	she was bad

3. Put the events in order
    a) Maddy was sentenced
       to 30 days in jail
    b) The women came to
       picket the persecution
       of Alice Paul
    c) Maddy was arrested
	a, b, c

4. What was a suffragist?	a bad person
5. What would be a good title for this passage?	Bed Bugs
6. What was the worst part about being in jail?	being away from home

7. Why would it be bad for
    the suffragists if Alice
    Paul were in the psychiatric
    ward?
	(student did not respond)

8. Will this experience turn
    Maddy against the suffrage
    movement? Why/why not?
	no, her mother came

9. Is the author of the story
    for or against the suffrage
    movement? How can you tell?
	(student did not respond)

10. The Commissioner said that
     Maddy was a rioter. Was she?
     How do you know?
	because

Table 4-16   Summary of Options—Hypothesizing Errors (Reading Comprehension)

Type of Error	Hypothesis	Next Step
Answers unrelated to questions	Passages inappropriate for student	Resurvey with different material a) lower reading level b) different topic
Answers wrong, but close to correct ones	Task too complex	Change conditions a) response level b) response mode
Some answers correct; others incorrect	Task too complex	Probe with shorter passage

needs to examine this student's responses to the survey questions to test out this hypothesis. If the answers seem quite unrelated to the comprehension questions, the teacher should consider another survey test using more familiar reading material.

Another possible explanation for answers that are completely wrong might be that the survey passage was at too difficult a reading level. In this case the teacher should re-survey reading comprehension using new material at a lower reading level.

One student's responses to the reading comprehension survey "Never Jam Today" (Figure 4-S) are presented in Table 4-15 as an illustration. To complete the survey, the student read each third of the passage to herself, then read the set of comprehension questions and wrote out her answers. The student's answers clearly indicate unfamiliarity with the material presented and suggest that the next step would be to re-survey reading comprehension with an entirely different set of passages.

If the student's responses seemed to be close to the correct response, the teacher might consider a different first step: a probe that would alter the conditions of the test. Since the questions in the survey required a recall response, a first probe for a student whose responses indicated some familiarity with the content might be to use the same reading materials but to require recognition responses instead. This probing decision would be based on the teacher's hypothesis that the errors on the survey were not a result of the survey materials but rather of the response requirements. Alternative probes might utilize shorter passages or oral rather than written responses. Table 4-16 summarizes three of the ways in which survey errors may be interpreted and the "next steps" implied by each interpretation.

Step 10: Probe (Comprehension/ Functional Readers)

Most probes in reading comprehension will be teacher-made, designed to measure a particular kind of comprehension (literal, inferential, or evaluative) at a particular level of response (recall, aided recall, recognition, or matching). Once the decision has been made about how to interpret survey errors, and what kinds of probes to develop, the teacher can find passages and prepare questions to accomplish specific purposes.

For example, a teacher's decision in Step 9—to follow up the "Never Jam Today" survey with probes at a lower response level—could have resulted in several different tests. The teacher could have rewritten the questions into a multiple choice format. The first two questions on this follow-up probe could read:

1. How old was Maddy Franklin?
    a)   10
    b)   17
    c)   31
2. Why was Maddy arrested?
    a)   She picketed in front of the White House.
    b)   She threw rocks at the police.
    c)   She carried her clothes in a bag.

Or, the teacher could have asked a student to answer the original comprehension questions by locating the correct answers in the text and showing the teacher where he/she found them. Or, the teacher could have given the student one question at a time before he/she began reading the passage, and had the student read until the answer was found.

In these three probes, the teacher used the same material as was used in the survey, but manipulated the test conditions to determine the conditions under which the student might be successful.

Step 11: Complete Recordkeeping Forms and Generate Teaching Objectives (Comprehension/Functional Readers)

Now the teacher would note, on the Assessment to Instruction Data Sheet for reading comprehension, the kinds of follow-up probes that had been administered, their conditions and their outcomes. Based on the information summarized on this record form, the teacher would establish teaching objectives for "skills not known."

Step 12: Start Teaching/Update Assessment Information (Comprehension/Functional Readers)

The teacher should begin to teach one comprehension skill at a time. Even when the survey and probes have indicated problems in more than one kind of comprehension, our experience has shown that it will be overwhelming for the student to have a variety of comprehension tasks presented all at once. The decision of which comprehension skill to teach first should be influenced both by the teacher's knowledge of the kinds of comprehension skills the student needs to master in order to be successful in the mainstream of his/her school, as well as by the hierarchy of skills reflected in the Assessment to Instruction Data Sheet. Once one skill has been mastered, the teacher can return to the recordkeeping form, update it with any new information that has been gathered in the course of instruction, and select the next skill to be taught.

ILLUSTRATION: GINA

The following example will take the reader through Steps 4 to 12 in the assessment strategy for gathering and interpreting comprehension data on a functional reader.

The teacher had the following information, based on a teacher-created IRI for Gina, a 6th grade student:

Independent reading level: grade 4.0

Instructional reading level: grade 4.5

The teacher also knew that Gina was interested in country music, animals, and roller skating and that she liked to read mystery stories.

Step 4: Select or Develop Survey Instrument (Gina)

The teacher decided to survey Gina using three separate passages, each no higher than a fourth-grade level. The passages she selected were based on her knowledge of Gina's interests. For the first passage, the teacher created 8 questions to assess the literal comprehension aspects of main idea (1), sequence (1), details (2), vocabulary meaning (2), and cause-effect relationships (2). The teacher created 6 questions from the second passage to tap inferential comprehension: interpretive (2), general inferential (2) and predictive (2). The three questions from the third passage were created to assess the evaluative aspects of judgment (2) and appreciation (1). Figure 4-V shows the survey passages selected and the comprehension questions created for Gina.

PART I

Saving Wild Animals*

Some people kill wild animals for food. Others hunt for the love of it. As a result, there are not many wild animals left. Millions of buffalo used to roam the western plains. Today they are found mainly in zoos and national parks. The forests used to be full of deer. These have been cruelly hunted. There were once many beavers too. They are nature's dam builders. Today there are few left. Lovers of these wild creatures soon began to worry. They saw that something had to be done. They didn't want these animals to be lost.

Many steps were taken to save all this wildlife. More national parks were started. This was good for animals. They cannot be hunted in national parks. Also, fees were charged for hunting licenses. Then, too, hunting seasons were set up. Hunting was allowed only during certain weeks or months. And more game wardens were hired. A game warden's job is to see that hunting laws are obeyed.

There is now another way to save wild animals. This is education of the public. Children in school are taught the value of these animals. The government prints many little books on the subject. These booklets reach millions of people. Museums also help. They prepare interesting nature magazines and films. Many people are working to save wild animals.

Figure 4-V Reading Comprehension Survey

*Robert Potter, *A Better Reading Workshop: Reading With Care.* Copyright © 1978 Globe Book Company, Inc. Used by permission.

Comprehension Questions

1. Choose an appropriate title for this story:

   a) Killing Wild Animals
   b) Hunting Wild Animals
   c) Saving Wild Animals

2. True or false:

   After the public was educated about wild animals, there were fewer animals left in the forests and plains.

3. Name three steps that were taken to save the wildlife:

   a)
   b)
   c)

4. Name two animals mentioned in the story that there are now fewer of:

   a)
   b)

5. Game wardens are people who:

6. Another word for creature used in the story is:

7. There are fewer animals on the plains today because:

8. The government educates people about wild animals so that:

PART II

The Tomato Plant*

A very old woman lived alone near the edge of town. She had just one friend--a tomato plant. The plant stood in a sunny spot in her back yard. Every morning and evening she watered it. She talked to it as she watered it.

"My, how strong you look today," she would tell the plant. "Would you like to have a little drink?"

The boy who lived next door laughed at the old woman and her plant. He made fun of her. She could hear him laughing at her at all hours of the day and night.

"Old lady," he would yell from his window. "Your plant is dying. Old lady, the birds are eating your tomatoes."

Near the end of the summer the tomatoes on the plant were soft and red. Every evening the old woman would go out and pick one of her tomatoes.

There was one tomato on the plant that the old woman never picked. It was the biggest tomato that she had ever seen. She was saving it for her birthday dinner.

Figure 4-V Reading Comprehension Survey—**Continued**

On the morning of her birthday, the old woman went out to water her plant. The big tomato was red and ripe. "Oh, my," she said to the plant. "You are the best friend anyone could ever have. What a beautiful birthday present." And she went inside to wait for evening, when she would pick the tomato. She did not see the boy next door watching her from his window.

That evening the old woman went out to pick her dinner. As she reached down to pick the tomato, she saw that it was gone. There were other, smaller tomatoes on the plant. But the old woman's large birthday tomato was not there. She looked at the plant for a long time, and then she went inside. That night the old woman did not feel like having any dinner.

The old woman was getting ready for bed when she heard the ambulance. It sounded very close. When it stopped outside her house, the old woman ran out to the street. The ambulance was parked in front of the house next door. She watched two men carry a stretcher out of the house.

"What is the matter?" she asked one of the men.

"It's the boy who lived here," he said. "And if you ask me, I would say it was something he ate that did him in."

Comprehension Questions

9. Circle the words that describe the woman in the story:

   a) elderly, lonely, friendless
   b) talkative, neighborly, happy
   c) ugly, mean, cruel

10. What do you think the author of the story is trying to say?

    a) Tomatoes make you sick.
    b) The boy was punished because he was cruel.
    c) The woman should have shared her tomatoes.

11. What happened to the woman's birthday tomato?

12. What information in the story gave you the answer for question 11?

13. How do you think the woman felt when she saw the boy on the stretcher?

14. What might happen next in the story?

PART III

The Johnny Cash Story*

When Johnny Cash sings, people listen. His big, deep voice rumbles out of radios and jukeboxes across North America. His records sell by the million. Country-music fans everywhere know his big hits. They love songs like "Hey Porter," "Ring of Fire," and "Folsom Prison Blues."

Figure 4-V Reading Comprehension Survey —**Continued**

*Robert Potter, *The Reading Road to Writing, Sentences.* Copyright ©
1977 Globe Book Company, Inc. Used by permission.

Johnny Cash sings about a hundred concerts a year. People like what they hear--and what they see, too. Rugged and big-shouldered, the singer stands six-two without his black boots on. He's a two-hundred-pound package of muscle and talent. And that scar on his cheek? It's a bullet hole, of course!

In the minds of most people, Johnny Cash is "Mr. Tough Guy." He's an ex-drug addict who once did a long stretch in jail. His grandmother was an Indian. To keep from starving, he once had to live on wild rabbits killed from forty feet away with a knife. Some people say he even killed a man.

In fact, most of the Johnny Cash story is just that--a story. True, years ago he had a "drug habit" for a short time. He "popped" pills. But he never used heroin or other "hard" drugs. Sometimes he'd go wild and get locked up for a few hours. But he never served a jail sentence. There's no Indian blood in his veins. He's been a killer only in song. As for the "bullet hole," it's an old scar left by a doctor who opened a cyst.

People who know Johnny Cash will say he's a "gentle guy," a "generous guy"--anything but a "tough guy." How did the stories get started? Some of them, like the story about the "Indian grandmother," he made up long ago to add excitement to his career. Others, like the "bullet hole," simply got started. Now there's little the singer can do to change people's minds. "They just want to believe it," he says.

Comprehension Questions

15. Why do people believe Johnny Cash is a tough guy?
   (You can mark more than one item)

   a) People are more interested in stars who have led exciting lives.
   b) He is a drug addict who spent a lot of time in jail.
   c) He is an Indian with a bullet hole in his cheek.
   d) He is large and rugged looking.

16. If you were to meet Johnny Cash, based on the story, choose three words that you think would describe him.

17. If you were writing a story about Johnny Cash, name three things you would do to find out if he's a tough guy or a gentle guy.

   a)
   b)
   c)

Figure 4-V Reading Comprehension Survey —**Continued**

Step 5: Get Ready to Test (Gina)

The teacher created questions at both the recall and recognition levels of response. She decided to survey Gina by having her read the three passages on three successive days. Gina was not permitted to go back into the material to locate the answers during the survey. She was instructed to read the questions and write out the answers. The teacher prepared Gina for the assessment by explaining that she was interested in how much Gina understands of what she reads. The teacher set up a carrel for Gina.

Step 6: Administer the Survey (Gina)

On each day of the survey, the teacher gave Gina a copy of the passage to be read and told her to announce quietly when she had finished reading. She explained to Gina that after reading the story, she was to return the story to the teacher and answer some questions. The teacher told Gina that she would be permitted to listen to an album for ten minutes after she had completed the questions. Gina went to the carrel to read the story, exchanged it for the questions when she had completed the reading, and returned to the carrel to answer the questions. She did this on three successive days until the survey was completed.

Step 7: Note Errors and Performance Style (Gina)

Figure 4-W is a copy of Gina's responses and the teacher's scoring. The teacher noted each error by circling it. She also noted if a response was incomplete.

Comprehension Questions

    1. Choose an appropriate title for this story:

        a) Killing Wild Animals
        b) Hunting Wild Animals
        (c) Saving Wild Animals

    2. True or false:

        After the public was educated about wild animals, there were fewer animals left in the forests and plains.

          T   (F)

    (3.) Name three steps that were taken to save the wildlife:

        a) stop shooting
        b) zoos
        c)

    4. Name two animals mentioned in the story that there are now fewer of:

        a) bufalos
        b) bevers

    5. Game wardens are people who: protect animals

    6. Another word for creature used in the story is: deer

    (7.) There are fewer animals on the plains today because: they run away

    (8.) The government educates people about wild animals so that: they know how to take care of pets

Figure 4-W Reading Comprehension Survey: Comprehension Questions

Comprehension Questions

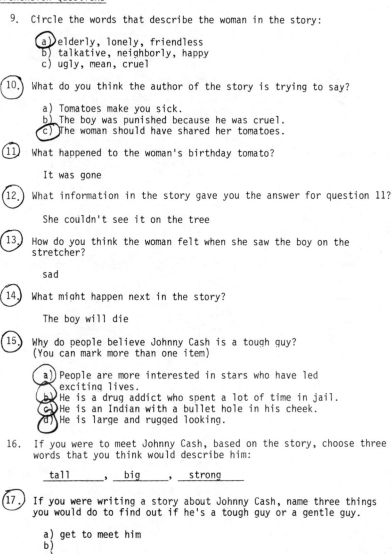

9. Circle the words that describe the woman in the story:

   (a) elderly, lonely, friendless
   b) talkative, neighborly, happy
   c) ugly, mean, cruel

10. What do you think the author of the story is trying to say?

    a) Tomatoes make you sick.
    b) The boy was punished because he was cruel.
    (c) The woman should have shared her tomatoes.

11. What happened to the woman's birthday tomato?

    It was gone

12. What information in the story gave you the answer for question 11?

    She couldn't see it on the tree

13. How do you think the woman felt when she saw the boy on the stretcher?

    sad

14. What might happen next in the story?

    The boy will die

15. Why do people believe Johnny Cash is a tough guy?
    (You can mark more than one item)

    (a) People are more interested in stars who have led
        exciting lives.
    (b) He is a drug addict who spent a lot of time in jail.
    (c) He is an Indian with a bullet hole in his cheek.
    (d) He is large and rugged looking.

16. If you were to meet Johnny Cash, based on the story, choose three
    words that you think would describe him:

    __tall__ , __big__ , __strong__

17. If you were writing a story about Johnny Cash, name three things
    you would do to find out if he's a tough guy or a gentle guy.

    a) get to meet him
    b)
    c)

Figure 4-W   Reading Comprehension Survey: Comprehension Questions—**Continued**

Step 8: *Analyze Findings and Summarize*
Outcomes (Gina)

The teacher recorded her findings on the Reading Comprehension Survey
Score Sheet found in Figure 4-T. Figure 4-X shows her notations. She then completed the Survey line of the Assessment to Instruction Data Sheet (Figure 4-Y).

Student ___Gina_____ Date ___11/4_____ Teacher ___Alberts_____

COMPREHENSION SKILLS	Complexity of Task				Conditions		
	Continuous text	Para-graphs	Sentences	Words	Response level	Mode of questions	Mode of responses
Literal	2						
Main Idea	✓				RG	W	W
Sequence	✓				RG	W	W
Details	X				RC	W	W
Vocabulary	✓				RC	W	W
Cause-effect	X				RC	W	W
Inferential	2						
Interpretive	✓				RG	W	W
General inferential	X				RG & RC	W	W
Predictive	X				RC	W	W
Evaluative	2						
Judgmental	X				RG	W	W
Appreciative	X				RC	W	W
Critical	–				RC	W	W

Code—Task
1 - Skill known @ 75% accuracy
2 - Skill not demonstrated to criterion
✓ - Skill tapped and known
X - Skill tapped and not known
— - Skill not tapped

Code—Conditions
RC - Recall response
RG - Recognition response
W - Written questions and responses
O - Oral questions and responses

Figure 4-X Reading Comprehension Survey: Score Sheet

Student _Gina_   School _Eisenhower_   Teacher _Alberts_

ASSESSMENT TASKS	Continuous text—evaluational	Continuous text—inferential	Continuous text—literal	Paragraphs—evaluational	Paragraphs—inferential	Paragraphs—literal	Sentences—literal	Words—vocabulary	Oral vocabulary	CONDITIONS Response level	Questions—mode	Responses—mode
Survey	3	4	3	5	5	5	5	5	5	RC	W	W
Initial Probe												
Further Probe												
Further Probe												
Further Probe												
UPDATE												

Code—Survey and Probe
1 - Skill known
2 - Skill known at lower level
3 - Need more information
4 - Skill not known
5 - Not assessed

Code—Conditions
RC - Recall response
RG - Recognition response
O - Oral questions and responses
W - Written questions and responses

Figure 4-Y Assessment to Instruction Data Sheet (Word Recognition)

Step 9: Hypothesize Reasons for Errors and
Determine Areas to Probe (Gina)

When the teacher looked over Gina's responses and the information recorded in Figures 4-X and 4-Y, it was clear that Gina was more accurate with recognition level questions, but that she was able to recall some information at the literal level. Her responses at the inferential and evaluative levels demonstrated that her comprehension skills in those areas were very weak.

The teacher hypothesized that, at the literal level, the materials were appropriate but that the conditions of the test might have constrained Gina's success. She further hypothesized that in the areas of inferential and evaluative comprehension, the task may have been too complex for Gina, in addition to the conditions being inappropriate. She decided to design different probes for literal comprehension and for inferential and evaluative comprehension.

Step 10: Probe (Gina)

The first probes created by the teacher utilized the same material as that on the survey, since there were no indications that this might be the source of Gina's lack of success.

For the initial probe, the teacher had Gina re-read the passage "Saving Wild Animals" and respond to questions 3, 7, and 8 from the original survey (Figure 4-V) by referring back to the text. In this probe, the teacher changed the original recall task to a recognition task. Under these conditions, Gina was able to demonstrate 100% accuracy on the literal questions.

For the second probe, the teacher used the same material from the survey. She asked Gina to re-read the story "The Tomato Plant" and told her that it was a mystery. She suggested that Gina look for clues that might tell her who took the tomato and why it was taken, and that she try to think about what happened from the viewpoint of the old woman in the story. After Gina had re-read the story, the teacher asked her the original survey questions and had Gina respond orally. The teacher determined from this probe that when Gina was given a set of questions before reading the story, and was allowed to respond in an oral mode, she was able to achieve a 75% mastery criterion. The teacher decided not to probe further at this time.

Step 11: Complete Recordkeeping Forms
and Generate Teaching Objectives (Gina)

The teacher added all the probe information she had gathered to the Assessment to Instruction Data Sheet given in Figure 4-T. The completed form is shown in Figure 4-Z.

Because Gina is a sixth-grade student, the conditions typically required of her in reading comprehension are written recall responses. The teacher's probing indicated that Gina was able to understand most literal and inferential questions if she could refer back to the passage and speak, rather than write, her responses. Therefore, teaching objectives for Gina will focus on helping Gina read for different kinds of meaning and respond in written form. The teacher developed six objectives for Gina, to be taught one at a time.

Student _Gina_   School _Eisenhower_   Teacher _Alberts_

ASSESSMENT TASKS	Continuous text—evaluational	Continuous text—inferential	Continuous text—literal	Paragraphs—evaluational	Paragraphs—inferential	Paragraphs—literal	Sentences—literal	Words—vocabulary	Oral vocabulary	CONDITIONS Response level	CONDITIONS Questions—mode	CONDITIONS Responses—mode
Survey	3	4	3	5	5	5	5	5	5	RC	W	W
Initial Probe			2							RG	W	W
Further Probe		2								RG	O	O
Further Probe												
Further Probe												
UPDATE												

Code—Survey and Probe
1 - Skill known
2 - Skill known at lower level
3 - Need more information
4 - Skill not known
5 - Not assessed

Code—Conditions
RC - Recall response
RG - Recognition response
O - Oral questions and responses
W - Written questions and responses

Figure 4-Z Assessment to Instruction Data Sheet (Word Recognition)

The student will:

1. Respond in writing to literal comprehension questions with 90% accuracy after referring back to the text as a check.
2. Respond in writing to literal comprehension questions with 75% accuracy without referring back to the text.
3. Respond orally to inferential comprehension questions with 90% accuracy after referring back to the text as a check.
4. Respond in writing to inferential comprehension questions with 90% accuracy after referring back to the text as a check.
5. Respond orally to inferential comprehension questions with 75% accuracy without referring back to the text.
6. Respond in writing to inferential comprehension questions with 75% accuracy without referring back to the text.

Step 12: Start Teaching/Update Assessment Information (Gina)

The teacher will begin to teach Gina literal comprehension skills at the written response level. Using material that interests Gina, her teacher will prepare comprehension questions (either by using published materials or by creating the questions) and, after Gina has responded, will have her refer back to the material to check her responses. As she moves Gina through the teaching objectives, the teacher will update the Assessment to Instruction Data Sheet, recording skills mastered and new skills not known.

If the information obtained in Step 3 of the comprehension assessment indicates that the student is a beginning reader, then the teacher executes Steps 4 through 12 of the assessment of reading comprehension in a slightly different manner, beginning at a point much lower on the skill hierarchy (Table 4-14). For students whose reading level is less than grade 2.5, but better than grade 1.5, the survey will be at the level of short paragraphs or sentences followed by literal comprehension questions (Level 4-C or 3-A on the hierarchy). Students with reading levels of less than grade 1.5 will be surveyed at the word meaning level of comprehension only.

We will now describe the procedures for assessment of beginning readers. The reader may wish to refer back to Figure 4-Q to see how this discussion of comprehension assessment of beginning readers fits into the total picture of reading assessment.

ASSESSMENT OF COMPREHENSION/BEGINNING READERS

Step 4: Select or Develop Survey Instrument (Comprehension/Beginning Readers)

As before, the reading level, length, and content of the materials to be used to survey reading comprehension skills in beginning readers depend on the student being tested. Typically, beginning readers become very frustrated if the passage is too complicated or too long. The teacher must take great care in selecting materials for these students.

As with functional readers, materials should be chosen at the student's independent reading level. Sentences, short paragraphs, or even words for the comprehension survey of beginning readers could be chosen from basal reading texts, from the reading tests found in Tables 4-2 and 4-3, or from popular materials of interest to the student. Actually, it is rather difficult to find reading material that is interesting at or below the 2.5 grade level. This presents a particular problem for older students who are beginning readers. Table 4-17 is a list of high interest/low vocabulary materials which are graded from grades 1.5 to 3.5. A teacher could choose passages of interest to older students from this set. Our experience with these materials is that, despite the readability level quoted by the publisher, beginning readers are often frustrated by them. The teacher should exercise judgment in presenting these materials for a reading comprehension survey; the teacher may find that the student's performance will indicate that even these passages were too difficult.

One way around this problem would be to establish the student's independ-

Table 4-17 High Interest/Low Vocabulary Reading Materials

Material	Publisher	Level
Action Kit	Scholastic	Unit Book 1-2
Action 25 Series	Rembert	—
American Adventure Series	Harper & Row	—
A Need to Read	Globe	A
Bowmar Reading Incentive Program	Bowmar Noble	—
Classmate Editions Developmental Reading Series	Lyons & Carnahan	—
Clue Magazine	Educational Progress	1
Hip Readers	Book-Lab	1-2
Know Your World	American Education Publications	—
Pal Paperbacks	Xerox	Yellow/Red
Pal Skills Kit	Xerox	Yellow/Red
Panorama Reading Series	Steck-Vaughn	1-3
Phoenix Reading Series	Prentice-Hall	—
Point 31 Readers	Reader's Digest	I
RD 2000	Reader's Digest	I
Scholastic Scope	Scholastic Magazines	—
Scope/Language Skills	Scholastic	1
Skillpacers	Random House	I
Spiral Individualized Reading Books	Continental Press	—
Sports Modules	Troll Associates	—
Sprint Library	Scholastic	Library I-II

Karen went for a ride to her friend Mike's house. On the way she
saw a black dog and two yellow ducks. They looked like they were having
a good time. Karen was going to hide from Mike but Mike saw her. The
children played a fast game of tag. Karen went home late.

Questions

1. Where did Karen go?

2. What did she see on the way?

3. What did the children play?

4. When did Karen go home?

5. Put the statements in order:

    a) The children played tag

    b) Karen went to see Mike

    c) Karen saw a dog and two ducks

6. What is another word for fast?

7. In the story, does <u>hide</u> mean

    a) The skin of an animal

    b) To try to not be seen

    c) To own something

Figure 4-AA Pre-Reader Comprehension Survey—Teacher-Made

ent reading level by using one of these books. The teacher could have the student
read a paragraph aloud from the material. If the student can decode 95% of the
words, the material will probably not be too difficult. If the student cannot meet a
95% criterion, easier material should be chosen for the comprehension survey.

The teacher who chooses to make up a text for the reading comprehension
survey will find it useful to include words that the student demonstrated he/she could
read on the earlier sight vocabulary assessment. The passage created should not
exceed 100 words.

Once the material has been selected or created, the teacher will need to generate comprehension questions for the survey. Passages appropriate for lower reading
levels seldom allow the teacher to generate questions at a more complex level than
the literal one. Questions will almost always be read to the student and answered
aloud to ensure that reading and writing problems do not interfere with the assessment of comprehension skills.

Figure 4-AA is an example of a teacher-made comprehension survey for
Karen, the beginning reader whose word recognition skills were described earlier in
this chapter.

Step 5: Get Ready to Test (Comprehension/
Beginning Readers)

The teacher should prepare one copy of the text for the student to read and a
copy of the questions for him/herself. The teacher should also have a sheet of paper
on which to record the student's answers.

Step 6: Administer the Survey
(Comprehension/Beginning Readers) and
Step 7: Note Errors and Performance Style
(Comprehension/Beginning Readers)

When administering the reading comprehension survey, the teacher should
write the student's answers to the questions, not just indicate whether the answer

Table 4-18 Karen's Answers

Questions	Answers
1. Where did Karen go?	to Mike
2. What did she see on the way?	dogs and ducks
3. What did the children play?	tag
4. When did Karen go home?	I don't know

5. Put the statements in order:
  a) The children played tag.
  b) Karen went to see Mike.
  c) Karen saw a dog and two ducks.
	a, b, c

6. What is another word for fast?	quickly

7. In the story, does *hide* mean—
  a) the skin of an animal
  b) to try to not be seen
  c) to own something
	b

was correct or incorrect. As with functional readers, the substance of the answers will help the teacher hypothesize about the causes of errors and decide about follow-up probes.

Step 8: Analyze Findings and Summarize Outcomes (Comprehension/Beginning Readers)

The score sheet introduced in Figure 4-T is useful for summarizing the results of the reading comprehension survey for beginning as well as functional readers. Table 4-18 provides Karen's answers to the teacher-made comprehension survey. The teacher noted that Karen could provide correct recall responses to questions of fact and detail, and to vocabulary items based on a single paragraph which she read silently (the checks on the score sheet). But he noted that she was unable to answer the sequence questions and that he needed to understand this further. He recorded these findings onto the score sheet (Figure 4-BB) and onto the Survey line of the Assessment to Instruction Data Sheet.

Step 9: Hypothesize Reasons for Errors and Determine Areas for Probes (Comprehension/Beginning Readers)

The same decision-making guides presented for functional readers (Table 4-16) are useful for beginning readers. If the student is unable to complete 75% of the comprehension questions, or if his/her responses are extremely inappropriate, the teacher should consider re-surveying with new (lower level) material. If the student answers some comprehension questions correctly and some incorrectly, the teacher should plan to follow up with probes that alter the test conditions.

Items that were answered incorrectly should be followed up with probes *down* the skill hierarchy, that is, with lower level comprehension tasks. Items that were answered correctly should be probed *up* the skill hierarchy systematically, with higher level tasks.

Student _Karen_ Date _2/20/81_ Teacher _Gibson_

COMPREHENSION SKILLS	Complexity of Task				Conditions		
	Continuous text	Para- graphs	Sentences	Words	Response level	Mode of questions	Mode of responses
Literal		2			RC	O	O
Main Idea		–					
Sequence		X					
Details		✓					
Vocabulary		✓					
Cause-effect		–					
Inferential							
Interpretive							
General inferential							
Predictive							
Evaluative							
Judgmental							
Appreciative							
Critical							

Code—Task
1 - Skill known @ 75% accuracy
2 - Skill not demonstrated to criterion
✓ - Skill tapped and known
X - Skill tapped and not known
— - Skill not tapped

Code—Conditions
RC - Recall response
RG - Recognition response
W - Written questions and responses
O - Oral questions and responses

Figure 4-BB Reading Comprehension Survey: Score Sheet

Step 10: Probe (Comprehension/ Beginning Readers)

In instances where the student answered comprehension questions incorrectly, the teacher could probe *down* by changing the questions to require recognition rather than recall responses. This can be done by changing open-ended questions to multiple choice, or by changing the requirement that the child answer from memory to permitting the child to search the paragraph for the answer.

Another way to probe down is to replace the reading material for the comprehension probe with a less lengthy, less complex text. If the student had to read a paragraph for the survey, the teacher might design a probe in which one literal comprehension question would be answered after reading a single sentence.

In instances where the student answered comprehension questions correctly, the teacher could probe *up* by asking more complex (inferential rather than literal) questions based on the original reading material, or by increasing the complexity and length of the reading passage on which more literal comprehension questions are based.

Referring back to Karen's responses to the comprehension survey, the teacher has noted that Karen could not recall the sequence of events, although she handled literal questions about facts and details quite adequately. Karen's teacher could decide to do two kinds of probes—one down the skill hierarchy to better understand Karen's problem with comprehension of sequence, and one up the skill hierarchy to see if Karen can handle even more complex questioning.

Table 4-19 shows the probes created for Karen, with her responses. In the first probe, the teacher examined comprehension of sequence through a recognition level question. In the second, the teacher asked inferential questions based on the survey paragraph. The teacher chose not to probe Karen's comprehension skills using more complex reading materials, because the earlier word recognition assessment showed her to have rather limited decoding skills.

Table 4-19 Probes for Karen

Probe 1	The teacher showed Karen the story and asked her which came first, next, and last using the items in question 5 from the survey. Karen was able to respond correctly by finding the items in the story and numbering them.
Probe 2	The teacher asked Karen some inferential questions:

    1) Do you think Karen likes to go to Mike's house? (yes); Why? (to play tag)

    2) Do you think Karen will go to play with Mike again? (yes); Why? (to play tag)

    3) What word would you use to describe Karen and Mike? (kids); [T. prompt—Do they like each other? (yes); Then what would you call them? (nice kids)]

    4) What might be an ending to the story since Karen came home late? (don't know); [T. prompt—What will Karen's mother say? (don't know)]

ASSESSMENT TASKS	Continuous text—evaluational	Continuous text—inferential	Continuous text—literal	Paragraphs—evaluational	Paragraphs—inferential	Paragraphs—literal	Sentences—literal	Words—vocabulary	Oral vocabulary	CONDITIONS Response level	Questions—mode	Responses—mode
Survey	5	5	5	5	5	3	5	5	5	RC	O	O
Initial Probe					2					RG	O	O
Further Probe					4					RC	O	O
Further Probe												
Further Probe												
UPDATE												

Code—Survey and Probe
1 - Skill known
2 - Skill known at lower level
3 - Need more information
4 - Skill not known
5 - Not assessed

Code—Conditions
RC - Recall response
RG - Recognition response
O - Oral questions and responses
W - Written questions and responses

Figure 4-CC Assessment to Instruction Data Sheet (Reading Comprehension)

Step 11: Complete Recordkeeping Form and Generate Teaching Objectives (Comprehension/Beginning Readers)

Information gathered in the survey and probes of reading comprehension in beginning readers can be summarized on the Assessment to Instruction Data Sheet. In Karen's case (Figure 4-CC) the assessment sheet shows that the initial survey was carried out at the paragraph level and that, while the survey needed to be followed up (2 in the square), it did indicate adequate knowledge of simple vocabulary words and some kinds of literal comprehension at the recall level. The initial probe showed that Karen could answer sequence questions at the recognition level. A further probe indicated that she was not successful with inferential questions.

Based on the findings on the Assessment to Instruction Data Sheet, the teacher can create objectives for reading comprehension skills along three dimensions: passage length, type of comprehension questions, and response conditions. Karen's teacher set 2 initial teaching objectives for reading comprehension.

The student will learn to:

1. Answer literal comprehension questions, at the recall level, in as complex material as can be developed from her word recognition vocabulary. (As word recognition skills improve, the complexity of the reading material on which literal comprehension questions will be based will increase.)

2. Answer interpretive questions, at the recognition level, in short passages.

Step 12: Start Teaching/Update Assessment Information (Comprehension/Beginning Readers)

As the beginning reading student responds to instruction in reading comprehension, the teacher should update the Assessment to Instruction Data Sheet, noting skills that are mastered and new areas that need instruction. New teaching objectives would be derived from a regular review of the recordkeeping form.

SUMMARY

In this chapter we have discussed two aspects of the components of reading that must be assessed: word recognition and comprehension. We have also treated functional readers and beginning readers separately for each component. The 12-step strategy for assessment for instructional planning, introduced in Chapter 3, has been applied to the assessment of reading.

We began this chapter by acknowledging that reading is a complex task. Our approach has been to simplify the assessment of reading so that even a teacher who is not yet experienced in assessment will be able to collect data that will lead to appropriate instructional objectives. It is likely that as teachers become more adept with the assessment process and the 12-step strategy, they will adapt and expand these assessment procedures to suit their individual styles and needs.

5

Assessment of Written Expression

Written expression is one of the most sophisticated and demanding forms of language, requiring the ability to combine several discrete and individually complex skills. Before students can express ideas in written form, they must have something to say. Students must be able to understand and use words and syntactical patterns in spoken language to generate something to communicate in print. They must also have organizational skills that will enable the words and ideas to develop a theme or make a point. Students who cannot organize their thoughts will be limited in their ability to communicate in written form. They may express their ideas in a disjointed fashion; their written stories may lack a main idea and be little more than a descriptive listing.

Written communication also requires knowledge of spelling, and this is a complex task because English is a complex language to spell. To spell phonetically predictable words, students must be able to determine the sounds heard in words and attach correct graphic symbols to those sounds. This requires adequate auditory analysis and discrimination skills as well as knowledge of sound-symbol correspondences. But not all English words are phonetically predictable, so students must also remember which letters or letter sequences are included in phonetically irregular or unpredictable spellings. Thus, visual memory skills are also necessary for accurate spelling. Finally, knowledge of morphological rules is required in order to alter basic forms of words, to make plurals, or to change verb tenses.

In order to write, students must be able to remember the visual forms of letters and translate those forms into motor plans. The sequence of movements necessary to reproduce each letter must be imagined and internalized so that it becomes an automatic pattern. "Good handwriting" also calls for motor fluency, which is dependent upon fine motor coordination.

Finally, for proper written expression, the student must know the conventions of print. These are the "rules of writing" that govern punctuation and capitalization usage, format conventions for identifying paragraphs or writing letters, guidelines for sentence structure and word order, and the use of various word forms (homonyms, such as their/there; subject/verb match; pronoun/referent match). Performance in this area is dependent on having an adequate oral language foundation; appropriate grammar and sentence structure in writing often reflects appropriate grammar and sentence structure in oral expression. But fluency in oral language is not enough. The student must also understand and use certain rules which apply only to the written form of communication.

If a child lacks skills in spoken language, organizing thoughts, spelling, writing, or knowledge of conventions of print, he/she will lack the ability to communicate well in print. The "product" the child generates will be inadequate in some way. Because so many teachers demand written work of their students from the early grades through high school, remedial teachers often feel responsible for helping children improve their written expression skills. Since assessment should be the foundation on which this help is built, we will apply the strategy for the assessment for instructional planning to the assessment of written expression skills. As in Chapter 4, we begin the discussion at Step 2.

Step 2: Select or Develop a Skill Hierarchy

We define written expression as the ability to express ideas or feelings in correct written form. Typically, written expression is considered that portion of the school curriculum referred to as composition. But it actually includes a full range of skills, especially those learned in handwriting, spelling and grammar lessons.

A variety of sources can be used to generate a skill hierarchy for written expression. Language arts scope and sequence charts or method textbooks for teaching reading and writing can be examined. In looking through these materials, the teacher should keep in mind that there are two dimensions to a written expression task: the amount that the student writes and the extent of the structure given by the teacher to guide the student's thinking and writing. The hierarchy presented in Table 5-1 reflects these two dimensions.

The highest level of performance indicated on the hierarchy is writing continuous text (Level 3). This may involve writing a series of thematically related paragraphs (that is, stories) or thematically related sentences (that is, paragraphs). Level 2 involves writing single sentences which are not organized into paragraphs or connected thematically. To meet the written language requirements of Levels 3 and 2, the student must think of something to say, write it down, spell the words correctly, and correctly apply the appropriate conventions of print.

At the lowest level of the hierarchy (Level 1), it is presumed that the student is unable to *combine* the discrete skills necessary to express ideas in written form, though he/she may have some capacity to perform these skills in isolation. Because the student has not yet integrated the skills, they are listed separately in the skill

Table 5-1 Written Expression Hierarchy

3. Writing Continuous Text

A. Generate a story (or series of paragraphs)
1. with no teacher direction
2. from topic
3. from story-starter
4. from picture
5. from sequence of pictures

B. Generate a paragraph
1. with no teacher direction
2. from topic
3. from topic sentence
4. from picture
5. from sequence of pictures

2. Writing Single Sentences

A. Generate a sentence
1. from topic
2. from word
3. from picture
4. from sentence starter

1. Demonstrating Component Skills of Written Expression

A. Generating ideas in oral language

B. Handwriting

C. Spelling

D. Knowing conventions of print

hierarchy. For the two highest levels, the dimension of structure is also incorporated into the hierarchy. Students may write about any theme or topic they choose, or they may be given some amount of direction and structure by the teacher: a specific topic to write about, a story-line starter, a picture that is to be the basis of the composition, a series of pictures that represents a sequence of events, or a sentence beginning.

Step 3: Decide Where to Begin

Now the teacher must decide where on the written expression hierarchy to initiate the assessment. The goal is to find the highest level of skill performance for the survey test without assigning the student too frustrating a task.

We suggest using two sources of information to determine where to begin the written language assessment: data which indicate the student's reading level and any available samples of student's written work. It is reasonable to differentiate students on the basis of their reading scores, since reading involves the same set of symbols necessary for writing and it is unusual to find a student in whom writing performance greatly exceeds reading ability. It is also useful to consider any available samples of the student's written work, because it is possible for a student to read much better than he/she can write.

As a rule, if the student is a functional reader (reading score of grade 2.5 or more) and work samples indicate that he/she is capable of generating sentences, the student would be classified as a functional writer. The written language assessment would then begin at the highest level of the hierarchy with a story or paragraph writing task. Students who meet these two criteria should be able to generate one or more paragraphs of written ideas.

If the student is a beginning reader, or has indicated on previous written work that he/she cannot compose a written sentence, the assessment should start at the lowest level of the hierarchy, where it is presumed that component skills have not yet been integrated into an adequate written expression capability. These beginning writers may be able to perform individual components of written expression adequately, but may not yet have learned to put them all together.

Because the written language assessment of functional and beginning writers proceeds from different levels on the hierarchy, the remainder of this chapter will deal with the two separately. First, we will follow Steps 4 through 12 of the Assessment for Instructional Planning for functional writers, then retrace Steps 4 through 12 for beginning writers.

ASSESSMENT OF WRITTEN EXPRESSION: FUNCTIONAL WRITERS

Step 4: Select or Develop Survey Instrument (Functional Writers)

For the functional writer, the survey will require the student to write a story (Level 3-A of the hierarchy presented in Table 5-1). In selecting or developing the specific survey to be used with a student, two factors should be considered. The first is the amount of structure to be provided to guide the student's thinking and writing. To write a story about "anything you like," the student must establish a focus and organize a story line. This is an extremely complex task. When the teacher assigns a topic, it is still difficult, because the student has to determine what aspects of the topic should be addressed, and in what order. Completing a story when the story line has been provided is somewhat less demanding because the task is already structured to some extent. Writing a story about a picture is less complex than that, because the picture helps to establish a story line and provides some specific details which can be included in the story. If a sequence of pictures is used, the task becomes even less demanding; the pictures illustrate a specific story line and provide an organizational framework. Thus, the writer has less responsibility for generating the ideas to be communicated.

To determine which of these task options would be the best choice for a particular student, the teacher should consider the student's oral language skills and his/her age. The teacher should ask, "Which task might this student be able to do *orally*?" The assumption is that if the child has enough organizational skill to perform the task in oral language, he/she could perform a similar task in writing. The teacher should listen to the student's conversation and his/her reporting on in-school or out-of-school events to judge how much structure the student needs in developing an idea to communicate. The written expression survey should require the student to take as much responsibility as possible for generating the ideas in the written language sample.

The second factor to consider in selecting or developing a survey of written

Table 5-2 List of Commonly Available Measures for Written Expression Survey

Test Name	Publisher	Writing Requirement	Structure
Picture Story Language Test	Grune & Stratton	Generate story	Single picture
Test of Written Language	Pro-Ed	Generate story	Sequence of pictures
Brigance Diagnostic Inventory of Essential Skills: Writing Subtest	Curriculum Associates	Generate sentences	Stimulus words

expression is the interests of the student. A longer writing sample is likely to be generated if the topic is one with which the student is familiar and in which the student is interested.

There are several commercially available tests of written expression which could be used as survey tasks. These are listed in Table 5-2. For each, we have identified the writing requirements of the tasks and the amount of structure provided in the test.

If the teacher would like to develop a survey using a picture as the story stimulus, there are several additional points to consider. First, the teacher should identify the topics of interest to students at particular ages (zoo animals, sports, neighborhood events, space, and so forth) and select several pictures for each age level. The pictures should include at least one central character and illustrate the character(s) engaged in some obvious activity. Care should be taken to avoid pictures with too much detail, as they may be confusing. Fantasy-like pictures should also be avoided because they may be difficult to interpret and may rely too heavily on the child's ability to fantasize.

Step 5: Get Ready to Test
(Functional Writers)

As in all assessment activities, it is important for both the teacher and the student to be well-prepared before the survey is administered. We have found it useful, when using a picture as the story stimulus, to have several pictures available, all meeting the guidelines outlined above, all representing age-appropriate themes and culture-appropriate experiences. Having several pictures available permits the teacher to give students a choice of what to write about.

The teacher should also be prepared to tape-record the student as soon as he/she has finished writing the story. The student should read the completed story into the recorder. This is an important part of the written language survey for functional writers, since it permits the teacher to know what the student *intended* to say. Analysis of error patterns is highly dependent on having an accurate text transcript which reflects the student's intentions. Students should be informed about the taping when the written language survey is being introduced, and the teacher should have the student tape-record his/her story immediately following its completion. (Students whose handwriting and/or spelling is difficult to decipher may not be able to read their own stories if too much time is allowed to elapse.) As well, students should be put at ease by a reassurance that the written language survey is not a test in the usual sense, and that their stories will not be graded. And the teacher should be prepared to offer a reinforcement to the student for completing the writing task.

Step 6: Administer the Survey
(Functional Writers)

Students should be given explicit instructions before they begin the written language survey task. First, the teacher should emphasize story quality. Students should be told that the objective of the activity is to determine how well they can write a story. They should be encouraged to write the best, most creative story possible, and to not be overly concerned about spelling unfamiliar words.

Second, neatness should be encouraged. Since handwriting will be evaluated through the story writing task, it is essential that students be asked to demonstrate their best writing/printing. This will help to insure that the sample obtained reflects the child's true ability. Students can be reminded to write carefully because they will be asked to read their stories aloud when they have been completed.

Third, students should be encouraged to try to spell words correctly, but they should understand that misspelled words are acceptable, because it is the story itself that is of principal concern. Students can be told that they should not avoid using particular words because they do not know how to spell them; rather, they should attempt to approximate the correct spelling.

Finally, teachers should introduce time guidelines. Students should be told that as much time as is necessary will be allowed for the story writing task. The only restriction is that a story must be completed on the same day it is started. Students should be encouraged to take their time to allow for maximum performance.

Step 7: Note Errors and Performance Style
(Functional Writers)

While the student is generating the story, and after it has been completed, the teacher should note the manner in which the student approached the task. Notes should be made of the apparent difficulties the student had in getting started, the amount of prodding and reinforcement needed to keep the student on-task, the number of times the student asked for a correct spelling, and the time taken by the student to complete the story. These performance patterns will be useful to the teacher in analyzing the error patterns.

Once the story has been written and the student has read the story onto a tape, the teacher should transcribe the student's oral version—onto the same page as the written sample, if possible. This will give the teacher a record of the child's intended story as compared to the written product.

Now the teacher should read through the story and identify the errors. Spelling errors should be numbered consecutively throughout the story. Omitted words should be identified with a caret (^) and superfluous words crossed out with a slash (/). Punctuation errors should also be marked: letters that should have been capitalized and punctuation marks that have been omitted should be circled (O). Examples of awkwardness in handwriting should be underlined. The markings should be done in colored pencil, clearly distinguishing them from the student's product. Figure 5-A shows a story that has been marked by the teacher. The markings appear in bold type. They show no omitted words, 1 superfluous word, 6 spelling errors, 8 punctuation errors, and 13 notations of poor handwriting.

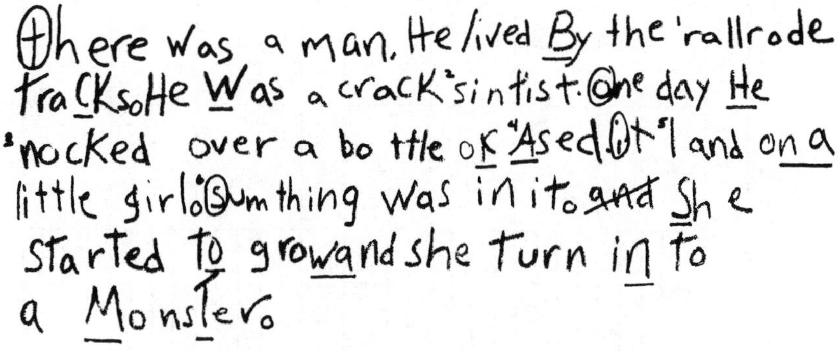

[Handwritten text:]
Where was a man. He lived By the 'rallrode
traCKsoHe Was a crack'sintist. One day He
'nocKed over a bo ttle of Ased ot'l and on a
little girl. Sumthing was in it, and She
started to growand she turn in to
a Monster.

There was a man. He lived by the railroad
tracks. He was a crack scientist. One day
he knocked over a bottle of acid. It landed
on a little girl. Something was in it and
she started to grow and she turned into a
monster.

Figure 5-A Written Language Sample

Step 8: Analyze Findings and Summarize Outcomes (Functional Writers)

The writing sample must be analyzed to determine which written language skills have been demonstrated adequately and which have not. In order to evaluate the student's story, we find it useful to consider separately each of the four components of written expression: generation of ideas, spelling, handwriting, and conventions of print.

Generation of ideas is used here to refer to aspects of written expression dealing with the thoughts and ideas communicated and their grammatical form. *Spelling* refers to the symbolic representation of words. *Handwriting* can be thought of as the "penmanship" aspect of written expression, and *conventions of print* involves the application of rules for writing.

The teacher should be prepared to read through the story four times, in order to evaluate the survey and complete the Written Language Survey Summary of Information (Figure 5-B). During the first reading, the teacher should evaluate generation of ideas. Our experience with evaluating written language samples has shown that students who have problems generating ideas are students who write stories that do not "tell a story." Their written expression is poorly organized and lacks a theme or central idea. They use immature and overly concrete vocabularies and inappropriate grammatical and syntactical patterns. The length of their written product is less than the average for students of that age. Figures 5-C and 5-D are stories written by students who seem to have poor "generation of ideas." In each figure a transcript of text accompanies a reproduction of the student's actual work.

Figure 5-C is a story written by an adolescent in response to a picture which showed a young man sitting near the edge of a lake. The story reads like a telegram. The sentence structure is concrete and the thoughts are poorly organized. It is also a rather short story for a student of this age.

Figure 5-D was written by a seven-year-old who has similar difficulties in

Name _____ School _____ Teacher _____ Date _____

Generation of Ideas	Summary of errors	Adequate	Inadequate
Vocabulary			
Productivity			
Story theme/ organization			
Grammar			

Handwriting	Summary of errors	Adequate	Inadequate
Remembering letter shapes			
Upper/lower case letters			
Reproducing letter shapes			

Conventions of Print	Summary of errors	Adequate	Inadequate
Punctuation			
Capitalization			
Sentence structure			
Word usage			

Spelling	Summary of errors	Adequate	Inadequate
Hearing sounds in words			
Sound/symbol correspondence			
Irregular spellings and letter sequences			
Morphological rules			

Figure 5-B Written Language Survey—Summary of Information

> *Go fishing, open the can of baked beans & go hunting with a knife Lonely. Look for other people. dig with my hands. Someone droppd a bome. no bildings.*

Go fishing, open a can of baked beans and go hunting with a knife. Lonely.
Look for other people. Dig with my hands. Someone dropped a bone. No
buildings.

Figure 5-C Written Language Sample

> *gril play with doys. boys rede oocks. little boys play with Tucks. little Doys play with bocks. gril with shos.*

Girls play with
dolls.
Boys read books.
Little boys play with
trucks.
Little boys play with
blocks.
Girl with shoes.

Figure 5-D Written Language Sample

oral language comprehension and use. It was written in response to the Picture Story Language Test stimulus picture. The sentence structure is concrete and articles are omitted. Further, the story is quite sparse and the story line is fragmented—it fails to establish a theme.

In evaluating the story for generation of ideas, the teacher should ask four questions:

1. What does the student have to say? (story theme)
2. Is the story long enough? (productivity)
3. Does the student use age- and experience-appropriate language? (vocabulary)
4. How well does the student tell the story? (grammar)

There are no specific guidelines for answering these questions. Teachers will have to use their best judgment, although seriously impaired performance should be quite obvious. Notations regarding each of these questions should be made on the Summary of Information (Figure 5-B).

Next, the teacher should review the story a second time, concentrating on handwriting. If a student's knowledge of correct letter forms is limited, the teacher is likely to note frequent letter reversals in the student's written work. Also, the student may use both upper and lower case letters within the same word. Forms which might best be described as "non-letters" may also be noted in written samples. These may be combinations of several letter parts or they may be combinations of letters and numbers. In either case, they suggest some confusion as to what the letters should look like (see Figure 5-E).

When a student is uncertain of the motor plan necessary to produce letters, his/her writing may be slow and quite laborious, with deep pencil grooves and numerous erasures noted. Additional strokes or connecting loops may be noted in

```
One day a mother told her
children to play so her children
played. The baby started to cry
because her brother hit her.
The mother gave her brother a
licking for hitting the baby.
```

Figure 5-E Written Language Sample

```
He is in a house in the city
The dog fell and ran to the wall
The end.
```

Figure 5-F   Written Language Sample

cursive samples, suggesting confusion as to how letters should be formed and joined. Noticeable variations in the size and shape of letters, and irregular spacing between words or among letters may also be seen (see Figure 5-F).

The teacher should note problems in remembering and reproducing letter shapes and, in general, motor fluency on the Written Language Survey Summary of Information (Figure 5-B).

The teacher reviews the story a third time to evaluate conventions of print. Punctuation errors should be counted and noted by type on the score sheet, including errors of capitalization. Sentence structure should also be evaluated. The teacher should note run-on sentences, sentence fragments, misplaced modifiers, and so on. Errors in use of homonyms and other word usage problems should be marked on the score sheet. Problems in format (i.e., paragraphing) should also be noted.

Figures 5-G, 5-H, and 5-I provide examples of problems with the conventions of print. They show several errors of punctuation, word form, and sentence structure (fragmentary and run-on sentences). In each figure the errors have been circled.

```
    This is Mark and I five years from now on a date at Parker Dam,
walking a trail. Mark asks me if I will marry him. I said, "Yes,
on one condition." Mark asked what it was. I said, "You don't join
the Navy." He said he wouldn't. A year later we got married. Joie
was the Bridesmaid. We have 3 boys and 2 girls. We named one boy
James, one Mark and the other one John. We named the girls Joie
and Jean.
```

Figure 5-G   Written Language Sample

Hey girl, what are you doing at the teacher's desk? Is you doing your homework? Tell that boy to stay down so you would get done with your work. Hey girl, I need a piece of paper to do my work. Can I see your pencil too? Hey, I like the way you write and read. Don't forget to do what I told you to do, ok? One more thing, would you put a point on my pencil? You have pretty eyes. I think I like you.

Figure 5-H Written Language Sample

Once upon a time there were three runaways. Their names were Judy, Kellie, and Nancy. They were only 15 or 16. Their parents were worried, especially Kellie's parents. They hired a special detective to find her. Two months later they found her. She was lying in a gutter, dead, along with her friends.

The moral of the story is, it don't pay to run away.

Figure 5-I Written Language Sample

Finally, the teacher should review the spelling found in the story. All misspelled words should be recopied onto the Analysis of Spelling Errors form (Figure 5-J), with the incorrect form in the first column and the correct form in the second. The teacher should attempt to categorize each spelling error as reflecting one of four types of problems: hearing sounds in words, sound/symbol correspondence, phonetically irregular spellings, letter sequences, or morphological rules.

		Error Categories			
Student's spelling	Correct spelling	Hearing sounds in words	Sound/ symbol	Irregular and sequence	Morphological rules
1.					
2.					
3.					
4.					
5.					
6.					
7.					
8.					
9.					
10.					
11.					
12.					
13.					
14.					
15.					
16.					
17.					
18.					
19.					
20.					
21.					
22.					
23.					
24.					
25.					

Figure 5-J Analysis of Spelling Errors

Spelling errors that show words combined or strung together as single units, as in the case of the student who writes, "Once *aponatime* there was," are categorized as problems in hearing sounds in words. Words spelled with individual sounds or full syllables missing, or with sounds (letters) added are categorized in the same way. In all three cases, the spelling error seems to reflect a difficulty in "mapping" the sounds of words.

Table 5-3 illustrates typical spelling patterns that would be categorized as problems in hearing sounds in words. The words reflect some confusion as to the auditory elements involved in the intended word. Entire syllables have been omitted and extra letters have been added. While most initial and final sounds are accurately identified, the child seems to consistently get "lost" within words.

Spelling that reflects inadequate mastery of sound-symbol correspondences will show a slightly different pattern. Students use the wrong letter or group of letters to represent a sound, even in phonetically regular words. In the extreme case, the spelling bears little or no relationship to the word the student intended to write.

Table 5-4 shows examples of these spelling errors. The first four samples are

Table 5-3 Examples of Problems Hearing Sounds in Words

Student Sample	Intended Word	Notice
canusee	can you see	Strung together
apunatime	upon a time	
cholat	chocolate	Sounds omitted
bantball	basketball	
dest	dressed	
cunterley	country	Sounds added
peresinits	presents	

Table 5-4 Examples of Problems with Sound-Symbol Relationships

Student Sample	Intended Word	Notice
plb	stop	No sound-symbol correspondence
ferg	fun	
rany	holding	
sootep	shelf	
cam	can	Error in particular sound-symbol correspondence
tem	them	
let	wet	
yelp	help	
ctop	chop	

cases where the student's spelling bears no resemblance to the intended word. The remaining samples show errors in selecting letters to represent particular sounds.

The third category of spelling errors involves words which are not spelled the way they sound or do not follow a predictable phonics rule. These are words that must be committed to memory. The spelling errors show an over-reliance on phonics, an attempt to "sound out" every word. Silent letters or unheard word parts are often omitted. Also, words may be written with all the correct elements included, but in the wrong sequence (e.g., rihgt for right). Table 5-5 illustrates these kinds of spelling errors.

A final type of error pattern reflects the student's limited mastery of morphological rules. These rules govern the spelling of a word formed by altering a root word, as in the case of adding affixes. The student may fail to double final letters or to drop the final vowel before attaching endings. Or, plural words may be misspelled consistently, with *s* and *es* inappropriately applied. Table 5-6 provides examples of spelling errors which reflect poor knowledge of morphological rules.

The teacher should review all the errors listed on the Analysis of Spelling Errors form and check the appropriate column to indicate error type. A single word, with misspellings in two different syllables or parts, may reflect more than one type

Table 5-5 Examples of Problems with Irregular Words

Student Sample	Intended Word	Notice
cud	could	Error in irregular vowel, consonant, phonogram or word
pepul	people	
wunce	once	
frum	from	
agin	again	
nite	night	
tho	though	
woh	who	Sequence error
saw	was	

Table 5-6 Examples of Problems with Morphological Rules

Student Sample	Intended Word	Notice
bated	batted	Failure to apply rules for verb tense and plurals
dreses	dresses	
comeing	coming	
flaten	flatten	
housses	houses	
storys	stories	

of spelling error. Each part of the misspelled word should be classified, and the appropriate error column checked. The teacher should total the checks in each column to indicate the distribution of spelling errors across types. Finally, the teacher should summarize the spelling errors onto the Written Language Survey Summary of Information sheet, noting how many and what types of spelling errors were most prevalent in the writing sample.

Now the teacher is ready to review all the errors and complete the Survey line of the Assessment to Instruction Data Sheet for written language (Figure 5-K). This sheet incorporates all the aspects of written expression that we have suggested

Student _____ School _____ Teacher _____

ASSESSMENT TASKS	Generation of ideas—vocabulary	Generation of ideas—productivity	Generation of ideas—story theme	Generation of ideas—grammar	Handwriting—remembering letters	Handwriting—upper/lower case letters	Handwriting—reproducing letters	Conventions of print—punctuation	Conventions of print—capitalization	Conventions of print—sentence structure	Conventions of print—word usage	Conventions of print—format	Spelling—hearing sounds in words	Spelling—sound/symbol correspondence	Spelling—irregular spellings and sequence	Spelling—morphological rules
Survey																
Initial Probe																
Further Probe																
Further Probe																
Further Probe																
UPDATE																

Code—Survey and Probe

1 - Skill known   3 - Need more information
2 - Skill known at lower level   4 - Skill not known   5 - Not assessed

Figure 5-K Assessment to Instruction Data Sheet (Curricular Area: Written Language)

are part of the assessment and error analysis. It is organized in a way that is similar to the reading Assessment to Instruction Data Sheets, and uses the same coding system. The form is designed to summarize information into three categories: skills known; skills not known; and skills for which information has not yet been gathered or is not yet complete.

Step 9: Hypothesize Reasons for Errors and Determine Areas to Probe (Functional Writers)

Using the information summarized on both the Summary of Information and the Assessment to Instruction Data Sheets, the teacher can see the student's pattern of errors. Now the teacher must try to hypothesize why the errors were made. Again, the four components of written expression are looked at separately.

If the student wrote a very short, very concrete story, and the teacher has made several notations in the category of generation of ideas, there are four hypotheses that could be tested. First, the student may have done poorly because the survey stimulus was inappropriate—either not interesting to the student or outside his/her range of experiences.

A second hypothesis would be that the composing task was too complex for the student. Acting independently, the student did not have sufficient organizational skills to develop a story or theme. The student needed more structure or direction to do a satisfactory job. In both these cases the teacher would want to re-survey, using different stimuli to elicit a written story.

A third hypothesis might be that the student's oral language skills are deficient and that this led to a limited story product. In general, sparse, fragmented stories, in which there are errors in vocabulary use or sentence structure, indicate oral communication deficits. The teacher could probe this hypothesis by dropping down the language hierarchy and having the student *tell* a story.

A fourth hypothesis to explain a survey that shows problems in generation of ideas could be that deficient spelling or motor skills and/or limited knowledge of conventions of print inhibited the student and were responsible for the limited sample. In this case the teacher might re-survey, while providing the student with as much assistance as he/she requests with spelling, handwriting, and punctuation.

In a similar way, hypotheses about errors and ideas for probes can be developed for the other three components of written language. Problems in handwriting could be attributed to the complexity of the composing task or to an uncertainty about letter forms. In the first case, the teacher would probe by having the student create single sentences instead of a complex story. In the second case, the probe would consist of copying tasks.

If the error patterns on the survey are clustered under conventions of print, the teacher might hypothesize that the student knows the rules but is unable to apply them in as complex a task as writing a story. The teacher would probe by reducing the complexity level of the task and using dictated rather than self-generated sentences.

Another hypothesis might be that the student either does not know the rules or has difficulty recalling them. The teacher might probe the student's memory by having him/her perform at a recognition level, correcting or editing a preprinted story.

Six hypotheses could be explored for spelling errors. A first hypothesis might be that the complexity of the survey made too many demands on the student, and that spelling errors simply reflect the student's response to an overwhelming task. The teacher would probe spelling by reducing the task demands for generating ideas and dictating sentences to the student.

A second hypothesis for spelling errors might be that the student is attempting to write words which he/she cannot read. The teacher could probe by having the student read the misspelled words printed in their correct form.

If the spelling errors are clustered in the hearing sounds in the words category, the teacher might suspect problems in auditory analysis skills and design probes to test out the student's capacity to discriminate sounds in words or word parts. If the spelling errors indicated problems in sound-symbol association, probes might involve the spelling of words or sentences from dictation. Similarly, errors that suggest problems in remembering unpredictable or phonetically irregular words might be followed up by probes that incorporate specific irregular words but that change the response requirements from recall to recognition level. Errors indicating that morphological rules are not being applied would be followed up by probes using root words in altered forms (with endings, plurals, etc.).

Summaries of all the hypotheses that could be generated from the error patterns in a survey of written expression are given in Tables 5-7 to 5-10. For each hypothesis the most likely focus for the probe is also given.

Table 5-7 Error Hypotheses and Possible Problems (Functional Writers/Generation of Ideas)

Error	Hypothesis	Probe
Very short story, concrete vocabulary	Topic/stimulus inappropriate	Re-survey with different topic/stimulus
Very short story, disorganized theme	Task too complex	Re-survey with less complex task
Vocabulary, grammar problems	Oral language deficits	Have a student tell a story
Short story, concrete (simple) vocabulary, correctly spelled	Deficits in spelling, handwriting, and conventions of print limit productivity	Have student tell story and write it down with teacher present

Table 5-8 Error Hypotheses and Possible Probes (Functional Writers/Handwriting)

Error	Hypothesis	Probe
Messy	Task too complex	Create or dictate sentences
Reversals, upper and lower case used inappropriately	Uncertain memory for letter forms	Copy sentences or single words
Size and spacing variations, deep pencil groves, erasures	Uncertain about motor plans	Dictate words or letters

Table 5-9 Error Hypotheses and Possible Probes
(Functional Writers/Conventions of Print)

Error	Hypothesis	Probe
All kinds	Task too complex	Dictate sentences
Punctuation and capitalization	Overwhelmed by writing requirement	Correct printed sentences
Sentence structure, word usage	Task too complex	Correct printed sentences; fill in blanks

Table 5-10 Error Hypotheses and Possible Probes (Functional Writers/Spelling)

Error	Hypothesis	Probe
All kinds of errors	Task too complex	Have student generate sentences Dictate sentences Dictate spelling list
All kinds of errors, especially sound symbol	Reading problems	Have student read misspelled words in correct forms
Errors of hearing sound in words	Auditory analysis deficits	Dictate isolated words part by part
Errors in sound/ symbols	Letter-sound combination problems	Dictate isolated words
Errors in nonphonetic word parts	Poor memory for word parts and letter sequences	Dictate words, list; recognition tasks
Errors in morphological rules	Poor knowledge of rule	Dictate word list

Step 10: Probe (Functional Writers)

Probing is carried out for each component of written language in which errors are detected in the survey. The probes verify the error patterns and clarify the level at which the student can perform in each skill area.

To get more information about generation of ideas, the teacher may want to probe with different test stimuli. A list of topics appropriate at different age levels is given in Table 5-11. Alternative pictures for use as stimuli, from which students may generate stories (written or oral), are available in commercial magazines or in a variety of published materials. The teacher could refer back to Table 5-2 and select a commercially available test which provides the student with additional task structure. The student could also be asked to develop single sentences about pictures or objects.

Handwriting probes may take several forms. The teacher could dictate words or sentences which the student is to write in his/her best handwriting. Or the student might copy samples of manuscript or cursive sentences, words, or letters. At an even lower level, the student might be asked to trace letter forms to determine the extent of eye-hand coordination.

Table 5-11   Topics for Probes at Various Grade Levels

Primary Grades	Intermediate Grades	Secondary Grades
Animals	Outer space	Music
Family trips	Science fiction	Cars
Television programs	Sports	Sports
Siblings	Television programs	Interpersonal relationships
Friends	Monsters	
Holidays	If I were. . .	Media
Ghost stories	Mysteries	Current events
		Food
		Ecology
		Careers
		College

Probes of knowledge of the conventions of print may make use of published tests on punctuation and capitalization or word usage. The teacher could dictate sentences which contain the elements on which the student made errors in the survey. The teacher could find or develop editing tasks to determine how well the student responds at the recognition rather than recall level.

Spelling probes will usually include spelling lists to be dictated to the student. The teacher may want to make up lists based on the error analysis done on the survey or use a published word list that includes certain word types. As the teacher continues to probe, tasks involving recognition rather than production responses (for example, multiple choice spelling tests) may be appropriate.

Many commercial resources are useful in probing written language skills. Table 5-12 lists some of these.

Step 11: Complete Recordkeeping Form and Generate Objectives (Functional Writers)

When probes have been administered and scored, the results should be added to the Assessment to Instruction Data Sheet for written language. Then, using the data on this form, the teacher can select teaching objectives (skills not known) and identify where further assessment data must be gathered in the course of teaching.

The subskills listed across the top of the form parallel the Written Expression Summary of Information that has guided our evaluation of the student's written language. To complete this form, the teacher uses the code printed at the bottom of the form. The *4* markings would be for skills that are not known (on the basis of evidence from a survey or a probe). These and the *2* skills (skills known at a lower level) would become teaching objectives. Each *3* (survey or probe completed, need more information) would serve to alert the teacher that more information should be gathered as the teaching of written expression progresses. Each *1* would indicate skills that do not need to be taught.

Table 5-12 Commercial Resources for Probes of Written Expression

Generation of Ideas	Spelling	Motor	Conventions of Print
Sequence Picture Cards (Levels 1 and 2); Teaching Resources	Spellmaster Diagnostic Spelling System; Curriculum Associates	Sequential Precision Assessment Resource Kit (SPARK II); Precision People, Inc.	SIMS Written Language Program; Minneapolis Public Schools
Story Starters (Primary/ Intermediate); Curriculum Associates	Prescriptive Spelling Program—Bks. 1-3; Barnell-Loft	Classroom Learning Screening Manual (Koenig and Kunzelmann); Chas. E. Merrill	Homonex; Curriculum Associates
SIMS Written Language Program; Minneapolis Public Schools	Spelling Vocabulary Workbooks— Levels A-B; Curriculum Associates	Penskill; Science Research Associates	Grammar and Mechanics Skills Skills Centers (Intermediate and Secondary); Curriculum Associates
	Working Words in Spelling; Curriculum Associates	Better Handwriting for You; Noble & Noble	Language Exercises Levels 1-8; Steck-Vaughn
	Basic Goals in Spelling— Grades 1-8; McGraw-Hill		
	Basic Spelling; J. B. Lippincott		
	Spelling Workbook Series; Educators Publishing Service		
	Better Spelling (Dolch, E. W.); Garrard		

Step 12: Start Teaching/Update Assessment
Information (Functional Writers)

The goal of instruction in written language is to have students master the ability to express their ideas effectively in written form. As instruction in specific subskills progresses, the teacher should keep in mind the "more information needed" areas on the Assessment to Instruction Data Sheet, and update the recordkeeping form when the information becomes available. When this new information moves the skill to the "skill not known" category, a new teaching objective might be generated.

ILLUSTRATION: ANDREW

To illustrate the steps in the written language assessment for instructional planning, we will move through Steps 4 through 12 for Andrew, an eight-year-old third grader. He has beginning third-grade reading skills. His teacher began the assessment at Step 4 because Steps 1, 2, and 3 had been completed: She had decided to assess written expression (Step 1—What to Assess); she had chosen the hierarchy presented in Table 5-1 to guide her assessment (Step 2—Select/Develop a Skill Hierarchy); she knew that Andrew was a functional reader and had collected some samples of last year's written work that showed he could generate sentences. She decided to have Andrew generate a story (Step 3—Decide Where to Begin).

Step 4: Select or Develop Survey Instrument
(Andrew)

Andrew's teacher had listened to his responses to questioning in class, and to Andrew's descriptions of what he likes to do after school. She had noted that he sometimes finds it difficult to get started, that he needs some prodding and some specific questioning before he can get the idea out. She decided that Andrew would probably not be able to "write about anything you like," but might respond to a picture stimulus for the written expression survey. She chose a picture of a family scene as the stimulus for Andrew. The picture met the criteria for a stimulus picture and seemed appropriate to Andrew's age and experiences.

Step 5: Get Ready to Test (Andrew)

After explaining the task to Andrew and giving him the picture, some lined paper, and a pencil, the teacher left Andrew at a desk in a quiet corner of the room. Andrew understood that he would have as much time as he needed, that he was to write the best story that he could, and that he would have five minutes of free time as a reward for completing the task.

The teacher had a tape recorder and blank tape ready to record Andrew's reading of his story after it had been written.

Step 6: Administer the Survey (Andrew)

Andrew took the picture and settled down to work. After 25 minutes he produced the written language sample shown in Figure 5-L. The teacher recorded Andrew's reading of the sample, then transcribed it onto the same page.

Owns apuna time   ther was
a little boy woh lived
in the Cuhterea. he had
a fother and a mother. it
was Cerigmis whaer he
lived. eley in the morning
he got dest opied his
peresints ahd startedt to
play. his mother woke up
ahd gave him somthing to eat
he aetit ahd went on
playing.

```
Once upon a time there was
a little boy who lived
in the country.  He had
a father and mother.  It
was Christmas where he
lived.  Early in the morning
he got dressed opened his
presents and started to
play.  His mother woke up
and gave him something to eat.
He ate it and went on
playing.
```

Figure 5-L Written Language Sample (Andrew)

Step 7: Note Errors and Performance Style (Andrew)

The teacher made a note of the fact that Andrew had no apparent difficulty in thinking up something to say. He started the task immediately and worked steadily, without asking questions and without being prodded by the teacher.

The teacher reviewed Andrew's story. She numbered the spelling errors, circled punctuation errors, and noted omitted and added words. She did not underline handwriting problems because they appeared throughout the story. The "scored" story is provided in Figure 5-M.

¹Owhs ²apuna time   ³ther was
a   little   boy ⁴Woh lived
in   the   ⁵Cuh terea. ⁶He had
a ⁷fother and a mother. ⁸It
was ⁹Cerigmis ¹⁰Whaer he
lived. ¹¹Oley in the morning
he   got ¹²deSto ¹³opied hi⁵
¹⁴peresints ahd ¹⁵Startedt to
play. ¹⁶His mother Woᴸe up
ahd gave him ¹⁷Somthing to eatₒ
¹⁸He ¹⁹aet it and went ₒn
playing.

Once upon a time there was
a little boy who lived
in the country. He had
a father and mother. It
was Christmas where he
lived. Early in the morning
he got dressed opened his
presents and started to
play. His mother woke up
and gave him something to eat.
He ate it and went on
playing.

Figure 5-M   Written Language Sample: Errors Noted

Step 8: Analyze Findings and Summarize Outcomes (Andrew)

To get a sense of Andrew's performance, the teacher followed the four-step analysis procedure. First, the teacher read through Andrew's entire story to get an impression of his capacity to generate ideas. The teacher noted that the quality of Andrew's story theme seemed to be quite adequate. A main idea or principle theme had been developed, and the story followed a reasonable sequence of events. The story line went beyond the picture and included events occurring before and after the portrayed scene. Also, the story seemed to be adequate in length and detail for a composition written by a child of this age. The teacher concluded that there was no evidence to suggest problems involving limited or inappropriate vocabulary usage, or poor grammar. The teacher recorded these findings on the Written Language Survey of Information (Figure 5-N).

Name _Andrew_   School _Park_   Teacher _Thomas_   Date _____

Generation of Ideas	Summary of errors	Adequate	Inadequate
Vocabulary		✓	
Productivity		✓	
Story theme/ organization		✓	
Grammar		✓	
Handwriting	Summary of errors	Adequate	Inadequate
Remembering letter shapes			
Upper/lower case letters			
Reproducing letter shapes			

Conventions of Print	Summary of errors	Adequate	Inadequate
Punctuation			
Capitalization			
Sentence structure			
Word usage			
Spelling	Summary of errors	Adequate	Inadequate
Hearing sounds in words			
Sound/symbol correspondence			
Irregular spellings and letter sequences			
Morphological rules			

Figure 5-N Written Language Survey—Summary of Information (Generation of Ideas) (Andrew)

The teacher reviewed the story a second time, concentrating on Andrew's handwriting. She saw no instances where inappropriate letter forms were used and concluded that Andrew had adequate knowledge of what the letters should look like. The teacher noted the variations in size, shape, and spacing of letters and words that appear throughout the story. She recorded these findings on the score sheet (Figure 5-O).

The teacher reviewed the story for the third time to evaluate conventions of print. She found that Andrew used periods appropriately throughout the story, except in the next to last sentence where the teacher circled the omission. She noted the one instance where Andrew failed to use commas to separate a series of clauses, and the several instances where Andrew failed to use capital letters at the beginning of sentences. She recorded these errors, and the number of times they occurred, on the score sheet (Figure 5-P).

In terms of other conventions of print, she recorded that sentence structure and word usage seemed to be adequate, especially in light of Andrew's age.

Now she reviewed the story a fourth time, concentrating on spelling errors. She copied the 15 spelling errors onto the Analysis of Spelling Errors form, writing Andrew's version, and then the correct spelling. She analyzed the errors and checked at least one category of spelling error for each word. Figure 5-Q shows the teacher's decisions.

She totaled the columns and noted that Andrew had the most errors in the third category—problems in spelling phonetically irregular words. He also had some errors that seemed to reflect failure to hear sounds in words, particularly parts of blends. He made very few errors involving application of morphological rules. The teacher added these findings to the Written Language Survey Score Sheet (Figure 5-R).

Now the analysis of Andrew's story was completed. The teacher looked over the score sheet and completed the Survey line of an Assessment to Instruction Data Sheet (Figure 5-S). In terms of generation of ideas, she determined that Andrew presented no serious problems; story theme, productivity, vocabulary, and grammar were all adequate. She recorded these as *1*, "skills known."

She noted adequate knowledge of letter shapes (*1*), along with the need for more information regarding the inconsistent use of upper and lower case letters and poor production of all letters (*3*). Punctuation and capitalization skills also required further information, although other conventions of print were adequate.

Under spelling, she indicated that more information was needed in each of the four areas.

Step 9: Hypothesize Reasons for Errors and Determine Areas to Probe (Andrew)

Andrew's teacher looked over the notations and saw that she had said "more information needed" in three of the four components of written expression: handwriting, conventions of print, and spelling. In handwriting, she considered that the irregular sizes and spacing of words and letters could be due to problems in reproducing letter shapes (i.e., in knowing the motor plans for letter shapes and reproducing them), or to problems in motor fluency (the automaticity of writing when many written expression skills must be brought into play at the same time). The teacher

Name *Andrew*   School *Park*   Teacher *Thomas*   Date _____

Generation of Ideas	Summary of errors	Adequate	Inadequate
Vocabulary		✓	
Productivity		✓	
Story theme/ organization		✓	
Grammar		✓	

Handwriting	Summary of errors	Adequate	Inadequate
Remembering letter shapes		✓	
Upper/lower case letters	*irregular use within sentences and words*		✓
Reproducing letter shapes	*irregular size and shape*		✓

Conventions of Print	Summary of errors	Adequate	Inadequate
Punctuation			
Capitalization			
Sentence structure			
Word usage			

Spelling	Summary of errors	Adequate	Inadequate
Hearing sounds in words			
Sound/symbol correspondence			
Irregular spellings and letter sequences			
Morphological rules			

Figure 5-O   Written Language Survey—Summary of Information (Handwriting) (Andrew)

Name _Andrew_   School _Park_   Teacher _Thomas_   Date _____

Generation of Ideas	Summary of errors	Adequate	Inadequate
Vocabulary		✓	
Productivity		✓	
Story theme/organization		✓	
Grammar		✓	

Handwriting	Summary of errors	Adequate	Inadequate
Remembering letter shapes		✓	
Upper/lower case letters	_irregular use within sentences and words_		✓
Reproducing letter shapes	_irregular size and shape_		✓

Conventions of Print	Summary of errors	Adequate	Inadequate
Punctuation	_1-comma omitted_ _1-period omitted_ _(but 5 correct)_		✓
Capitalization	_5-caps. omitted at beginnings of sentences_		✓
Sentence structure		✓	
Word usage		✓	

Spelling	Summary of errors	Adequate	Inadequate
Hearing sounds in words			
Sound/symbol correspondence			
Irregular spellings and letter sequences			
Morphological rules			

Figure 5-P Written Language Survey—Summary of Information (Conventions of Print) (Andrew)

154

Error Categories

	Student's spelling	Correct spelling	Hearing sounds in words	Sound/ symbol	Irregular and sequence	Morphological rules
1.	owns	once			√	
2.	apunatime	upon a time	√ strung together	√ vowel		
3.	ther	there			√	
4.	woh	who			√ seq.	
5.	cunterea	country		√ vowel √ vowel		
6.	fother	father		√ vowel		
7.	cerismis	Christmas			√	
8.	whaer	where			√	
9.	eley	early	√ mid. cons.	√ vowel		
10.	dest	dressed	√ mid. cons			√ past tense
11.	opied	opened	√ mid. cons	√ vowel		
12.	peresints	presents		√ r √ vowel		
13.	startedt	started				√ past tense
14.	somthing	something			√	
15.	aet	ate			√ seq.	
16.						
17.						
18.						
19.						
20.						
21.						
22.						
23.						
24.						
25.						
			4	6	7	2

Figure 5-Q Analysis of Spelling Errors

Name Andrew   School Park   Teacher Thomas   Date

Generation of Ideas	Summary of errors	Adequate	Inadequate
Vocabulary		✓	
Productivity		✓	
Story theme/organization		✓	
Grammar		✓	

Handwriting	Summary of errors	Adequate	Inadequate
Remembering letter shapes		✓	
Upper/lower case letters	irregular use within sentences and words		✓
Reproducing letter shapes	irregular size and shape		✓

Conventions of Print	Summary of errors	Adequate	Inadequate
Punctuation	1-comma omitted / 1-period omitted (but 5 correct)		✓
Capitalization	5-caps. omitted at beginnings of sentences		✓
Sentence structure		✓	
Word usage		✓	

Spelling	Summary of errors	Adequate	Inadequate
Hearing sounds in words	omits medial consonants		✓
Sound/symbol correspondence	vowels; r		✓
Irregular spellings and letter sequences	sight words: once, there, some sequences: who, ate		✓
Morphological rules	past tense		✓

Figure 5-R Written Language Survey—Summary of Information (Spelling) (Andrew)

Student _____ *Andrew* _____ School _____ *Park* _____ Teacher _____ *Thomas* _____

ASSESSMENT TASKS	Generation of ideas—vocabulary	Generation of ideas—productivity	Generation of ideas—story theme	Generation of ideas—grammar	Handwriting—remembering letters	Handwriting—upper/lower case letters	Handwriting—reproducing letters	Conventions of print—punctuation	Conventions of print—capitalization	Conventions of print—sentence structure	Conventions of print—word usage	Conventions of print—format	Spelling—hearing sounds in words	Spelling—sound/symbol correspondence	Spelling—irregular spellings and sequence	Spelling—morphological rules
Survey	1	1	1	1	1	3	3	3	3	1	1	1	3	3	3	3
Initial Probe																
Further Probe																
Further Probe																
Further Probe																
UPDATE																

Code—Survey and Probe

1 - Skill known   3 - Need more information

2 - Skill known at lower level   4 - Skill not known   5 - Not assessed

Figure 5-S Assessment to Instruction Data Sheet (Curricular Area: Written Language)

determined that further analysis of handwriting would be possible in future written language samples, and decided not to develop a special probe for handwriting.

The second area of concern was conventions of print, specifically capitalization and punctuation. She decided to probe knowledge of these rules in a recognition task because Andrew had demonstrated problems in these areas in spontaneous production.

The third area of concern was spelling. The teacher hypothesized that the spelling errors could reflect either satisfactory spelling knowledge that could not be demonstrated in so complex a generative writing task, or unsatisfactory knowledge of particular spelling skills. The teacher decided to begin with a spelling probe which would require Andrew to spell the words he misspelled in the survey without the complication of generating ideas at the same time.

Step 10: Probe (Andrew)

The teacher developed spelling probes first. In the initial probe the teacher selected words Andrew misspelled in the survey and dictated them in isolation. Figure 5-T shows the results of that probe.

Of the 15 words presented, Andrew was able to spell 6 correctly in isolation. This information told the teacher that Andrew does have some spelling skills but needs practice in applying this knowledge in a complex generative writing task. After analyzing the words misspelled on the probe, the teacher also discovered that Andrew spells phonetically and has most difficulty with phonetically irregular words. On this probe, he showed none of the earlier problems of hearing sounds in words. This added further weight to the conclusion that the complexity of the task may have been a factor in Andrew's spelling problems.

In a further effort to gather information on what spelling skills to teach, the teacher decided to probe down the language hierarchy to determine if Andrew could read the words he had misspelled. (The teacher knew that it is possible for words to be in a student's oral vocabulary but not in his reading vocabulary.) The teacher

		ANALYSIS	
Word Dictated	*Andrew's Response*	*Correct*	*Error Type*
once	wunce		*nonphonetic*
upon	upon	✓	
there	ther		*nonphonetic*
who	who	✓	
country	cuntere		*vowel; r*
father	father	✓	
Christmas	Chrismis		*nonphonetic*
where	whear		*nonphonetic*
early	erly		*vowel*
dressed	dresst		*past tense*
opened	opened	✓	
presents	peresints		*r; vowel*
started	started	✓	
something	somthing		*nonphonetic*
ate	ate	✓	

Figure 5-T Probe of Andrew's Spelling Errors

determined that Andrew could, in fact, read all of the misspelled words, except "country" and "presents." The last step the teacher took to probe Andrew's spelling problems was to test down the response hierarchy to determine if Andrew could recognize the correct representation of the words he misspelled. This probe, shown in Table 5-13, required that Andrew look at three words and circle the one the teacher said. Andrew was able to recognize all of the words but "country."

Now Andrew's teacher moved to probes of conventions of print. The teacher created sentences for Andrew to correct. Table 5-14 shows the probe. The teacher limited the probe to capitalization errors and punctuation items requiring the use of periods, commas, and question marks. She probed at the recognition level because Andrew had already demonstrated problems with self-generated sentences.

Table 5-13 Recognition Level Probe

(1)	(once)	wunce	owns
(2)	ther	(there)	theer
(3)	cuntere	country	(cunterea)
(4)	cerismis	Crismis	(Christmas)
(5)	whear	whaer	(where)
(6)	(early)	erly	eley
(7)	dresst	(dressed)	dest
(8)	(presents)	perisints	presints
(9)	somthing	sumthing	(something)

Table 5-14 Conventions of Print Probe

Directions: Correct these sentences.

1. andrew mark and josh went to raccoon state park on thursday for a picnic

2. mrs johnson went on main st to pick up luke

3. do you think the boys had enough food drinks and candy

4. my dog lester likes to play fetch roll over and catch a frisbee

Figure 5-U Conventions of Print Probe (Andrew's Responses)

Directions: Correct these sentences.

    A   *M*   *J*
1. andrew mark and josh went to raccoon state park on thursday for a picnic •

       J   *L*
2. mrs johnson went on main st to pick up luke.

3. do you think the boys had enough food drinks and candy •

4. my dog lester likes to play fetch roll over and catch a frisbee •

Figure 5-U Conventions of Print Probe (Andrew's Responses)

Figure 5-U shows Andrew's responses. It indicates that Andrew used periods to end all sentences, including interrogative ones. He capitalized people's names but applied no other capitalization rules. He did not use commas at all.

Step 11: Complete Recordkeeping Forms and Generate Objectives (Andrew)

Andrew's teacher now completed the Probe lines of the Assessment to Instruction Data Sheet. Figure 5-V shows her notations. Under spelling, she indicated that Andrew should be taught to recognize and reproduce the correct spellings of phonetically irregular words and to use the rules of morphology. He also needed to be taught the rules regarding capitalization, commas, and question marks. More information was needed in the area of handwriting, but she decided that the information could be gathered as Andrew continued to write.

Looking over the Assessment to Instruction Data Sheet, the teacher outlined three teaching objectives for Andrew:

1. Andrew will increase his spelling skills in isolation by spelling words appropriate to his reading level with 90% accuracy.

2. Andrew will edit his own stories and compositions, and identify the misspelled words with 90% accuracy. (It may be necessary, because of his age, that he seek help from the teacher or be taught dictionary skills in order to correct his errors.)

3. Andrew will apply the grade-appropriate conventions of print, including capitalization and use of commas and question marks, with 100% accuracy. (Some conventions of print, such as paragraph indentation, use of dialogue, and certain punctuation rules, have not been introduced by third grade. The teacher would expect Andrew to be able to apply only those rules which have been taught.)

Student _____Andrew_____ School _____Park_____ Teacher _____Thomas_____

ASSESSMENT TASKS	Generation of ideas—vocabulary	Generation of ideas—productivity	Generation of ideas—story theme	Generation of ideas—grammar	Handwriting—remembering letters	Handwriting—upper/lower case letters	Handwriting—reproducing letters	Conventions of print—punctuation	Conventions of print—capitalization	Conventions of print—sentence structure	Conventions of print—word usage	Conventions of print—format	Spelling—hearing sounds in words	Spelling—sound/symbol correspondence	Spelling—irregular spellings and sequence	Spelling—morphological rules
Survey	1	1	1	1	1	3	3	3	3	1	1	1	3	3	3	3
Initial Probe													1	1		
Further Probe															2	
Further Probe								4	4							
Further Probe																
UPDATE																

Code—Survey and Probe

1 - Skill known   3 - Need more information

2 - Skill known at lower level   4 - Skill not known   5 - Not assessed

Figure 5-V Assessment to Instruction Data Sheet (Curricular Area: Written Language)

Step 12: Start Teaching/Update Assessment Information (Andrew)

The overall goal in teaching written expression is to allow students to express their ideas in written form. Although the teaching objectives focus on individual components of written expression, some time will be devoted to generative writing. The teacher will also take opportunities during writing lessons to observe and evaluate Andrew's handwriting and update the Assessment to Instruction Data Sheet as new information appears.

ILLUSTRATION: GEORGE

To further illustrate the steps in a written language assessment for instructional planning, we will move through this process a second time for George, a fourteen-year-old eighth-grader, who is reading at the fifth-grade level. His teacher will begin the assessment at Step 4, having completed Steps 1, 2, and 3. That is, she decided that written expression should be part of her assessment plan for George (Step 1—What to Assess); she selected the hierarchy, presented in Table 5-1, to guide the assessment (Step 2—Select or Develop a Skill Hierarchy); she classified George as a functional writer, capable of generating stories on the basis of his reading level and some samples of his written work (Step 3—Decide Where to Begin).

Step 4: Select or Develop Survey Instrument (George)

George's teacher listened to his conversations with friends, and to his comments in class, and felt that George was able to express his ideas with minimal teacher direction. She decided that the survey should require George to write a story about a particular topic. She knew that George was interested in minibikes, so she intended to have him write a story on that topic.

Step 5: Get Ready to Test (George)

The teacher explained the nature of the task to George and provided him with lined paper, pencil, and a quiet work space. He understood that he would be given as much time as necessary to write the best story he could. The teacher explained that correct spelling was encouraged, but was not essential. George also knew that upon completion of the task, he would be allowed to listen to popular music tapes for ten minutes.

The teacher prepared a tape recorder and blank tape to record George's reading of his story after it had been written.

Step 6: Administer the Survey (George)

George began writing his story almost immediately and, within fifteen minutes, produced the sample shown in Figure 5-W. He read the story aloud and his teacher recorded it on tape. Later, she transcribed the text onto the same page.

Step 7: Note Errors and Performance Style (George)

The teacher noted that George had no apparent problem in thinking up something to say. The teacher reviewed George's story, numbered the spelling errors, circled the errors in punctuation, capitalization, and verb-tense agreement, and underlined some handwriting problems (Figure 5-X).

When I turned 13 I wanted a mini bike and I asked
my mom and she said she'll will pay for half and
I would have to pay for half so I started saving
my money and so I'm still saving for it.

The End

Figure 5-W Written Language Sample (George)

When I turned 13 I wanted a mini bike and I asked
my mom and she said she'll will pay for half and
I would have to pay for half so I started saving
my money and so I'm still saving for it.

The End

Figure 5-X Written Language Sample: Errors Noted

Step 8: Analyze Findings and Summarize Outcomes (George)

To evaluate George's written expression abilities, the teacher followed the 4-step procedure. First, she read George's story to get an impression of his capacity to generate ideas. She noted that George's overall level of productivity was somewhat limited, particularly in view of his age and his expressed interest in the topic. Further, he failed to really develop a story line or theme. She evaluated George's performance, with respect to the other aspects of generation of ideas, as generally adequate.

He did not seem to have significant problems with vocabulary usage or grammar. (While she noted that his story was written as one run-on sentence, she believed that this type of error was more related to difficulties with the conventions of print, because run-on sentences and sentence fragments are common occurrences in oral language.) She recognized the errors involving verb tense (*want* for wanted; *start* for started), but noted that the text transcript showed that George used the past tense appropriately when he read back his work. Since he generally used appropriate forms in his oral language, she concluded that these might be problems in spelling or word usage—conventions of print—and not basic grammar problems to be noted in the generation of ideas category. She recorded these impressions on a Written Expression Survey Summary of Information (Figure 5-Y).

She reviewed George's story a second time, concentrating on handwriting. She saw this as an area of difficulty for George. In several instances, he had used an inappropriate letter form. Specifically, she noted that George did not seem to know what the upper case cursive /I/ looks like; he consistently substituted a cursive /t/ in its place. She also noted that he appeared to have considerable difficulty connecting one letter to the next and that, frequently, strokes were added to or omitted from letters, as in the cases of *mom* (line 3), *will* (line 4), *my* (line 7), and *and* (line 7). The teacher saw that George knew the correct forms of these letters, since he used them in the sample. George also seemed unable to produce some letters easily without beginning them on the line. The teacher noted, for example, the way he moved from one letter to the next in the words *want* and *pay*. As well, his repeated trials with the letter /s/ (lines 3 and 8) suggested confusion about how to produce that symbol. Finally, she noted his irregular use of upper and lower case letters. She recorded these findings on the score sheet (Figure 5-Z).

The teacher reviewed George's story a third time to evaluate conventions of print. She saw that George failed to capitalize the first word of a sentence or to use capitals in writing "the end." In both instances where an apostrophe was necessary, it was either placed incorrectly or omitted entirely. His story consisted of one run-on sentence, when at least three sentences would have been appropriate. Finally, errors involving tense agreement suggested possible word usage problems. She recorded these errors on the score sheet (Figure 5-AA).

Finally, she reviewed George's story a fourth time, concentrating on spelling errors. She copied the 19 spelling errors onto the Analysis of Spelling Errors form, writing George's versions, followed by the correct spellings. She analyzed the errors and checked the category of spelling error for each misspelled word or word part. Figure 5-BB shows that George had spelling errors of all types. The teacher added these findings to the score sheet (Figure 5-CC). Then she summarized her survey findings onto the Survey line of the Assessment to Instruction Data Sheet (Figure 5-DD).

Generation of Ideas	Summary of errors	Adequate	Inadequate
Vocabulary	generally adequate	✓	
Productivity	limited		✓
Story theme/organization	fails to develop story		✓
Grammar	errors corrected in oral form	✓	

Handwriting	Summary of errors	Adequate	Inadequate
Remembering letter shapes			
Upper/lower case letters			
Reproducing letter shapes			

Conventions of Print	Summary of errors	Adequate	Inadequate
Punctuation			
Capitalization			
Sentence structure			
Word usage			

Spelling	Summary of errors	Adequate	Inadequate
Hearing sounds in words			
Sound/symbol correspondence			
Irregular spellings and letter sequences			
Morphological rules			

Figure 5-Y Written Language Survey—Summary of Information (Generation of Ideas) (George)

Name George   School Westover   Teacher Perkins   Date _____

Generation of Ideas	Summary of errors	Adequate	Inadequate
Vocabulary	generally adequate	✓	
Productivity	limited		✓
Story theme/ organization	fails to develop story		✓
Grammar	errors corrected in oral form	✓	

Conventions of Print	Summary of errors	Adequate	Inadequate
Punctuation			
Capitalization			
Sentence structure			
Word usage			

Handwriting	Summary of errors	Adequate	Inadequate
Remembering letter shapes	uses inappropriate forms		✓
Upper/lower case letters	mixed use within sentences and words		✓
Reproducing letter shapes	difficulty producing and connecting letters		✓

Spelling	Summary of errors	Adequate	Inadequate
Hearing sounds in words			
Sound/symbol correspondence			
Irregular spellings and letter sequences			
Morphological rules			

Figure 5-Z Written Language Survey—Summary of Information (Handwriting) (George)

Name _George_   School _Westover_   Teacher _Perkins_   Date _____

Generation of Ideas	Summary of errors	Adequate	Inadequate
Vocabulary	generally adequate	✓	
Productivity	limited		✓
Story theme/ organization	fails to develop story		✓
Grammar	errors corrected in oral form	✓	

Handwriting	Summary of errors	Adequate	Inadequate
Remembering letter shapes	uses inappropriate forms		✓
Upper/lower case letters	mixed use within sentences and words		✓
Reproducing letter shapes	difficulty producing and connecting letters		✓

Conventions of Print	Summary of errors	Adequate	Inadequate
Punctuation	apostrophe misplaced and omitted		✓
Capitalization	begins sentence without capital; no caps. on "The End"		✓
Sentence structure	writes 1 run-on sentence		✓
Word usage	tense agreement error		✓

Spelling	Summary of errors	Adequate	Inadequate
Hearing sounds in words			
Sound/symbol correspondence			
Irregular spellings and letter sequences			
Morphological rules			

Figure 5-AA Written Language Survey—Summary of Information (Conventions of Print) (George)

167

	Student's spelling	Correct spelling	Hearing sounds in words	Sound/ symbol	Irregular and sequence	Morphological rules
1.	terned	turned		✓ vowel		
2.	want	wanted				✓ past tense
3.	minney	mini		✓ vowel		
4.	bicke	bike		✓ cons.		
5.	askt	asked				✓ past tense
6.	mam	mom		✓ vowel		
7.	sed	said		✓ vowel		
8.	foer	for		✓ vowel		
9.	hgh	half			✓	
10.	wolled	would			✓	
11.	hyft to	have to			✓	
12.	foer	for		✓ vowel		
13.	haf	half			✓	
14.	start	started				✓ past tense
15.	sury	saving	✓			
16.	muny	money		✓ vowel		
17.	amd	and		✓ cons.		
18.	shung	saving	✓			
19.	foer	for		✓ vowel		
20.						
21.						
22.						
23.						
24.						
25.						
			2	10	4	3

Error Categories

Figure 5-BB Analysis of Spelling Errors

Name _George_ School _Westover_ Teacher _Perkins_ Date _____

Generation of Ideas	Summary of errors	Adequate	Inadequate
Vocabulary	generally adequate	✓	
Productivity	limited		✓
Story theme/organization	fails to develop story		✓
Grammar	errors corrected in oral form	✓	

Handwriting	Summary of errors	Adequate	Inadequate
Remembering letter shapes	uses inappropriate forms		✓
Upper/lower case letters	mixed use within sentences and words		✓
Reproducing letter shapes	difficulty producing and connecting letters		✓

Conventions of Print	Summary of errors	Adequate	Inadequate
Punctuation	apostrophe misplaced and omitted		✓
Capitalization	begins sentence without capital / no caps. on "The End"		✓
Sentence structure	writes 1 run-on sentence		✓
Word usage	tense agreement error		✓

Spelling	Summary of errors	Adequate	Inadequate
Hearing sounds in words	saving have to		✓
Sound/symbol correspondence	vowel sounds		✓
Irregular spellings and letter sequences	phonetically irregular (would, half)		✓
Morphological rules	past tense		✓

Figure 5-CC Written Language Survey—Summary of Information (Spelling) (George)

Student ___George___   School ___Westover___   Teacher ___Perkins___

ASSESSMENT TASKS	Generation of ideas—vocabulary	Generation of ideas—productivity	Generation of ideas—story theme	Generation of ideas—grammar	Handwriting—remembering letters	Handwriting—upper/lower case letters	Handwriting—reproducing letters	Conventions of print—punctuation	Conventions of print—capitalization	Conventions of print—sentence structure	Conventions of print—word usage	Conventions of print—format	Spelling—hearing sounds in words	Spelling—sound/symbol correspondence	Spelling—irregular spellings and sequence	Spelling—morphological rules
Survey	1	3	3	1	3	3	3	3	3	3	3	3	3	3	3	3
Initial Probe																
Further Probe																
Further Probe																
Further Probe																
UPDATE																

Code—Survey and Probe

1 - Skill known

2 - Skill known at lower level

3 - Need more information

4 - Skill not known

5 - Not assessed

Figure 5-DD Assessment to Instruction Data Sheet (Curricular Area: Written Language)

Step 9: Hypothesize Causes for Errors and Determine Areas to Probe (George)

The teacher looked over George's score sheet and saw that she had made notations of errors in all components of written expression. She considered two explanations for the limited productivity and story theme: George may have had more difficulty in organizing and developing his ideas than she had originally thought, or George may have written little because of his apparent difficulties in spelling and other skills. She decided that she would have to probe in this area.

She reviewed her analysis of George's handwriting and drew several conclusions. First, considering his errors involving letter shapes and capitalization, she decided that there may be upper case cursive letters he does not know. She planned to probe this area further. George's problems in reproducing letters led her to hypothesize that George lacked a consistent motor plan for writing certain letters, although she realized that his performance could have been influenced by other task demands—generating ideas and spelling. She decided to probe the last alternative first, by administering a follow-up assessment in which George would have to concentrate only on writing, and not on the other components of written expression.

The teacher reviewed George's errors involving conventions of print and decided that, since his story was so short and since relatively few errors of each type had occurred, she would probe this area. She determined that the probe should not require simultaneous generation of ideas.

The teacher also decided that, given George's extensive spelling difficulties, she must evaluate his spelling skills, free of the complications of generation of ideas and handwriting. She planned to develop a spelling probe in which she would dictate words and George would spell them aloud or type them.

Step 10: Probe (George)

The teacher developed the generation of ideas probe first. She asked George to *tell* a story about another topic, eliminating the need for him to spell, write, or punctuate. This probe was an example of testing down the language hierarchy. It was designed to assess organization and theme development at the level of oral language, rather than at the level of print. It helped determine the extent to which motor and/or spelling problems had affected George's survey performance. However, George's performance on the oral story was very similar to his performance on the written story. The teacher concluded that George had problems in organization at both the oral and written levels. She decided that she would have to follow up with further probes down the skill hierarchy, introducing more structure or teacher direction into the written expression assignment. This would be done as she began teaching.

Turning her attention to handwriting, the teacher developed and administered the probe shown in Figure 5-EE to determine if George knew upper case cursive symbols. His performance showed that he did not form the letters /I/, /J/, /Q/, and /Z/ correctly. She then administered the follow-up probe shown in Figure 5-FF to determine if George could identify the correct form of these letters at a recognition level. His performance on the probe indicated that he could. In the course of teaching him, the teacher planned to explore George's ability to reproduce and connect letters.

The teacher borrowed from a number of commercial sources to develop the probe for conventions of print shown in Figure 5-GG. Each section sampled different skills. George's performance demonstrated that he had difficulty only in using punc-

Directions: Write these capital letters in cursive form.

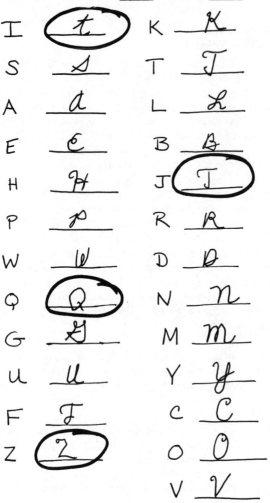

I (t)   K *K*

S *A*   T *J*

A *a*   L *L*

E *E*   B *B*

H *H*   J (J)

P *P*   R *R*

W *W*   D *D*

Q (Q)   N *n*

G *G*   M *m*

U *u*   Y *y*

F *F*   C *C*

Z (2)   O *O*

        V *V*

Figure 5-EE Handwriting Skills Probe

Directions: Circle the correct way to write the letter shown in the box.

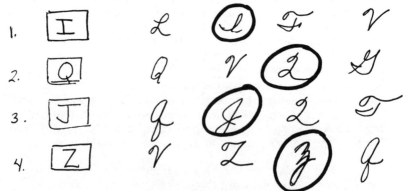

1. [I]   *L* (*L*) *F* *V*

2. [Q]   *Q* *V* (*Q*) *G*

3. [J]   *J* (*J*) *L* *J*

4. [Z]   *V* *Z* (*Z*) *q*

Figure 5-FF Handwriting Skills Probe

Part I - Knowledge of Punctuation and Capitalization Conventions

(Teacher reads directions and/or sentences to the student)

These sentences were written without any punctuation or capital letters. Please rewrite each sentence using correct punctuation and capitalization.

1. the book is red _____

_____

2. im sure his name is mr smith _____

_____

3. my sister goes to washington high school _____

_____

4. we re meeting with the boy scouts 4 30 p m _____

_____

5. yes john did sail on the pacific ocean _____

_____

6. shell bring the following people john sally mary and bill _____

_____

7. you run fast but the russian was the fastest runner of them all

_____

_____

8. oh lauras mother said in surprise _____

_____

Part II - Knowledge of Word Usage Conventions

These sentences have one word missing. Please write in the missing word.

1. Jim is very tall. Jim has _____ three inches since I last saw him.

2. John is a good player. Bill is a better player. But Ann is the _____ player of them all.

3. It is autumn. The _____ on the trees are turning brown.

4. What time does the sun _____ in the morning?

Figure 5-GG Probe (Conventions of Print)

5. One woman was talking to another woman. The two _____ were talking to each other.

6. One deer is by the barn. Two other _____ are by the trees.

7. I wish I _____ seen the movie.

8. Joe throws a ball every day. Yesterday, he _____ a ball.

Part III - Knowledge of Sentence Structure Conventions

Some of these groups of words make a complete sentence and some of them do not. Some of them are really <u>more than one</u> sentence.

If the group of words is one complete sentence, put a ✓ in the box.

If the group of words is an incomplete sentence, put an <u>X</u> in the box.

If the group of words is really more than one sentence, show how to write them correctly.

1. A strange spaceship landed. ☐

_____

2. Since it was in the field. ☐

_____

3. She was too afraid to run so she just stood there shaking. ☐

_____

4. A clam can weigh over 225 kilograms they live in the ocean. ☐

_____

5. When mother found out what the children were doing. ☐

_____

6. He will take a trip before he starts his new job. ☐

_____

7. We are going to my Grandmother's and she lives on a farm and we will have lots of fun. ☐

_____

8. The game was tied until the last inning our team scored a run. ☐

_____

Figure 5-GG Probe (Conventions of Print)—**Continued**

tuation and capitalization conventions correctly. She developed the follow-up probe in Figure 5-HH based on his errors, to determine if George's performance improved at the recognition level. She found that he was still unable to demonstrate adequate knowledge of most of the punctuation/capitalization rules assessed (proper names, abbreviations, and commas).

Put a check (✓) next to the sentence which follows correct punctuation/ capitalization rules.

1. They will be back September 15.
   They will be back September, 15.

2. His name is Bill J. Jones.
   His name is, Bill J Jones.

3. "Have you completed your work? asked the teacher."
   "Have you completed your work?" asked the teacher.

4. The biggest game of the season is next Friday.
   The biggest game of the Season is next Friday.

5. At Easter we go on a short vacation to the Ocean.
   At Easter we go on a short vacation to the ocean.

6. They live at 230 Oak Street.
   They live at, 230, Oak Street.

Circle the correct answer.

1. Smith High School
   Smith high school
   Smith High school

2. She'll tell the Principal.
   She'll tell the principal.
   Shell' tell the principal.

3. It is the Christmas Season.
   It is the christmas season.
   It is the Christmas season.

4. I'm going to be a Sailor.
   Im' going to be a sailor.
   I'm going to be a sailor.

5. Mr and Mrs Smith
   Mr. and Mr.s Smith
   Mr. and Mrs. Smith

6. Its' not 2:30 yet.
   It's not 2:30 yet.
   It's not 23:00 yet.

Figure 5-HH Recognition Probe (Capitalization/Punctuation)

To probe spelling, the teacher created a dictated spelling test from the words George had misspelled on the survey. George was asked to spell the words aloud, and the teacher recorded his responses (Figure 5-II).

Of the 14 words presented, George was able to spell 5 correctly in isolation. The teacher now knew that George needed practice spelling these words in generative writing tasks. From her analysis of the words he missed, the teacher saw that George had most difficulty with sight words, and that he had problems adding affixes. She administered a follow-up probe to see if George could recognize the correct forms of the misspelled words. George's performance on the probe, shown in Figure 5-JJ, indicated that he could correctly recognize all the probed words.

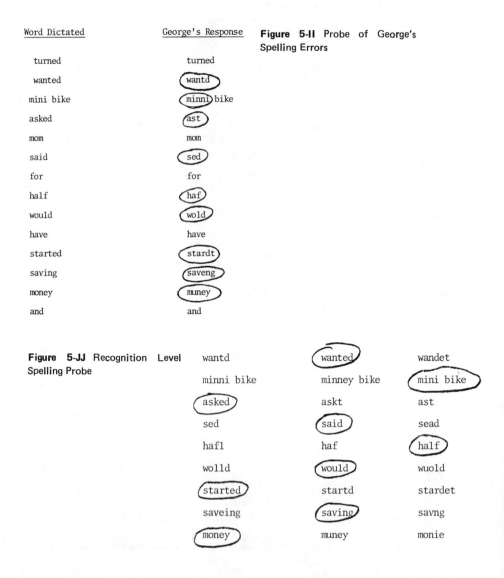

Figure 5-II Probe of George's Spelling Errors

Figure 5-JJ Recognition Level Spelling Probe

Step 11: Complete Recordkeeping Forms and Generate Teaching Objectives (George)

George's teacher now completed the Assessment to Instruction Data Sheet (Figure 5-KK) to summarize all the assessment information gathered from the probes. In the area of generation of ideas, she concluded that George's vocabulary usage and grammar were adequate. She indicated that she still planned to gather additional information about George's organization and productivity problems. This

Student ___George___ School ___Westover___ Teacher ___Perkins___

ASSESSMENT TASKS	Generation of ideas—vocabulary	Generation of ideas—productivity	Generation of ideas—story theme	Generation of ideas—grammar	Handwriting—remembering letters	Handwriting—upper/lower case letters	Handwriting—reproducing letters	Conventions of print—punctuation	Conventions of print—capitalization	Conventions of print—sentence structure	Conventions of print—word usage	Conventions of print—format	Spelling—hearing sounds in words	Spelling—sound/symbol correspondence	Spelling—irregular spellings and sequence	Spelling—morphological rules
Survey	1	3	3	1	3	3	3	3	3	3	3	3	3	3	3	3
Initial Probe		4	4		4	4	3	3	3	1	1	1	1	1	4	4
Further Probe					2	2		4	4						2	2
Further Probe																
Further Probe																
UPDATE																

Code—Survey and Probe

1 - Skill known   3 - Need more information
2 - Skill known at lower level   4 - Skill not known   5 - Not assessed

Figure 5-KK Assessment to Instruction Data Sheet (Curricular Area: Written Language)

would be done, in time, through writing assignments providing him with varying amounts of teacher direction and structure.

Her notations concerning his handwriting skills indicated that he must be taught several upper case cursive letters. His performance in reproducing and connecting letter shapes must still be probed. The teacher indicated that George must be taught most rules regarding correct punctuation and capitalization.

In spelling, the teacher noted that George needs to be taught how to spell phonetically irregular words from memory and how to correctly apply the morphological rules for spelling.

Reviewing the Assessment to Instruction Data Sheet, the teacher outlined five beginning teaching objectives for George.

1. George will increase his spelling skills by spelling, in isolation, all unknown words from the Dolch basic sight vocabulary list with 90% accuracy. (The first words taught will be those missed in the written expression survey.)
2. George will correctly apply the affixes *ed, ing, s,* and *es* with 90% accuracy to root words he can already spell.
3. George will reproduce, from memory, the upper case cursive letters /I/, /J/, /Q/, and /Z/ with 100% accuracy.
4. George will spell contractions with 100% accuracy.
5. George will apply the rules for capitalizing proper names with 100% accuracy.

Step 12: Start Teaching/Update Assessment Information (George)

The teacher planned to introduce each of these component skills individually and to provide George with every opportunity to practice each skill in isolation. At the same time, she would work to improve George's generative writing skill, since the ultimate goal in teaching written expression is to improve students' ability to express themselves. The generative writing tasks would also be used to provide George with opportunities to apply the skills he masters in isolation. She would update the Assessment to Instruction Data Sheet as new information is obtained.

ASSESSMENT OF BEGINNING WRITERS

The assessment of written expression of beginning writers begins at the lowest level of the skill hierarchy (Table 5-1), where component skills have not yet been integrated into a written expression capability. Therefore, the components cannot be assessed with a single survey. We will review the assessment for instructional planning strategy separately for generation of ideas and conventions of print, and together for spelling and handwriting. In each case we begin at Step 4, because the teacher has decided what to test, has developed a skill hierarchy, and has classified the student as a beginning writer. We will describe Steps 4–10 for the components of written expression, then put all the information together in a single discussion of Steps 11 and 12.

ASSESSMENT OF BEGINNING WRITERS: GENERATION OF IDEAS

Step 4: Select or Develop a Survey (Beginning Writers/Generation of Ideas)

Following the same guidelines suggested for selecting a topic of interest and for providing structure to the functional writer, the teacher can survey the beginning writer's ability to generate ideas by having him/her *tell* a story about a topic or a picture. This survey will allow the teacher to determine if the student has the oral language prerequisites for written language.

Step 5: Get Ready to Test (Beginning Writers/Generation of Ideas)

The teacher should be prepared to tape-record the student's story-telling. This will permit the teacher to transcribe it, and evaluate it at a later time. The teacher should have available several interesting, age-appropriate pictures which could serve as stimuli for the oral language sample. A tape recorder, microphone, and blank tape should also be on hand. And, as always, the teacher should find a quiet, comfortable place in which to administer the survey, and be prepared to reinforce successful student performance.

Step 6: Administer the Survey (Beginning Writers/Generation of Ideas)

The teacher should explain the purpose of the story-telling and the reasons for taping it. The student should be given a choice of pictures to use as the stimulus and should try out the tape recorder before beginning the "real story."

Step 7: Note Errors and Performance Style (Beginning Writers/Generation of Ideas)

While the student is telling the story, the teacher should note the manner in which the student approached the task, the apparent difficulties he/she had getting started, and the amount of prodding needed to keep the student on-task. After the student has completed the story, the tape should be transcribed, verbatim, and filed for future reference.

Step 8: Analyze Findings and Summarize Outcomes (Beginning Writers/Generation of Ideas)

The teacher evaluates the oral story by listening to the tape. The story should be evaluated along the same dimensions as a written story. Are the vocabulary and grammar age-appropriate? Does the grammar suit the student's cultural background? Is the story organized well, around a central theme or story line? Answers to these questions should be noted on the Written Language Survey Summary of Information. A special notation should indicate that the generation of ideas component was evaluated at the oral language level. Then the results of the survey should be summarized in the Survey line of the Assessment to Instruction Data Sheet.

Table 5-15   Error Hypotheses and Possible Probes
(Beginning Writers/Generation of Ideas)

Error	Hypothesis	Probe
Grammar and vocabulary usage	Oral expressive or receptive language problems	Specific language tests: first in the expressive area, then in receptive, if indicated
Story theme	Organizational problems	Telling a story based on an outline or sequence of pictures
Productivity	Oral expressive language problems	Specific oral language tests
	Original task not stimulating	Re-survey with more appropriate task

Step 9: Hypothesize Reasons for Errors and Determine Areas to Probe (Beginning Writers/Generation of Ideas)

If the student's oral story was weak in vocabulary use and grammar, the teacher may suspect specific oral receptive or expressive language problems. An appropriate next step would be a more comprehensive assessment of oral language.

If the student's oral story was weak in theme or productivity, the teacher would suspect problems in organizational skills or in thinking up things to say. An appropriate follow-up would be a story-telling task that had more teacher direction and structure.

Table 5-15 summarizes these alternatives.

Step 10: Probe (Beginning Writers/Generation of Ideas)

To probe receptive and expressive oral language skills, the teacher may want to use one of the commercially available tests listed in Table 5-16. Or, the teacher may choose to create an informal oral language probe by selecting or developing an oral language hierarchy and creating items which test down the hierarchy.

If the student was weak in story theme, the teacher might design a probe that utilized a series of pictures that "tell a story," a set of questions, or an outline in order to prompt a more organized or longer story. Poor productivity may be the result of an unmotivating survey, and the teacher could probe by changing the topic and/or by introducing motivators.

Table 5-16 Tests of Oral Language

Test	Aspects		Publisher
Test of Oral Language Development	Expressive	syntax semantics/vocabulary	Pro-Ed
	Receptive	syntax semantics/vocabulary	
Test of Adolescent Language	Expressive	syntax semantics/vocabulary	Pro-Ed
	Receptive	syntax semantics/vocabulary	
Clinical Evaluation of Language Functions: Diagnostic Battery	Expressive	syntax semantics/vocabulary	Chas. E. Merrill
	Receptive	syntax/morphology semantics/vocabulary	
Northwestern Syntax Screening Test	Expressive	syntax	Northwestern University Press
	Receptive	syntax	
Carrow Elicited Language Inventory	Expressive	syntax	Learning Concepts
Carrow Test for Auditory Comprehension of Language	Receptive	syntax	Learning Concepts
Assessment of Children's Language Comprehension	Receptive	syntax	Consulting Psychologists Press
Boehm Test of Basic Concepts	Receptive	semantics/vocabulary	Psychological Corporation

ASSESSMENT OF BEGINNING WRITERS: SPELLING AND HANDWRITING

Step 4: Select or Develop a Survey (Beginning Writers/Spelling and Handwriting)

The initial assessment of spelling, even in a beginning writer, should utilize a dictation format at the recall level of memory. Within this format, there are several ways to survey spelling skills. A formal, commercially available test, selected from the list provided in Table 5-17, offers two advantages. The words in the list are generally graded, allowing the teacher to stop after a certain number of errors. And, more importantly, some tests (particularly the Test of Written Spelling) are divided into lists of predictable and unpredictable words, allowing for more efficient analysis of the student's errors.

A second way to survey spelling would be to construct a word list from a basal spelling text. Five words would be chosen from the mid-year and end-of-year lists at each of three grade levels—beginning one year below the grade in which the student is placed. These thirty words would be dictated to the student.

In either case, the teacher could concurrently analyze the student's handwriting based on his/her performance on the dictated spelling test.

Table 5-17 Dictated Spelling Tests

Test	Publisher
Test of Written Spelling	Pro-Ed
Test of Written Language (Spelling Subtest)	Pro-Ed
Wide Range Achievement Test (Spelling Subtest)	Guidance Associates
Diagnostic Achievement Test in Spelling	Barnell-Loft
Kottmeyer Diagnostic Spelling Test	Webster Publishing
Lincoln Diagnostic Spelling Test	Bobbs-Merrill
Durrell Analysis of Reading Difficulty (Spelling Subtests)	Harcourt Brace Jovanovich
Brigance Diagnostic Inventory of Basic Skills (Spelling Subtest)	Curriculum Associates
Brigance Inventory of Essential Skills (Spelling Subtest)	Curriculum Associates
Gates-McKillop Reading Diagnostic Test (Supplemental Spelling Subtest)	Teachers College Press

Step 5: Get Ready to Test (Beginning Writers/Spelling and Handwriting)

The teacher will need lined paper and pencils of the appropriate thickness for the age and experience of the student. Pencils without erasers are preferable.

Step 6: Administer the Survey (Beginning Writers/Spelling and Handwriting)

Formal spelling tests should be administered following the guidelines given in the teacher's manual. For an informal survey, the teacher should say the word, use it in a sentence, and then repeat it. In either case the teacher should create a comfortable environment in which the student can demonstrate his/her maximum effort. In order to assess handwriting along with spelling, the teacher should remind the student to write in his/her best manuscript or cursive lettering. Students should also be advised to cross out errors with single lines—no scribbling over or erasing—and to write corrections carefully above or next to the first attempts.

Step 7: Note Errors and Performance Style (Beginning Writers/Spelling and Handwriting) and Step 8: Analyze Findings and Summarize Outcomes (Beginning Writers/Spelling and Handwriting)

The scoring and analysis of spelling performance in beginning writers should follow the same procedures used for functional writers. Each spelling error should be rewritten onto the Analysis of Spelling Errors form, and categorized into one of the four error patterns: problems in hearing sounds in words; problems with sound/symbol association; problems with phonetically irregular words or sequencing; or poor application of morphological rules. As a pattern of spelling weaknesses emerges, the results should be transcribed onto the Written Language Survey Summary of Information. The teacher should indicate in the spelling section that the survey tested "dictated words in isolation."

The spelling performance should be reviewed for handwriting errors as well. As with functional writers, the teacher looks for evidence of problems in remembering letter shapes, in reproducing upper and lower case letters, and in fluency of writing. Areas of weakness should be noted on the Written Language Survey Summary of Information. Survey performance in both spelling and handwriting should then be added to the Survey line of the Assessment to Instruction Data Sheet.

Step 9: Hypothesize Reasons for Errors and Determine Areas to Probe (Beginning Writers/Spelling and Handwriting)

One explanation for spelling errors, particularly on a commercially available test, is that the spelling pattern or rule has not yet been introduced in the curriculum. The spelling errors of beginning writers need to be checked against the scope and sequence chart of the spelling program in order to be certain that the student has, in fact, been taught the words he/she has misspelled.

If misspelled words were indeed part of the spelling curriculum, an analysis of categories of spelling error should lead the teacher to specific probes for more complete and definitive information. The guidelines for interpreting spelling errors and selecting probes presented in Table 5-10 apply equally well for assessment of beginning writers.

Handwriting problems would be interpreted by using the guidelines in Table 5-8. It is unlikely that task complexity would be a factor in the writing of single words from dictation. But the alternative explanations for handwriting problems should be explored.

Table 5-18 Spelling for Probing Recognition Response or Dictation of Sounds

Test	Aspects	Publisher
Peabody Individual Achievement Test (Spelling Subtest)	Recognition of correct spelling	American Guidance Services
Sequential Test of Educational Progress (Spelling Subtest)	Recognition of correct spelling	Educational Testing Service
SRA Achievement Series (Spelling Subtest)	Recognition of correct spelling	Science Research Associates
Gates-Russell Spelling Diagnostic Test	Writing sounds from dictation	Teachers College Press
Brigance Diagnostic Inventory of Basic Skills (Readiness and Spelling Subtests)	Writing sounds from dictation	Curriculum Associates
Brigance Inventory of Essential Skills (Spelling Subtest)	Writing sounds from dictation	Curriculum Associates

Table 5-19 Copying Tests/Subtests

Test	Publisher
Screening Test for Identifying Children with Specific Language Disabilities (Handwriting Subtest)	Educators Publishing Service
Zaner-Bloser Evaluation Scales	Zaner-Bloser
Brigance Diagnostic Inventory of Basic Skills (Readiness Subtest)	Curriculum Associates
Durrell Analysis of Reading Difficulty (Handwriting Subtest)	Harcourt Brace Jovanovich

Step 10: Probe (Beginning Writers/Spelling and Handwriting)

Since the spelling survey utilized dictation of single words, the spelling probe could do one of two things: change the response requirement from recall to partial recall or recognition; or change the complexity of the dictation from word to sound. Spelling tests or subtests which probe in this manner are listed in Table 5-18.

A handwriting probe should require that the student copy from a model rather than write from memory. There are very few commercially available copying tests (Table 5-19), so the teacher may have to develop his/her own.

ASSESSMENT OF BEGINNING WRITERS: CONVENTIONS OF PRINT

Step 4: Select or Develop Survey (Beginning Writers/Conventions of Print)

Formal surveys of conventions of print can be found in subtests of several commercially available materials (Table 5-20). In general, separate tests should be administered to assess word usage, sentence structure, and punctuation/capitalization.

A teacher-made survey could be developed, based on that portion of the scope and sequence chart of a language arts curriculum that deals with word usage, sentence structure, and writing mechanics. The teacher would create two or three items for every skill on the chart, at the grade level up to which the student has been taught. The survey should require that the student produce correct forms of words, punctuation, or sentence structure. Recognition level tests are not as useful as recall tasks. The tests listed in Table 5-20 are identified by the response requirements for each subtest of conventions of print.

Step 5: Get Ready to Test (Beginning Writers/Conventions of Print)

Since the survey will be a pencil and paper task, the teacher will have to decide whether to have the student work independently or under teacher direction.

Table 5-20   Tests of Conventions of Print

Test	Publisher	Aspect	*Response Requirements*
Test of Adolescent Language	Pro-Ed	Capitalization and punctuation, word usage, sentence structure	Production and recognition
Test of Written Language	Pro-Ed	Capitalization and punctuation, word usage, sentence structure	Production and recognition
California Test of Basic Skills	McGraw-Hill	Capitalization and punctuation, word usage, sentence structure	Recognition
Iowa Test of Basic Skills	Houghton Mifflin	Capitalization and punctuation, word usage	Production and recognition
SRA Achievement Series	Science Research Associates	Capitalization and punctuation, sentence structure	Production and recognition
Sequential Test of Educational Progress	Educational Testing Service	Capitalization and punctuation, word usage, sentence structure	Recognition
Brigance Inventory of Basic Skills	Curriculum Associates	Capitalization and punctuation, parts of speech	Recognition
Brigance Inventory of Essential Skills	Curriculum Associates	Capitalization and punctuation	Production

Since most beginning writers will also be beginning readers, the decision will usually be to have the student work with the teacher.

Step 6: Administer the Survey (Beginning Writers/Conventions of Print)

The teacher should be prepared to help the student read the survey text, so that the student's performance on tasks that measure punctuation, word usage, or sentence structure skills is not limited by poor reading ability.

Step 7: Note Errors and Performance Style (Beginning Writers/Conventions of Print)

Once the student has completed the survey, the teacher should score all items as correct or incorrect. Any help that was given, such as reading the test items to the student, should be noted on the student response form and on the Written Language Survey Summary of Information.

Step 8: Analyze Findings and Summarize Outcomes (Beginning Writers/Conventions of Print)

The results of the survey test(s) should be summarized on the Written Language Survey Summary of Information. The teacher should indicate the response mode if it was not recall. To the extent that it is possible, notations should be made in each skill area: punctuation, capitalization, sentence structure, and word usage. Then the information should be added to the Survey line of the Assessment to Instruction Data Sheet.

Step 9: Hypothesize Reasons for Errors and Determine Areas to Probe (Beginning Writers/Conventions of Print)

Errors in this component of written expression may stem from several causes.

1. The student may not have been able to read the text well enough to respond appropriately.
2. The student may not have remembered the rules he/she should have applied.
3. The student may never have been taught the conventions on which he/she was being tested.

If the student gave up on the task, the first hypothesis is likely. If the student's performance was inconsistent, the second or third hypothesis could apply.

Step 10: Probe (Beginning Writers/Conventions of Print)

If the teacher hypothesized that the student could not read the survey, a first probe might ask the student to read the test aloud. Then the teacher could ask the student about the rule that was being tested. For example, if the survey errors had been related to capitalization, the teacher could query the student about the rules for using capital letters. If the student knows that proper names require capital letters, errors may have been made on the survey because the student did not read the words correctly or did not grasp the context well enough to recognize the proper names. If the student can verbalize correct rules, probing might continue by having the teacher administer the survey by reading the items aloud as the student follows along. If the student is not successful at this level, further probing could occur using a less complex task. For example, if the student was surveyed with sentences requiring the addition of capital letters, a word list containing proper and common nouns could be presented as a probe.

Step 11: Complete Recordkeeping Forms and Generate Teaching Objective (Beginning Writers)

As the teacher completes the assessment of all four components of written expression, the results of all probes would be added to an Assessment to Instruction

Data Sheet. This record of each student's assessment data permits the teacher to make appropriate instructional decisions for teaching written expression.

Step 12: Start Teaching/Update Assessment Information (Beginning Writers)

The long term goal of instruction for beginning writers is to have them integrate the component skills of written language into the capability to express ideas in written form. As instruction proceeds towards that goal, the teacher should record skills that are mastered on the Assessment to Instruction Data Sheet and identify new skills that are "not known" and need to be taught.

ILLUSTRATION: HUGO

The following example will follow Hugo from initial surveys through recordkeeping and teaching objectives to illustrate the assessment of a beginning writer. Hugo is a fourth-grade student with beginning second-grade reading skills. He has been assigned to a resource room for remedial help in reading and language arts. The illustration begins at Step 4 because Steps 1, 2, and 3 had already been completed. The teacher had decided to assess Hugo's written expression skills (Step 1); had selected the hierarchy provided in Table 5-1 to guide the assessment (Step 2); and had categorized Hugo as a beginning writer based on his reading level of grade 2 and the report of his second-grade teacher that Hugo performs written work very poorly (Step 3).

The teacher decided to assess the components of written expression in the following order: first, generation of ideas, then spelling and handwriting and, finally, conventions of print. He planned to go through Steps 4–10 for each component separately, then to pull the information together in Steps 11 and 12.

Step 4: Select or Develop Survey Instrument (Generation of Ideas) (Hugo)

The teacher decided to begin the assessment by asking Hugo to tell what he would do if he were given $50.00 and had to spend it on Saturday.

Step 5: Get Ready to Test (Generation of Ideas) (Hugo)

The teacher found a tape recorder and blank tape and set it up in a corner of the resource room. He also had a tape of popular music to use as a reinforcer for Hugo at the end of the testing.

Step 6: Administer the Survey (Generation of Ideas) (Hugo)

The teacher presented Hugo with the task: "I've just given you $50 and you have to spend it all on Saturday. What would you do?" He tape-recorded Hugo's response.

Step 7: Note Errors and Performance Style (Generation of Ideas) (Hugo)

Hugo had no trouble getting started. When Hugo left the resource room, the teacher transcribed the story. The transcription is presented in Table 5-21.

Table 5-21 Transcription of Hugo's Story

"Well, me and my brother we would go to Great Adventure.
We'd do all the rides and stuff and eat and stuff and play
and stuff and have fun and not take nobody but maybe my
dad would drive us."

Step 8: Analyze Findings and Summarize Outcomes (Generation of Ideas) (Hugo)

The teacher listened to Hugo's tape several times to get an impression of his oral language ability. He noted on a Written Language Survey Summary of Information that Hugo told a very brief story, with no theme or organization. His vocabulary was quite limited, and his grammatical errors reflected how he spoke in daily conversation (Figure 5-LL). The teacher summarized these findings on an Assessment to Instruction Data Sheet by placing a *3* in each box on the Survey line that related to generation of ideas.

Step 9: Hypothesize Reasons for Errors and Determine Areas to Probe (Generation of Ideas) (Hugo)

Hugo's teacher suspected problems in oral language comprehension and usage, as well as in organizing ideas. He wondered if the task might have been too unstructured for Hugo. He decided to probe with a more structured task.

Step 10: Probe (Generation of Ideas) (Hugo)

The teacher decided to return to the survey task but asked Hugo specific questions that would guide his thinking and his story. He created the questions found in Table 5-22. The teacher wrote each question on a strip of oak tag and numbered the strips. He read each question to Hugo and made certain that Hugo could read each one. Then the teacher explained to Hugo that he was to answer each question with one or more sentences as he told his story, and that he could not answer "yes" or "no," although he might turn the questions into statements for his responses. He again taped Hugo's story. The transcription is given in Table 5-23.

The teacher determined that Hugo's oral language productivity and organization could be improved if he were given a structure for telling a story, but that his vocabulary was limited and his grammar poor.

Now the teacher turned to an evaluation of Hugo's spelling and handwriting.

Step 4: Select or Develop Survey Instrument (Spelling and Handwriting) (Hugo)

The teacher selected the Test of Written Spelling to survey Hugo's spelling and handwriting skills.

Step 5: Get Ready to Test (Spelling and Handwriting) (Hugo) and Step 6: Administer the Survey (Spelling and Handwriting) (Hugo)

The teacher had lined paper and a sharpened pencil ready for Hugo. He reviewed the section in the teacher's manual for administering the TWS. Without

Name **Hugo** School **Reynolds** Teacher **Engel** Date _____

Oral _____

Generation of Ideas	Summary of errors	Adequate	Inadequate	Conventions of Print	Summary of errors	Adequate	Inadequate
Vocabulary	limited for age		✓	Punctuation			
Productivity	limited		✓	Capitalization			
Story theme/ organization	poor		✓	Sentence structure			
Grammar	me and my brother we ... not take nobody ... run-on sentence		✓	Word usage			
Handwriting	Summary of errors	Adequate	Inadequate	**Spelling**	Summary of errors	Adequate	Inadequate
Remembering letter shapes				Hearing sounds in words			
Upper/lower case letters				Sound/symbol correspondence			
Reproducing letter shapes				Irregular spellings and letter sequences			
				Morphological rules			

Figure 5-LL Written Language Survey—Summary of Information (Generation of Ideas) (Hugo)

Table 5-22   Generation of Ideas—Probe (Hugo)

1. How did you get the $50.00?
2. What was your reaction?
3. What did you decide to do? Why?
4. Who did you do it with? Why?
5. Describe exactly what happened next.
6. Did you have a good time?
7. Were you glad you spent the money that way?

Table 5-23   Transcription of Probe—Generation of Ideas (Hugo)

My uncle Oscar he's from Buffalo sent me $50.00 for my birthday.
I was real happy cause I ain't never seen so much money ever. I went
to Great Adventure because on television they show rides and stuff
and I ain't never been to Great Adventure or anything. Me and my
brother went because he is in the Army and home and I don't never
see him and he is fun and takes me to the store sometimes. So me and
him got in the car and went to Great Adventure. I had a good time
it was fun and next time If somebody gives me money I would give it
to my mother to buy stuff.

deviating from the printed instructions, the teacher administered the dictated spelling test, stopping after five consecutive errors in each category.

Step 7: Note Errors and Performance Style (Spelling and Handwriting) (Hugo) and Step 8: Analyze Findings and Summarize Outcomes (Spelling and Handwriting) (Hugo)

Hugo's performance on the spelling test is shown in Table 5-24. The teacher scored the spelling test, recopied the misspellings onto an Analysis of Spelling Errors score sheet, and categorized the errors (Figure 5-MM). The tallies in the four columns indicate that most of Hugo's spelling errors clustered in the category of hearing sounds in words. The teacher noted these findings on the Written Language Survey Summary of Information (Figure 5-NN), noting also that spelling of words modified by morphological rules was not tested. The teacher also noted that the spelling findings were from "dictated words in isolation."

A further analysis of Hugo's performance on the TWS indicated that his handwriting was quite adequate. These findings were also noted on the Summary of

Table 5-24 Spelling Performance (Hugo)

Words	Hugo's response	Words	Hugo's response
up	up	trip	tip
that	dat	left	lef
it	it	went	wet
bed	bed	when	wen
dog	dog	myself	mist
this	dis	people	peoel
had	had	knew	new
him	him	uncle	oncl
plant	pat	music	musac

Information (Figure 5-OO). The survey results for spelling and handwriting were now added to the Assessment to Instruction Data Sheet.

Step 9: Hypothesize Reasons for Errors and Generate Areas to Probe (Spelling and Handwriting) (Hugo)

The teacher focused attention on the errors attributed to problems with hearing sounds in words, and hypothesized that Hugo's errors were the result of difficulties in breaking words into component sounds. He decided to probe by having Hugo write words dictated syllable by syllable or sound by sound.

Step 10: Probe (Spelling and Handwriting) (Hugo)

The teacher probed spelling by using the words that Hugo had missed on the spelling test. He asked Hugo to repeat the parts of the word after the teacher and then write what he had heard. They did the first one together to be certain that Hugo understood the task. Hugo's performance on this probe is given on Table 5-25. The teacher then asked Hugo to write the letters which represented the sounds that he said. This probe and Hugo's responses are given in Table 5-26.

The teacher's final probe was to determine if Hugo could recognize phonetically irregular words and words he had missed earlier. The teacher designed a multiple choice task with one correct and two incorrect representations of the target word. Hugo was asked to circle the word the teacher said from among the three choices. The probe and Hugo's responses are shown in Figure 5-PP. Based on these spelling probes, the teacher concluded that Hugo heard most sounds in words correctly (the exceptions were th and wh) if the word was broken apart. At the recognition level, he identified some irregular spellings and earlier misspellings correctly.

Next the teacher assessed Hugo's grasp of the conventions of print, returning to Step 4 of the assessment strategy.

		Error Categories			
Student's spelling	Correct spelling	Hearing sounds in words	Sound/ symbol	Irregular and sequence	Morphological rules
1. dis	this		✓		
2. pat	plant	✓			
3. tip	trip	✓			
4. lef	left	✓			
5. wet	went	✓			
6. wen	when			✓	
7. mist	myself	✓			
8. pepel	people			✓	
9. new	knew			✓	
10. oncl	uncle		✓		
11. musac	music		✓		
12. dat	that		✓		
13.					
14.					
15.					
16.					
17.					
18.					
19.					
20.					
21.					
22.					
23.					
24.					
25.					
		5	4	3	

Figure 5-MM Analysis of Spelling Errors (Hugo)

Name Hugo   School Reynolds   Teacher Engel   Date _____

Generation of Ideas	Summary of errors	Adequate	Inadequate
Oral			
Vocabulary	limited for age		✓
Productivity	limited		✓
Story theme/organization	poor		✓
Grammar	me and my brother we ... / not take nobody ... / run-on sentence		✓

Handwriting	Summary of errors	Adequate	Inadequate
Remembering letter shapes			
Upper/lower case letters			
Reproducing letter shapes			

Conventions of Print	Summary of errors	Adequate	Inadequate
Punctuation			
Capitalization			
Sentence structure			
Word usage			

Spelling *Dictated in isolation*	Summary of errors	Adequate	Inadequate
Hearing sounds in words	'd' for 'th', wet/went, pat/plant, tip/trip, lef/left, mist/myself		✓
Sound/symbol correspondence		✓	
Irregular spellings and letter sequences	new/knew, wen/when, pepil/people		?
Morphological rules	did not survey		

Figure 5-NN Written Language Survey—Summary of Information (Spelling) (Hugo)

Name **Hugo** School _____ Teacher **Reynolds** _____ **Engel** _____ Date _____

Oral

Generation of Ideas	Summary of errors	Adequate	Inadequate
Vocabulary	limited for age		✓
Productivity	limited		✓
Story theme/ organization	poor		✓
Grammar	me and my brother we ... / not take nobody ... / run-on sentence		✓

Handwriting	Summary of errors	Adequate	Inadequate
Remembering letter shapes		✓	
Upper/lower case letters		✓	
Reproducing letter shapes		✓	

Conventions of Print	Summary of errors	Adequate	Inadequate
Punctuation			
Capitalization			
Sentence structure			
Word usage			

Spelling (*Dictated in isolation*)	Summary of errors	Adequate	Inadequate
Hearing sounds in words	'd' for 'th', wet/went, pat/plant, tip/trip, lef/left, mist/myself		✓
Sound/symbol correspondence		✓	
Irregular spellings and letter sequences	new/knew / wen/when / pepil/people		?
Morphological rules	did not survey		

Figure 5-OO Written Language Survey—Summary of Information (Handwriting) (Hugo)

Table 5-25   Spelling Probe (Hugo)

Word	Oral Response	Written Response
that	th at	th at
this	d is	dis
there	d ere	d are
plant	pl an t	p an t
trip	tr ip	trip
left	lef t	lft
went	w ent	wnt
when	w en	wen
myself	my se f	mi se f
uncle	unc le	unk el
music	mu sic	mu zik

Table 5-26   Spelling Probe (Hugo)

Sound	Hugo's response
/sh/ as in *shut*	sh
/st/ as *stop*	st
/pl/ as in *plant*	pl
/th/ as in *that*	d
/wh/ as in *while*	w
/ch/ as in *church*	ck

1.	fite	(fight)	fitgh
2.	(there)	dere	tere
3.	enough	enuf	(enouf)
4.	(wen)	when	went
5.	know	(now)	noe
6.	oncle	onkle	(uncle)
7.	thru	throut	(through)
8.	(miself)	misef	myself
9.	(phone)	fone	fune
10.	muzik	musik	(music)

Figure 5-PP   Recognition Spelling Probe (Hugo)

Step 4: Select or Develop Survey
(Conventions of Print) (Hugo)

Hugo's teacher selected the Word Usage and Style subtests of the Test of Written Language (TOWL) to survey Hugo's knowledge of word usage and punctuation/capitalization rules. Both subtests require knowledge of the conventions of print but do not require spelling or generation of ideas.

Step 5: Get Ready to Test (Conventions of
Print) (Hugo) and Step 6: Administer the
Survey (Conventions of Print) (Hugo)

The teacher obtained a record form for the TOWL and reviewed the section of the test manual for administering the two TOWL subtests. He had several sharpened pencils ready, as well.

The teacher administered each of the two subtests without deviating from the instructions provided in the test manual. On each of the subtests the teacher stopped at item 10.

Step 7: Note Errors and Performance Style
(Conventions of Print) (Hugo) and Step 8:
Analyze Findings and Summarize Outcomes
(Conventions of Print) (Hugo)

Hugo's responses on the two subtests are provided in Figures 5-QQ and 5-RR. The teacher scored the two subtests following the instructions in the test manual. The teacher noted that Hugo only used capital letters for the first word of each sentence and that the only punctuation mark he used was a period at the end of each sentence. He was consistent with these two rules but applied no others.

Instructions. The sentences written below have one word missing. Read each sentence and fill in the missing word. Be sure to write or print neatly.

1. Sally has a party dress and a school dress. She has two _dress_ .

2. We have done that work already. We _don_ it yesterday.

3. Jim is very tall. Jim has _taller_ three inches since I last saw him.

4. Before dinner Mother asked Brenda to _set_ the table.

5. John is a good player. Bill is a better player than John. But Tom is the _good_ player of them all.

6. Bob is a child. Mary is a child. They are two _childs_ .

7. It is autumn. The _tree_ on the trees are turning brown.

8. Will you _tech_ me how to read?

9. I wish I _wood_ seen the movie.

10. The brown dog is small; the gray dog is smaller; but the white one is the _best_ .

Figure 5-QQ Word Usage Probe (Hugo)

Instructions. These sentences are written without any punctuation or
capital letters. Rewrite each sentence in the space provided.
Be sure to use correct punctuation and capitals. Please write
or print neatly.

1. the boy ran _The boy ran._

2. the book is red _The book is red._

3. her name is mary _Her name is mary._

4. today is tuesday _Today is tuesday._

5. he is mr smith _He is mr smith._

6. i was born on may 4 1972 _I was born on may 4 1972._

7. didnt tom live in canada _Didn't tom live in canada._

8. its a sad day _Its a sad day._

9. he joined the british team _He joined the british team._

10. his name is john t hill _His name is john t hill._

Figure 5-RR   Style Probe (Hugo)

The teacher also noted that Hugo's performance on the Word Usage subtest
was very poor. The teacher summarized these findings on the Written Language Survey, noting also that sentence structure was not surveyed (Figure 5-SS). He added
these findings to the Survey line of the Assessment to Instruction Data Sheet.

Step 9: Hypothesize Reasons for Errors and
Determine Areas to Probe (Conventions of
Print) (Hugo)

The teacher hypothesized that Hugo may not have learned any more punctuation and capitalization rules than he was demonstrating, given his consistent tendency to use capital letters to start sentences and periods to end them.

Furthermore, the teacher wondered how his poor reading skills affected his
performance on the Word Usage probe, since his performance on the generation of
ideas survey and probe was much better than his performance on the TOWL subtest. The teacher decided to probe both hypotheses.

Step 10: Probe (Conventions of Print)
(Hugo)

In talking with Hugo, the teacher discovered that he knew no capitalization
or punctuation rules, except the ones he had already demonstrated. The teacher
decided not to probe this area further.

To probe word usage the teacher readministered the survey orally. The
teacher read each item to Hugo and asked him to fill in the missing word. The

Name Hugo School Reynolds Teacher Engel Date _____

Oral

Generation of Ideas	Summary of errors	Adequate	Inadequate
Vocabulary	limited for age		✓
Productivity	limited		✓
Story theme/organization	poor		✓
Grammar	me and my brother we … / not take nobody … / run-on sentence		✓

Handwriting	Summary of errors	Adequate	Inadequate
Remembering letter shapes		✓	
Upper/lower case letters		✓	
Reproducing letter shapes		✓	

Conventions of Print	Summary of errors	Adequate	Inadequate
Punctuation	only used periods at sentence ending—no other punctuation used (periods only)	✓	
Capitalization	capitalizes first word only		✓
Sentence structure	did not survey		
Word usage			✓

Dictated in isolation — Spelling	Summary of errors	Adequate	Inadequate
Hearing sounds in words	'd' for 'th', wet/went, pat/plant, tip/trip, lef/left, mist/myself		✓
Sound/symbol correspondence		✓	
Irregular spellings and letter sequences	new/knew / wen/when / pepil/people		?
Morphological rules	did not survey		

Figure 5-SS Written Language Survey—Summary of Information (Conventions of Print) (Hugo)

198

Instructions. The sentences written below have one word missing. Read each sentence and fill in the missing word. Be sure to write or print neatly.

1. Sally has a party dress and a school dress. She has two _dress_ .
   [dresses]

2. We have done that work already. We _done_ it yesterday. [done]

3. Jim is very tall. Jim has _grode_ three inches since I last saw him. [growed]

4. Before dinner Mother asked Brenda to _set_ the table. [set]

5. John is a good player. Bill is a better player than John. But Tom is the _best_ player of them all. [best]

6. Bob is a child. Mary is a child. They are two _chidrun_ . [children]

7. It is autumn. The _leafs_ on the trees are turning brown. [leaves]

8. Will you _show_ me how to read? [show]

9. I wish I _cod_ seen the movie. [could]

10. The brown dog is small; the gray dog is smaller; but the white one is the _hest_ . [best]

11. I have one mouse here and one mouse there. I have two _mise_ . [mice]

12. If you are tired, _sit_ down on the chair. [sat]

13. Joe throws a ball every day. Yesterday, he _lost_ the ball. [lost]

14. Yesterday Tina and Marie _was_ walking down the street. [was]

15. What time does the sun _shine_ in the morning? [shine]

16. One woman was talking to another woman. The two _wumn_ were talking to each other. [women]

17. Bill has a sheep. Patti has a sheep. Together they have two _sheep_ .

18. When the game ended, two men _was_ left on base.

19. One deer is by the barn. Two other _deers_ are by the trees.

20. The hungry dogs have _took_ all the food. [took]

21. One child is throwing the ball to the other child. The two _brtrs_ are playing with the ball. [brothers]

22. Dad gave the present to us. He gave it to Sandy and _Hugo_ . [Hugo]

23. I know you gave the doll away. To _____ did you give it?
    [could not answer]

24. We built the bridge all by _the river_ . [the river]

25. The clowns were so funny that Jack _fell_ out laughing. [fell]

Figure 5-TT Word Usage Probe (Hugo)

teacher recorded Hugo's responses on a piece of paper and, at the same time, asked Hugo to write in the answer on a fresh TOWL record form. The results are shown in Figure 5-TT. Hugo's oral responses are shown in brackets after each item. While he continued to make many errors, it was clear to the teacher that Hugo's reading deficiencies had affected his responses to the survey. But many of the persistent errors were consistent with errors made on the oral survey and reflected how he speaks.

Step 11: Complete Recordkeeping Forms and Generate Teaching Objectives (Hugo)

Using the Assessment to Instruction Data Sheet for written expression, the teacher recorded his probe findings on Hugo. Figure 5-UU shows all the information that was gathered. The form indicates that the teacher surveyed generation of ideas and needed more information. Initial probes of story theme and productivity showed adequate performance with teacher cueing. Vocabulary and grammar skills needed to be taught. In spelling, application of morphological rules was not assessed, sound-symbol association skills were known, but more information was needed on hearing sounds in words and spelling of irregular words. Probes in these areas indicated that performance was improved when the teacher provided cues. Handwriting presented no problems. Survey results on conventions of print indicated a need for more information. Probes of punctuation, capitalization, and word usage showed that these skills needed to be taught.

Based on this assessment, the teacher generated the following teaching objectives as first goals for Hugo:

1. The student will tell an organized story of appropriate length by creating a questioning sequence.
2. The student will represent the sounds heard in phonetically regular words with 90% accuracy.
3. The student will spell sight words presented in his reading curriculum with 90% accuracy.
4. The student will apply all capitalization rules with 100% accuracy.
5. The student will use periods, commas, and question marks with 100% accuracy.

Step 12: Start Teaching/Update Assessment Information (Hugo)

Long term goals for Hugo will be:

1. To increase his oral vocabulary to include more age-appropriate words.
2. To improve his oral grammar in the areas of verb and pronoun usage.
3. To write short paragraphs which have a theme and use appropriate vocabulary and grammar.
4. To increase his spelling skills as his reading skills increase.

As teaching progresses, the teacher will update the Assessment to Instruction Data Sheet, remembering to record information on skills that were not assessed on the initial surveys or probes.

Student ___Hugo___   School ___Reynolds___   Teacher ___Engel___

ASSESSMENT TASKS	Generation of ideas—vocabulary	Generation of ideas—productivity	Generation of ideas—story theme	Generation of ideas—grammar	Handwriting—remembering letters	Handwriting—upper/lower case letters	Handwriting—reproducing letters	Conventions of print—punctuation	Conventions of print—capitalization	Conventions of print—sentence structure	Conventions of print—word usage	Conventions of print—format	Spelling—hearing sounds in words	Spelling—sound/symbol correspondence	Spelling—irregular spellings and sequence	Spelling—morphological rules
Survey	3	3	3	3	1	1	1	3	3	5	3	5	3	1	3	5
Initial Probe	4	2	2	4												
Further Probe													2		2	
Further Probe								4	4		4					
Further Probe																
UPDATE																

Code—Survey and Probe

1 - Skill known

2 - Skill known at lower level

3 - Need more information

4 - Skill not known

5 - Not assessed

Figure 5-UU Assessment to Instruction Data Sheet (Curricular Area: Written Language)

SUMMARY

In this chapter we have described and illustrated procedures for assessing written expression. We have suggested different assessment strategies for students who are functional writers (by virtue of their reading and writing abilities) and for students who are beginning writers. Functional writers began with a survey task that required integration of the four component skills (generation of ideas, handwriting, spelling, and knowledge of the conventions of print); follow-up probes examined each component of written expression separately. Beginning writers were assumed to be not yet capable of integrating the component skills of written expression, and, for them, separate surveys were administered.

Many students who are in remedial or special education programs have serious difficulties in expressing their ideas in correct written form. Yet there are very few curriculum guides on the market to help teachers design remedial programs, and even fewer formal tests of written expression which can be used to assess entering levels of ability. We believe that the strategies outlined in this chapter provide a framework that can be used by teachers to guide not only their assessment process but their remedial planning as well.

6

Assessment of Mathematics

Many students have difficulty becoming proficient at mathematics. Some may not acquire basic computation skills. Others may fall behind in their understanding of mathematical concepts. Still others may be unable to apply their math knowledge to solve mathematical problems. Although math performance is not required in as many school subjects as is reading or written expression, mathematics is, nevertheless, a basic skill subject of principal importance for a successful school or life experience. Special education and remedial teachers often encounter students who need help learning mathematics, and, since this help should be grounded in an assessment, this chapter is devoted to the application of our assessment strategy in mathematics.

We will deal with three areas of mathematics: concepts, computation, and problem solving. These three areas were selected because they involve the skills taught in the most widely used basal mathematic texts and because many math educators believe there should be "an emphasis on problem solving and application, as well as concept development and computation" (Underhill, Uprichard, and Heddens, 1980, p. 3).

The area of *concepts* will include whole number concepts, time, measurement, money, and geometry. Whole number concepts are prerequisite to a student's understanding of all aspects of mathematics and to the development of skills in whole number computation. Telling time and using money are essential for daily functioning. Skills in the areas of measurement and geometry are necessary in everyday life and are applied in other content areas. We have deliberately excluded concepts in the areas of equations, graphing, probability, and ratio and proportion, despite their inclusion in most basal math textbooks. Remedial teachers constantly have to make decisions about which deficit areas to emphasize. We have chosen to emphasize only those skills which seem to have the most application to real-life experiences.

The area of *computation* includes whole number computation in addition, subtraction, multiplication, and division, and computation skills involving decimals and fractions.

The area of *problem solving* includes the ability to apply skills covered in concepts and computation to problems which resemble real-life situations. This area covers "story problems," as well as logical reasoning, puzzles, games, sports, careers, and calculator "applications."

Because we believe that the assessment of concepts and computation should be carried out separately from the assessment of problem solving, we have organized this chapter into two parts. First, we will review the assessment for instructional

Table 6-1   Skill Hierarchy—Math Concepts

	Whole Number Concepts	*Time*	*Measurement*	*Money*	*Geometry*
8	Square roots Scientific notation Powers of 10 Negative exponents Expanded notation with exponents		Volume of cylinders, cones, and pyramids Surface of cones Area of trapezoid Precision		Right triangle geometry – sine, cosine, and tangent – pythagorean relation
7	Tests for divisibility		Surface area of pyramids and cylinders Area using formulas – parallelogram and circle Perimeter using formulas		Constructions Chord and arc of angles Angle measurement of triangles Regular polygons
6	Least common multiple Exponents Prime factors Primes and composites Greatest common factor Place value: 10-digit numbers	Time zones	Volume using formulas Surface area of prisms Area using formulas – rectangle, square, triangle Circumference		Polygons in circles Planes
5-2			Angle measurement Volume by multiplying Area of rectangles and triangles		Polyhedrons Perpendicular lines Angles – sums of angles in a triangle – central angles – congruence of – measuring and drawing – acute and obtuse
5-1	Place value: 9-digit numbers Expanded form		Metric units—millimeter		
4-2			Area of a triangle by counting Customary units—weight Metric units – cubic centimeter – degrees celsius – milliliter – decimeter		Naming angles Circles—radius and diameter Parallelogram Points, lines, segments, parallel lines, intersecting lines
4-1	Rounding Place value: 7- and 8-digit numbers				

planning strategy for the assessment of concepts and computation, moving from Step 2 through Step 12. Then, we will turn to a discussion of assessment of problem solving beginning again at Step 2 and working through Step 12.

ASSESSMENT OF CONCEPTS AND COMPUTATION

Step 2: Select or Develop a Skill Hierarchy (Concepts and Computation)

Most textbook series in mathematics present a scope and sequence chart for the material presented in the various levels. We have adapted the scope and sequence of the concept and computation strands of the math textbooks from Scott, Foresman, and Company and from Macmillan to create the hierarchies presented in Tables 6-1 and 6-2. These hierarchies are unique in two ways. First, they include an

Table 6-1 Skill Hierarchy—Math Concepts (continued)

	Whole Number Concepts	Time	Measurement	Money	Geometry

3-2			Volume by counting
			Area by counting
			  – square and
			    ½ square
			    nonstandard unit
			Metric unit—square centimeter
				Making change	

3-1		One-minute
		  intervals
		Five-minute
		  intervals
			Customary units
			  – cup and gallon
			  – foot, yard, and mile
			Metric units
			  – gram and kilogram
			  – meter and kilometer
					Right angles
					Recognizing angles
					Polygons: pentagons, hexagons,
					  octagons

2-2	Counting and ordering 4-digit
	  numbers
	Place value: 4-, 5-, and 6-digit
	  numbers
				Counting of money
				Dollar
				Quarter
					Congruence of segments

2-1	Renaming tens and ones Counting money Ordering 3-digit numbers Place value: 3-digit numbers	Quarter- hour			

1-2	Counting by tens, fives, and twos
	Ordered pairs
	Ordinal numbers: first through
	  fifteenth
			Customary units
			  – quarts
			  – pints
			  – inches
			Metric units
			  – liters
			  – centimeters
				Comparison
				Equivalent
				  amounts
					Symmetry

1-1	One greater and one less Place value: 2-digit numbers Teen numbers Grouping and recording tens	Calendar Half-hour			Congruent figures Three-dimensional shapes

K	Counting by ones
	Number line
	Ordering
	Comparing greater than and less
	  than
	Numbers through 12
	One-to-one correspondence
		Hour	Readiness for perimeter and
			  area by counting
			Nonstandard units of length
			Comparison of lengths
				Penny, nickel, dime
				Counting
					Circles
					Polygons: triangles, squares,
					  rectangles

Table 6-2 Skill Hierarchy—Math Computation

	Whole Number Addition	Whole Number Subtraction	Whole Number Multiplication	Whole Number Division	Decimals	Fractions
					Percents greater than 100% and less than 100%	
8					Rational numbers – multiplying and dividing – adding and subtracting – comparing and ordering – meaning Finding a number when a percent of it is known	Rational numbers – multiplying and dividing – adding and subtracting – comparing and ordering – meaning
7	Addition property of zero Commutative and associative properties Missing minuends	Missing minuends	Property – of one – distributive – associative – commutative	Missing dividends Dividing by a 3-digit number	Terminating and repeating decimals Estimating products	
6-2					Finding what percent one number is of another Finding a percent of a number Changing percents to fractions Changing percents to decimals Meaning Percents and decimals Changing fractions to decimals Dividing – by 10, 100, and 1000 – rounding quotients – zeros in dividend – by a decimal – zeros in quotient – until remainder is zero – by a whole number	Percents and fractions Subtracting fractions and mixed numbers with different denominators, renaming Dividing – mixed numbers – with whole numbers – using pictures – reciprocals Changing fractions to decimals by dividing
6-1			Least common multiple Greatest common factor	3- and 4-digit quotients Short division	Estimating sums and differences Rounding Place value through millionths	

Table 6-2 Skill Hierarchy—Math Computation (continued)

	Whole Number Addition	Whole Number Subtraction	Whole Number Multiplication	Whole Number Division	Decimals	Fractions

5-2				Missing factors
				Dividing by a 2-
				  digit number
				  – zero in
				    quotients
				  – 3-digit
				    quotients
					Mixed number
					  quotients
					Changing fractions
					  to decimals
					Multiplying
					  – by 10, 100,
					    and 1000
					  – with zeros in
					    products
					  – by a decimal
					  – by a whole
					    number
					  – counting
					    decimals
						Subtracting mixed
						  numbers
						  – different
						    denominators,
						    no renaming
						  – from a whole
						    number
						  – same denominator
						Subtracting fractions
						  with different
						  denominators
						Adding mixed numbers
						  – different
						    denominators
						  – same
						    denominator
						Adding fractions
						  with different
						  denominators
						Ordering fractions
						Different
						  denominators
						Common denominators
						Multiplying
						  – mixed numbers
						  – fractions and
						    whole numbers
						  – fractions
						Changing fractions
						  to decimals
						Mixed numbers
						  – as quotients
						  – as improper
						    fractions
						  – measurement
						Finding equal
						  fractions using
						  multiplication
						  and division

5-1			Missing factors
			Multiplying
			  – more than
			    two factors
			  – with a 3-digit
			    number
			Multiples
					Finding equal
					Ordering
					Place value
					  – thousandths	

4-2			Estimating products
			Multiplying with a
			  2-digit factor
			  – 2-digit factors
			  – multiples of 10
				Dividing by a 2-
				  digit number
				  – adjusting
				    quotients
				  – 2-digit
				    quotients
				  – 1-digit
				    quotients
				  – multiples
				    of 10
				Dividing by a 1-
				  digit number
				Dividing money
				  – zero in
				    quotients
				  – checking
				  – 3-digit,
				    quotients
						Adding and
						  subtracting
						  – different
						    denominator,
						    using number
						    line
						  – same
						    denominator
						    without
						    renaming
						Finding equal
						  fractions
						  – using number
						    line
						  – using pictures
						Mixed numbers
						  – related to
						    fractions
						  – in measurement
						  – meaning
						Fraction of an inch

Table 6-2 Skill Hierarchy—Math Computation (continued)

	Whole Number Addition	Whole Number Subtraction	Whole Number Multiplication	Whole Number Division	Decimals	Fractions
4-1		Missing addends Estimating differences	Multiplying with a 1-digit factor Multiplying money – more than one renaming – with zero		Subtracting Adding Place value – hundredths	
3-2	4-digit numbers Checking	Computation – with two renamings – with zero 4-digit numbers Checking	Multiplying with a 1-digit factor – 3-digit factors – one renaming, 2-digit factors – no renaming – multiples of 10 and 100 Families of facts Names for numbers Basic facts with a factor of – six, seven, eight, nine – zero or one – three, four, five	Remainders Dividing by a 1- digit number – 2-digit quotients – 1-digit quotient Families of facts Names for numbers Basic facts with a divisor or quotient of – six, seven, eight, nine – zero – two, three, four, five	Comparing Place value—tenths	Comparing Part of a set
3-1	Three or more addends Renaming tens	Subtraction of money		Meaning of division		
2-2	Relating addition and multiples Computation with one renaming – 3-digit	Computation with one renaming – 3-digit	Products through eighteen Relating addition and multiplication Meaning of multiplication			Parts of a whole— tenths
2-1	Computation with one renaming – 2-digit Renaming ones	Computation with one renaming – 2-digit Renaming tens				
1-2	Computation without renaming Basic facts: sums – of three numbers – through eighteen – through twelve	Computation without renaming Basic facts: minuends – through eighteen – through twelve				
1-1	Families of facts Basic facts: sums – through nine – with zero – through six Names for numbers	Families of facts Basic facts: minuends – through nine – with zero – through six				Parts of a whole— one-fourth and, one-third Equal parts
K	Meaning of addition	Meaning of subtraction				Parts of a whole— one-half

approximate grade level (divided by half years, when appropriate) for when a skill is typically presented. Second, they present the components of concepts and computation in parallel fashion, allowing the teacher to determine, at a glance, not only the prerequisite skills for each component, but also the breadth of skills a student would have been exposed to by a certain level.

Of course, the hierarchies are not precise. Not all mathematics series present skills in the same order as the ones we examined, nor is new content presented at exactly the same grade level in all series. However, the hierarchies are not intended to be exact. Rather, they are intended as a guide to help the teacher to organize some portion of the mathematics domain and to decide where to begin the assessment.

The hierarchies presented in Tables 6-1 and 6-2 will be most helpful to special education and remedial mathematics teachers who do not rely on a single basal series and who teach a variety of math skills. Teachers who do use one particular series could create a hierarchy based on the scope and sequence of the particular math series used in their classrooms.

Step 3: Decide Where to Begin (Concepts and Computation)

The teacher will need two pieces of information in order to know where to begin: the current grade level placement of the student in mathematics and an estimate of the student's present functioning math level. The latter can be determined by searching the student's permanent records for a math score from the most recently administered standardized test. If the student is in special education, that information may be available on the report of the most recent educational evaluation. Using these two pieces of information, the teacher would select a grade level at which to begin the assessment.

If the two pieces of information indicate the same grade level, the selection of where to begin is simple: the assessment begins at that grade level. If there is a discrepancy between the grade placement of the student and the grade level of his/her test performance, the teacher should select a point midway between the two grade levels at which to begin the assessment.

The reason for choosing the midpoint is that students do not necessarily learn all of the skills in the order in which they are presented, but they may know more than is measured on the test. For example, a student who is beginning the fourth grade could have test scores which indicate math skills at the 2.2 grade level. These scores might have been derived from the student's performing some third-grade skills adequately but failing some second-grade skills; that is, he/she may have learned basic multiplication facts (a third-grade skill) but not how to regroup in subtraction (a second-grade skill). Beginning the assessment for this student at the early fourth-grade level (his/her grade placement) would probably be too frustrating. Beginning the assessment at early second grade (his/her test score level) would probably result in the need to probe up. We have found that an appropriate and efficient starting point is midway between the student's grade placement and standardized test score.

Step 4: Select or Develop Survey Instrument (Concepts and Computation)

The teacher has several options in selecting a survey. If the teacher uses a math series which includes end-of-unit or placement tests, he/she may want to use

Table 6-3 Math Survey Tests

Name	Publisher	Grade Levels
Basic Educational Skills Inventory: Math	Brad Winch	Primary grade levels
Individual Pupil Monitoring Systems: Mathematics	Houghton Mifflin	1-8
Key Math Diagnostic Arithmetic Test	American Guidance Services	1-9
Stanford Diagnostic Mathematics Test	Harcourt Brace Jovanovich	2-12
Wide Range Achievement Test	Guidance Associates	Preschool and up

them as survey materials. The teacher may want to use one of the several commercially available mathematics tests which yield diagnostic information. Table 6-3 lists these resources and the grade levels for which they are appropriate. Finally, the teacher may want to construct a teacher-made survey. We suggest that a teacher-made survey be developed by selecting test items from across the hierarchies presented in Tables 6-1 and 6-2, at the appropriate grade level. Several items could be developed for each skill listed at the particular grade level.

In developing a survey the teacher has to make decisions not only about what to test but about the number of items to include for each skill on the hierarchy, whether the responses should require production or multiple choice, whether the computation items should require written or oral responses, whether manipulatives

Table 6-4 Decision-Making Guidelines for Teacher-Made Math Survey (Concepts and Computations)

Decision	Information needed	Decision process
Number of items	Age of student, attention span of student, number of skills to be surveyed	Range from 2-4 per skill for survey. The younger the student, the shorter the attention span and/or the more skills to be surveyed the fewer items per skill.
	Nature of the skill	Some skills cannot easily generate more than one item (i.e., matching numerals to names). Develop two items whenever possible.
Blank cell in hierarchy	Complexity of the next higher skill, time gap to next items, student's grade placement	If the next skill at the higher level is at a grade level beyond where student has been taught, drop down. If the next skill at the higher level is very complex, drop down. Otherwise, move up.
Production or multiple choice, written or oral	Nature of the skill, age of the student	For computation tasks, written production is first choice (test down model), followed by oral production, then multiple choice. Some concepts are more amenable to multiple choice or matching responses, and oral or demonstration. When possible, written production is first choice.

should be available to the student, and what to do if a particular cell on the hierarchy is blank. Table 6-4 presents guidelines for making these decisions.

Figure 6-A is an example of a teacher-made survey for the beginning third-grade level. The survey includes two items for each computation problem. All these problems require production and written computation. The concepts section includes only one item to survey some concepts (e.g., shapes) and both production and recognition responses. These decisions were based on the nature of the skills being assessed.

Once the survey has been selected or developed, the teacher should prepare a Concepts and Computation Survey Analysis form. A blank copy of the form is

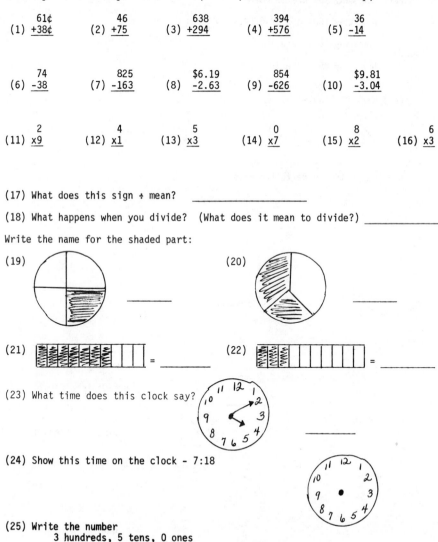

(1) $\begin{array}{r} 61¢ \\ +38¢ \\ \hline \end{array}$ (2) $\begin{array}{r} 46 \\ +75 \\ \hline \end{array}$ (3) $\begin{array}{r} 638 \\ +294 \\ \hline \end{array}$ (4) $\begin{array}{r} 394 \\ +576 \\ \hline \end{array}$ (5) $\begin{array}{r} 36 \\ -14 \\ \hline \end{array}$

(6) $\begin{array}{r} 74 \\ -38 \\ \hline \end{array}$ (7) $\begin{array}{r} 825 \\ -163 \\ \hline \end{array}$ (8) $\begin{array}{r} \$6.19 \\ -2.63 \\ \hline \end{array}$ (9) $\begin{array}{r} 854 \\ -626 \\ \hline \end{array}$ (10) $\begin{array}{r} \$9.81 \\ -3.04 \\ \hline \end{array}$

(11) $\begin{array}{r} 2 \\ \times 9 \\ \hline \end{array}$ (12) $\begin{array}{r} 4 \\ \times 1 \\ \hline \end{array}$ (13) $\begin{array}{r} 5 \\ \times 3 \\ \hline \end{array}$ (14) $\begin{array}{r} 0 \\ \times 7 \\ \hline \end{array}$ (15) $\begin{array}{r} 8 \\ \times 2 \\ \hline \end{array}$ (16) $\begin{array}{r} 6 \\ \times 3 \\ \hline \end{array}$

(17) What does this sign ÷ mean? _____

(18) What happens when you divide? (What does it mean to divide?) _____

Write the name for the shaded part:

(19) _____

(20) _____

(21) _____

(22) _____

(23) What time does this clock say? _____

(24) Show this time on the clock - 7:18

(25) Write the number
     3 hundreds, 5 tens, 0 ones _____

Figure 6-A Teacher-Made Survey (Computation and Concepts; Early 3rd Grade)

(26) In this number, 56,493

what number is in the thousands place _____

tens place _____

hundreds place _____

ones place _____

ten thousands place_____

(27) How many 10s are in 4378 _____

how many 100s are in 68042 _____

how many 1000s are in 903,148 _____

how many ones are in 627 _____

(28) Mark the angles:

(29) Match the shape to its name:

pentagon

triangle

octagon

square

circle

hexagon

rectangle

(30) How many:

feet in a yard? _____

meters in a kilometer? _____

pints in a quart? _____

(31) Which is larger?

gram or kilogram?

foot or yard?

quart   or cup?

Figure 6-A   Teacher-Made Survey (Computation and Concepts; Early 3rd Grade) —**Continued**

given in Figure 6-B. The form provides space for the teacher to record which skills are to be measured on the survey, and what level of the hierarchy they represent. The remainder of the form will be completed in Step 8. A Concepts and Computation Survey Analysis form to accompany the survey presented in Figure 6-A is provided in Figure 6-C.

	Survey			Student Performance		
Item number	Level	Area	Skill	Correct	Incorrect	Error pattern

Notes:

Figure 6-B Concepts and Computation—Survey Analysis Form

Survey				Student Performance		
Item number	Level	Area	Skill	Correct	Incorrect	Error pattern
1	1-2	addition money	2-digit without renaming			
2	2-1	addition	2-digit renaming			
3, 4	3-1	addition	3-digit renaming			
5	1-2	subtraction	2-digit without renaming			
6	2-1	subtraction	2-digit renaming			
7-10	3-1	subtraction	3-digit renaming			
11-16	3-2	multi-plication	basic facts			
17, 18	3-1	division	meaning			
19, 20	1-1	fractions	parts of a whole			
21, 22	2-2	fractions	parts of a whole			
23, 24	3-1	time	one-minute intervals			
25-27	2-2	whole number concepts	place value			
28	3-1	geometry	angles			
29	3-1	geometry	shapes			
30, 31	3-1	measure-ment	metric and cues— to many units			

Notes:

Figure 6-C Concepts and Computation—Survey Analysis Form Matched to Teacher-Made Survey

Step 5: Get Ready to Test (Concepts and Computation)

If a commercially available test is to be used, the teacher should review the test manual, and become thoroughly familiar with the directions for administering the test. If a teacher-made test has been constructed, the teacher should gather together any materials that will be needed by teacher and student to complete the test. The teacher will need to have a copy of the test answer key, which should be prepared before the test is administered. The teacher should also have a copy of the skill hierarchy being used to guide the assessment in an easily accessible place. Of course, pencils and paper should be available, along with a suitable place for the student to take the test. The teacher should have considered how the testing will be introduced to the student and what reinforcers will be offered to keep the student on-task.

Step 6: Administer the Survey (Concepts and Computation)

We strongly suggest that the teacher administer the survey one-to-one. We recommend this procedure for two reasons. First, the teacher can observe the student's behavior during the testing and can interview the student immediately after the test to determine how she/he arrived at an answer. The observation and interview are critical to the interpretation of a student's math performance.

The second advantage to administering the math concepts and computation survey one-to-one is that, after some practice, the teacher can usually eliminate some of the steps in the assessment strategy by gathering "on the spot" information. Through observation, interview, and scoring, the experienced teacher will often be able to move from survey (Step 6) to probe (Step 10) without some of the intermediate steps.

When sitting with the student, the teacher should have the answer key at hand. If it becomes obvious to the teacher that the student cannot succeed with a particular skill, and there are more items measuring the skill at a higher level, the teacher should direct the student to skip those items and move on to the next skill area on the survey. By observing the survey process, the teacher can prevent unnecessary frustration and failure for the student.

Figure 6-D is a record of one student's responses to the survey presented in Figure 6-A. The asterisk (*) at item 6 marks the place where the teacher suggested that the student skip some items.

61¢ (1) +38¢ 99¢	46 (2) +75 121	638 (3) +294 8132	394 (4) +576 8170	36 (5) -14 22
74 * (6) -38 44	825 (7) -163	$6.19 (8) -2.63	854 (9) -626	$9.81 (10) -3.04
2 (11) x9 18	4 (12) x1 4	5 (13) x3 15	0 (14) x7 7	8 (15) x2 16

6
(16) x3
18

Figure 6-D Teacher-Made Survey (Computation and Concepts; Early 3rd Grade) (Student's Response)

(17) What does this sign ÷ mean?   _divide_

(18) What happens when you divide? (What does it mean to divide?)   _to split_

Write the name for the shaded part:

(19)   _1/4_

(20)   _2/3_

(21) =   _7/10_

(22) =   _3/10_

(23) What time does this clock say?   _5:10_

(24) Show this time on the clock - 7:18

(25) Write the number
    3 hundreds, 5 tens, 0 ones   _300 5100_

(26) In this number, 56,493

        what number is in the thousands place   _56_

                                tens place   _9_

                      hundreds place   _493_

                           ones place   _3_

                  ten thousands place _56493_

(27) How many 10s are in 4378   _7_

    how many 100s are in 68042   _042_

    how many 1000s are in 903,148   _903_

    how many ones are in 627   _7_

(28) Mark the angles:

Figure 6-D   Teacher-Made Survey (Computation and Concepts; Early 3rd Grade)
(Student's Response)—**Continued**

(29) Match the shape to its name:

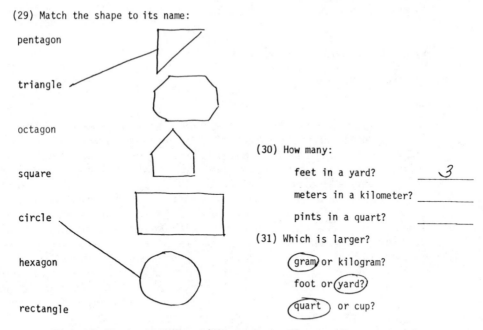

pentagon

triangle

octagon

square

circle

hexagon

rectangle

(30) How many:

feet in a yard?   _3_

meters in a kilometer? _____

pints in a quart?   _____

(31) Which is larger?

(gram) or kilogram?

foot or (yard?)

(quart) or cup?

Figure 6-D Teacher-Made Survey (Computation and Concepts; Early 3rd Grade)
(Student's Response)—**Continued**

Step 7: Note Errors and Performance Style
(Concepts and Computations)

When the survey has been completed, the teacher should score the items, using the answer key that was created previously. The teacher should note on the Concepts and Computation Survey Analysis form any significant student behaviors observed during the survey, such as counting on fingers, making numerous erasures, being inattentive to the task, getting frustrated, and so forth.

Step 8: Analyze Findings and Summarize
Outcomes (Concepts and Computation)

The teacher learns little about the student's abilities in mathematics by simply scoring the responses as correct or incorrect and recording the scores. It is essential for the teacher to ascertain *why* incorrect responses were made and to classify each of the errors. In interpreting errors on items involving concepts, the teacher needs to discover whether the student has no understanding of the concept, or has some understanding but only at a simple level, or whether the student cannot perform the task at the required level of response. Observation and questioning can lead the teacher to the correct interpretation of the student's error.

For example, if a student identifies a circle, square, triangle, and rectangle but not a pentagon, octagon, or hexagon, the teacher could assume that the student had learned the names for simple figures. But without conducting an interview, the teacher would not know whether the student had not been exposed to the more complex shapes or had been taught but could not remember them.

	Problem	Student's response
	56	$\overset{4}{\cancel{8}}6$
Figure 6-E Example of Math	$-\ 29$	$-\ 29$
Computation Error Completed		37
from Student's Response		

In interpreting errors in computation, Roberts (1968) suggests four reasons why students make errors: wrong operation, wrong basic facts, defective algorithm (procedure for carrying out the computation), and random response. We would add a fifth and sixth reason to this list: carelessness and not understanding the concept. By observing a student and asking how he/she arrived at a certain answer, the teacher should be able to attribute each error to one of these six reasons.

For example, Figure 6-E presents a math computation problem and a student's response. The teacher could generate several hypotheses based on the student's answer. The student either was careless, or didn't know basic facts, or went about the computation in the wrong way (defective algorithm). Had the teacher observed the student or questioned him/her after the test was scored, it would have been discovered that the student began working the problem from the left (the tens column, in this case) rather than the right (the ones column). The teacher would then have known that the error resulted from a defective algorithm.

Once the survey is scored, the teacher needs to interview the student to determine how he/she arrived at the incorrect answers. This will permit the teacher to analyze the findings properly. The teacher should begin by showing the student a problem that was answered incorrectly and asking the student to tell the teacher how he/she got the answer. The teacher must ask the student to "walk through" the steps. If the student's initial response is, "I added," the teacher should say, "Tell me what numbers you added first and what your answer was." Figure 6-F is an example of an interview based on the survey responses shown in Figure 6-C. It shows that the errors in problems 3, 4, and 6 seem to be the result of faulty algorithms, and that the error in problem 26 seems to represent poor understanding of place value.

To complete the analysis of error patterns, the teacher now returns to the Concepts and Computation Survey Analysis form and indicates, for each skill tested, whether the items were scored as correct or incorrect and, if incorrect, which of the error types is represented (Table 6-5). Each concept error is marked as either not understanding the concept, understanding at a simpler level, or not able to meet the response requirement. Each computation error is marked as either wrong operation, wrong basic facts, faulty algorithm, carelessness, random response, or no understanding of the concept. Figure 6-G matches examples of computation errors with reasons for the errors, as indicated by observation of the student and follow-up interviews. Figure 6-H shows the completed Concepts and Computation Survey Analysis form presented in Figure 6-C, with each error classified by type.

At this point the teacher would also complete the Survey line of the Assessment to Instruction Data Sheet for concepts and computation (Figures 6-I, 6-J). These forms do not attempt to break down each step in every operation. Rather, next to the skill assessed, the teacher records the highest level at which the student could perform the operation, that is, the most complex item in that component of the

T: Tell me what you did in problem 3, step by step.

S: I added 8 and 4, put down the 2 and carried the 1.   1 and 3 is 4
   and 9 is 13.   6 and 2 is 8.

T: Why did you carry the one when you added 3 and 4 (points to ones column)
   and not when you added 4 and 9 (points to tens column)?

S: I think you only do that here (points to ones column).

T: OK, now tell me what you did in problem 6.

S: 8 take away 4 is 4.   7 take away 3 is 4.

T: Now go to number 26. How do you know which is the ones place?

S: It's the first place.

T: What do you mean?

S: It's always over here (points to the number on the right).

T: How do you know which is the tens place?

S: It's next to the ones.

T: What about the hundreds place?

S: I don't know. I forget.

T: Can you write the number 100?

S: (writes) 100

T: Can you write one hundred thirty-six?

S: (writes) 10036

T: Can you write forty-two?

S: (writes) 42

T: Sixty seven?

S: (writes) 67

Figure 6-F Example of Math Interview

hierarchy which the student could successfully complete. For example, if a student is unable to solve whole number subtraction problems with regrouping, but has mastered subtraction of two-digit numbers without regrouping, the teacher would fill in the Survey line of Figure 6-J, under whole number subtraction: a *2* to indicate skill known at lower level, and, under level known, *2 places without regrouping*. (Typically, this would be abbreviated as *2 pl w/o reg*.) By noting the level at which the survey was tested and, in the level known column, the highest level of the skill which the student performed correctly, the teacher can refer back to the skill hierarchy to identify the next skill to be probed.

Table 6-5 Error Types in Concepts
and Computation

Concepts:

1. Not understanding the concept
2. Understanding at a simpler level
3. Not able to meet response requirements

Computation:

1. Wrong operation
2. Wrong basic facts
3. Defective algorithm
4. Random response
5. Carelessness
6. Not understanding the concept

Examples of Error			Reason for Error
1. 47 $\frac{-63}{110}$	82 $\frac{-19}{111}$		1. wrong operation
2. 64 $\frac{+12}{77}$	$\overset{8}{\cancel{9}}1$ $\frac{-36}{56}$	28 $\frac{\times\ 9}{104}$	2. computation errors
3. 16 $\frac{+\ 9}{115}$	34 $\frac{-18}{24}$	78 $\frac{\times 12}{716}$	3. faulty algorithm
4. 34 $\frac{+12}{93}$	71 $\frac{+23}{36}$	50 $\frac{-28}{94}$	4. random response
5. 6894 $\frac{+3047}{10941}$	746 $\frac{-331}{15}$	46 $\frac{\times\ 3}{128}$	5. carelessness
6. 3.2 $\frac{+.17}{49}$	$7\frac{5}{6}$ $\frac{-\ 3\frac{1}{3}}{4\ ^4/_3}$		6. not understanding the concept

Figure 6-G Computation Error Patterns

Survey				Student Performance		
Item number	Level	Area	Skill	Correct	Incorrect	Error pattern
1	1-2	addition money	2-digit without renaming	✓		
2	2-1	addition	2-digit renaming	✓		
3, 4	3-1	addition	3-digit renaming		✓	faulty algorithm
5	1-2	subtraction	2-digit without renaming	✓		
6	2-1	subtraction	2-digit renaming		✓	faulty algorithm
7-10	3-1	subtraction	3-digit renaming	✓		
11-16	3-2	multi-plication	basic facts	✓		
17, 18	3-1	division	meaning	✓		
19, 20	1-1	fractions	parts of a whole	✓		
21, 22	2-2	fractions	parts of a whole	✓		
23, 24	3-1	time	one-minute intervals	✓		
25-27	2-2	whole number concepts	place value		✓	not understanding concepts
28	3-1	geometry	angles		✓	—
29	3-1	geometry	shapes		✓	random response
30, 31	3-1	measure-ment	metric and cues— to many units		✓	random response

Notes:

Figure 6-H Concepts and Computation—Survey Analysis Form

Student _____ Teacher _____ Date _____

ASSESSMENT TASKS	Whole number	Level known	Time	Level known	Measurement	Level known	Money	Level known	Geometry	Level known
*Survey Level _____										
Initial Probe										
Further Probe										
Further Probe										
Further Probe										
UPDATE										

Code—Survey and Probe

1 - Skill known   3 - Need more information

2 - Skill known at lower level   4 - Skill not known   5 - Not assessed

Figure 6-I Assessment to Instruction Data Sheet (Curricular Area: Math Concepts)

Student _____ Teacher _____ Date _____

ASSESSMENT TASKS	Whole number +	Level known	Whole number −	Level known	Whole number X	Level known	Whole number ÷	Level known	Decimals +	Level known	Decimals −	Level known	Decimals X	Level known	Decimals ÷	Level known	Fractions +	Level known	Fractions −	Level known	Fractions X	Level known	Fractions ÷	Level known
Survey Level ___																								
Initial Probe																								
Further Probe																								
Further Probe																								
Further Probe																								
UPDATE																								

Code—Survey and Probe

1 - Skill known   3 - Need more information   5 - Not assessed
2 - Skill known at lower level   4 - Skill not known

Figure 6-J Assessment to Instruction Data Sheet (Curricular Area: Math Computation)

223

Step 9: Hypothesize Reasons for Errors and Generate Areas to Probe (Concepts and Computation)

The teacher must now interpret the error patterns and generate a plan for the next steps. If the student made many errors, and most of them were random or careless responses, the teacher should consider two possibilities. First, the student may not have been motivated when performing the survey task. In that case, the teacher should plan to resurvey using more explicit or more powerful reinforcers. Second, the survey may have been too difficult for the student, requiring performance of skills at too high a level. In this case the teacher would have to drop down one grade level and develop or select a new survey.

If the student made very few errors of any type, the teacher should consider resurveying with problems at a higher level.

If the student's errors were of the wrong operation, the teacher might consider that the student could not interpret the printed word or sign indicating which type of computation was called for. The teacher would want to check this by administering a probe.

If the student made errors in basic facts, the next step would be to explore which number facts are and are not known. A probe of basic fact knowledge would be appropriate.

If the student used a faulty algorithm, the teacher would want to probe down the computation hierarchy to be certain that the student used the correct algorithm on simpler, prerequisite computation skills.

If the student made an isolated, random response to a particular problem on the survey, the teacher might hypothesize that the student had never been taught that particular skill. Referring back to the skill hierarchy generated in Step 2, the teacher would probe earlier skills to discover where teaching should begin. Table 6-6

Table 6-6 Hypothesizing Reasons for Computation Errors

Error Pattern	Hypothesis	Next Step
Many errors, careless and/or random	Unmotivated	Re-survey with appropriate motivators
Many errors, careless and/or random	Survey too difficult	Re-survey down the math hierarchy
Few errors	Survey too easy	Re-survey up the math hierarchy
Wrong operation	Cannot interpret process words or signs	Probe meaning of computation signs or words
Computation errors	Does not know basic facts	Probe basic computation facts
Faulty algorithms	Does not know procedures	Probe down computation hierarchy to check prerequisite skills
No understanding of concept; particular random responses, item left blank	Never taught	Probe down to test prerequisite skills

summarizes the hypotheses generated on the basis of errors made on the survey, as well as possible next steps for the teacher to take.

Step 10: Probe (Concepts and Computation)

Once the teacher has determined what skills are to be probed, he/she must select or develop measures of those skills.

Probes of specific skills can be drawn from published tests, or subtests. Table 6-7 is a list of published instruments which measure mathematical skills. Some of these, such as the SRA Diagnosis Kits, allow the teacher to choose a lengthy probe in a specific area. In addition, survey tests listed in Table 6-3 might provide the teacher with a few items for each skill area in which he/she wishes to probe.

Teachers can create their own probes by developing items to test the next step(s) up or down the hierarchies that interest them. Figure 6-K is an example of a teacher-made probe of beginning multiplication and division skills. Figures 6-L and 6-M are examples of commercially available probes of fraction and measurement skills. Probes may also be generated by moving from computation to number concepts. For example, a student who used a faulty algorithm for regrouping in addition may not have grasped the concept of place value, which is prerequisite to regrouping. The teacher might design a probe of place value concepts for this student.

Table 6-7   Published Math Tests for Probes (Concepts and Computation)

Name	Publisher	Areas Assessed
Brigance Diagnostic Inventory of Basic Skills	Curriculum Associates	Number concepts, operations with whole and fractional numbers, applications
Brigance Diagnostic Inventory of Essential Skills	Curriculum Associates	Number concepts, operations with whole and fractional numbers, applications
Diagnostic Tests and Self-Helps in Arithmetic	California Test Bureau/ McGraw-Hill	Operations with whole and fractional numbers
Individualized Computation Skill Series (diagnostic tests included)	Holt, Rinehart & Winston	Operations with whole and fractional numbers
Individualized Math Drill and Practice Kits (diagnostic tests included)	Random House-Singer	Operations with whole and fractional numbers
Sequential Mathematics (diagnostic tests included)	Harcourt Brace Jovanovich	Operations with whole numbers
SRA Diagnosis Kits (Math)	Science Research Associates	Number concepts, operations with whole and fractional numbers
Kraner Tests of Mathematics	C.C. Publications	Number concepts, operations with whole and fractional numbers, applications

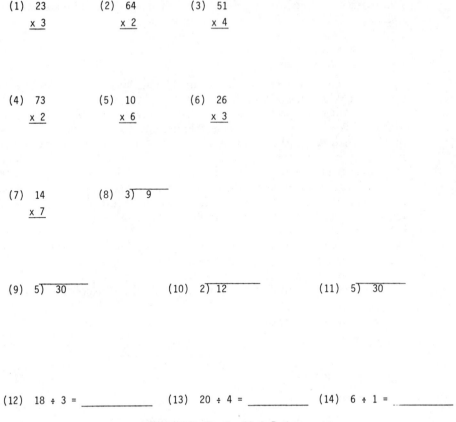

Figure 6-K Teacher-Made Probe

Step 11: Complete Recordkeeping Forms
and Generate Teaching Objectives
(Concepts and Computation)

The results of probe testing should be added to the Assessment to Instruction Data Sheets for math concepts and math computation (Figures 6-I and 6-J).

Figures 6-N and 6-O are Assessment to Instruction Data Sheets completed for the student whose survey we presented in Figures 6-D and 6-H. The student can add by regrouping in the ones place and subtract to 2 places without regrouping. He/she knows the multiplication tables, fractional concepts, and place values to ten, and can identify a rectangle, circle, square, and triangle.

From the information summarized on these Assessment to Instruction Data Sheets, the teacher can generate teaching objectives and become aware of the areas in which more information is needed. The teacher could begin instruction at every point where there is a notation of *2* (skill known at lower level) or *4* (skill not known). Instruction would begin at the lowest point at which skill breakdown occurred in each component.

Probe 2

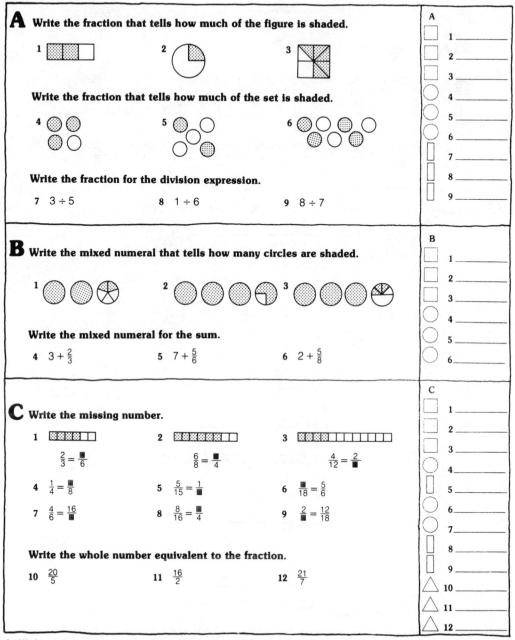

A Write the fraction that tells how much of the figure is shaded.

1   2   3

Write the fraction that tells how much of the set is shaded.

4   5   6

Write the fraction for the division expression.

7 $3 \div 5$ 8 $1 \div 6$ 9 $8 \div 7$

B Write the mixed numeral that tells how many circles are shaded.

1   2   3

Write the mixed numeral for the sum.

4 $3 + \frac{2}{3}$ 5 $7 + \frac{5}{6}$ 6 $2 + \frac{5}{8}$

C Write the missing number.

1   2   3

$\frac{2}{3} = \frac{\blacksquare}{6}$ $\frac{6}{8} = \frac{\blacksquare}{4}$ $\frac{4}{12} = \frac{2}{\blacksquare}$

4 $\frac{1}{4} = \frac{\blacksquare}{8}$ 5 $\frac{5}{15} = \frac{1}{\blacksquare}$ 6 $\frac{\blacksquare}{18} = \frac{5}{6}$

7 $\frac{4}{6} = \frac{16}{\blacksquare}$ 8 $\frac{8}{16} = \frac{\blacksquare}{4}$ 9 $\frac{2}{\blacksquare} = \frac{12}{18}$

Write the whole number equivalent to the fraction.

10 $\frac{20}{5}$ 11 $\frac{16}{2}$ 12 $\frac{21}{7}$

A
1 _____
2 _____
3 _____
4 _____
5 _____
6 _____
7 _____
8 _____
9 _____

B
1 _____
2 _____
3 _____
4 _____
5 _____
6 _____

C
1 _____
2 _____
3 _____
4 _____
5 _____
6 _____
7 _____
8 _____
9 _____
10 _____
11 _____
12 _____

Figure 6-L Fractions and Mixed Numerals Probe*

*From *diagnosis: an instructional aid; Mathematics Level B, Lab B2.*
© 1980, Science Research Associates, Inc. Reprinted by permission.

A How many paper clips long?

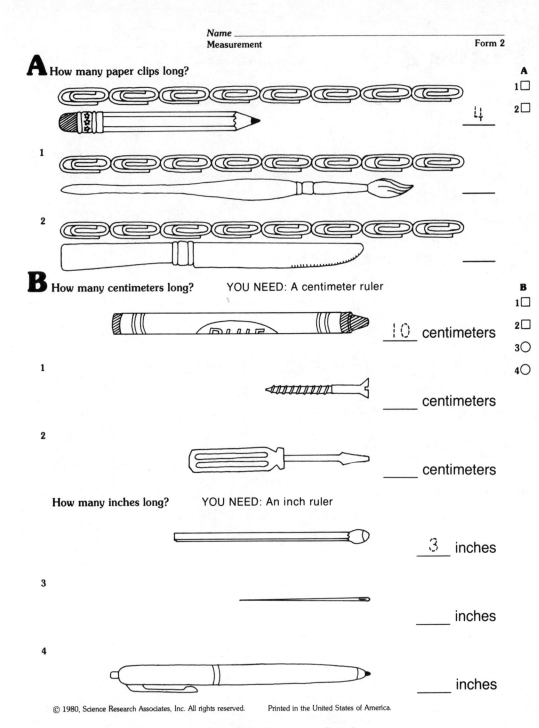

A

1 ☐
2 ☐

4

1

___

2

___

B How many centimeters long?   YOU NEED: A centimeter ruler

B

1 ☐
2 ☐
3 ○
4 ○

10 centimeters

1

___ centimeters

2

___ centimeters

How many inches long?   YOU NEED: An inch ruler

3 inches

3

___ inches

4

___ inches

Figure 6-M Measurement Probe*

*From *diagnosis: an instructional aid; Mathematics Level A.* © 1979, Science Research Associates, Inc. Reprinted by permission.

Student _____ Teacher _____ Date _____

ASSESSMENT TASKS	Whole number	Level known	Time	Level known	Measurement	Level known	Money	Level known	Geometry	Level known
Survey Level _3-1_	3		1		3		4		3	
Initial Probe	2	place value to 10's pl.							2	rec., sq., tri., circle
Further Probe										
Further Probe										
Further Probe										
UPDATE										

Code—Survey and Probe

1 – Skill known   3 – Need more information
2 – Skill known at lower level 4 – Skill not known   5 – Not assessed

Figure 6-N Assessment to Instruction Data Sheet
(Curricular Area: Math Concepts)

Figure 6-O Assessment to Instruction Data Sheet (Curricular Area: Math Computation)

Student _____ Teacher _____ Date _____

ASSESSMENT TASKS	Whole number +	Level known	Whole number −	Level known	Whole number X	Level known	Whole number ÷	Level known	Decimals +	Level known	Decimals −	Level known	Decimals X	Level known	Decimals ÷	Level known	Fractions +	Level known	Fractions −	Level known	Fractions X	Level known	Fractions ÷	Level known
Survey Level _3.1_	2	2 pl w/regr.	2	2 pl w/o regr.	3	tables	3		4		4		4		4		3	con-cept	4		4		4	
Initial Probe					2	tables																		
Further Probe																								
Further Probe																								
Further Probe																								
UPDATE																								

Code—Survey and Probe

1 - Skill known
2 - Skill known at lower level
3 - Need more information
4 - Skill not known
5 - Not assessed

For the student whose performance is summarized in Figures 6-N and 6-O, the next skill to teach in addition is renaming tens; in subtraction, renaming ones; in multiplication, multiplying with a ones factor; in fractions, comparing; in place value, three-digit numbers; in geometry, three-dimensional shapes.

Step 12: Start Teaching/Update Assessment
Information (Concepts and Computation)

As skills are mastered, the Assessment to Instruction Data Sheet should be updated, and new teaching objectives should be defined. Periodically, the teacher should deliberately introduce some skills not tested in the original survey or those on which more information is needed, so that the Assessment to Instruction Data Sheet can be completed.

SURVEYING
LOW-FUNCTIONING STUDENTS

Teachers whose research of the cumulative records yields student math scores below second grade may want to survey with a diagnostic interview. One such survey (Crown, 1980) can be found in Appendix E. This survey provides information in the areas of number concepts, addition, and subtraction. Built into this survey are interview questions and directed observations for the teacher. We recommend the use of Crown's Diagnostic Arithmetic Interview, or a similar measure, as a survey for young students (first or second grade) and for students up to sixth grade with first- or second-grade math skills, or as a probe, when the initial survey indicates that the student's skills in mathematics are at a very low level.

ILLUSTRATION: CHRIS

The following example illustrates Steps 2 to 12 of the assessment model in concepts and computation. It begins at Step 2 because the teacher decided that math assessment information was needed on this student (Step 1).

Chris was a seventh grader. He had been assigned to a resource room for math remediation. His score on the math section of the Wide Range Achievement Test (WRAT) was grade 3.5. He scored in the 14th percentile of the seventh-grade level Metropolitan Achievement Test in mathematical concepts and computation. He had been taught to the end of the sixth-grade basal math textbook and had received a failing grade in mathematics at the end of sixth grade.

Step 2: Select or Develop a Skill Hierarchy
(Chris)

The teacher was one who created her own remedial math program. She used a variety of texts, workbooks, teacher-made materials, and games. Therefore, she selected the "generic" skill hierarchy found in Tables 6-1 and 6-2 to guide her assessment of concepts and computation.

Step 3: Decide Where to Begin (Chris)

With the information about Chris available to the teacher, she decided to test him at the end of fourth-grade level. Her decision was based on "splitting the difference" between the grade level to which he had been taught (end of sixth grade) and his WRAT score (grade 3.5).

Step 4: Select or Develop Survey Instrument (Chris)

The teacher decided to develop her own survey by creating items to test the skills that are typically learned by the end of fourth grade. Based on the skills identified in the hierarchies in Tables 6-1 and 6-2, she created two items each in the areas of whole number computation involving addition, subtraction, multiplication, and division. She used one item each for addition and subtraction of decimals because she was only interested in determining if Chris could set up the problems appropriately; the addition and subtraction skills would have been surveyed in whole number computation. She created two items each in addition and subtraction of fractions and three in improper fractions, in order to survey different aspects of the skill. The

(1)   487
     +368

(2) 8693
    +4748

(3)   902
    - 367

(4) 4162
    -1864

(5) 26
    x46

(6) 49
    x62

(7) 5) 768

(8) 23) 917

(9). Work this problem: 4.2 + 3.37 + .61

(10) Work this problem: 3.7 - .16

(11) $\dfrac{3}{8}$
     $+\dfrac{2}{8}$

(12) $\dfrac{2}{3}$
     $+\dfrac{2}{3}$

(13) $\dfrac{6}{10}$
     $-\dfrac{2}{10}$

(14) $\dfrac{4}{5}$
     $-\dfrac{1}{5}$

(15)   Show these fractions another way:

$\dfrac{7}{5}$ = $\dfrac{6}{2}$ = $\dfrac{4}{4}$ =

(16)   Reduce these fractions:

$\dfrac{2}{4}$ = $\dfrac{5}{15}$ = $\dfrac{4}{12}$ =

(17) What time do these clocks say?

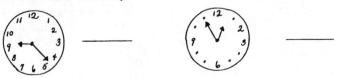

Figure 6-P End of 4th Grade Survey Prepared for Chris

(18) 11 cm = ___ dm ___ cm

23 cm = ___ dm ___ cm

Each ☐ is 1 square foot. Write the area in square feet.

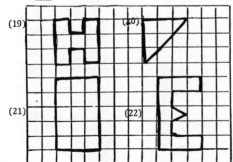

(19) _____

(20) _____

(21) _____

(22) _____

(23) Given one dollar, tell me how much change you would receive if you bought something for 33¢? _____

Given one dollar, tell me how much change you would receive if you bought something for 52¢? _____

Given five dollars, tell me how much change you would receive if you bought something for $1.39? _____

Given five dollars, tell me how much change you would receive if you bought something for $3.75? _____

In the picture find two:

(24) rays _____ _____

(25) right angles _____ _____

(26) angles that are not right angles _____ _____

(27) lines that are parallel _____ _____

(28) lines that are perpendicular

_____ _____

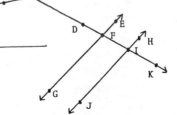

(29) Round these numbers to the nearest ten:

67 = _____

45 = _____

311 = _____

(30) Round these numbers to the nearest hundred:

421 = _____

838 = _____

1471 = _____

(31) Round these numbers to the nearest thousand:

1099 = _____

57502 = _____

Figure 6-P End of 4th Grade Survey Prepared for Chris—**Continued**

Survey				Student Performance		
Item number	Level	Area	Skill	Correct	Incorrect	Error pattern
1, 2	3-2	addition	3- and 4-digit numbers with renaming			
3, 4	3-2	subtraction	3- and 4-digit numbers with renaming			
5, 6	4-2	multi-plication	2-digit by 2-digit numbers			
7	4-2	division	1-digit number with 3-digit quotient			
8	4-2	division	2-digit number with 2-digit quotient			
9, 10	4-1	decimals	adding and subtracting			
11-14	4-2	fractions	addition and sub-traction with like denominator			
15	5-2	fractions	improper			
16	5-2	fractions	reducing			
17	3-1	time	one minute			
18	4-2	measure	metric units			
19-22	4-2	measure	areas by counting			
23	4-2	money	making change			
24-28	4-2	geometry	lines, rays, angles, parallel, perpendicular			
29-31	4-1	whole number concepts	rounding			

Notes: *Knows number facts*
Works quickly—skips over things he doesn't know
Tries what he thinks he can do
Complains ("this is hard")
Stayed with task

Figure 6-Q Concepts and Computation—Survey Analysis Form (Chris)

number of items used to survey concepts varied, depending on the nature of the skill. Because of Chris's age and skill level, the teacher created a survey which required written production at a recall level of response. The survey she created is shown in Figure 6-P. Figure 6-Q is the Concepts and Computation Survey Analysis form she prepared for this survey.

Step 5: Get Ready to Test (Chris)

The teacher prepared the survey on a ditto master. She gave one copy to the student and used a second copy to create a "key," in order to simplify scoring.

Step 6: Administer the Survey (Chris)

The teacher administered the survey one-to-one with Chris at a table in a quiet corner of the classroom. The other students were working independently in a different area of the room. The teacher gave Chris the survey and several sharpened pencils. She asked him to show all of his work and to do the best he could. She reminded him that if she saw him trying his best, the next day he would be able to play Quinto with another student. (Quinto is a math game which Chris particularly enjoys.)

The teacher sat across the table from Chris in order to observe and note, on the Concepts and Computation Survey Analysis form, any behaviors of interest to her. For example, she noted that Chris used no manipulatives for number facts, that he worked quickly, skipping items he did not know but attempting all those that he seemed to think he might know, and that he occasionally looked at the teacher and said, "This is hard."

Step 7: Note Errors and Performance Style (Chris)

Figure 6-R shows Chris's responses to the survey. When Chris was done, the teacher used the answer key created earlier to quickly determine which responses were correct and which were incorrect.

Step 8: Analyze Findings and Summarize Outcomes (Chris)

In order to understand how Chris arrived at his responses, the teacher interviewed him by showing him his copy of the survey and asking him to recreate his problem-solving strategies. The interview is presented in Figure 6-S. (The reader should refer back to Chris's survey in Figure 6-R to follow the interview.)

The interview with Chris demonstrated that he used a faulty algorithm for long multiplication and long division and that his knowledge of fractions was rudimentary. The teacher also determined that he had not tried to do any problems requiring knowledge of geometry.

On the basis of the interview, the teacher completed the Concepts and Computation Survey Analysis form for Chris (Figure 6-T). She also completed the Survey lines of the Assessment to Instruction Data Sheets for concepts and computation (Figure 6-U and 6-V).

(1)   487
      +368
      ─────
      855

(2)   8693
     +4748
     ──────
     13441

(3)   902
      -367
      ─────
      535

(4)   4162
     -1864
     ──────
     2298

(5)   26
      x46
      ────
       36
       80
      ────
      116

(6)   49
      x62
      ────
       18
      240
      ────
      258

(7)   15 r 243
       5) 768
          5
          ───
          268
          25
          ───
          243

(8)   45 r 107
      23) 917
           8
          ────
          117
           10
          ────
          107

(9) Work this problem: 4.2 + 3.37 + .61

        4.2
        3.37
        .61
        ─────
        4.40

(10) Work this problem: 3.7 - .16

        3.7
       -.16
       ─────
        .21

(11) $\frac{3}{8}$

     $+\frac{2}{8}$
     ─────
      5/8

(12) $\frac{2}{3}$

     $+\frac{2}{3}$
     ─────
      4/3

(13) $\frac{6}{10}$

     $-\frac{2}{10}$
     ─────
      4/10

(14) $\frac{4}{5}$

     $-\frac{1}{5}$
     ─────
      3/5

(15) Show these fractions another way:

     $\frac{7}{5}$ = $\frac{6}{2}$ = $\frac{4}{4}$ = 1

(16) Reduce these fractions:

     $\frac{2}{4}$ = 2 $\frac{5}{15}$ = 3 $\frac{4}{12}$ = 3

(17) What time do these clocks say?

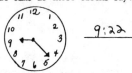   9:22      6 to 1

(18) 11 cm = __1__ dm __1__ cm
     23 cm = __2__ dm __3__ cm

Each ☐ is 1 square foot. Write the area in square feet.

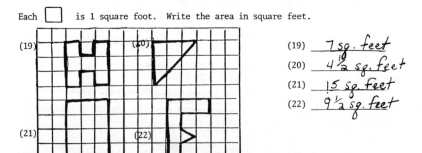

(19) __7 sq. feet__
(20) __4½ sq. feet__
(21) __15 sq. feet__
(22) __9½ sq. feet__

Figure 6-R End of 4th Grade Survey Prepared for Chris—Responses

(23) Given one dollar, tell me how much change you would receive if you bought something for 33¢? _67¢_

Given one dollar, tell me how much change you would receive if you bought something for 52¢? _48¢_

Given five dollars, tell me how much change you would receive if you bought something for $1.39? _$3.61_

Given five dollars, tell me how much change you would receive if you bought something for $3.75? _$1.25_

In the picture find two:

(24) rays _____   _____

(25) right angles _____   _____

(26) angles that are not right angles _____   _____

(27) lines that are parallel _____   _____

(28) lines that are perpendicular

_____   _____

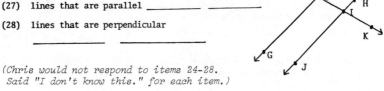

(Chris would not respond to items 24-28. Said "I don't know this." for each item.)

(29) Round these numbers to the nearest ten:

67 = __70__

45 = __50__

311 = __310__

(30) Round these numbers to the nearest hundred:

421 = __400__

838 = __800__

1471 = __1500__

(31) Round these numbers to the nearest thousand:

1099 = __1000__

57502 = __58000__

Figure 6-R End of 4th Grade Survey Prepared for Chris—Responses—**Continued**

T: Tell me how you did #5.

S: 6 times 6 is 36. Put a 0 to hold the place. 2 times 4 is 8. Then add.
   6 and nothing is 6, 3 and 8 is 11.

T: How did you do #6?

S: 9 times 2 is 18. Put a 0, 6 times 4 is 24. Add 8 and 0 is 8, 4 and 1
   is 5, 2 and nothing is 2.

T: How did you do #7?

S: 5 into 7 goes 1, 1 times 5 is 5, subtract and bring down the 68.
   5 into 26 goes 5, 5 times 5 is 25, subtract and what's left over
   goes on the top with an /r/.

T: How about #8?

S: 2 into 9 goes 4, 4 times 2 is 8. Subtract, bring down the 17,
   5 into 11 goes 2, 2 times 5 is 10. Subtract and put what's left
   on top with an /r/.

T: For #15, can you draw a picture that shows 7/5 and 6/2?

S:

T: How would you read these pictures?

S: 5/7ths   2/6ths

T: What did you do in #16?

S: Divided 2 into 4, 5 into 15, and 4 into 12.

Figure 6-S Follow-Up Interview (Chris)

Survey				Student Performance		
Item number	Level	Area	Skill	Correct	Incorrect	Error pattern
1, 2	3-2	addition	3- and 4-digit numbers with renaming	✓		
3, 4	3-2	subtraction	3- and 4-digit numbers with renaming	✓		
5, 6	4-2	multi-plication	2-digit by 2-digit numbers		✓	faulty algorithm
7	4-2	division	1-digit number with 3-digit quotient		✓	faulty algorithm
8	4-2	division	2-digit number with 2-digit quotient		✓	faulty algorithm
9, 10	4-1	decimals	adding and subtracting		✓	not understanding concept
11-14	4-2	fractions	addition and subtraction with like denominator	✓		
15	5-2	fractions	improper		✓	not understanding concept
16	5-2	fractions	reducing		✓	not understanding concept
17	3-1	time	one minute	✓		
18	4-2	measure	metric units	✓		
19-22	4-2	measure	area by counting	✓		
23	3-2	money	making change	✓		
24-28	4-2	geometry	lines, rays, angles, parallel, perpendicular		✓	not understanding concept
29-31	4-1	whole number concepts	rounding	✓		

Notes: *Knows number facts*
Works quickly—skips over things he doesn't know
Tries what he thinks he can do
Complains ("this is hard")
Stayed with task

Figure 6-T Concepts and Computation—Survey Analysis Form (Chris)

Student _Chris_____   Teacher _Cornwell_____   Date _9/25/81_____

ASSESSMENT TASKS	Whole number	Level known	Time	Level known	Measurement	Level known	Money	Level known	Geometry	Level known
Survey Level _4-2_	1		1		1		1		3	
Initial Probe										
Further Probe										
Further Probe										
Further Probe										
UPDATE										

Code—Survey and Probe

1 - Skill known   3 - Need more information
2 - Skill known at lower level   4 - Skill not known   5 - Not assessed

Figure 6-U Assessment to Instruction Data Sheet
(Curricular Area: Math Concepts) (Chris)

Student **Chris** Teacher **Cornwell** Date **9/25/81**

ASSESSMENT TASKS	Whole number +	Level known	Whole number −	Level known	Whole number X	Level known	Whole number ÷	Level known	Decimals +	Level known	Decimals −	Level known	Decimals X	Level known	Decimals ÷	Level known	Fractions +	Level known	Fractions −	Level known	Fractions X	Level known	Fractions ÷	Level known
Survey Level **4-2**	1		1		3		3		4		4		5		5		3		3		4		4	
Initial Probe																								
Further Probe																								
Further Probe																								
Further Probe																								
UPDATE																								

Code—Survey and Probe
1 - Skill known
2 - Skill known at lower level
3 - Need more information
4 - Skill not known
5 - Not assessed

Figure 6-V Assessment to Instruction Data Sheet (Curricular Area: Math Computation)

Step 9: Hypothesize Reasons for Errors and Determine Areas to Probe (Chris)

Given the grade level to which Chris had been taught and his responses to the survey and interview, the teacher hypothesized that Chris had not yet mastered the procedures for carrying out long multiplication and long division problems. She decided to probe lower level multiplication and division skills to see if Chris had properly learned some lower level algorithms. She also hypothesized that Chris had only rudimentary knowledge of fractions and again decided to probe down the skill hierarchy in the fractions column. She felt certain that Chris had not yet learned any concepts involving decimals and decided not to probe this area further. She believed that she would need to probe down the skill hierarchy in geometry in order to understand what Chris knows and does not know in this area.

Step 10: Probe (Chris)

Figures 6-W and 6-X show the following: the probes the teacher created and selected for Chris, Chris's responses, and the teacher's interview with him.

The teacher administered the probes, staying with Chris to watch him work. The interviews she conducted with him, following items 5 and 9, were lengthy, but they revealed where the breakdowns in both long multiplication and division were occurring. The teacher determined that Chris understood multiplication and division, and the prerequisite place value skills needed to do the tasks, although he did not apply them. Once the teacher reminded him, Chris was able to perform the operations correctly. Therefore, the teacher knew she would have to re-teach long multiplication and division with cues and allow Chris a great deal of practice in those areas.

The fraction probe, taken from the SRA Diagnosis Kit, Level B, Lab B2 revealed that Chris did not have a clear understanding of the concept of fractions. He was able to perform rote tasks (on the survey he could add and subtract fractions with like denominators), and he could represent fractions pictorially. But he only understood comparisons when he was directed in the task by the teacher, using manipulatives.

Given the number of computation skills that Chris had difficulty with, the teacher decided to postpone probing in geometry.

Step 11: Complete Recordkeeping Forms and Generate Teaching Objectives (Chris)

Figure 6-Y shows how the teacher added the probe information gathered about Chris to the Assessment to Instruction Data Sheet for computation. Based on these data, the teacher was able to establish the following teaching objectives for Chris:

The student will be able to:

-solve 3- by 3-digit multiplication problems, without cues, with 90% accuracy

-solve division problems with 2-digit divisors and 3-digit quotients, without cues, with 90% accuracy

-represent mixed fractions and improper fractions pictorially with 100% accuracy

12	23	41	92	17
(1) x 4	(2) x 3	(3) x 4	(4) x 3	(5) x 3
48	69	164	276	321 *

*T: Tell me what you did in #5.

S: 7 times 3 is 21. 3 times 1 is 3.

T: Here are 17 sticks (shows S 17 popsicle sticks). If you had 2 more
   piles of 17 sticks each, would you have 321 altogether?

S: I don't think so.

T: Show me how you could do this problem as an addition problem.

S: 17 + 17 + 17.

T: Right! And what's the answer?

S: 51

T: Good. Multiplying is just a simpler way to do that. Look at
   the problem again. When you multiplied 7 times 3 and got 21,
   how many ones did you get?

S: One

T: Right. And how many tens?

S: Two

T: Well, you can't put the 2 tens in the ones place. What should
   you do?

S: Carry?

T: Right. Show me how that would go.

S: 7 times 3 is 21, put down the 1 and carry the 2. 1 times 3 is 3
   plus 2 is 5.

T: Very good. Now you got the same answer that you got when you added.
   Do the next 3 problems, remembering to carry.

25	46	67	1 r6
(6) x 2	(7) x 4	(8) x 6	(9) 3) 36
50	184	402	3
			06 *

*T: Tell me what you did in #9

S: 3 into 3 goes 1. 1 times 3 is 3. Subtract and bring down.
   What's left goes on top with an /r/.

T: If you have 36 sticks (shows student 36 popsicle sticks) and
   wanted to divide them among 3 people, would you give each person
   1 and have 6 left over?

S: No

Figure 6-W Multiplication and Division Probe and Student's Response

T: You divided 3 into 3 (shows with sticks) and forgot the rest of the problem. What place is the 3 in?

S: 10s

T: What does that mean?

S: 30

T: How many sticks would each student get if you divided 30 by 3?

S: (without using sticks) 10

T: How many are left?

S: 6

T: Can you divide those among the 3 people?

S: 2 to each

T: How many would each person have altogether?

S: 12

T: Twelve is the correct answer. Doing the problem like this: $3\overline{)\,36}$ is an easier way to divide than counting sticks. You started the problem correctly (shows student) but forgot the next step. You have to divide the 3 into the 6 that you brought down.

S: I always forget to do that.

T: Now try to remember and do the next three problems.

(10)
$$
\begin{array}{r}
12 \\
4\overline{)\,48} \\
4 \\
\hline
08 \\
8 \\
\hline
0
\end{array}
$$

(11)
$$
\begin{array}{r}
431 \\
2\overline{)\,862} \\
8 \\
\hline
06 \\
6 \\
\hline
02 \;**
\end{array}
$$

(12)
$$
\begin{array}{r}
312 \\
3\overline{)\,936} \\
9 \\
\hline
03 \\
3 \\
\hline
06 \\
6
\end{array}
$$

(13)
$$
\begin{array}{r}
24 \\
4\overline{)\,96} \\
8 \\
\hline
16 \\
16
\end{array}
$$

(14)
$$
\begin{array}{r}
13 \\
7\overline{)\,91} \\
7 \\
\hline
21 \\
21
\end{array}
$$

(15)
$$
\begin{array}{r}
75 \; r1 \\
3\overline{)\,226} \\
21 \\
\hline
16 \\
15 \\
\hline
1
\end{array}
$$

(16)
$$
\begin{array}{r}
15 \; r4 \\
6\overline{)\,94} \\
6 \\
\hline
34 \\
30 \\
\hline
4
\end{array}
$$

(17) $10\overline{)\,200}$

(18) $30\overline{)\,600}$ (19) $12\overline{)\,24}$ (20) $15\overline{)\,45}$

** The teacher stopped the student when he tried to bring down 62 and reminded him to only bring down 1 number. He then successfully completed problems 12-16. The teacher stopped the survey after item 16.

Figure 6-W Multiplication and Division Probe and Student's Response—**Continued**

Probe 2

A Write the fraction that tells how much of the figure is shaded.

1   2   3

Write the fraction that tells how much of the set is shaded.

4   5   6

Write the fraction for the division expression.

7 $3 \div 5$ 8 $1 \div 6$ 9 $8 \div 7$

A

1. 2/3
2. 1/4
3. 5/7
4. 3/4
5. 2/5
6. 4/7
7. 3/5
8. 1/6
9. 8/7

B Write the mixed numeral that tells how many circles are shaded.

1   2 3

Write the mixed numeral for the sum.

4 $3 + \frac{2}{3}$ 5 $7 + \frac{5}{6}$ 6 $2 + \frac{5}{8}$

B

1. 2 2/5
2. 3 1/4
3. 3 3/5
4. _____
5. _____
6. _____

C Write the missing number.

1   2   3

$\frac{2}{3} = \frac{\blacksquare}{6}$ $\frac{6}{8} = \frac{\blacksquare}{4}$ $\frac{4}{12} = \frac{2}{\blacksquare}$

4 $\frac{1}{4} = \frac{\blacksquare}{8}$ 5 $\frac{5}{15} = \frac{1}{\blacksquare}$ 6 $\frac{\blacksquare}{18} = \frac{5}{6}$

7 $\frac{4}{6} = \frac{16}{\blacksquare}$ 8 $\frac{8}{16} = \frac{\blacksquare}{4}$ 9 $\frac{2}{\blacksquare} = \frac{12}{18}$

Write the whole number equivalent to the fraction.

10 $\frac{20}{5}$ 11 $\frac{16}{2}$ 12 $\frac{21}{7}$

C

1. 4/6
2. 6/8
3. 4/12
4. 1/8
5. 1/15
6. 5/18
7. 16/6
8. 8/4
9. 2/18
10. 4
11. 8
12. 3

Figure 6-X Fraction Probe and Student's Response*

*From *diagnosis: an instructional aid; Mathematics Level B, Lab B2.*
© 1980, Science Research Associates, Inc. Reprinted by permission.

Student _Chris_   Teacher _Cornwell_   Date _9/25/81_

ASSESSMENT TASKS	Whole number +	Level known	Whole number −	Level known	Whole number X	Level known	Whole number ÷	Level known	Decimals +	Level known	Decimals −	Level known	Decimals X	Level known	Decimals ÷	Level known	Fractions +	Level known	Fractions −	Level known	Fractions X	Level known	Fractions ÷	Level known
Survey Level _4-2_	1		1		3		3		4		4		5		5		3		3		4		4	
Initial Probe					2	1 x 2 w/regr & cues	3	3 ÷ 1 w/regr & cues									4/2	conc/ same den.	4/2	conc/ same den.				
Further Probe																								
Further Probe																								
Further Probe																								
Further Probe																								
UPDATE																								

Code—Survey and Probe

1 - Skill known

2 - Skill known at lower level

3 - Need more information

4 - Skill not known

5 - Not assessed

Figure 6-Y Assessment to Instruction Data Sheet (Curricular Area: Math Computation)

-find equal fractions using pictures and a number line with 100% accuracy
-compare fractions with different denominators with 90% accuracy
-add and subtract fractions with different denominators with 90% accuracy

Step 12: Start Teaching/Update Assessment Information (Chris)

The teacher planned to have Chris practice the algorithms for long multiplication and division, first by cueing him and then by fading the cues. She planned to create teaching sequences in fractions that moved from concrete representations to more abstract ones. As Chris demonstrated mastery with the various skills, the teacher would update the Assessment to Instruction Data Sheets. She would next introduce decimals and probe in the area of geometry to continue Chris's math program.

ASSESSMENT OF PROBLEM SOLVING

Once the assessment of concepts and computation has been completed, and the teacher has a clear picture of a student's competence level in basic computation algorithms and basic computation facts, the assessment of problem solving can be undertaken. *Problem solving* involves the solution of story problems which describe real or imaginary events and require the application of computation skills, or concepts of time, measurement, money, geometry, and so on in the solution of the problems.

Step 2: Select or Develop a Skill Hierarchy (Problem Solving)

The skill hierarchy presented in Table 6-8 was adapted from the problem-solving and applications components of the scope and sequence charts of the Scott, Foresman and Company and the Macmillan math programs. It is not organized by grade level because, in problem solving, many of the same skills are presented at each grade level, the difference among grades being the computation skill or concept applied, and the complexity of the language used.

There are three levels to the problem-solving hierarchy. At the highest level, the student can solve story problems involving several steps. At each step the student can choose the correct operation from the information given, write the number sentence, apply computation skills to solve the problem, and attach the correct units to the final answer. At the second level, the student can solve two step story problems by selecting the appropriate operation for step one, write the number sentence, apply computation skills and then repeat the entire process for step two, attaching the correct units to the final answer. At the lowest level, the student can solve one-step problems by understanding the language, selecting the correct operation, developing the number sentence, executing the computation, and assigning the correct units to the answer. Again, at each of these levels the story problems may require application of knowledge about math concepts (Table 6-1) in the solution of the problem.

As with concepts and computation, the teacher could use the skill hierarchy shown in Table 6-8 to guide the assessment of problem solving, or develop a skill hierarchy from the scope and sequence chart of a basal math series, or create a skill hierarchy based on the problem solving and application skills he/she expects the student to master.

Table 6-8 Skill Hierarchy in Problem Solving

3. Solve multi-step problems and application tasks*
   a. when unnecessary (distracting) information is provided
   b. when only necessary information is provided

2. Solve two-step problems and application tasks*
   a. when unnecessary (distracting) information is provided
   b. when only necessary information is provided.

1. Solve single-step problems and application tasks*
   a. when unnecessary (distracting) information is provided
   b. when only necessary information is provided

*Typical application tasks may include but are not limited to the following:

1. *Time*
   weather calendar
   time zones
   bus schedules
   time cards

2. *Money*
   comparing money
   spending money
   making change
   checkbook

3. *Measurement*
   calories
   recipes
   map scale
   scale drawings

4. *Geometry*
   puzzles
   blueprints
   Venn diagrams
   classification

5. *Consumer applications*
   reading a menu
   finding sale price
   sales tax
   unit pricing
   cash register tapes
   discounts/interest
   catalog ordering
   installment buying

6. *Leisure time activities*
   magic squares
   codes
   riddles
   sports
   music
   cars
   food
   recreation
   travel

7. *Career application*
   calculators
   statistics
   taxes
   forms

8. *Life-skill applications*
   completing tasks
   using maps
   tallying
   census
   savings accounts
   long distance calling
   order forms
   budgets
   payroll records
   transportation

See Table 6-1 for the approximate grade levels at which these concepts are introduced

Step 3: Decide Where to Begin
(Problem Solving)

The assessment of problem solving will begin at either Step 3, 2 or 1 of the hierarchy, i.e., with either multi-step, two-step or single step problems. Using the information gathered in the assessment of concepts and computation, the teacher would determine whether the student had mastered math concepts and computation skills to the fifth-grade level. If so, the assessment of problem solving would begin at level 1 of the skill hierarchy and would include multi-step problems. If computation skills and concepts are at the third- and fourth-grade levels, only two-step and one-step problem solving would be assessed. If skills are not solidly established at the third-grade level, the assessment of problem solving would begin at level 1 and include only single step problems.

Step 4: Select or Develop Survey Instrument
(Problem Solving)

The problem solving survey should contain two types of problems: story problems appropriate to the student's level in computation, and application tasks matched to the student's skills in math concepts. That is, the survey of problem solving ability, selected or developed by the teacher, should contain only those mathematical computation skills or concepts on which the student has already demonstrated competence. It would be a waste of time to ask a student to solve a word problem requiring subtraction with regrouping, or telling time, if the student could not perform subtraction problems on the computation test or could not do "time" problems on the concepts survey.

The problem-solving survey should also be within the reading capabilities of the student. If the student cannot read the narrative of the story problem, it is unlikely that the teacher will get a valid picture of his/her problem-solving skills. For a student who has adequate reading skills, the issue of reading is not a concern, and a commercially available test like one of those listed in Table 6-9, or subtests of some of those listed in Table 6-3, may be selected. For the student with reading problems,

Table 6-9 Problem-Solving Tests

Source	Publisher	Subskills Measured
Kraner Tests of Mathematics	C.C. Publications	Time, geometry, measurements, money, charts, and graphs
Skills for Arithmetic	The Ohio State University	Measurement and geometry
I.E.P. Educational Diagnostic Inventories	National Center for Learning Disabilities	Statement problems, money, time, measurement
Brigance Diagnostic Inventory of Basic Skills	Curriculum Associates	Money, time, linear measurement, geometry
Brigance Diagnostic Inventory of Essential Skills	Curriculum Associates	Money, time, linear measurement
SRA Diagnosis Kits (Math)	Science Research Associates	Problem solving, measurement, geometry

or for the student whose reading level is considerably lower than his/her math level, certain adjustments will have to be made, especially if a commercially available test is to be used. Most formal tests match the reading level to the mathematics skill level. For example, computation with decimals is typically introduced in fourth or fifth grade, and the word problems in a commercially available test requiring the use of decimals are generally written at a fourth- or fifth-grade reading level. The teacher will need to create a survey, or rewrite a commercially available survey, for any primary age student whose reading score is more than 0.5 grade levels below the math score, for any intermediate age student reading more than 1 grade level below the math score, and for any secondary age student reading more than 2 years below his/her math level. Or, the teacher will have to tape-record the story problems, or arrange to read the problems to the student, so that his/her limited reading skills will not interfere with math performance.

If the teacher chooses to create a survey, he/she should include two to four items involving each type of computation skill at the highest level at which the student has demonstrated competence. For example, if the student can do four-place addition with regrouping, two-place subtraction with regrouping, simple one-digit multiplication and division, and no fractions or decimals, the teacher would develop eight to sixteen story problems, some involving four-place addition, two-place subtraction, simple multiplication, and simple division. There would be no story problems requiring computation of decimals or fractions. Since these computation skills place the student in the third- to fourth-grade levels, there would be some one-step and two-step problems, but no multi-step problems.

If the teacher decides to use a commercially available survey, he/she must review each problem, rewriting those using words too difficult to read and eliminating those involving computations beyond the scope of the student.

Step 5: Get Ready to Test (Problem Solving)

The teacher should prepare one copy of the survey for the student and one copy to be used as the answer key. It is often useful to put the survey onto a ditto master so that all or part of the test can be used at another time as a survey or probe for a different student. As always, the teacher should plan for the student to work in a quiet place and should be prepared to offer motivators in order to elicit the student's best performance.

Step 6: Administer the Survey (Problem Solving)

If the teacher administers a lengthy survey, we suggest giving it in two sittings. The decision to administer the survey in this way will depend upon both the length of the test and the age and attention span of the student being tested.

As with the concepts and computation survey, the teacher may want to administer the survey by remaining with the student. This would allow the teacher to observe the student's work habits, to pace the survey, and to offer help where it is needed.

The student should be reminded to show all his/her work, and to seek help from the teacher if he/she cannot read any of the problems.

If the survey has been tape-recorded, or the teacher is reading the problems aloud, the student should be instructed to follow the printed text as he/she is listening.

Step 7: Note Errors and Performance Style (Problem Solving)

Once the student has completed the survey, each item should be scored as correct or incorrect.

Step 8: Analyze Findings and Summarize Outcomes (Problem Solving)

The survey should be analyzed to determine why the student made the errors.

Problem-solving tasks in mathematics require a step-by-step procedure. The student must read the problem and interpret the language to decide what operation is implied. The student needs to understand the meanings of phrases like "how many more," "distributed evenly," and "twice as many," before he/she can choose the operation to solve the problem. Many students make mistakes on story problem tasks because they cannot read, or, having read correctly, they misinterpet the words and choose the wrong operation.

Next, the student must construct a number sentence using the facts from the problem and the correct operation. Sometimes more information than is necessary to solve the problem is given, often in the form of extra, irrelevant numbers or facts. Some students have difficulty selecting the pertinent information and ignoring the distractors in order to generate the correct number sentence.

An error in a story problem may be the result of carelessness in computation. This type of error should not be the result of an inability to perform the computation task, because only computation skills performed adequately on the computation assessment are to be embedded in word problems.

Finally, the student may not understand how to interpret the answer using the correct units, that is, the student does not really understand whether he/she has traveled 8 hours or 8 miles, has 3 lollipops or 3 girls, and so forth.

In two-step or multi-step problems, the student may perform the first step correctly but be unaware that a second or third step is required. For example, given the following problem:

A store advertises 20% off during a sale. What would be the sale price of an item regularly priced at $42.00?

the student has to be able to calculate 20% of $42.00. He/she must also know that the answer obtained is not the answer to the problem. The correct answer cannot be obtained until the "discount" is subtracted from the regular price to obtain the sale price.

Table 6-10 summarizes the steps involved in solving word problems.

Table 6-10 Sequence of Steps in Solving Word Problems

In single-step problems:
1. Read story problem and understand language.
2. Choose the operation.
3. Write number sentence selecting only necessary information.
4. Apply computation algorithm.
5. Attach correct units to answer.

In multi-step problems, repeat steps 2 to 5 as needed.

Name _____ Date _____

Test items		Performance		Error categories					
Number	Type	Correct	Incorrect	Language	Choosing operation	Number sentence	Computing	Attaching units	Integrating steps

Figure 6-Z Problem-Solving Survey Analysis Form

Figure 6-Z is an example of a recordkeeping form which could be used to summarize the information the teacher gathers from the survey. To complete the form, the teacher would record the number of each problem presented in the survey and identify, in shorthand, each problem by type (one-step, two-step, or multi-step, involving addition, subtraction, multiplication, or division of whole numbers, fractions or decimals/money). Then the teacher would indicate by a checkmark whether each problem was performed correctly or incorrectly. Finally, for each problem done incorrectly, the teacher would mark the steps at which the student seemed to have made mistakes.

Then the survey information would be coded onto the Survey line of an Assessment to Instruction Data Sheet for problem solving (Figure 6-AA).

Step 9: Hypothesize Reasons for Errors and Determine Areas to Probe (Problem Solving)

By completing the Problem Solving Analysis form, the teacher has already made some initial hypotheses regarding the student's errors. As can be seen in Table 6-11, these hypotheses are almost always followed up by a structured interview, used as a probe. For example, if the teacher suspected that the student may not have understood the words which implied the several-step process in multi-step problems, the interview would probe the student's knowledge of the language of the math problems.

If the teacher suspected a language problem, the interview would consist of having the student work some problems aloud, up to the point of telling what operation is required—not working out the number sentence and computing the answer. An interview would also uncover problems in selecting the appropriate information for the number sentence or in attaching the correct units to the problem.

Finally, if the errors were in application tasks, the teacher might conclude that the concepts had not been mastered and might follow up with an interview using lower level concept tasks.

In some cases, however, follow-up testing would be appropriate. For example, if most of the student's errors occurred in multi-step problems, the teacher might suspect that the problem-solving tasks were too complex. Then a probe of simpler one-step problems may be necessary.

If the errors were in choosing the correct operation, the teacher might suspect reading problems. Then, the teacher could readminister the survey by reading each item aloud to the student.

If the teacher suspected computation problems, the next step would be to re-check computation skills.

Step 10: Probe (Problem Solving)

If an interview probe is needed, the teacher would have to construct it on the spot and focus the questioning on the specific concerns raised in the survey. The structured interview is aimed at determining what the student was thinking when he/she solved a particular problem. Often, having the student talk through a problem with the teacher will be more revealing than having the student complete some formal or informal probes.

But if testing probes are needed, these may be found in unit tests of basal math series, in workbooks, or as subtests of formal math tests available commercially. Many of the tests listed in Tables 6-3 and 6-9 provide sources for problem

Name _____ Teacher _____ Date _____

Computation skills known: Reading level: _____

    Addition _____ Concepts known:

    Subtraction _____   Time _____

    Multiplication _____   Money _____

    Division _____   Measurement _____

    Decimals _____   Geometry _____

    Fractions _____   Numeration _____

	Multi-step word problems			Multi-step applications	Two-step word problems			Two-step applications	Single-step word problems			Single-step applications
	Whole Numbers	Fractions	Decimals	Concepts	Whole Numbers	Fractions	Decimals	Concepts	Whole Numbers	Fractions	Decimals	Concepts
Survey												
Initial Probe												
Further Probe												
Further Probe												
Further Probe												
UPDATE												

Code—Survey and Probe

  1 - Skill known   **3** - Need more information

  2 - Skill known at lower level   **4** - Skill not known   **5** - Not assessed

Figure 6-AA Assessment to Instruction Data Sheet
(Curricular Area: Problem Solving)

Table 6-11 Error Types and Hypotheses (Problem Solving)

Error	Hypotheses	Next Step
Multi-step operations	Task too complex Comprehension problem	Choose/create simpler task Interview student
Selecting correct operation	Reading/language problem Comprehension problem	Read problem to student Interview student
Selecting appropriate information	Task too complex Comprehension problem	Choose/create simpler task Interview student
Computation	Carelessness Facts and/or algorithms not know	Provide reinforcers Test down computation hierarchy
Attaching units	Carelessness Comprehension problem	Provide reinforcers Interview student
Application task	Task too complex Comprehension problem Material inappropriate	Choose/create simpler task Interview student Select more familiar material

solving probes. The teacher will have to judge what information would be most useful to gather, and how detailed that information must be.

Step 11: Complete Recordkeeping Forms and Generate Teaching Objectives (Problem Solving)

When probing has been completed, the teacher would complete the Assessment to Instruction Data Sheet for problem solving. This form serves to summarize the areas in which testing has taken place and the areas for which more information is needed. It helps the teacher to keep track of skills known and skills that need to be taught. As before, the Assessment to Instruction Data Sheet guides the teacher's plans for what to teach in the areas of problem solving.

Step 12: Start Teaching/Update Assessment Information (Problem Solving)

The most salient point for the teacher to keep in mind when teaching problem solving is that, as the student's computational skills and concepts increase, problem solving and application tasks which use those skills should be introduced. The integration of computation and problem solving activities will serve a two-fold purpose: students will have practice in more reality-based math tasks, and the usefulness of math will be made more clear to the student.

ILLUSTRATION: CHRIS

The following example follows Chris, the student introduced earlier, as his teacher assessed his skills in problem solving. The example begins with Step 3, because the teacher elected to use the hierarchy presented in Figure 6-8 to guide the assessment.

Step 3: Decide Where to Begin (Chris)

The teacher referred to the information she recorded on Chris in Figures 6-U and 6-Y. She noted that Chris had a grasp of math concepts and computation skills from the first- through the fourth-grade levels. She decided that the assessment of problem solving would involve one- and two-step story problems.

Step 4: Select or Develop Survey Instrument (Chris)

The teacher knew that Chris could handle a variety of addition and subtraction problems, including those requiring regrouping to four digits, but could only do simple multiplication and division problems, and that he had no competence in decimals and fractions. She also reviewed Chris's records and found evidence of fifth-grade reading abilities. Given this spread of ability in computation, she decided to create her own probe.

Figure 6-BB is the problem solving survey the teacher created for Chris. The teacher created story problems which utilize the skills Chris should be able to do, given his present computation and concepts skill levels. The choice of a recipe and train schedule as application tasks were based on Chris's interests and experiences, and on the evidence that he had mastered concepts of measurement and time.

Work these problems. Show your work.

1. A school has 173 students in ninth grade, 166 in tenth grade, 94 in eleventh grade, and 85 in 12th grade. How many students are in the school?   _____

2. In question 1, how many more students are in the 9th grade than in the 12th grade?   _____

3. Judy, Ed, and Terry are going to share a piece of cheese which weighs 71 ounces. How many ounces will each of them get?   _____

4. Karen is painting the steps. If it takes her 21 minutes to paint the first step, how long will it take her to paint 4 steps?
                                                         ____hr. ____min.

Figure 6-BB Problem-Solving and Application Survey

5. Jim spent $17.45 and bought a sweater, a belt, and a tie. The sweater cost $9.95 and the belt cost $5.25. How much did the tie cost?   _____

6. Kevin and Larry had the following recipe for a milkshake:

> Banana-Strawberry Milkshake
>
> serves 1
>
> 1 cup milk
> 2 scoops strawberry ice cream
> 1 banana, cut into pieces
> 6 strawberries, cut in half
>
> Put all the ingredients into a blender and blend on high speed until smooth.

Rewrite the recipe to show how it would read to make 4 milkshakes.

7.   TRAIN SCHEDULE   Philadelphia - New York

Train number	#121	#131	#141	#151	#161	#171	#181	#191	#201
	a.m.	a.m.	a.m.	a.m.	p.m.	p.m.	p.m.	p.m.	p.m.
Philadelphia	6:00	7:05	8:20	10:00	12:20	2:52	4:09	5:00	6:01
Trenton	6:25	7:39	8:53	10:28	1:30	3:20		5:28	6:34
Princeton	6:36	7:49	9:02		1:40			5:36	
New Brunswick	6:58	8:07			1:55	3:50		5:49	
Newark	7:07	8:32	9:38	11:05	2:25	4:00	5:25	6:08	7:20
New York (ar)	7:21	8:47	9:54	11:17	2:42	4:17	5:41	6:22	7:37

a. What time would you leave Philadelphia to arrive in New York at 11:17 a.m.?   _____

b. Which trains do not stop in either Princeton or New Brunswick? _____

c. Which train takes the shortest time to travel between Philadelphia and New York?   _____   the longest time?   _____

d. If I took #171, how long would it take me to travel between New Brunswick and New York?   _____

e. If I live in New Brunswick and want to be home from Philadelphia by 5:00 p.m., what train should I take?   _____

Figure 6-BB Problem-Solving and Application Survey—**Continued**

Step 5: Get Ready to Test (Chris)

First, the teacher made one copy of the survey for Chris and one for herself to use as an answer key. She put the survey on a ditto master, so that she could use all or part of it with another student of similar skill levels. She gave Chris the survey, had him work in a carrel in a quiet corner of the classroom, and told him that he would be permitted to clean the fish tank the following day if he completed the test. She also reminded him to do his best work.

Step 6: Administer the Survey (Chris)

Because the problem-solving survey (unlike the concepts and computation one) does not require that the teacher remain with the student during administration, the teacher had Chris work alone. She knew that Chris would remain on-task when left alone to work, and that the opportunity to clean the fish tank was highly motivating to him.

Step 7: Note Errors and Performance Style (Chris)

When Chris had finished the survey, his teacher scored his performance using the answer key she had made (Figure 6-CC). Then, she completed the Problem Solving Survey Analysis form (Figure 6-DD).

Work these problems. Show your work.

1. A school has 173 students in ninth grade, 166 in tenth grade, 94 in eleventh grade, and 85 in 12th grade. How many students are in the school?

$$\begin{array}{r} 173 \\ 166 \\ 94 \\ 85 \\ \hline 518 \end{array}$$

_518_

2. In question 1, how many more students are in the 9th grade than in the 12th grade?

$$\begin{array}{r} 173 \\ -\ 85 \\ \hline 88 \end{array}$$

_88_

3. Judy, Ed, and Terry are going to share a piece of cheese which weighs 71 ounces. How many ounces will each of them get?

$$\begin{array}{r} 2 \\ 3\overline{)71} \\ 6 \\ \hline 65 \end{array}$$

_2 r. 65_

4. Karen is painting the steps. If it takes her 21 minutes to paint the first step, how long will it take her to paint 4 steps?

$$\begin{array}{r} 21 \\ \times\ 4 \\ \hline 84 \\ 60 \\ \hline 24 \end{array}$$

_1_ hr. _24_ min.

Figure 6-CC Problem-Solving and Application Survey—Student's Response (Chris)

5. Jim spent $17.45 and bought a sweater, a belt, and a tie. The sweater cost $9.95 and the belt cost $5.25. How much did the tie cost?

$2.25

9.95
5.25
15.20

17.45
15.20
2.25

6. Kevin and Larry had the following recipe for a milkshake:

```
Banana-Strawberry Milkshake
                                serves 1

1 cup milk
2 scoops strawberry ice cream
1 banana, cut into pieces
6 strawberries, cut in half

Put all the ingredients into a blender and blend
on high speed until smooth.
```

milk - 4 cups
ice cream - 8 scoops
bananas - 4
strawberries - 24
blend.

Rewrite the recipe to show how it would read to make 4 milkshakes.

7.   TRAIN SCHEDULE   Philadelphia - New York

Train number	#121	#131	#141	#151	#161	#171	#181	#191	#201
	a.m.	a.m.	a.m.	a.m.	p.m.	p.m.	p.m.	p.m.	p.m.
Philadelphia	6:00	7:05	8:20	10:00	12:20	2:52	4:09	5:00	6:01
Trenton	6:25	7:39	8:53	10:28	1:30	3:20		5:28	6:34
Princeton	6:36	7:49	9:02		1:40			5:36	
New Brunswick	6:58	8:07			1:55	3:50		5:49	
Newark	7:07	8:32	9:38	11:05	2:25	4:00	5:25	6:08	7:20
New York (ar)	7:21	8:47	9:54	11:17	2:42	4:17	5:41	6:22	7:37

a. What time would you leave Philadelphia to arrive in New York at 11:17 a.m.?   *10:00*

b. Which trains do not stop in either Princeton or New Brunswick? _____

c. Which train takes the shortest time to travel between Philadelphia and New York? *#121* the longest time? *#201*

d. If I took #171, how long would it take me to travel between New Brunswick and New York? *67 min.*

e. If I live in New Brunswick and want to be home from Philadelphia by 5:00 p.m., what train should I take? *none*

Figure 6-CC Problem-Solving and Application Survey—Student's Response (Chris)—Continued

Name _Chris_   Date _____

| Test items | | Performance | | Error categories | | | | | |
Number	Type	Correct	Incorrect	Language	Choosing operation	Number sentence	Computing	Attaching units	Integrating steps
1	single-step addition	✓						✓	
2	single-step, subtraction	✓						✓	
3	single-step, division		✓				✓	✓	
4	two-step, X & −	✓						✓	
5	two-step, + & −	✓						✓	
6	recipe	✓							
7a	applications— train	✓							
b	"		✓						
c	"		✓						
d	"		✓						
e	"		✓						

Figure 6-DD Problem-Solving Survey Analysis Form (Chris)

Step 8: Analyze Findings and Summarize
Outcomes (Chris)

After analyzing his answers, the teacher noted that Chris chose the operation correctly and applied the computation skills of addition, subtraction, and multiplication in word problems. He failed, however, to attach any units to his responses. His error in problem 3 appeared to be with the division algorithm rather than with the problem solving. Chris had demonstrated this same problem with the division algorithm during the computation survey.

Chris demonstrated errors in one of the application tasks. While he was able to correctly adjust the ingredients in the milkshake recipe, he had considerable difficulty in reading the train schedule. Chris successfully answered the simplest question but did not respond correctly to those items (7b, 7c, 7d, 7e) which require more complex analyses.

The teacher completed the Survey line of an Assessment to Instruction Data Sheet (Figure 6-EE) with the information she had thus far.

Step 9: Hypothesize Reasons for Errors and
Determine Areas to Probe (Chris)

Since Chris made so few errors on the story problems in the survey, the teacher suspected that the problems may have been too simple. She decided to probe at the level of multi-step problems.

She also hypothesized that the errors on the application tasks were not the result of a lack of familiarity with the material. She decided that she must probe Chris's competence in applying concepts of time with an interview, in which she broke the task down into simpler steps and had Chris demonstrate his reasoning.

Step 10: Probe (Chris)

The teacher designed two probes. In the first (Figure 6-FF), she tried to determine whether Chris was able to tell what to do in multi-step problems. She began with two-step problems (there had been one on the survey), then moved to a three-step problem. She determined that he got confused when more than two steps were required.

For the second probe, the teacher returned to survey item 7, which required Chris to read the train schedule. Her probe consisted of an interview with Chris in which she attempted to establish why he had been unsuccessful with certain items. Her interview and Chris's responses are given in Figure 6-GG.

The probe is a good example of how informal the assessment procedure can be. The teacher knew that she would have gathered much less information about Chris if she had given him new application tasks to solve. She understood that probing in problem solving is often more revealing if it consists of a structured interview with the student.

The teacher also knew when to stop probing. When Chris did not understand the concept of 4:00 being the same as 3 hours and 60 minutes, the teacher moved on, knowing that she had discovered a teaching objective.

Name _____Chris_____ Teacher _____Cornwell_____ Date ___9/25/81___

Computation skills known: Reading level: _____5.1 grade_____

   Addition ____highest level____   Concepts known:

   Subtraction ____highest level____   Time ____to minute____

   Multiplication ___2 × 1 without regrp.___   Money ____some concepts____

   Division ____3 ÷ 1 with remainder____   Measurement ___some concepts___

   Decimals ____not known____   Geometry ___some concepts___

   Fractions ____not known____   Numeration___OK___

	Multi-step word problems			Multi-step applications	Two-step word problems			Two-step applications	Single-step word problems			Single-step applications
	Whole Numbers	Fractions	Decimals	Concepts	Whole Numbers	Fractions	Decimals	Concepts	Whole Numbers	Fractions	Decimals	Concepts
Survey	5	5	5	5	1 (X, −) (Time)	5	1 $ (+, −)	3 (Time)	1 (+, −) 4 (÷)	5	5	1(Measurement)
Initial Probe												
Further Probe												
Further Probe												
Further Probe												
UPDATE												

Code—Survey and Probe

  1 - Skill known   3 - Need more information

  2 - Skill known at lower level   4 - Skill not known   5 - Not assessed

Figure 6-EE Assessment to Instruction Data Sheet
(Curricular Area: Problem Solving)

Read the following problems. Tell how many steps are required to solve the problem and describe the operation you would perform for each step. DO NOT WORK THE PROBLEM. Example: List was the winning pitcher in a ball game that lasted 3 hours and 16 minutes. How many minutes did she pitch altogether?

Step	Operation
1	Multiply 3 x 60
2	Add answer from step 1 to 16

1. Allan had $10.00. He bought a book for $1.99, spent $2.75 for lunch and bought a frisbee for $2.10. How much money does he have left?

Step	Operation
1	add $1.99 + 2.75 + 2.10
2	subtract answer from step 1 from $10.00

2. A school bus has 26 rows of seats and 4 people can sit in each row. How many buses will be needed to take 650 students and teachers to the circus? How many seats will be empty?

Step	Operation
1	multiply 26 x 4
2	subtract answer from 650

3. A & P is selling an 8-slice pizza for $1.00 and 2 pizzas for $1.50. The Pizza Hut sells a 14-slice pizza for $1.30. What place offers the better buy? How much better?

Step	Operation
1	subtract 1.30 from $1.50
2	Subtract 14 from 16
3	divide answer from 2 into answer from one.

Figure 6-FF Probe

T: Find the column which shows train #141. What does the blank space beside New Brunswick mean?

S: I don't know.

T: What does the 9:02 beside Princeton mean?

S: That's when the train gets to Princeton.

T: If there is no time beside a station, that means that train does not stop there.

S: You mean trains don't stop at every station.

T: That's right. You can tell if a train stops at a certain station by whether or not there is a time beside the station. What other trains do not stop at every station?

S: 151, 171, 181, and 201

T: Good. Now, of the trains which don't stop everywhere, which ones skip both Princeton and New Brunswick?

S: 151, 181, and 201

T: Why didn't you say #171?

S: Well... because it stops in New Brunswick.

T: Good! Now, tell me how long it would take train #171 to get from New Brunswick to New York?

S: (calculates on scratch paper) 67 minutes.

T: How long would it take train #171 to get from New Brunswick to Newark?

S: 50 minutes

T: What's another way to say 3:50?

S: Ten to four.

T: Right. Now if it's ten to four (or 3:50) in how many minutes will it be 4:00?

S: Ten.

T: Then how could it take 50 minutes for the train to get from New Brunswick to Newark if it leaves New Brunswick at ten to four and arrives in Newark at 4:00?

S: I don't know.

T: I can show you what you are doing wrong. You are subtracting from 100 instead of 60. There are 60 minutes in an hour. So 4:00 is the same as 3:60. If you subtract 3:50 from 3:60, you get 10.

S: I don't understand that.

Figure 6-GG Probe—Interview

T: OK - let's move on and come back to that. Let's say you are coming from Philadelphia and you have a doctor's appointment at 4:00 in New York. Which train would you take to get to New York in time for your appointment?

S: No train gets in at 4:00.

T: Right, so you have to select the train that gets in closer to 4:00 than any other, but not later than 4:00. Which train would that be?

S: #161.

T: Right... but it looks like you don't like that.

S: You get in too early.

T: That's right, but what else can you do if the train is your only choice?

S: I'd buy a car.

T: Right... now tell me what train you would take if you were coming from Princeton and wanted to be in Newark at 12:00?

S: #141 - that's terrible.

T: I agree, but now you can read the schedule to tell how bad it is!

Figure 6-GG Probe—Interview—**Continued**

Step 11: Complete Recordkeeping Forms and Generate Teaching Objectives (Chris)

In Figure 6-HH, the teacher has added the probe data to her Assessment to Instruction Data Sheet for problem solving shown in Figure 6-EE. The teacher is ready to teach those skills marked with a *2* or a *4*. Based on information she gathered, the teacher has created the following teaching objectives for Chris:

1. As his computation skills in long multiplication, division, decimals, and fractions reach pre-established criteria, the student will be able to apply these computational skills in one- and two-step word problems with 90% accuracy.
2. The student will be able to solve multi-step word problems, using known computational skills, with 90% accuracy.
3. The student will use known problem-solving skills in simple application activities with 100% accuracy.
4. The student will use known problem solving skills in increasingly complex application activities with 90% accuracy.

Step 12: Start Teaching/Update Assessment Information (Chris)

Information on the skills noted with a *3* or *5* on the Assessment to Instruction Data Sheet for problem solving will be obtained either through a survey given at a later date or in the course of instructing Chris toward other math objectives. As

Name _Chris_   Teacher _Cornwell_   Date _9/25/81_

Computation skills known: Reading level: _5.1 grade_

Addition _highest level_   Concepts known:

Subtraction _highest level_   Time _to minute_

Multiplication _2 × 1 without regrp._   Money _some concepts_

Division _3 ÷ 1 with remainder_   Measurement _some concepts_

Decimals _not known_   Geometry _some concepts_

Fractions _not known_   Numeration _OK_

	Multi-step word problems			Multi-step applications	Two-step word problems			Two-step applications	Single-step word problems			Single-step applications
	Whole Numbers	Fractions	Decimals	Concepts	Whole Numbers	Fractions	Decimals	Concepts	Whole Numbers	Fractions	Decimals	Concepts
Survey	5	5		5	1 (X,−1) (Time)	5	1 $ (+, −)	3 (Time)	1 (+, −) 4 (÷)	5	5	1 (Measurement)
Initial Probe			4 $		1		1 $	4 (Time)				
Further Probe												
Further Probe												
Further Probe												
UPDATE												

Code—Survey and Probe

1 - Skill known   3 - Need more information

2 - Skill known at lower level   4 - Skill not known   5 - Not assessed

Figure 6-HH Assessment to Instruction Data Sheet (Curricular Area: Problem Solving)

new areas in need of instruction are revealed, they will be added to the list of instructional objectives. As skills are mastered, the recordkeeping form will be updated to reflect the new skills.

SUMMARY

The 12-step strategy of an assessment for instructional planning in mathematics may be cumbersome to an experienced math teacher. Such a teacher may find that by administering either the concepts and computation or problem-solving math surveys one-to-one, he/she can score the survey items as the student completes them and can immediately interrupt the survey with interview questions to understand how answers were obtained. The combination of one-to-one testing, monitoring responses, and interviewing would permit the experienced teacher to combine Steps 6 through 9, and even begin some probing (Step 10) before the survey testing has been completed.

However, we suggest that teachers not do that until they are very familiar with the steps in the assessment strategy. Experienced assessors will know that they are gathering all necessary information and collecting data which will lead to teaching decisions. Teachers new to the assessment strategy may not be so sure. Nevertheless, even new teachers will find that once they are familiar with the procedures outlined in this chapter, they may be able to move through the assessment process more quickly than we have presented it.

7

Assessment of Learning Style, Interest, and Motivators

Assessment for instructional planning has traditionally focused on the cognitive abilities of students. The purpose of the assessment has been to collect information on *what* to teach, and the assessment procedures we have described in the last three chapters were developed to accomplish that purpose. In this chapter we move from an emphasis on *what* to teach to an emphasis on *how* to teach. We will detail some assessment procedures which help the teacher find out under what conditions a student should be taught.

Although there are numerous student characteristics which might affect learning, we have identified three which we feel are of particular significance: the student's *learning style*, the student's *interests*, and the student's response to *motivators*. Attention to these three would influence how the teacher arranges instruction, selects materials, and organizes a management and reinforcement system. Failure to attend to these three might result in inappropriate or negative conditions for learning in which little progress can be realized.

Because we believe that it is part of the teacher's responsibility to design learning environments which maximize the likelihood of each student's achievement, we believe that the assessment of *how* to teach is as important as the assessment of *what* to teach. Therefore, the focus of this chapter is on assessment of students' learning style, interest, and preference for motivators.

We must concede at the outset that there is no irrefutable evidence to support a claim that achievement growth is enhanced when teaching style, materials, and reinforcers are manipulated to match a student's profile. We postulate, however, that the teacher who includes information on *how* to teach in his/her planning will increase the likelihood of students becoming actively involved in the learning process. And the more actively students participate, the greater the opportunity for them to benefit from a remedial program.

In this chapter we will present separately each of the three aspects of assessment of *how* to teach, beginning with learning style. The 12-step procedure for assessment which has guided our discussion in the last few chapters has been modified slightly for this chapter. There are no skill hierarchies to develop for the assessment of learning style, interest, and motivators, so Steps 2 and 3 are omitted. In selecting a survey (Step 4), the teacher relies heavily on observation, interview, and anecdotal recordings of student in-class behavior, instead of on tests to gather initial information. Information on learning style is collected most efficiently through observation. Data on interest and motivators are gathered through questionnaires or structured interviews as well as through observation. Steps 5, 6, and 7 remain intact. Step 5 involves the preparations before administering the survey, Step 6 is the administering of the survey, and Step 7 involves the recording of results. Steps 8 and 9 are combined into a single step. The teacher reviews the results of the survey, hypothesizes why the results were obtained, and determines what further information is needed. Step 10 involves developing, administering, and interpreting probes which the teacher will use to uncover this additional information. Step 11 has the teacher completing recordkeeping forms. And in Step 12, the findings from the assessment of learning style, interest, and motivators are incorporated into teaching plans.

ASSESSMENT OF LEARNING STYLE

Learning style refers to personal differences vis-à-vis learning (Charles, 1980). It is a construct which reflects the notion that, for most of us, learning may be much harder under certain conditions and much easier under other conditions. By "condition" some authors have meant the kinds of instruction delivered (auditory vs. visual, concrete vs. abstract), or the physical characteristics of the learning environment (lighting, temperature, noise), or the social dimension of instruction (size of group, amount of teacher direction). In fact, Dunn and Dunn (1975) have outlined eighteen elements of learning style which they believe are important in understanding the instructional needs of individual students.

While all aspects of learning style may be of interest in a clinical description of the unique learning preferences of each individual student, we believe that it would be impossible for a teacher to attend to all of them in designing remedial instruction. Some aspects of learning style are not easy to change for a single student (e.g., lighting, temperature, or time schedules) and others are based on immutable characteristics of the teacher, the learner, or the environment. Therefore, we have narrowed the focus of the learning style assessment to three interrelated dimensions: size of instructional group; mode of instruction; and frequency and intensity of teacher contacts. We have decided to emphasize these three aspects of learning style because they are amenable to adaptation, and because they have received considerable attention in the literature on effective teaching. We recognize, however, that modifications made in these three dimensions of learning style may not solve a student's learning problem, or they may only succeed in helping to reach a student on one day and not on another, or they may be influenced by factors of which we are unaware at the time of the assessment.

The "size of instructional group" dimension refers to the number of students who are participating in the lesson at one time. Students can be taught in one large group, in several small groups, or individually. Often, teachers introduce a lesson or a new concept to a large group, then assign independent practice or test activities to each of the students, to be performed at his/her desk. Most students can handle the variety in instructional group size and can work adequately under each condition. Other students cannot. They may be unable to follow a lesson given to one large group, or they may be unable to work independently on practice activities. One goal of the assessment of learning style is to determine the size-of-group conditions under which certain students perform best.

Teachers also vary the mode of instruction in ways that can enhance or impede learning for certain students. The mode may be predominantly oral (lecture, verbal questions and answers, tapes), written (text or handouts, written questions and answers, overhead transparencies, chalkboard), or a combination of oral and written activities (films, filmstrips, lecture with chalkboard or transparencies as supplement). The instructional mode may also utilize demonstration, either exclusively or in combination with oral or visual inputs (teacher demonstrates while students observe; teacher demonstrates while students take turns participating; teacher demonstrates and every student does what the teacher does; student or students demonstrate with teacher direction). Most students can learn adequately regardless of the mode, as long as the instruction is explicit and at the appropriate level of difficulty. But some students may have particular difficulty with one or more of these approaches. A second goal of the assessment of learning style is to determine if "mode of instruction" seems particularly important for a given student.

The frequency and intensity of the teacher's involvement can also vary from activity to activity, and is often affected by the size of instructional group. During large-group instruction and individual pencil and paper tasks, students generally receive fewer direct teacher contacts. However, during small-group, teacher-directed activities, students tend to receive more frequent corrective feedback and a greater number of teacher contacts. Most students can adjust their need for teacher presence, teacher involvement, and corrective feedback to the structure the teacher has imposed. But some cannot. They need to feel the teacher's physical presence to stay on-task. They need immediate feedback to avoid making errors. They need teacher direction to move from one step to the next. Therefore, the third goal of the assessment of learning style is to determine whether, for certain students, "frequency and intensity of teacher contacts" is a significant dimension.

Table 7-1 summarizes the three dimensions of learning style with which we will be concerned in the assessment. Information gathered about a particular student's learning style will allow the teacher to make a conscious effort to structure the environment, so that there is a greater likelihood of success for that student. Because information on learning style is needed for all students (Step 1—Decide What to Assess), and because we omit Steps 2 and 3 in the assessment of *how* to teach, our discussion of the assessment procedure begins at Step 4.

Table 7-1   Dimensions of Learning Style

I.   Size of Instructional group
   A. Large-group instruction
   B. Small-group instruction
   C. Individual without teacher
   D. One to one task with teacher

II.   Mode of Instruction
   A. Oral
   B. Written
   C. Combination oral and written
   D. Demonstration

III.   Frequency and Intensity of Teacher Contacts
   A. Teacher present
   B. Teacher involved
   C. Corrective feedback given

Step 4: Select or Develop Survey Instrument (Learning Style)

Assessment of learning style can be accomplished through observation and note-taking. The teacher collects information during a series of teaching situations in which dimensions of group size, mode of instruction, and amount of teacher involvement are varied systematically. The teacher keeps notes on student reactions and student accomplishments under the different conditions. The experienced teacher may find it possible to complete the entire assessment (survey and probes) in a single session—by creating a situation in which one or more conditions can be observed, noting the outcomes for specific students under these conditions, and then changing the conditions systematically and noting changes in student behaviors.

For most teachers, however, we suggest that the assessment be spread out over several lessons. The first lesson would be taught under "normal" conditions, and student behaviors would be noted. Over the next several days, certain dimensions of the learning environment would be changed systematically and student responses noted each time. By the third or fourth lesson, sufficient information should have been gathered for a preliminary analysis of learning style. Assessments of learning style done in this way are records of classroom situations in which the teacher has gathered specific information on students' behavior under particular conditions.

Most surveys of learning style should involve the entire class, although probes may focus on small groups of students or individuals. The teacher would select a particular lesson, taught in a particular way, to serve as the learning style survey, and plan to keep accurate, comprehensive notes on student reactions. The teacher would also establish a criterion level by which to judge successful and unsuccessful performance, so he/she can assess whether the survey condition produces appropriate learning for each student. For example, a teacher of a compensatory English class had twelve seventh- and eighth-grade students during third period and was trying to teach them reference skills. The teacher was uncertain about the extent to which learning style was an important consideration in their achievement. She selected as a survey a dictionary skills task. She usually introduced the skill to the entire group and followed it with a worksheet which was done individually by each student at his/her desk. She established a criterion for success (75% correct on the practice task) to enable her to determine which students had and had not been successful under the standard conditions.

Step 5: Get Ready to Test
(Learning Style)

Once the teacher has chosen the activity which will be used to gather survey information, he/she should prepare a simple recordkeeping form on which to record observed student behaviors. This can be done when the materials for the lesson are being readied. No standard recordkeeping form will be appropriate for all surveys of learning style. Rather, the form should reflect the characteristics of the particular activity being observed. All forms should have a place for writing the subject matter being taught, the survey conditions along each of the three dimensions (size of group, mode of instruction, and intensity of teacher contact), and the student performance under these conditions. Figure 7-A is an example of a Learning Style Survey Observation form.

Step 6: Administer the Survey
(Learning Style)

To administer the survey, the teacher should engage the students in the selected activity in the typical fashion. The compensatory English teacher taught the lesson in her usual way. She introduced the unit on dictionary skills by explaining to the entire group how guide words in the dictionary are organized and used. She took about ten minutes to present the lesson, and had the students refer to the examples on the chalkboard and use the dictionaries at their desks to follow along. She then distributed a worksheet containing twenty vocabulary words and a set of twenty dictionary guide words. The students had fifteen minutes to match the vocabulary words with the appropriate guide words.

Step 7: Note Performance
(Learning Style)

While the students are performing the survey activity, the teacher would record observations on the recordkeeping form. Once the students have completed the task, the teacher would add an indication to his/her notes of whose performance met the established criterion. The completed observation form provides the basis for the analysis of student performance and the determination of next steps. Figure 7-B shows a completed observation form for the dictionary skills survey presented to the students in the compensatory English class.

Survey Conditions: Task: _____

   Size of group: _____   Criterion level: _____

   Mode of instruction: _____

   Teacher involvement: _____   Date: _____

| Student | Survey Results | | Notes | Follow Up Probes—Conditions and Notes | | |
	Number attempted	Number correct		1	2	3

Figure 7-A Learning Style Survey—Observation Form

Survey Conditions:

  Size of group: _lrg grp instr; indep. pract._

  Mode of instruction: _oral_

  Teacher involvement: _minimal_

Task: _Dictionary task_

Criterion level: _75% (15/20)_

Date: _Oct. 14, 1981_

| Student | Survey Results | | Notes | Follow Up Probes—Conditions and Notes | | |
	Number attempted	Number correct		1	2	3
Gretchen	19	4	stayed with task—didn't understand?			
Bob	20	18	OK			
Michael	20	20	OK			
Yvonne	17	6	attempted task—understanding			
Karl	20	8	attempted task—understanding?			
Jerry	19	5	attempted task—understanding?			
Lee	20	16	OK			
Allan	5	5	barely tried, but those done are OK			
June	20	16	OK			
Bill	20	15	OK			
George	7	5	barely tried, but got most right			
Martha	3	3	barely tried, but those done OK			

Figure 7-B Learning Style Survey—Observation Form Example

Steps 8 and 9: Analyze Findings and Determine Areas to Probe (Learning Style)

Based on the findings from the survey, the teacher would determine who was successful on the task under the survey conditions. The performances of those students who were not successful would be reviewed carefully to try to establish whether the failure could be attributed to size of group, mode of instruction, or intensity of teacher contact. For these unsuccessful students, follow-up probes in which the teacher alters one, two, or all three dimensions of the task would need to be developed. The teacher would rate the effects on students' performance. Table 7-2 summarizes the hypotheses which a teacher might consider in designing follow-up probes for the unsuccessful students.

In the example that we have been following, the recordkeeping form in Figure 7-B shows that seven of the students did not meet the success criterion established by the teacher. Four of the students (Gretchen, Yvonne, Karl, and Jerry) attempted to complete the task but made many errors. Three other students (Allan, George, and Martha) completed very few of the items but were successful with those they did complete. The teacher decided to explore further the effects of size of group, mode of instruction, and intensity of teacher contact on student performance. After consulting Table 7-2, she decided to get some sense of how the seven unsuccessful students respond to small group instruction. For those whose performance did not improve with small groups, she would continue to probe using one-to-one instruction. The change in size of group also changed the intensity of teacher contact. The teacher decided not to change mode of instruction until the effects of the changes in the other two dimensions were clearer.

Step 10: Probe (Learning Style)

Having decided whose performance to probe and what dimensions to vary, the teacher would design some new lessons to be carried out over the next several days. After each lesson, the teacher would note on the recordkeeping form the conditions under which the lesson was taught and the student behaviors and performances observed.

The teacher of the compensatory English class decided to probe two groups of students separately. The first group would be made up of the four students who attempted to complete the task but made many errors; the second group would be the three students who did very few problems but were accurate on those they completed. She called the first group—Gretchen, Yvonne, Karl and Jerry—to a table in the rear of the classroom, and she re-explained the lesson on dictionary skills. In the small group setting, Gretchen and Karl seemed to understand the lesson. They returned to their seats, ready to complete the worksheet.

Jerry and Yvonne remained with the teacher. The teacher asked Yvonne to work on another task, and, sitting alone with Jerry, she went through the lesson and the worksheet one more time. Now that she was able to maintain Jerry's attention throughout the lesson, she found that he finally understood the task. He remained at the table with her (in case he needed further support) as he completed the rest of the worksheet. The teacher then worked individually with Yvonne. After a few minutes, it became clear that Yvonne could not alphabetize and that the task was simply too difficult for her. During this time, Jerry had asked several questions of the teacher, Karl had completed the task without too much difficulty, and Gretchen had worked but had completed only seven items correctly.

Table 7-2 Hypotheses and Next Steps for Assessment of Learning Style

Survey Conditions	Hypothesis	Next Step
Size of Group		
Large-group instruction	Directions confusing Pace too fast Social envrionment threatening	Try small group
Small-group instruction	Pace too fast Social environment threatening	Try one-to-one
Individual task without teacher	Distracted/inattentive Directions confusing Needs reinforcement/ encouragement	Try one-to-one

One to one task
with teacher
	Does not have prerequisite
	   skills for subject
	   matter
		Try easier task
		Review academic
		   assessment data

Mode of Instruction		
Oral	Inattentive Needs visual cues Pace too fast	Try visual cues Try different size group
Visual	Inattentive Needs auditory cues Pace too fast	Try auditory cues Try different size group
Combined	Overstimulated Inattentive Pace too fast	Try different size group Vary questioning techniques

Demonstration	Needs auditory or
	   visual cues
	Inattentive
	Pace too fast
		Break instruction into
		   smaller units

Frequency and Intensity of Teacher Contacts		

Teacher gives directions
General corrective
   feedback
No specific individual
   feedback
	Environment too
	   unstructured
	Needs individual attention
		Try small group task
		Try teacher monitoring
		Try immediate feedback

Teacher monitors
   performance
Gives feedback
	Task too difficult	Try easier task
		Review academic
		   assessment data

Teacher present No feedback	Needs reassurance Task too difficult	Try feedback Try easier task
Student-directed Independent No feedback	Cannot work independently Needs more structure	Try teacher monitoring Try feedback

Survey Conditions:

Size of group: *lrg grp instr; indep. pract.*

Mode of instruction: *oral*

Teacher involvement: *minimal*

Task: *Dictionary task*

Criterion level: *75% (15/20)*

Date: *Oct. 14, 1981: Oct. 15*

Small group or indiv. reteach

Student	Survey Results		Notes	Follow Up Probes— Conditions and Notes		
	Number attempted	Number correct		1	2	3
Gretchen	19	4	*stayed with task— didn't understand?*	*still unsuccess, need > info*		
Bob	20	18	*OK*			
Michael	20	20	*OK*			
Yvonne	17	6	*attempted task— understanding?*	*lacked prerequis., no info on L.S.*		
Karl	20	8	*attempted task— understanding?*	*improves with small grp instr.*		
Jerry	19	5	*attempted task— understanding?*	*needs 1:1 and direct tchr contact*		
Lee	20	16	*OK*			
Allan	5	5	*barely tried, but those done are OK*			
June	20	16	*OK*			
Bill	20	15	*OK*			
George	7	5	*barely tried, but got most right*			
Martha	3	3	*barely tried, but those done OK*			

Figure 7-C Learning Style Survey—Observation Form (First Probe)

With the probing of this group of four students completed, the teacher recorded her actions and her observations of the students on the probes section of the Learning Style Survey Observation form (Figure 7-C).

On the next day, she gathered her follow-up information on the second group of students. She gave Allan, George, and Martha another copy of the

Survey Conditions:

Task: *Dictionary task*

Size of group: *lrg grp instr; indep. pract.*

Criterion level: *75% (15/20)*

Mode of instruction: *oral*

Teacher involvement: *minimal*

Date: *Oct. 14, 1981: Oct. 15: Oct. 16*

Small group or indiv. reteach

| Student | Survey Results | | Notes | Follow Up Probes—Conditions and Notes | | |
	Number attempted	Number correct		1	2	3
Gretchen	19	4	stayed with task— didn't understand?	still unsuccess, need > info		
Bob	20	18	OK			
Michael	20	20	OK			
Yvonne	17	6	attempted task— understanding?	lacked prerequis, no info on L.S.		
Karl	20	8	attempted task— understanding?	improves with small grp instr.		
Jerry	19	5	attempted task— understanding?	needs 1:1 and direct tchr contact		
Lee	20	16	OK			
Allan	5	5	barely tried, but those done are OK		improves in quiet area, no distrac- tions	
June	20	16	OK			
Bill	20	15	OK			
George	7	5	barely tried, but got most right		still unsuccess, need > info	
Martha	3	3	barely tried, but those done OK		improves in small grp with tch contact	

Figure 7-D Learning Style Survey—Observation Form (Second Probe)

worksheet, asking them to try it again at a table with no one else around. Martha went right to work, but Allan and George did not. The teacher asked Allan to move to a carrel to do the sheet, and sat down beside George to offer assistance. At the end of the period, she added her new findings to those of the previous day (Figure 7-D). She concluded that Karl, Jerry, Allan, and Martha were able to meet the success criterion for the task after specific conditions had been changed for each of them. Gretchen, Yvonne, and George continued to be unsuccessful. The teacher knew that Yvonne's lack of success was due to her lack of prerequisite skills for the task, and the teacher had, therefore, discovered *what* to teach Yvonne but not *how*. She also noted that she needed more information about Gretchen's and George's learning styles.

Step 11: Complete Recordkeeping Forms (Learning Style)

Once the teacher has manipulated the conditions of the task, has gathered preliminary and follow-up information on students, and has recorded his/her observations on the Learning Style Survey Observation form, one final recordkeeping

Figure 7-E Summary of Information (Learning Style)

STUDENTS		Size of instructional group				Mode of instruction				Frequency and intensity of teacher contacts					
										Proximity		Contact		Feedback	
		Large group	Small group	Individual without teacher	1:1 with teacher	Oral	Written	Combination O & W	Demonstration	Minimal	Considerable	Minimal	Considerable	Minimal	Considerable
Gretchen	?	X	✓	X		✓				X	✓		?		?
Bob		✓				✓				✓		✓		✓	
Michael		✓				✓				✓		✓		✓	
Yvonne	?														
Karl		X	✓	✓		✓				X	✓	✓		✓	
Jerry		X	X	X	✓	✓				X	✓	X	✓	X	✓
Lee		✓				✓				✓		✓		✓	
Allan		X	X	✓		✓				✓		✓		✓	
June		✓				✓				✓		✓		✓	
Bill		✓				✓				✓		✓		✓	
George	?	X			X	?					?		?		?
Martha		X	✓	✓		✓				✓		✓		✓	

✓ - Works to criterion under these conditions
? - Need more information
X - Does not work to criterion under these conditions
Blank - Not assessed

form should be completed. On it the teacher notes for whom conditions of learning seem to make a significant difference, and what particular conditions seem to enhance performance. Figure 7-E shows this Summary of Information—Learning Style form completed for the students in the compensatory English class.

Step 12: Incorporate Findings into Teaching Plans (Learning Style)

The teaching plan for each student should include information on both what to teach and how to teach it. Learning style is assessed so that the teacher can identify the conditions under which the student is "easier to teach" and therefore more likely to learn, and the conditions under which the student is "harder to teach" and therefore less likely to profit from instruction.

In making use of learning style information, the teacher need not necessarily change the classroom conditions for everyone, but may choose to alter some specific procedures for some specific students. For example, in the compensatory English class, the teacher continued to present information to the total group, although she was aware that Karl, Jerry, Allan, and Martha might require some reteaching. She continued to assign practice assignments to be done independently, understanding that Martha, and especially Jerry, would probably need extra teacher contacts and that Allan would need to work without distraction whenever possible.

ILLUSTRATION: MR. SIMON'S CLASS

The following scenario shows how one teacher applied the modified 12-step strategy to an assessment of learning style. It involves Mr. Simon's class of twelve intermediate-age learning-disabled students. Mr. Simon had observed that most of his students did not complete their assignments to his satisfaction and that some of the students required attention from him or from other students to stay on-task during independent work. He decided that he needed more information on learning style, particularly with respect to the dimension of intensity of teacher contacts. Because he had decided to assess learning style (Step 1), and because Steps 2 and 3 are omitted, the illustration begins with Step 4.

Step 4: Select or Develop Survey Instrument (Mr. Simon's Class)

Mr. Simon decided to survey learning style by giving his students an independent assignment to complete. As they worked, he would observe them and take notes on their performance. Mr. Simon selected a creative writing assignment that he knew his students would be able to perform, and he set aside twenty minutes for that task. He chose this particular assignment for the survey because it provided him with an opportunity to observe the conditions under which students were successful or unsuccessful.

Step 5: Get Ready To Test (Mr. Simon's Class)

Mr. Simon chose a time when all the students were in the class. He prepared a recordkeeping form (Figure 7-F) on which he would make notes under

Survey Conditions:

Size of Group: _____

Mode of Instruction: _____

Teacher Involvement: _____

Task: _____

Criterion: _____

Date: _____

Students	Time required for task	Seeks help from teacher	Requires corrective feedback	Works independently	Completes task

Figure 7-F Learning Style Survey—Observation Form

the following headings: time required for the task; seeks help from the teacher; requires corrective feedback; works independently; completes task. Mr. Simon's version of a Learning Style Survey Observation form fit the learning style survey task he had decided upon. While it differed from the form used by the compensatory English teacher, it was appropriate for Mr. Simon's purposes. He had a clock handy so he could see how much time each student took to complete the task.

Step 6: Administer the Survey
(Mr. Simon's Class)

Mr. Simon administered the survey by assigning the topic "What I Would Do If I Were Principal for a Day" to his students. He explained that the students would have twenty minutes to do the assignment and that he would grade the papers solely on the basis of the ideas and the creativity with which the ideas were presented. He distributed writing materials, then sat at his desk with the blank observation form.

Step 7: Note Performance
(Mr. Simon's Class)

Mr. Simon noted his findings in the following manner: "Time required for the task" was recorded as each student handed in his or her completed paper. "Seeks help from the teacher" was checked if a student requested teacher direction. If the student also requested corrective feedback (as indicated by questions such as "Am I doing this right?" or "Is this the right spelling?"), the teacher marked in that column as well. Students were given "yes" for working independently if they did not attempt to disturb or question their peers and/or if the help they sought from the teacher was appropriate to the task. "Completes task" was recorded after Mr. Simon had read the papers and had determined if the task was completed to his satisfaction.

Figure 7-G shows the completed survey observation form for Mr. Simon's class.

Steps 8 and 9: Analyze Findings
and Determine Areas to Probe
(Mr. Simon's Class)

Mr. Simon decided to reorganize the information shown in Figure 7-G by separating the students who were successful (those who completed the task) from those who were unsuccessful (those who did not complete the task). Figure 7-H shows how he reorganized the information.

Next, he analyzed the findings to try to draw some conclusions. He noticed that of the twelve students in the class, only four completed the assignment to his satisfaction. None of these students completed the task in less than ten minutes (but three of the students who worked for more than ten minutes did not complete the task). While not all students who requested teacher help required corrective feedback, the need for such feedback was demonstrated by one of the four students who completed the task, and by three of the eight who did not. Of the four students who completed the task, three had been observed to be working independently, and five of the eight who did not complete the task had been working independently.

Mr. Simon now made some general observations about the differences and similarities between the two groups. The students who were successful stayed on-task nearly twice as long as those who were not. In each group, however, there were students who needed help from the teacher and those who did not; there were students who worked independently and those who did not; and there were students who required corrective feedback and those who did not.

Mr. Simon decided he would look more closely at those eight students who were unsuccessful to try to uncover the important dimensions of their learning styles.

Survey Conditions:

Task: _Creative Writing_

Size of Group: _(large grp): independent work_

Criterion: _20 min.: creative_

Mode of Instruction: _written_

Teacher Involvement: _minimal_

Date: _Nov. 9, 1981_

Students	Time required for task	Seeks help from teacher	Requires corrective feedback	Works independently	Completes task
Abby	12 min	I	0	yes	yes
Brian	16 min	0	0	yes	no
Chuck	3 min	IIII	III	yes	no
Ellen	13 min	0	0	no	no
Harriet	4 min	II	I	no	no
Ira	6 min	III	0	yes	no
Jackie	12 min	II	0	no	yes
Ken	3 min	++++ II	III	no	no
Lee	7 min	I	0	yes	no
Monica	12 min	0	0	yes	yes
Nick	10 min	III	0	yes	no
Peter	20 min	II	II	yes	yes

Figure 7-G Learning Style Survey—Observation Form (Mr. Simon's Class)

Completed task	Time in minutes	Seeks help	Feedback	Independent
Abby	12	1	0	yes
Jackie	12	3	0	no
Monica	12	0	0	yes
Peter	20	2	2	yes
Did not complete task				
Brian	16	0	0	yes
Chuck	3	4	3	yes
Ellen	13	0	0	no
Harriet	4	2	1	no
Ira	6	3	0	yes
Ken	3	7	3	no
Lee	7	1	0	yes
Nick	10	3	0	yes

Figure 7-H Reorganization of Survey Observation Data (Mr. Simon's Class)

He reviewed the survey information one more time. He found that five students (Brian, Ellen, Ira, Lee, and Nick) requested no corrective feedback and sought help from the teacher only a few times. Five other students (Chuck, Harriet, Ira, Ken, and Lee) had been unable to stay on-task for (at least) ten minutes. Another five (Brian, Chuck, Ira, Lee, and Nick) had worked independently but were not successful. Based on the overlap among the dimensions surveyed, Mr. Simon decided to create a single follow-up task for all eight students, in which he would observe the effect on student performance of increased teacher presence, increased number of teacher contacts, and a move from an individual to a small group activity.

Step 10: Probe (Mr. Simon's Class)

Bringing the eight students together, Mr. Simon assigned them a writing task with the following directions: Each student was to write a four-sentence paragraph describing his/her favorite holiday. Students were to raise a hand after finishing each sentence so the teacher could check it. Students were permitted to pair up with one another to exchange ideas and/or to seek help. Mr. Simon decided to put no time limit on the activity, because he had already limited the number of sentences to be completed for the task. As students raised their hands, Mr. Simon read their sentences, corrected them, and encouraged the students to continue. He then noted the following results on an observation form he created for recording follow-up findings (Figure 7-I). Within fifteen minutes, all of the students, except Ken and Chuck, had completed the assignment. Two students (Ellen and Nick) had written more than was required. Three students (Brian, Lee, and Nick) had stopped raising their hands after they had completed the second sentence of the assignment. None of the students actually "paired up," but Ellen and Ira, and Lee and Nick had talked to one another as they worked.

Mr. Simon drew the following tentative conclusions: He would have to probe further with Chuck and Ken. Not all the students seemed to need the additional feedback, the limited task, and/or the small group, but none of the conditions

Conditions:

Size of group: *Independent—with option for small group*

Mode of instruction: *Written*

Teacher involvement: *Considerable*

Task: *Write 4 sentences: get corrective feedback after each*

Criterion: *Complete task (check at 15 min.)*

Students	At 15 min. completed task	Conditions of Learning		
		Uses feedback	Uses task structure	Prefers small group
Brian	yes	at first, then not	yes	no
Chuck	no	–	–	–
Ellen	yes	yes	goes beyond	yes
Harriet	yes	yes	yes	no
Ira	yes	yes	yes	yes
Ken	no	–	–	–
Lee	yes	at first	yes	yes
Nick	yes	at first	goes beyond	yes

Figure 7-I Learning Style Observation Data Probe (Mr. Simon's Class)

had a negative impact on the six students who were able to achieve success with the probe.

Step 11: Complete Recordkeeping Forms
(Mr. Simon's Class)

Mr. Simon completed a Summary of Information—Learning Style form for his whole class, to assist him in making decisions about how to organize his teaching. His notes are shown in Figure 7-J.

STUDENTS	Large group	Small group	Individual without teacher	1:1 with teacher	Oral	Written	Combination O & W	Demonstration	Proximity Minimal	Proximity Considerable	Contact Minimal	Contact Considerable	Feedback Minimal	Feedback Considerable
Abby			✓			✓			✓		✓			
Brian		X	✓			✓				✓		✓		?
Chuck ?														
Ellen		✓	X			✓				✓		?		✓
Harriet		X	✓			✓				✓		✓		✓
Ira		✓	X			✓				✓		✓		✓
Jackie			✓			✓			✓		✓			
Ken ?														
Lee		✓	X			✓				✓		✓		?
Monica			✓			✓			✓		✓			
Nick		✓	X							✓		?		?
Peter			✓			✓			✓		✓			

Conditions of Learning — Size of instructional group — Mode of instruction — Frequency and intensity of teacher contacts

✓ - Works to criterion under these conditions
? - Need more information
X - Does not work to criterion under these conditions
Blank - Not assessed

Figure 7-J Summary of Information (Learning Style) (Mr. Simon's Class)

Step 12: Incorporate Findings into Teaching
Plans (Mr. Simon's Class)

Based on the information gathered from the survey and the follow-up probe, Mr. Simon made the following decisions. During large group activities, he would encourage students to work together if they wished to. He would limit the time and scope of independent assignments for Brian, Harriet, Ira, and Lee, who seemed to need more teacher contact than the others. Ellen and Nick would be observed in this area. More corrective feedback would be built into tasks for Ellen, Harriet, and Ira. Brian, Lee, and Nick would be observed further in this area. More information on learning style would be gathered on Chuck and Ken.

The learning style information gathered by Mr. Simon will be useful in two ways. First, Mr. Simon can now create situations in which students can be successful. Second, he can develop some long term plans to slowly change his students' behaviors. He can guide Ellen, Harriet, and Ira to be more self-directing and to delay their need for teacher feedback. He can gradually increase the length of assignments for Brian, Harriet, Ira, and Lee. He can teach Ellen, Ira, Lee, and Nick to work more independently.

ASSESSMENT OF INTEREST

The purpose of the assessment of students' *interests* is to provide the teacher with some direction for developing lessons that engage students in the learning process. Teachers who have some flexibility in the use of instructional materials can identify topics which interest a student and use this information to select appropriate materials. Or, information on interest can be used to make rote or drill work more appealing by pairing the routine tasks with effective reinforcers.

Information on interest will be needed for all students (Step 1), and, since we omit Steps 2 and 3 in our assessment of *how* to teach, we will begin our discussion of assessment of interest at Step 4.

Step 4: Select or Develop Survey Instrument
(Interest)

Information on interest can be gathered through the use of questionnaires and/or observation. Questionnaires require students to respond to items about themselves. They can be administered as pencil and paper tasks done independently by the students or as interviews, with the teacher asking the questions and recording the student's responses.

Observation requires that the teacher observe a student making choices. The teacher may create the situation; for example, the teacher might give the student free time, and observe and record what he/she elects to do. Or, the teacher may simply record anecdotally, whenever information on student interest presents itself in the natural course of events. Most teachers will use a combination of questionnaires and observation of contrived and natural situations to gather information on students' interests.

Several published interest surveys or inventories which are available for teachers to use or adapt are listed in Table 7-3. Figure 7-K is an example of one of them—a reading interest inventory developed by Fry (1977). Depending on the

Table 7-3 Interest and Reinforcement Inventories

Alexander Interest Inventory

Alexander, J. E. (Ed.) *Teaching Reading.* Boston: Little, Brown, 1979, pp. 333-334.

A Children's Reinforcement Survey Schedule

Phillips, D., Fischer, S. C., and Singh, R. *Journal of Behavior Therapy and Experimental Psychiatry,* 1977, *8,* 131-134.

Edwards Personal Preference Schedule

Edwards, A. *Edwards Personal Preference Schedule.* New York: Psychological Corporation. 1959.

Intermediate Interest Inventory

LaPray, M. H. *On the Spot Reading Diagnosis File.* New York: Center for Applied Research in Education, Inc., 1978.

Kuder Personal Preference Record

Kuder, R. *Kuder Personal Preference Record.* Chicago: Science Research Associates, 1954.

Methods of Identifying Potential Reinforcers for Children

Blackman, G. J. and Silverman, A. *Modification of Child and Adolescent Behavior.* Belmont, Calif.: Wadsworth, 1975.

Primary Interest Inventory

LaPray, M. H. *On the Spot Reading Diagnosis File.* New York: Center for Applied Research in Education, Inc., 1978.

Reading Interest Inventory

Fry, E. *Elementary Reading Instruction.* New York: McGraw Hill, 1977, p. 222.

The Reinforcement Inventory

Steller, J., Vasa, S., and Little, J. *Introduction to Diagnostic-Prescriptive Teaching and Programming.* Glen Ridge, N.J.: Exceptional Press, 1976.

Reinforcement Surveys

Swanson, H. L. and Reinert, H. R. *Teaching Strategies for Children in Conflict.* St. Louis: C. V. Mosby, 1979.

School Interest Inventory

Cottle, W. *School Interest Inventory.* Boston: Houghton Mifflin, 1966.

School Motivation Analysis Test

Sweney, A., Cattell, R., and Krug, S. *School Motivation Analysis Test.* Champaign, Ill.: Institute for Personality and Ability Testing, 1970.

Strong-Campbell Interest Inventory

Campbell, D. P. *Strong-Campbell Interest Inventory.* Stanford, Calif.: University of Stanford Press, 1974.

Upper Grade Interest Inventory

LaPray, M. H. *On the Spot Reading Diagnosis File.* New York: Center for Applied Research in Education, Inc., 1978.

My name is _____

I am _____ years old.

Outside of school the thing I like to do best is _____

_____

In school the thing I like best is _____

If I had a million dollars I would _____

When I grow up I will _____

I hate _____

My favorite animal is _____

The best sport is _____

When nobody is around I like to _____

The person I like best is _____

Next summer I hope to _____

My father's work is _____

My mother's work is _____

When I grow up I will be _____

I like to collect _____

The things I like to make are _____

My favorite place to be is _____

The best book I ever read is _____

The best TV show is _____

What's funny? _____

Figure 7-K   Reading Interest Inventory*

student's age and experiences, a survey such as this one may be useful. Alternatively, using published materials as a guide, the teacher could delete and/or add questions to make a survey particularly appropriate for his/her students. Whether the survey is selected, adapted, or created, it should be quite specific, so that the teacher gathers the information he/she needs.

If the teacher were interested in finding appropriate reading material, the survey in Figure 7-K would be fine. However, if the teacher wanted to determine what would be suitable free time activities for students, the teacher-made survey found in Figure 7-L would be more helpful. To develop it, the teacher first listed

*Reprinted from: Fry, E., *Elementary Reading Instruction.* New York: McGraw-Hill Book Co., 1977, p. 222.

Check the things you like to do during free time.

____1. Play games	____Scrabble	____Battleship
	____checkers	____Othello
	____chess	____Backgammon
____2. Read books	____animal stories	____space/sci-fi
	____sports stories	
	____adventure stories	
____3. Read magazines	____sports	____Mad
	____cars	____TV/movie
	____comic books	____news
____4. Use AV equipment	____tapes	____record player
	____filmstrips	____typewriter
____5. Make things	____puzzles	____erector set
	____lego	____models
	____lincoln logs	____art projects
____6. Help the teacher	____clean boards	____run dittos
	____water plants	____clean fish bowl

____7. List other things you would like to do during free time.

_____   _____   _____

_____   _____   _____

Figure 7-L Teacher-Made Survey of Free-Time Interests

possible free time activities available within the classroom and then created a multiple choice worksheet. Observation could also have provided the teacher with the same information on free time interests. The teacher could have observed the students as they chose activities during several free time periods and noted the activities and materials chosen by each.

Step 5: Get Ready to Test (Interest)

If the teacher is going to use a pencil and paper survey, he/she will need sufficient copies of the task for all the students. The teacher will have to decide whether to read the survey to the students, to have the students work independently, or to interview the students one at a time. If the students have reading skills below the fourth-grade level, the teacher should be prepared to read the survey aloud to the group of students as they follow along and mark their responses. If students can read at or above the fourth-grade level, they can probably work at the survey independently. The teacher will have to be certain that the reading level of the survey (particularly one that is commercially available) is well within the capabilities of the students. If the students are very poor readers, or newcomers to this teacher's class, the teacher will probably want to treat the survey instrument as an interview. In that case the teacher will have to schedule meetings with individual students to complete the survey.

If the interest survey will take the form of an observation, the teacher will have to schedule activities into the lesson plan that would give him/her the information being sought. The teacher will also have to create a recordkeeping form to permit easy recording of the activities students engage in. Figure 7-M is an example of a form developed by a teacher who plans to assess interest by observing students during free time activities. The teacher planned to offer the students several possible choices each day and to note the choices they made.

Step 6: Administer the Survey (Interest)

Survey administration will depend upon the type of survey chosen. If a questionnaire is to be completed by the entire group, the teacher should clearly explain the purpose for the activity and be available to answer questions and explain items. If the survey is to be administered as a one-to-one interview, the teacher will have to plan to involve the other students in independent activities while he/she is

Teacher _____Jones-LD_____   Date _____Sept. 22_____

Students	Games	Books	Magazines	A-V	Make Things
Kevin					
Larry					
Scott					
Mark					
Richard					
Eric					
Jeff					
Andrew					
Barry					

Figure 7-M   Observation Form (Free-Time Interests)

interviewing. For an observation, the teacher will need to create the situation, then observe and note students' choices and activities in an unobtrusive manner.

Step 7: Note Performance (Interest)

If the teacher has used a pencil and paper survey (completed by either the students or the teacher), each student's survey itself is a recordkeeping form. However, the teacher may want to condense the information onto a single chart to make analysis easier.

If the teacher has surveyed by observing the students in some activity, the observation form on which the information was recorded may serve as a summary sheet as well (Figure 7-N).

Steps 8 and 9: Analyze Findings and Determine Areas to Probe (Interest)

Probing in the area of interest will be necessary only if the survey has not yielded sufficient information, or if the data from the survey need to be confirmed. In the example shown in Figure 7-N, the teacher may want to probe with Scott and Barry, Scott because he chose so few things that he wanted to do, and Barry because he seemed tempted by every possible choice. It is clear that, in these two cases, the survey did not provide enough useful information, and a follow-up is needed.

If the teacher feels that it is necessary to confirm the survey information for the whole class or for a few target students, a pencil and paper survey may be followed by an observation, or an observation may be followed by a questionnaire.

Teacher _____ Jones-LD _____ Date _____ Sept. 22 _____

Students	Games	Books	Magazines	A-V	Make Things
Kevin	Checkers Battleship	no	no	all A-V	Art Projects Lego Logs Erector Set
Larry	Checkers Backgammon	sci-fi	Mad	tape recorders	no
Scott	Checkers	no	no	no	Art materials
Mark	Scrabble Othello	sports adventure	sports	tapes	Art projects Lego
Richard	Chess Scrabble	space adventure	Mad news	all A-V	no
Eric	Checkers Chess Backgammon	all books	Mad news sports	typewriter	puzzles
Jeff	Scrabble Checkers	sports adventure	comics sports	tapes records	all
Andrew	Othello Battleship	no	comics	tapes	Art projects Lego
Barry	all games	all books	all magazines	all A-V	all

Figure 7-N Summary of Information (Free-Time Interests)

Step 10: Probe (Interest)

The probes should look very different from the survey. If the student worked independently on the survey, the teacher should probe using a face-to-face interview. If the survey asked general questions, the probe should be more specific.

In the case of Scott, who was observed to make few choices of tasks during the free time survey, the teacher would want to have an informal conversation with him to try to determine the types of activities that are really of interest to him. The teacher would also want to interview Barry, in order to get him to be more specific about his choices. Or, a probe for Barry might consist of having him complete a form on which he orders, by rank, his favorite games, types of books, magazines, and so on.

Step 11: Complete Recordkeeping Forms (Interest)

Once the teacher has gathered more specific information or data which corroborate the survey findings, that new information should be added to the recordkeeping form on which survey data were summarized. For example, at this point the teacher could update Figure 7-J to reflect the new information gathered on Scott and Barry in the probes. No new forms need to be created, as long as the teacher has maintained a record of the interests of each student in the class.

Step 12: Incorporate Findings into Teaching Plans (Interest)

The purpose of assessing students' interests is to use the information in developing teaching plans. Interest information is very easily incorporated into instruction in reading. An adolescent who is interested in cars, but who has very poor reading skills, may not perceive a need for learning to read until he/she is presented with a driver's manual and realizes that reading will be needed in order to earn a license. A student who is interested in science fiction might balk at learning traditional sight words but might be willing to learn sight words which are related to science fiction. With a little thought, math and written expression activities can also be made more attractive to students by incorporating information on interest areas into teaching plans. Sports, card and dice activities, cooking, and consumer tasks are all appropriate tasks for mathematics teaching. Writing projects, such as composing letters for "giveaways," to one's Congressman or "to the editor," publishing a classroom newspaper, completing application forms, or creating a radio show, may entice otherwise reluctant students into participating in writing tasks.

If the information gathered in the assessment of interest is to be used, the teacher must be willing to substitute an unusual activity for a more traditional one. The advantage will be that the reluctant student is more likely to participate in the unusual and interesting task.

ILLUSTRATION: MS. PATTON'S CLASS

The following example shows how Ms. Patton applied the modified 12-step strategy for an assessment of interest. Ms. Patton's middle school learning disabilities classroom serves ten students, ages eleven to fourteen. Ms. Patton teaches them reading, math, and language arts. She has a variety of materials and equipment available, and the flexibility to plan her own remedial curriculum. Most of her students are at least two years below grade placement in reading and math skills, and some are working at the primary level.

As part of her assessment for instructional planning, Ms. Patton wanted to assess her students' interests in order to select and/or develop appropriate materials for them. As well, she wanted to identify activities or topics that she might use to stimulate the students to participate more willingly in their learning. Having decided to assess interest for all of her students, and remembering that in assessment of *how* to teach we skip Steps 2 and 3, she began her assessment at Step 4.

Step 4: Select or Develop Survey Instrument
(Ms. Patton's Class)

Ms. Patton decided to use an interest inventory which each student would complete individually. She chose to develop her own survey, creating some of her own items and adapting some items from the interest inventory shown in Figure 7-K. Her survey can be seen in Figure 7-O. She used open-ended questions so as not to limit the students' responses. She added a checklist at the end for students who might not be able to think of answers in the first part of the survey.

Step 5: Get Ready to Test
(Ms. Patton's Class)

Ms. Patton prepared the survey on a ditto master and ran off enough copies for the entire group. She chose a time to administer the survey when everyone was in the room and when there were no distractions and no time limits.

Step 6: Administer the Survey
(Ms. Patton's Class)

Ms. Patton gave the survey to the entire group. She explained that the answers would be private and that she did not care about spelling in the responses. She offered to help anyone who was having problems filling out the survey. Before administering it, she read each item aloud. Then she told the students to take as much time as they needed to fill in the items.

Step 7: Note Performance
(Ms. Patton's Class)

After the students had completed the survey, Ms. Patton read each one and circled any responses that yielded the information she was seeking. She had already organized the academic assessment information for each student into individual file folders. On the inside cover of each folder, she had a space marked "topics of interest." She filled it in for each student, based on his/her response to the survey. Unlike the previous example, Ms. Patton did not use a group recordkeeping form to note her student's interests. Because she did her daily lesson plans based on information kept in individual student folders, she preferred to record her findings on these same folders. Her example serves to illustrate that recordkeeping systems can, and will, vary from teacher to teacher, depending on individual styles and needs. Each teacher must select one that serves him/her best.

Name _____ Date _____

1. If I could do anything I wanted, I would _____
   _____

2. When I grow up I would like to _____
   _____

3. My favorite movies are _____
   _____

4. My favorite TV shows are _____
   _____

5. The books I like to read are about _____
   _____

6. I think the most interesting job is _____
   _____

7. If I had $100.00 I would spend it on _____
   _____

8. When I am with my friends I like to _____
   _____

9. When I am with my family I like to _____
   _____

10. When I am alone I like to _____
    _____

11. Put a check (√) beside the things that interest you.

    ___cars   ___music   ___radio   ___puzzles   ___fashion

    ___sports   ___movies   ___acting   ___food/cooking ___CB

    ___animals   ___TV   ___books   ___news   ___body building

    others _____

Figure 7-O Teacher-Created Survey (Interest Inventory)

Steps 8 and 9: Analyze Findings and Determine Areas to Probe (Ms. Patton's Class)

Upon reviewing the information gathered on the survey, Ms. Patton found that she had useful information from all but one student. Jenny completed only a few of the questions on the first part of the survey, and did not check any items in question 11. Ms. Patton decided to probe further with Jenny.

Step 10: Probe (Ms. Patton's Class)

Ms. Patton's probe took the form of an individual interview, in order to gather information not yielded by the survey. She sat down with Jenny and explained that she wanted to select materials that Jenny would like. Ms. Patton asked Jenny questions similar to the ones on the survey until two topics of interest were generated. She found that Jenny liked to explore caves and build things like bird houses. She recorded these two items in Jenny's file folder.

For Jenny, and the other nine students in her class, Ms. Patton decided to verify the information obtained on the survey by selecting a reading book for each student based on the survey findings. She would ask the students if they thought they would enjoy reading the books. Ms. Patton looked through her collection of low vocabulary, high interest books, and also borrowed some books from the library. She planned to incorporate this "probe" into her next reading lesson.

Step 11: Complete Recordkeeping Forms (Ms. Patton's Class)

As she completed her probe, Ms. Patton updated her notes in each student's file folder.

Step 12: Incorporate Findings into Teaching Plans (Ms. Patton's Class)

Ms. Patton understood that the goal of the assessment of interest was to provide her with the information she needed to make learning experiences more meaningful, more interesting, and more appropriate for each student. Once she had this information, she made choices about instructional materials that were guided by individual student's interests.

To use Jenny as an example, Ms. Patton referred to Jenny's interest in building bird houses as she created a teaching sequence to remediate a weakness in the area of measurement. Ms. Patton found a blueprint for building a bird house and planned a series of measurement lessons around that blueprint. Once Jenny had completed the various measurement activities, she was able to apply these skills by actually constructing a bird house. Into this final activity Ms. Patton incorporated a variety of math skills on which Jenny needed practice by making the final bird house a different size from the one in the original blueprint. Jenny remained actively engaged in the lessons because they were of interest to her and because they would result in a product she could use.

In the case of John, another of her students, whose interests were rock music, football, basketball, and photography, Ms. Patton's job was even easier. She was able to assign reading activities in the Troll Associates' "Sports Modules" and the Economy Company's "Rock 'n Pop Stars" and "Superbowl Champions." Math activities for John were based on his interest in sports.

The teacher followed this same method of choosing or creating materials based on interest for each of her students, knowing that, by doing so, the students were more likely to stay on-task and were therefore more likely to make progress.

ASSESSMENT OF MOTIVATORS

For many students, especially those who are successful in academic tasks, learning is motivating. For these students, it may be unnecessary to entice them into engaging in new academic pursuits. However, for a population of underachieving students, the process of learning is seldom rewarding in and of itself. Often a teacher must make deliberate attempts to use motivators to help these students to engage in learning tasks.

There are two general types of remedial activities the teacher can design: those which are intrinsically motivating because they contain materials of interest to the student, and those which are not intrinsically interesting but which, upon completion, lead to an interesting reinforcement. Assessment of interest leads the teacher to create tasks which the student will engage in because they are interesting to the student. However, it is unlikely that the teacher will always be able to select or create tasks and materials which are of interest to students; some drill and practice activities defy even the most innovative teacher's ability to stimulate the students' interest. For those situations, assessment of motivators can guide the teacher to create a learning situation which will engage the student, despite the inherently dull or repetitive nature of the learning task.

Because most underachieving students need to be motivated to engage in academic tasks, the assessment of motivators should be carried out on all students. Knowing that, and because we omit Steps 2 and 3 in the assessment of *how* to teach, our discussion of assessment of *motivators* begins with Step 4.

Step 4: Select or Develop Survey Instrument (Motivators)

Before the assessment begins, the teacher needs to identify the set of available materials, classroom activities, or events that could be used as rewards for appropriate academic and/or social behaviors. Some of these motivators may have been identified as part of the assessment of interest and are on the list of things students say they like to do. Others to be added to the list are: positive teacher reaction to appropriate behavior, graphic symbols (stars, smiling faces, grades, or positive comments), token or prize systems, graphing and charting of progress, displaying completed work, success-o-grams sent home or displayed in the classroom, sharing completed work with the entire class, and helping the teacher. The list will vary, of course, depending on the age and maturity level of the students. This list of "available rewards" will be the basis for the assessment of motivators.

Throughout the assessment of motivators, the teacher will be concerned with the power of a certain reward or reward system to affect the student's learning and behavior. The most efficient way to assess this power will be through systematic observation of students' performance when certain motivators are being used. For example, if the teacher is already using graphic symbols on the students' work as rewards for task completion and accuracy, the teacher could chart task completion rates of students for a few days. Then, to survey the power of the reward, he/she could omit the symbols for a few days and chart the effects on student performance. The teacher may also want to create survey situations in which new motivators or motivation systems are introduced, and then observe and chart their effects. However, if the survey is to utilize observation, the teacher must be confident that the motivator, and not the task, is leading to the results. Therefore, the teacher will need to utilize a task which is not intrinsically rewarding. This will guarantee that the students who complete the task are either self-motivated or responsive to the motivator being assessed.

Another way of gathering survey information on the relative usefulness of various motivators is through structured interviews. The teacher could poll students to determine if they like to have their work displayed, if they want their parents to receive "good work" notices, or if they consider certain prizes or tokens to be rewarding.

There are no formal instruments for assessment of motivators as we are defining it. The teacher will need to decide what information is being sought and create his/her own survey. The survey could take the form of a systematic or informal observation, an interview, or a combination of these.

Step 5: Get Ready to Test (Motivators)

The preparation for the survey will differ depending on the form the survey will take. For a systematic observation, the teacher will have to structure a task with which the particular motivation system is to be assessed. The teacher will also have to arrange to carry out the observation when all the students are present. Finally, the teacher will have to develop a recordkeeping form on which to record the observation findings.

For an interview, the teacher will have to arrange to meet with each student individually and to have a copy of the interview for each student.

Step 6: Administer the Survey (Motivators)

The method of administration will depend on the type of survey the teacher has decided to use. If an observation will be used, the teacher will have to be certain that the students understand the task and that the motivation system being assessed has been explained adequately. If the teacher has selected an interview, arrangements will have to be made to keep the remaining students on an independent task while the one-to-one interviews take place.

Step 7: Note Performance (Motivators)

If the survey is a systematic observation, the teacher would record notes and observations on the recordkeeping form created in Step 5. If the teacher has used an interview format for the survey, the students' responses can be recorded on the interview form.

Steps 8 and 9: Analyze Findings and
Determine Areas to Probe (Motivators)

Additional information might be sought to validate the findings obtained on the survey, or to uncover information the survey did not yield. The teacher will certainly want to probe with those students whose responses on the survey were incomplete or inconclusive.

Step 10: Probe (Motivators)

If the purpose of probing is to validate survey information, the teacher would want to observe the students informally, to see if they respond in unstructured situations as they did in the structured observation or interview. The probe, therefore, would consist of the teacher using the motivator he/she found to be successful in the survey, and observing its effectiveness in typical classroom situations.

If the purpose of the probe is to gather new information, the teacher will probably want to meet individually with some students to establish what might be appropriate motivators. The extent of the probe(s) will be determined by the adequacy of the survey information.

Step 11: Complete Recordkeeping Forms (Motivators)

As the teacher confirms the original information or discovers new data, the findings should be recorded. We suggested earlier that interest information could be recorded on individual students' folders or on a single summary sheet for the whole class. The same options are available for recording information derived from the assessment of motivators. It is appropriate, however, to record the findings on interest and motivators together, because the decisions which utilize information on interest and motivators often overlap. It is efficient to have the information on interest and motivators in the same place.

Step 12: Incorporate Findings into Teaching Plans (Motivators)

As with all areas assessed, information is only meaningful if it guides teaching decisions. Information gathered from an assessment of motivators should direct the teacher to the organization of a reward system, either for individual students or for the whole group. If students find graphic symbols rewarding, the teacher would check work immediately and return it with an appropriate response. If students are motivated by seeing their work displayed, a bulletin board or an area of the room would be set aside for display purposes and work would be hung promptly. If appropriate motivators are tokens or prizes, the teacher would award these systematically and fairly. Whatever the system, if rewards are appropriate and if they are matched to the information found during the assessment of motivators, the teacher is more likely to create learning conditions under which students will be diligent in carrying out tasks.

ILLUSTRATION: MR. DAWSON'S CLASS

The following is an example of the modified 12-step procedure for assessment of motivators for the students who are taught in Mr. Dawson's resource room during second period. There are six students, ages six to eight, in the classroom. The entire 45-minute class period is devoted to mathematics remediation.

Mr. Dawson presents a remedial curriculum to his second period class, and most of the work requires drill and repetition. He had already assessed mathematics ability, learning style, and interest, and was able to maintain a high level of activity during tasks that the students liked. However, since many activities that were appropriate for his students were not inherently interesting, Mr. Dawson wanted to determine which external motivators would stimulate his students to engage in the duller activities. He had used verbal reinforcement and graphic symbols but with inconsistent results. Therefore, he decided to conduct an assessment to determine if charting progress and displaying work would motivate his students. He began at Step 4.

Step 4: *Select or Develop Survey Instrument*
(Mr. Dawson's Class)

One of the activities that Mr. Dawson had determined was instructive for his students, but which his students found to be least interesting, was drill in addition and subtraction number facts. Mr. Dawson decided to use this activity while systematically observing the students to see whether they could be motivated to improve performance with a charting and graphing reinforcer. He decided to dispense with the stickers he had used on perfect practice sheets and began, instead, to chart the students' progress and display perfect papers.

Mr. Dawson created his own survey. He determined that three steps were required to obtain accurate information. First, he would determine a base line of behavior on the drill and practice task, before he tried a new set of motivators. Next, he would offer the new motivators with the same drill and practice task. Last, he would observe over several days, to see if the new system made a difference in any student's performance.

Step 5: *Get Ready to Test*
(Mr. Dawson's Class)

Since all of the students needed practice in basic facts, Mr. Dawson prepared several drill sheets, appropriate for each student. Each drill sheet consisted of twenty-five items. He also prepared a recordkeeping form on which he would note three aspects of each student's work: how long the student worked, how many items the student completed, and the success percentage.

Step 6: *Administer the Survey*
(Mr. Dawson's Class)

On Monday, Mr. Dawson explained to the class that the first activity each day that week would be a drill sheet in number facts. This announcement was greeted with moans and protests. Ignoring the response, Mr. Dawson continued by telling the students that the activity would only require about five minutes, but that students could take as much time as they needed. He then handed out the papers.

On Tuesday, and for the remainder of the week, Mr. Dawson made the same announcement but also explained a new charting system. He had a sheet of quarter-inch quadrille-lined paper for each student, with the student's name written boldly at the top. The vertical column was numbered 1–25, from the bottom up, and a place for the date was left at the top of each column (Figure 7-P). Mr. Dawson explained that each student would chart his/her own progress, and he showed the students how the charting was to be done. He also told the students that perfect papers would be displayed. He showed them a bulletin board he had created exclusively for their work. He then handed out the practice drill sheet for that day.

Step 7: *Note Performance*
(Mr. Dawson's Class)

Mr. Dawson transferred the information from each child's practice sheets onto the master recordkeeping form he had created in Step 5, so that he was able to see if there were differences in "minutes to complete task," "number completed," and "percent correct" as a result of the charting. The summary of his findings can be seen in Figure 7-Q.

Student's Name _____

Date	9/21																
25																	
24																	
23																	
22																	
21																	
20																	
19																	
18																	
17																	
16																	
15																	
14																	
13																	
12																	
11																	
10																	
9																	
8																	
7																	
6																	
5																	
4																	
3																	
2																	
1																	

Figure 7-P Example of Mr. Dawson's Charting System

Student	Minutes to Complete					Number Completed					Percentage Correct					Comments	
	9/20	9/21	9/22	9/23	9/24	9/20	9/21	9/22	9/23	9/24	9/20	9/21	9/22	9/23	9/24	Survey	Probe
Wendy	12	13	15	16	16	15	17	20	25	25	40	56	80	88	96	Taking a lot of time but improving	
Bruce	3	6	7	7	8	25	25	25	25	25	88	96	100	100	100	Improvement! Checking work	
Chris	4	6	7	3	3	20	25	25	20	20	76	100	100	80	72	Short term change	
Jamie	4	4	5	6	5	25	25	25	25	25	100	100	100	100	100	She's always great	
Bill	4	5	5	6	5	25	25	25	25	25	88	100	84	100	92	Inconclusive	
Pam	2	3	5	8	8	15	19	25	25	25	56	68	88	100	100	Dramatic Improvement! Checking her work	

Figure 7-Q Summary of Findings (Mr. Dawson's Survey)

Steps 8 and 9: Analyze Findings and Determine Areas to Probe (Mr. Dawson's Class)

When Mr. Dawson looked at the results summarized in Figure 7-Q, he saw that Jamie continued to perform at a consistent rate, and that all the other students showed some change as a result of the charting. For Wendy, the change was in a positive direction, but she seemed to be working very slowly. Bruce and Pam showed steady and ongoing positive change. Chris responded immediately but then began falling back. Bill's performance was erratic. Mr. Dawson decided that he needed more information on Wendy, Chris, and Bill. In Wendy's case, he planned to continue the charting and try to speed her up by introducing some additional reinforcers. He decided on interviews for Chris and Bill.

Step 10: Probe (Mr. Dawson's Class)

Mr. Dawson probed with Wendy by praising her progress and building in an additional motivator: he had her begin to record her time. He started a new chart, divided into half-minute intervals. Once she had reached 100% accuracy on two consecutive drill sheets with no time limit, she and Mr. Dawson set ten minutes as the goal for completion of each worksheet. Mr. Dawson found that when Wendy recorded both the number of correct answers and the time taken, she was able to decrease the number of minutes she took to complete the task.

Mr. Dawson probed with Bill by meeting with him and going over his chart. Bill made it clear that he thought charting was a waste of time, and that he was embarrassed to have his work displayed. He felt it was "baby stuff" and reported to Mr. Dawson that friends who came into the resource room at other times during the day had teased him about his work. Mr. Dawson agreed to stop displaying Bill's work and to keep his chart private. He also praised Bill for his progress and proposed to let Bill take the attendance sheet to the office on each day that his chart showed a 100% score.

When Mr. Dawson interviewed Chris, Chris told him that he would rather work on math puzzles than see his progress charted and his work displayed. Since it was clear that charting was not a motivator for Chris and that the math puzzles might be, Mr. Dawson decided to make work on the puzzles contingent on Chris's doing the drill sheet quickly and accurately.

Step 11: Complete Recordkeeping Forms (Mr. Dawson's Class)

Mr. Dawson filled in the information from his probes on the recordkeeping form he had completed with the survey information (Figure 7-R). He also recorded the information in each student's assessment folder.

Step 12: Incorporate Findings into Teaching Plans (Mr. Dawson's Class)

Mr. Dawson had learned several things about his students from the assessment of motivators, and he planned to use that information in planning work assignments for different students. Since some of his second period students come back later in the day for reading, he decided to introduce a charting system for progress on sight words to those who had been responsive to charting as a motivator in the math

| Student | Minutes to Complete | | | | | Number Completed | | | | | Percentage Correct | | | | | Comments | |
	9/20	9/21	9/22	9/23	9/24	9/20	9/21	9/22	9/23	9/24	9/20	9/21	9/22	9/23	9/24	Survey	Probe
Wendy	12	13	15	16	16	15	17	20	25	25	40	56	80	88	96	Taking a lot of time but improving	Charting time and accuracy useful
Bruce	3	6	7	7	8	25	25	25	25	25	88	96	100	100	100	Improvement! Checking work	
Chris	4	6	7	3	3	20	25	25	20	20	76	100	100	80	72	Short term change	Charting not a motivator. Try praise and helping teacher.
Jamie	4	4	5	4	5	25	25	25	25	25	100	100	100	100	100	She's always great	
Bill	4	5	5	6	5	25	25	25	25	25	88	100	84	100	92	Inconclusive	Do not chart or display work. Try math puzzles as reward.
Pam	2	3	5	8	8	15	19	25	25	25	56	68	88	100	100	Dramatic, Improvement! Checking her work	

Figure 7-R Summary of Findings (Mr. Dawson's Survey)

class. He planned to continue to look for different motivators for Bill and Chris and to be particularly sensitive to Bill's feelings about the level of work he is required to do. Finally, as other motivational strategies were tried, he planned to update his recordkeeping so that he would be better able to control the conditions under which his students learned. He believed that he was on his way to creating the most appropriate learning environments for all his students.

SUMMARY

In this chapter we have discussed assessment of *how* to teach, focusing on the aspects of learning style, interest, and motivators. The 12-step sequence for assessment for instructional planning was modified slightly and then applied to these three areas.

We emphasized in this chapter that by assessing *how* to teach and by planning instruction which incorporates that information, the teacher might actively engage more students in the learning process. It is important that we reiterate an earlier caution. Students who are underachieving present complex problems to teachers. There are no simple solutions to these problems. In our experience, a motivator which was successful with a student on one day may not be motivating on another day. Finding materials which are of interest to a student may not be enough to break a pattern of failure. Reorganizing teaching arrangements to accommodate different learning styles may not lead to improved skills or increased attention. Moreover, what is effective for one teacher in one environment may prove to be ineffective for a different teacher in a different environment.

Nonetheless, while recognizing these cautions, we still believe that assessment of learning style, interest, and motivators can lead to improved teaching practices and may make classrooms more appropriate learning environments for underachieving students.

8

Organizing and Managing the Assessment Process

To carry out an assessment for instructional planning with a group of students, the teacher needs to know what tasks to give each student and how to organize and manage the entire assessment process, so that teacher and students get everything done. Thus far, we have focused on the first problem: selecting, administering, and interpreting assessment tasks for individual students. Now we turn our attention to the second problem: organizing and managing the assessment for instructional planning for groups of students. We will begin by discussing how a teacher can make the assessment process manageable. Then we will describe how the student data gathered through assessment can be organized for easy access and use. We will also discuss how the information derived from the assessment can be used to generate or improve the Individualized Educational Program plan (IEP), and to develop instructional groups within a classroom.

MAKING THE ASSESSMENT PROCESS MANAGEABLE

In Chapters 4, 5, 6, and 7, we have suggested a variety of tasks, tests, and activities which could be administered to determine students' instructional needs. Table 8-1 provides a summary of the survey options for each area of assessment. It also lists the conditions under which survey tests are generally administered.

Table 8-1 Summary of Survey Options and Conditions

Area of Interest	Survey Options	Test-Selection Criteria and Guidlines	Conditions
Reading: Word Recognition	Oral Reading/Tape	Instructional level approximately 2.5 or better	Teacher-directed; requires tape recorder
	Decoding Skills Survey and Sight Vocabulary Test	Instructional level below 2.5 grade level	Teacher-directed
Reading: Comprehension	Reading five pages of continuous text	Independent reading level 5.0 or better	Student-directed silent reading
	Reading three single selections	Independent reading level below 5.0	Teacher-directed questions; or questions can be recorded on tape or card reader
	Reading up to 100-word passage	Independent reading level below 2.5	Teacher-directed
Written Expression	Story writing; given story starter, picture, sequence of pictures	Reading approximately 2.5 or better; can write sentences	Student-directed
	Component Skills Survey (with oral story)	Reading below 2.5 grade level; cannot write sentences	Teacher-directed
Math: Concepts and Computation	Pencil and paper tasks	Select point midway between present level of functioning and level to which taught; sample from hierarchy of skills	Teacher-directed
Math: Problem Solving	Pencil and paper tasks	Based on results of concepts and computation testing	Student-directed
Learning Style	Observation	First measure for all students	Student-directed individual and/or group activities; teacher observes and takes notes
Interest	Observation	First measure for all students	Student-directed individual and/or group activities
	Interview/Questionnaire	Individual or group measure	Teacher-directed
Motivators	Observation	First measure for all students	Student-directed individual and/or group activities
	Interview/Questionnaire	Individual or group measure	Teacher-directed

It is clear from this table that a wide variety of tasks can be used as survey instruments, and that each task requires a particular set of task conditions. Some surveys are teacher-directed, i.e., they call for the teacher to work with the child individually. To carry out these assessments, the teacher must assign non-teacher-directed work to the rest of the students, so that he/she can be free to work one-to-one. Other surveys require the use of special equipment, such as a tape recorder or a card reader. For these tasks the teacher must be certain to schedule only one child at a time to each piece of equipment. Some surveys can be completed independently while others call for the student to work with other students. The teacher must know in advance who is going to do what, so that the appropriate assignments can be made.

Clearly, to get everything done, the teacher must engage in some "logistical" planning before initiating the assessment activities. Once each student's assessment needs have been identified and the appropriate types of surveys have been selected (Steps 1 through 3), an assessment schedule can be planned. Teacher time can be allocated for assessment tasks which require teacher direction. Independent work can be selected for other students to complete during those times that the teacher is assessing individuals. Group activities can be planned as needed. The teacher's planning should consider the physical space of the classroom and how it will be arranged to provide easy access to equipment and to permit various groupings. With careful preparation, the assessment for instructional planning will run smoothly. Without careful pre-planning, it could easily become chaotic. Three elements of careful planning are important: summarizing student assessment needs, scheduling teacher and student time, and structuring classroom space. Suggestions for each of these elements are given below.

Summarize Student Assessment Needs

As we have said before, it is reasonable to assume that in any classroom, some students may have problems in *all* basic skill areas while others may have difficulty in only a *few* areas. The scope of a student's problem will, of course, dictate the range of the assessment activities which must be planned. That is why determining what to assess for each student is the first step in the 12-step assessment strategy. For purposes of organizing an assessment schedule, the teacher might find it helpful to expand the Step 1 recordkeeping form (Figures 3-A and 3-B) so that it reflects decisions made through Step 3 for all students in each area. This can be accomplished by using a planning guide such as the one presented in Figure 8-A. Across the top of the form, each of the areas which might be assessed has been listed. Down the side are the names of all students in the group who will be assessed. Space has also been provided for recording any current achievement data available on the students directly on this Pre-Assessment Planning Guide. These data provide a point of reference for decisions made about where to begin some of the assessments. (Decision-making guidelines that have been suggested in previous chapters have been summarized in Table 8-1.)

In each box on the guide, the teacher would indicate the survey option which will be employed (e.g., taped oral reading, story writing, component skill surveys, observation, interview) and, wherever possible, the grade level or hierarchy level at which the assessment will begin. This information will help the teacher

Student	Reading: Word Recognition	Reading: Comprehension	Written Expression	Math	Learning Style	Interest	Motivators
1. Chuck Rdg. Rec. ____ Rdg. Compr. ____ Math ____ Spelling ____							
2. Anthony Rdg. Rec. ____ Rdg. Comp. ____ Math ____ Spelling ____							
3. John Rdg. Rec. ____ Rdg. Comp. ____ Math ____ Spelling ____							
4. Vickie Rdg. Rec. ____ Rdg. Comp. ____ Math ____ Spelling ____							
5. Ronnie Rdg. Rec. ____ Rdg. Comp. ____ Math ____ Spelling ____							
Rdg. Rec. ____ Rdg. Comp. ____ Math ____ Spelling ____							

Figure 8-A   Pre-Assessment Planning Guide

to plan appropriate activities and to schedule his/her time and student time accordingly.

The importance of engaging in pre-assessment planning cannot be overemphasized. While it is true that it takes time to complete the Pre-Assessment Planning Guide, the finished product makes the effort worthwhile. The overview it provides greatly facilitates implementation of our suggested approach to assessment, and it is an enormous help in organizing the teacher.

Illustration: Resource Room—First Period Class. Two examples which illustrate the use of this Pre-Assessment Planning Guide are presented below. The first of these comes from a resource room teacher, Ms. Barth, who works in grades 7 to 9. Figure 8-B shows the assessment plan outlined for the five students in her first period class.

Looking down the student column (far left), we can see that Ms. Barth recorded available achievement data for each of her students. She also indicated skill areas which would not be assessed (Step 1). For instance, John and Ronnie will not receive assessments in math because the resource room teacher is not responsible for math instruction for these students.

Now, using both the achievement information and the Test Selection Criteria and Guidelines in Table 8-1, she chose an appropriate survey for each child. For students who had reading achievement scores of 2.5 or better, she noted that she would have them do an oral reading tape. Those students who fell below the 2.5 grade level were scheduled for surveys of decoding and sight vocabulary. Appropriate options for assessing reading comprehension, written expression, math concepts and computation, and math problem solving and applications were selected in a similar fashion and recorded on the Pre-Assessment Planning Guide.

The next area Ms. Barth considered was learning style. She noted her plans to observe students to determine how well they followed various types of directions, how they responded to various grouping conditions, and how well they worked independently.

The last thing Ms. Barth did was to consider the tasks she would have students perform to provide information on interests and motivators. In the final columns of the Pre-Assessment Planning Guide, she indicated her intention to observe students as they engaged in three types of activities. Each student would be asked to select a book to read independently from among many choices. Ms. Barth hoped this would provide insight into topics that interested each child. As well, students would be asked to decorate their class assignment folders in a way that "told" something about themselves (e.g., hobbies, sports, favorite foods, etc.). Further, on several occasions, they would be given free time to work on whatever activities they chose, either alone or with classmates. Ms. Barth planned to observe students during these free time activities to derive information on possible motivators and grouping arrangements which might be used or which should be avoided.

The completed Pre-Assessment Planning Guide provides the teacher with an overview of all assessments which must be completed for the first period class. It is a "picture" showing who will be assessed, in which areas, using which tools. Once this information is on paper, the teacher can schedule the assessment activities more easily and keep track of her progress. Similar planning forms, of course, would be generated for each of the resource room teacher's other classes.

Student	Reading: Word Recognition	Reading: Comprehension	Written Expression	Math	Learning Style	Interest	Motivators
1. Chuck Rdg. Rec. _3.5_ Rdg. Compr. _3.0_ Math _2.5-3.0_ Spelling _—_	Oral reading tape	3 selections (3rd grade level)	picture story	Survey skill hierarchy items between grades 2.5-4	Observation: —Following directions —grouping pref. —independent work skills	Observation: —book selection —Folder decorations —Free-time choices	Observation: Same
2. Anthony Rdg. Rec. _4.5-5.0_ Rdg. Comp. _4.0_ Math _3-3.5_ Spelling _—_	Oral reading tape	3 selections (4th grade level)	write a story on a theme	(") Grades 4-6	(")	(")	(")
3. John Rdg. Rec. _2.0-2.5_ Rdg. Comp. _2.5_ Math _7.0_ Spelling _2.0_	Decoding skill survey Sight vocabulary test	3 selections (2nd-3rd grade level)	picture story	Performance at grade level	(")	(")	(")
4. Vickie Rdg. Rec. _3.5-4_ Rdg. Comp. _3.0_ Math _2.5-3_ Spelling _3.0_	Oral reading tape	3 selections (3rd grade level)	picture story about sequence of pictures	Survey skill hierarchy items between grades 3-4	(")	(")	(")
5. Ronnie Rdg. Rec. _1.5_ Rdg. Comp. _?_ Math _6.0_ Spelling _—_	Decoding skill survey Sight vocabulary test	Sentence level survey	Component skills survey (with oral story)	Performance at grade level	(")	(")	(")
Rdg. Rec. _____ Rdg. Comp. _____ Math _____ Spelling _____							

Figure 8-B Pre-Assessment Planning Guide (Resource Room) (First Probe)

Illustration: Self-Contained Class. The second illustration of pre-assessment planning comes from a teacher, Mr. Sellers, serving ten students in a self-contained special education class (Figure 8-C).

Figure 8-C Pre-Assessment Planning Guide (Self-Contained Class)

Student	Reading: Word Recognition	Reading: Compre-hension	Written Expression	Math	Learning Style	Interest	Motivators
1. Billy Rdg. Rec. ___1.5___ Reg. Comp. ___1.5___ Math ___2.0___ Spelling ___—___	decoding survey & sight voc. test	sentence level survey	component skills—oral story	Skill hier-archy gr 2-4	Observation: . directions . grp. . independent work	Observa-tion: . book . folder . free time	Observation: same
2. Stephen Rdg. Rec. ___2.0___ Rdg. Comp. ___2.5___ Math ___2.0___ Spelling ___—___	decoding survey & sight voc. test	3 selections (2nd gr. level)	"	" gr 2-4	"	"	"
3. Carolyn Rdg. Rec. ___3.0___ Rdg. Comp. ___2.0___ Math ___3.0___ Spelling ___2.0___	oral reading/ tape	3 selections (2nd gr. level)	"	" gr 3-5	"	"	"
4. Karen Rdg. Rec. ___3-3.5___ Rdg. Comp. ___3.0___ Math ___3.5___ Spelling ___3.0___	oral reading/ tape	3 selections (3rd gr. level)	picture story	" gr 3-5	"	"	"
5. Ted Rdg. Rec. ___1.5-2.0___ Rdg. Comp. ___1.5___ Math ___2.0___ Spelling ___—___	decoding survey & sight voc. test	sentence level survey	compon-ent skills— oral story	" gr 2-5	"	"	"
6. Eric Rdg. Rec. ___3.0-3.5___ Rdg. Comp. ___2.5___ Math ___4.0___ Spelling ___2.5___	oral reading/ tape	3 selections (2nd-3rd gr. level)	picture story w/seq-uence	" gr 4-6	"	"	"
7. Ron Rdg. Rec. ___3.5___ Rdg. Comp. ___4.0___ Math ___4.0___ Spelling ___3.0___	oral reading/ tape	3 selections (3rd-4th gr. level)	picture story	" gr 4-6	"	"	"
8. Sue Ellen Rdg. Rec. ___1-1.5___ Rdg. Comp. ___1-1.5___ Math ___1.5___ Spelling ___—___	decoding survey & sight voc. test	sentence level survey	compon-ent skills- oral story	" gr 1	"	"	"
9. Doyle Rdg. Rec. ___3.5___ Rdg. Comp. ___3.0___ Math ___4.0___ Spelling ___3.5___	oral reading/ tape	3 selections (3rd gr. level)	picture story	" gr 4-6	"	"	"
10. Mark Rdg. Rec. ___2.5___ Rdg. Comp. ___2.0___ Math ___2.5___ Spelling ___2.0___	oral reading/ tape	3 selections (2nd gr. level)	compon-ent skills— oral story	" gr 2-4	"	"	"

Mr. Sellers has completed the Pre-Assessment Planning Guide by considering student achievement scores and the suggested decision rules for selecting survey tasks summarized in Table 8-1. As we read down the first five columns, we see that a variety of tasks has been selected. In each case, the particular task selected for a student reflects his/her apparent level of performance.

The final columns of the form indicate that learning style, interest, and motivators will be assessed in the same fashion as that outlined for the resource room students. Again, notice that Mr. Sellers has specified both the behaviors of interest and the manner of data collection (i.e., observation).

Two differences between this guide and the resource room guide should be noted. First, the teacher of the self-contained class made plans to assess *all* of his students in *all* areas. This is because Mr. Sellers' students will receive all of their academic instruction in the self-contained class. Second, for the resource room teacher, there will be several guides developed, one for each class period; the teacher of the self-contained class will make only one plan to accommodate all of his students.

Schedule Teacher and Student Time

Once a Pre-Assessment Planning Guide has been generated, it can be used to develop an implementation schedule. Such a schedule is quite simple to prepare, if the teacher sees students individually; it involves little more than indicating the days and times when particular tests will be administered. However, most teachers see students in groups, and for them, the scheduling task is slightly more difficult. The resource room or self-contained class teacher must not only allocate his/her time for testing a particular student, but must also plan appropriate activities to keep the other students busy while he/she is occupied.

The precise method of scheduling that a teacher employs can vary. However, several features of the schedule are important. First, the teacher must plan many activities which students can work on independently, so that he/she is free to conduct assessments. The activities must be designed so as to require very little teacher direction. At the same time, the activities should be meaningful, either yielding new assessment data or providing skill review for the students. They should not be simply "busy work" tasks. Also, the schedule must allocate both teacher time and equipment resources, so that students are not kept waiting. Finally, the teacher should develop a procedure for letting students know what they are to do, so that they can move through the schedule independently and smoothly.

Illustration: Resource Room—First Period Class. We can take a closer look at how this type of scheduling actually might be accomplished by returning to our classroom examples. We will begin by describing how the resource room teacher, Ms. Barth, planned the assessment schedule for her first period class.

She started by making two lists. The first was a list of activities which students could be asked to complete *independently* (Table 8-2). This first list was divided into two categories: activities which would provide *assessment data*, and activities which were *review or enrichment tasks*. Her second list outlined assessment tasks which required *teacher direction* or called for use of *special equipment* (Table 8-3). Using these two lists and her Pre-Assessment Planning Guide (Figure 8-B), Ms. Barth began to prepare a schedule for assessment.

Table 8-2 Independent Student-Directed Activities

ACTIVITIES YIELDING ASSESSMENT DATA

Area	Activity
Reading (Comprehension)	– Read selection silently and answer questions (on paper or at tape recorder).
Written Expression	– Write a story about a topic, a picture, or a sequence of pictures. – Tell a story about a topic, a picture, or a sequence of pictures (record on tape).
Learning Style (Grouping)	– Complete packets of math puzzles and activities independently. (The difficulty level will vary.) – Complete an appropriate packet of math puzzles and activities in a small group. (Performance and on-task behavior will be compared to independent work.)
Learning Style (Following oral and written directions)	– Listen to a set of simple directions on tape and carry them out on paper. – Complete a written "Following Directions" packet independently.
Learning Style (Mode of instruction)	– Five new words taught to mastery level. Practice activities emphasize auditory aspects of the words. (Language master cards and cassette tapes will be used.) – Five new words taught to mastery level. Practice activities emphasize visual aspects of the words. (Teacher-made filmstrips will be used.)
Interest	– Select an independent reader from choices. – Decorate class assignment folders to illustrate interests.

PLANNED REVIEW AND ENRICHMENT TASKS

Area	Activity
Reading	– Work packets developed for individual students. Each contains tasks, activities, games, and puzzles, which students can complete independently. Most involve review material.
Written Expression	– Work packets developed for individual students. Each contains tasks, activities, games, and puzzles, which students can complete independently. Most involve review material.
Math	– Work packets developed for individual students. Each contains tasks, activities, games, and puzzles, which students can complete independently. Most involve review material.

Table 8-3   Teacher-Directed and Special Equipment Tasks

Teacher-Directed Assessment Tasks	Special Equipment Tasks
Word Recognition—Oral Reading Tape	Word Recognition—Oral Reading Tape
Word Recognition—Decoding Skills Survey	Reading Comprehension—Questions on tape or card reader
Skill Survey and Sight Vocabulary Test	Written Expression—Oral stories on tape
Reading Comprehension—Survey at Sentence Level	Learning Style—Modality preference task
	• card reader
Written Expression—Component Skills Survey	• filmstrip viewer
Math—Survey Interviews	Learning Style—Following oral directions task
	• tape recorder and tape

She decided to concentrate her efforts on gathering reading data first, beginning with word recognition assessments. Looking down the appropriate column of the Pre-Assessment Planning Guide, she found that three students were to do oral reading tapes and two were to be given decoding surveys and sight vocabulary tests. She realized that none of these activities could be student-directed and that she would have to schedule her time to work with each of the five students individually. She also realized that the other students would have to be scheduled for tasks which did not require teacher direction each time she planned a reading assessment.

Ms. Barth wrote each student's name in her daily planning book (Figure 8-D). Then she scheduled herself to work with Ronnie on his decoding and sight vocabulary surveys. She estimated that this would keep her and Ronnie busy for the entire class. Referring to her activity list (Table 8-2), she selected tasks for the other four students to complete independently. She scheduled John and Vickie to work on writing stories (a student-directed assessment task), and Chuck and Anthony to work on a "following directions" activity. Then, in case these activities did not require the entire class period, she selected a second independent activity for each student to be assigned, if time permitted.

At the end of the class period, Ms. Barth checkmarked all of the activities that had been completed. She used this information in developing a plan for Tuesday's class meeting. For Tuesday (Figure 8-E) Ms. Barth planned to continue gathering reading assessment data: John would work with her on decoding and sight vocabulary surveys; the others would do independent tasks. Following the pattern from the previous day, she assigned the story writing task to Chuck and Anthony and scheduled Vickie and Ronnie to the "following directions" activities. She again planned for a follow-up task for each child, in case the initial assignment was finished early.

The same procedure was followed in planning the schedule for the remainder of the week. The teacher began by reviewing the tests to be administered and allocating *her* time. Then she assigned independent activities, either new activities or incomplete work from the previous day, to the rest of the students. When activities called for special equipment, she monitored the allocation of these resources so that students' schedules would not conflict.

Period   *1—9:00-9:40*   Week of: *9-1*

Monday

Chuck—Following <u>oral</u> directions | tape | *; pick an independent reader (if time)*

Anthony—Following <u>written</u> directions packet; pick an independent reader (if time)

John—Write a picture story; work on independent math puzzle pack

Vickie—Write a picture story (use sequence of pictures); work on independent math puzzle pack

Ronnie—Work with (teacher) on reading decoding skills survey/sight vocabulary test

Tuesday

Wednesday

Thursday

Friday

Finish Next Week:

Figure 8-D   Ms. Barth's Daily Plan Book (Monday)

Period <u>1—9:00-9:40</u>　　　　　　　　　　　　　Week of: <u>9-1</u>

Monday	Tuesday
Chuck—Following <u>oral</u> directions ✓ `tape` *; pick an independent reader (if time)* ✓	*Chuck—Write a picture story; work on independent math puzzle pack*
Anthony—Following <u>written</u> directions packet; ✓ *pick an independent reader (if time)* ✓	*Anthony—Write a story on a theme (football); work on independent math puzzle pack*
John—Write a picture story; ✓ *work on independent math puzzle pack*	*John—Work with* (teacher) *on reading decoding skills survey/sight vocabulary test*
Vickie—Write a picture story ✓ *(use sequence of pictures); work on independent math puzzle pack*	*Vickie—Following written directions packet; pick an independent reader*
Ronnie—Work with (teacher) *on reading* ✓ *decoding skills survey/sight vocabulary test*	*Ronnie—Following oral directions* `tape` *; pick an independent reader*

Wednesday	Thursday

Friday	Finish Next Week:

Figure 8-E　Ms. Barth's Daily Plan Book (Tuesday)

　　Figure 8-F illustrates the daily plans generated for the entire week. At the end of the week, Ms. Barth checked all completed tasks on her Pre-Assessment Planning Guide (Figure 8-G). She noticed that she had now completed all of the word recognition surveys and most of the reading comprehension assessments she had

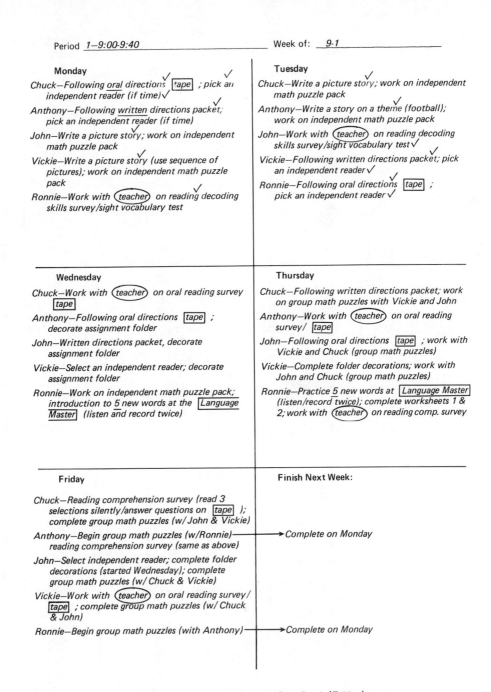

Period _1—9:00-9:40_   Week of: ___9-1___

Monday

Chuck—Following <u>oral</u> directions [tape] *; pick an independent reader (if time)*✓

Anthony—Following <u>written</u> directions packet; pick an independent reader (if time)

John—Write a picture story; work on independent math puzzle pack

Vickie—Write a picture story (use sequence of pictures); work on independent math puzzle pack

Ronnie—Work with (teacher) *on reading decoding skills survey/sight vocabulary test*

Tuesday

Chuck—Write a picture story; work on independent math puzzle pack

Anthony—Write a story on a theme (football); work on independent math puzzle pack

John—Work with (teacher) *on reading decoding skills survey/sight vocabulary test*✓

Vickie—Following written directions packet; pick an independent reader ✓

Ronnie—Following oral directions [tape] *; pick an independent reader* ✓

Wednesday

Chuck—Work with (teacher) *on oral reading survey* [tape]

Anthony—Following oral directions [tape] *; decorate assignment folder*

John—Written directions packet, decorate assignment folder

Vickie—Select an independent reader; decorate assignment folder

Ronnie—Work on independent math puzzle pack; introduction to <u>5</u> new words at the [Language Master] *(listen and record twice)*

Thursday

Chuck—Following written directions packet; work on group math puzzles with Vickie and John

Anthony—Work with (teacher) *on oral reading survey/* [tape]

John—Following oral directions [tape] *; work with Vickie and Chuck (group math puzzles)*

Vickie—Complete folder decorations; work with John and Chuck (group math puzzles)

Ronnie—Practice <u>5</u> new words at [Language Master] *(listen/record twice); complete worksheets 1 & 2; work with* (teacher) *on reading comp. survey*

Friday

Chuck—Reading comprehension survey (read 3 selections silently/answer questions on [tape] *); complete group math puzzles (w/ John & Vickie)*

Anthony—Begin group math puzzles (w/Ronnie)——→ reading comprehension survey (same as above)

John—Select independent reader; complete folder decorations (started Wednesday); complete group math puzzles (w/ Chuck & Vickie)

Vickie—Work with (teacher) *on oral reading survey/* [tape] *; complete group math puzzles (w/ Chuck & John)*

Ronnie—Begin group math puzzles (with Anthony)——→

Finish Next Week:

→ *Complete on Monday*

→ *Complete on Monday*

Figure 8-F Ms. Barth's Daily Plan Book (Friday)

planned. She still needed to administer several math surveys and a series of written expression tests to the beginning writer. However, if she continued her scheduling pattern, she could anticipate completing all initial surveys within the next week. The follow-up probing might take another two weeks.

Figure 8-G Pre-Assessment Planning Guide (Ms. Barth's Accomplishments)

Student	Reading: Word Recognition	Reading: Comprehension	Written Expression	Math	Learning Style	Interest	Motivators
1. Chuck Rdg. Rec. _3.5_ Rdg. Compr. _3.0_ Math _2.5-3.0_ Spelling _—_	✓ Oral reading tape	✓ 3 selections (3rd grade level)	✓ picture story	Survey skill hierarchy items between grades 2.5-4	Observation: —Following directions ✓ —grouping pref. —independent ✓ work skills	Observation: —book selection ✓ —folder decora- tions —free-time ✓ choices	Observation: Same
2. Anthony Rdg. Rec. _4.5-5.0_ Rdg. Comp. _4.0_ Math _3-3.5_ Spelling _—_	✓ Oral reading tape	✓ 3 selections (4th grade level)	✓ write a story on a theme	(") grades 4-6	(")	(")	(")
3. John Rdg. Rec. _2.0-2.5_ Rdg. Comp. _2.5_ Math _7.0_ Spelling _2.0_	✓ Decoding skill survey Sight vocabulary test	✓ 3 selections (2nd-3rd grade level)	✓ picture story	Performance at grade level	(")	(")	(")
4. Vickie Rdg. Rec. _3.5-4_ Rdg. Comp. _3.0_ Math _2.5-3_ Spelling _3.0_	✓ Oral reading tape	✓ 3 selections (3rd grade level)	✓ picture story about sequence of pictures	Survey skill hierarchy items between grades 3-4	(")	(")	(")
5. Ronnie Rdg. Rec. _1.5_ Rdg. Comp. _?_ Math _6.0_ Spelling _—_	✓ Decoding skill survey Sight vocabulary test	✓ Sentence level survey	Component skills survey (with oral story)	Performance at grade level	(")	(")	(")
Rdg. Rec. _____ Rdg. Comp. _____ Math _____ Spelling _____							

Period _Chuck_   Week of: _9/1_

Monday	Tuesday
— Complete the _Following Oral Directions_ tape/activity — Pick your next book to read (choose one from the blue boxes)	— Write a story about the "fishing" picture. (Check w/ teacher before you begin.) — Work on your _Independent Math_ puzzle pack
Wednesday	**Thursday**
Work w/ teacher on _reading_	— Complete the _Following Written Directions_ packet — Work on your _Group Math_ puzzles w/Vickie & John
Friday	**Finish Next Week:**
— Read stories #1, #2, & #3 to yourself at tape recorder. Listen to questions for each story & answer them on tape — Complete your _Group Math_ puzzles w/Vickie and John	

Figure 8-H Assignment Schedule for One Resource-Room Student

In order that her schedule of student activities run smoothly, Ms. Barth decided that each student needed to know what he or she was supposed to be doing at any given time. Therefore, she provided each student with an assignment schedule. These were simply spirit master forms placed inside individual student folders. The students' assignments were written on the forms in the order that the students were to do them. Materials needed to carry out each task were also placed inside the folder, so that the students could be fairly independent. Figure 8-H is a copy of Chuck's assignment schedule for the week of 9–1. Only Monday's assignments were on Monday morning's schedule. Each subsequent day's assignments were added as they were planned.

Illustration: Self-Contained Class. The teacher in the self-contained classroom, Mr. Sellers, planned his assessment schedule in a slightly different way. He began by developing a general daily schedule for the whole class, which showed how students would spend their time over the course of an entire day (Figure 8-I, left column). He planned student-directed assessment tasks or other independent activities for most of the morning. Each student would be given an appropriate packet of review activities in the areas of reading and written expression. They would also receive a set of "following directions" tasks to be completed independently. After the lunch break, one of several special class options, such as gym or music, was scheduled. Then he planned to have students work independently again, this time on appropriate review packets in math. Instruction in social studies or science would follow, and the last period of the day would be devoted to language development activities.

Once a general schedule had been mapped out, Mr. Sellers prepared

Daily Schedule		Equipment Schedule		Teacher's Assessment Schedule	
9–9:45	Reading—Work on independent seatwork review packets	9:00	"Following oral directions" tape and activities (at the listening post) [*Ted *Sue Ellen *Stephen]	9:00	*Billy—Decoding skills survey, sight vocabulary, sentence level comprehension test
9:45–10:30	Written Language/Language Arts —work on independent seatwork, review packets —Story Writing *Eric & *Karen	9:45	"Following oral directions" tape and activities (at the listening post) [*Billy *Mark *Carolyn]	9:45	*Ted—Decoding skills survey, sight vocabulary, sentence level comprehension test
10:30–11:00	Following Directions —work on "Following written directions" packet	10:30	"Following oral directions" tape and activities (at the listening post) [*Karen *Ron *Eric *Doyle]	10:30	*Sue Ellen—Decoding skills survey, sight vocabulary, sentence level comprehension test
11–11:15	Rest Rooms/Clean Up/ Free Time				
11:15–11:45	LUNCH ☺				
12–12:45	Gym				
12:45–1:30	Math—Work on independent seatwork, review packets			1:30	*Carolyn—Oral reading survey and tape
1:30–2:00	Social Studies—Begin unit on the Civil War				
2:00–2:45	Language Development				
2:45–3:00	Clean Up/Dismissal				

Figure 8-I Daily Schedule (Self-Contained Class) (Plans for Monday)

schedules for equipment use and teacher-directed assessments for Monday (see Figure 8-I, center and right columns). His plan was that students would be pulled away from their independent activities to be assessed by him or to complete activities involving equipment.

Because the general schedule was posted on the chalkboard at the front of the room, Mr. Sellers did not make individual assignment schedules for each child. He went over the plan each morning and guided students along over the course of the day. He explained the nature of each activity and reviewed the directions for completing each task at the start of each 45-minute period. Necessary materials were provided at the appropriate work areas or in individual student folders. Considerable extra time was built into Mr. Sellers' assessment schedule, so that he could monitor the class and give assistance between one-to-one assessments.

Figures 8-J and 8-K show Mr. Sellers' projected schedule for Tuesday and Wednesday. If he actually accomplishes all he has planned, his survey assessment will be completed in very little time. (Figure 8-L shows what he would have accomplished by the end of Wednesday.) Indeed, even if the schedule overestimates the amount which can be completed each day, his initial assessments could still be completed in approximately ten days. The follow-up probing would take another two weeks.

Daily Schedule		Equipment Schedule		Teacher's Assessment Schedule	
9–9:45	Reading—Work on independent seatwork review packets	9:00	Read story #1, #2, and #3 to yourself—answer questions on the tape recorder *Carolyn	9:00	*Karen—Oral reading survey and tape
9:45–10:30	Written Language/ Language Arts -Work on independent seatwork, review packets -Story Writing *Doyle & * Ron			9:45	*Eric—Oral reading survey and tape
10:30–11:00	Following Directions -Work on "Following Written Directions" packet	10:30	Read story #1, #2, and #3 to yourself—answer questions on the tape recorder *Karen	10:30	*Stephen—Decoding skills survey & sight vocabulary
11–11:15	Rest Rooms/Clean Up/Free Time				
11:15–11:45	LUNCH ☺				
12–12:45	Art—Decorate class assignment folders				
12:45–1:30	Math—Work on independent seatwork, review packets	12:45	Read story #1, #2, & #3 to yourself—answer questions on the tape recorder *Eric	12:45	*Ron—Oral reading survey and tape
1:30–2:00	Social Studies—Civil War film, group discussion activities				
2–2:45	Language Development				
2:45–3:00	Clean up/Dismissal				

Figure 8-J Daily Schedule (Self-Contained Class) (Plans for Tuesday)

Daily Schedule			Equipment Schedule		Teacher's Assessment Schedule	
9–9:45	Reading–Work on independent seatwork, review packets		9:00	Read story #1, #2, & #3 to yourself–answer questions on the tape recorder, *Stephen	9:00	*Doyle–Oral reading survey and tape
9:45–10:30	Written Language/ Language Arts -Work on independent seatwork, review packets		9:45	Read story #1, #2, & #3 to yourself–answer questions on the tape recorder *Ron	9:45	*Mark–Oral reading survey and tape
10:30–11:00	Book selection Pick a book to read from choices in the boxes				10:30	*Billy–Written expression component skills survey and oral story
RED BOXES	BLUE BOXES	GREEN BOXES				
* Billy	* Stephen	* Karen				
* Ted	* Mark	* Eric				
* Sue Ellen	* Carolyn	* Doyle				
		* Ron				
11–11:15	Rest Rooms/Clean Up/ Free Time					
11:15–11:45	LUNCH ☺					
12–12:40	Music					
12:45–1:30	Math–Work on group puzzle packs		12:45	Read story #1, #2, & #3 to yourself–answer questions on the tape recorder *Doyle	12:45	*Stephen–Written expression component skills survey and oral story
Group 1	Group 2	Group 3			1:10	*Carolyn–Written expression component skills survey and oral story
* Billy	* Stephen	* Carolyn				
* Eric	* Karen	* Sue Ellen				
* Mark	* Ron	* Ted				
1:30–2:00	Science					
2–2:45	Language Development					
2:45–3:00	Clean Up/Dismissal					

Figure 8-K Daily Schedule (Self-Contained Class) (Plans for Wednesday)

Structure Classroom Space

A final concern in organizing the assessment process is the physical plan of the classroom. Because the assessment schedule will involve several types of activities going on in the classroom at the same time, the teacher should consider how to arrange the room and its furniture so that these activities will not interfere with each other.

Several factors should be considered in organizing the classroom space. There should be a quiet, out-of-the-way area designated for teacher-directed assessment. Space for using equipment should be provided as far away from the teacher-directed assessment area as possible. Students will need places for completing independent activities. Space for small-group work should also be available.

How the teacher chooses to arrange these areas within the classroom can vary considerably. Clearly, the specific room arrangement will depend, in part, on teacher preferences, availability of furniture, and the dimensions of the classroom space.

Student	Reading: Word Recognition	Reading: Comprehension	Written Expression	Math	Learning Style	Interest	Motivators
1. *Billy* Rdg. Rec. ___1.5___ Reg. Comp. ___1.5___ Math ___2.0___ Spelling ___—___	✓ *decoding survey & sight voc. test*	✓ *sentence level survey*	✓ *component skills—oral story*	*skill hierarchy* *gr 2-4*	*Observation:* *. directions* ✓ *. grp.* ✓ *. independent work* ✓	*Observation:* *. book* ✓ *. folder* ✓ *. free time*	*Observation: same*
2. *Stephen* Rdg. Rec. ___2.0___ Rdg. Comp. ___2.5___ Math ___2.0___ Spelling ___—___	✓ *decoding survey & sight voc. test*	✓ *3 selections (2nd gr. level)*	" ✓	" *gr 2-4*	"	"	"
3. *Carolyn* Rdg. Rec. ___3.0___ Rdg. Comp. ___2.0___ Math ___3.0___ Spelling ___2.0___	✓ *oral reading/ tape*	✓ *3 selections (2nd gr. level)*	" ✓	" *gr 3-5*	"	"	"
4. *Karen* Rdg. Rec. ___3-3.5___ Rdg. Comp. ___3.0___ Math ___3.5___ Spelling ___3.0___	✓ *oral reading/ tape*	✓ *3 selections (3rd gr. level)*	✓ *picture story*	" *gr 3-5*	"	"	"
5. *Ted* Rdg. Rec. ___1.5-2.0___ Rdg. Comp. ___1.5___ Math ___2.0___ Spelling ___—___	✓ *decoding survey & sight voc. test*	✓ *sentence level survey*	*component skills- oral story*	" *gr 2-5*	"	"	"
6. *Eric* Rdg. Rec. ___3.0-3.5___ Rdg. Comp. ___2.5___ Math ___4.0___ Spelling ___2.5___	✓ *oral reading/ tape*	✓ *3 selections (2nd-3rd gr. level)*	*picture story w/sequence* ✓	" *gr 4-6*	"	"	"
7. *Ron* Rdg. Rec. ___3.5___ Rdg. Comp. ___4.0___ Math ___4.0___ Spelling ___3.0___	✓ *oral reading/ tape*	✓ *3 selections (3rd-4th gr. level)*	✓ *picture story*	" *gr 4-6*	"	"	"
8. *Sue Ellen* Rdg. Rec. ___1-1.5___ Rdg. Comp. ___1-1.5___ Math ___1.5___ Spelling ___—___	✓ *decoding survey & sight voc. test*	✓ *sentence level survey*	*component skills- oral story*	" *gr 1*	"	"	"
9. *Doyle* Rdg. Rec. ___3.5___ Rdg. Comp. ___3.0___ Math ___4.0___ Spelling ___3.5___	✓ *oral reading/ tape*	✓ *3 selections (3rd gr. level)*	✓ *picture story*	" *gr 4-6*	"	"	"
10. *Mark* Rdg. Rec. ___2.5___ Rdg. Comp. ___2.0___ Math ___2.5___ Spelling ___2.0___	✓ *oral reading/ tape*	✓ *3 selections (2nd gr. level)*	*component skills- oral story*	" *gr 2-4*	"	"	"

Figure 8-L Pre-Assessment Planning Guide (Self-Contained Class)
(Mr. Seller's Accomplishments)

The room plans provided in Figures 8-M and 8-N are two of many possible options. In the resource room plan (Figure 8-M), there are no student desks in the classroom. Instead, the teacher, Ms. Barth, has students complete all of their work at "centers." She provided tables for independent assignments in reading, math, and written expression, and labeled each table accordingly. At these "centers," she placed materials she thought would aid students in completing their work. For example, at the math center, number lines, rulers, a hand calculator, and graph paper were available.

Figure 8-M Resource-Room Floor Plan

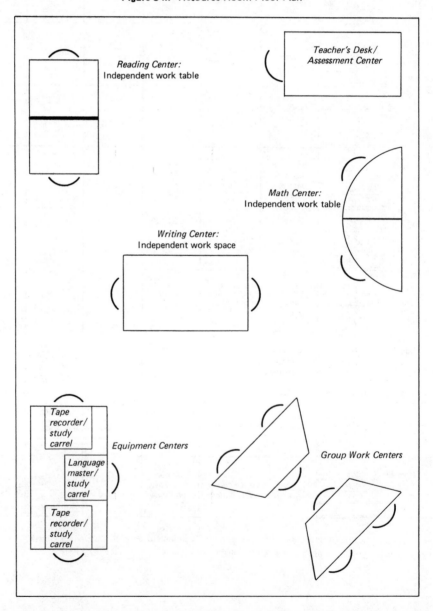

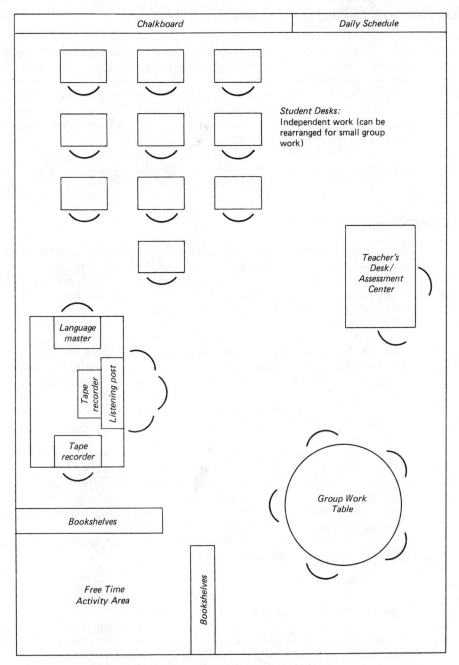

Figure 8-N Self-Contained Class Floor Plan

She also provided an "equipment center," where tape recorders and card readers were kept. She placed each piece of equipment in a study carrel to minimize any distractions it might create.

The plan also shows a space for students to work in small groups. Ms. Barth will use her desk for one-to-one assessment and instruction.

In contrast, Mr. Sellers arranged his self-contained classroom somewhat differently (Figure 8-N). Since his students remain in the classroom throughout the day, he thought it important to give them permanent work spaces. So he assigned each student to a desk. Students kept work materials and aids in their desks, and moved from this "home base" to alternative work stations as necessary. Mr. Sellers also arranged for separate areas for small group work, equipment use, and one-to-one assessment and teaching.

While the two room plans differ, both teachers' plans accommodate the range of activities likely to be going on simultaneously in the classroom. In so doing, each helps to insure smooth implementation of the daily plans.

ORGANIZING STUDENT DATA

When the assessment for instructional planning has been carried out as we have suggested, a composite instructional profile of each student will soon emerge from the set of Assessment to Instruction Data Sheets. Before the teacher actually initiates instruction, however, it will probably be useful to organize each student's instructional profile further into a "master plan" for instruction. The set of instructional objectives derived from the various assessments would be organized, sequenced, and recorded in a single place, instead of on several pieces of paper. One form this "master plan" might take is presented in Figure 8-O. Intructional objectives for each basic skill area would be recorded in the order in which they will be taught. Spaces have been provided for noting materials which might be used and for specifying criteria for skill mastery. As the teacher prepares to teach each objective listed on the form, the missing information would be filled in. The form could provide enough space for adding additional objectives as they are identified during instruction.

Another place to record the "master plan" would be on the IEP developed for each student. Indeed, specification of a "master plan" for instruction is precisely what the IEP calls for. The teacher must not only establish annual goals for each student, but must also identify a sequence of specific short-term objectives which will lead to the accomplishment of these goals. While it may not always be possible to complete the entire assessment for instructional planning in time to meet school deadlines for submitting IEPs, data derived from the assessment can be used to refine the initial plan and make it more specific.

Illustration: Resource Room—First Period Class. To illustrate the process of organizing assessment data and translating it into a specific instructional plan, we will describe the steps that the resource room teacher, Ms. Barth, followed.

She began by pulling together all the assessment data she had gathered on her student, Chuck. Figure 8-P shows fragments of the Assessment to Instruction Data Sheets on which she had summarized the results of surveys and probes completed on Chuck. Only the codes *2* and *4* (skills which need to be taught) are reprinted, for ease of reading.

Ms. Barth's next step was to transfer this information from the set of summary sheets to a "master plan" and, at the same time, to detail the specific skills which would be addressed in their correct order. As she did this, she began to specify instructional materials which could be used, based on the information she had gath-

Student _____ Date _____

Reading

Objectives	Material	Mastery criteria

Written Expression

Objectives	Materials	Mastery criteria

Math

Objectives	Materials	Mastery criteria

Figure 8-O Master Plan of Instructional Objectives

Student _Chuck_   Date _September_

Figure 8-P Composite Assessment Summary

Reading: Word Recognition (recorded codes shown at left)

Code	Item
	Reading continuous text (a,b,c)*
4	Reading sentences
4	Reading words (a,)b,c,(d,)e)*
	Reading word parts, affixes (a,b)*
2	Reading word parts, irregular phonograms
4	Reading word parts, vowels ((a,)(b,)c,d)*
4	Reading word parts, consonants (a,(b,)c)*
	Reading single letters, vowels (a,b,c)*
	Reading single letters, consonants (a,b)*
	Hearing sounds in words
	Recognizing letter shapes
4	High frequency words, phonetically predictable
	High frequency words, phonetically irregular
	System for attacking unknown words

Reading Comprehension

Code	Item
	Continuous text—evaluational
4	Continuous text—inferential
	Continuous text—literal
	Paragraphs—evaluational
	Paragraphs—inferential
	Paragraphs—literal
	Sentences—literal
	Words—vocabulary
	Oral—vocabulary

Written Expression

Code	Item
	Generation of ideas—vocabulary
	Generation of ideas—productivity
	Generation of ideas—story theme
	Generation of ideas—grammar
	Handwriting—remembering letters
	Handwriting—upper/lower case letters
	Handwriting—reproducing letters
4	Conventions of print—punctuation
4	Conventions of print—capitalization
	Conventions of print—sentence structure
	Conventions of print—word usage
	Conventions of print—format
4	Spelling—hearing sounds in words
4	Spelling—sound/symbol correspondence
4	Spelling—irregular spellings and sequence
	Spelling—morphological rules

Math Concepts

Item	Notes	Status
Whole number		Level known
Time	4	Level known
Handwriting / ¼ hr.		Level known
Measurement	4 / Chg.	Level known
Money		Level known
Geometry		Level known

Math Computation

Item	Notes	Status
Whole number +		Level known
Whole number −		Level known
Whole number X	4 fcts.	Level known
Whole number ÷	4 fcts.	Level known
Decimals +		Level known
Decimals −		Level known
Decimals X		Level known
Decimals ÷		Level known
Fractions +		Level known
Fractions −		Level known
Fractions X		Level known
Fractions ÷		Level known

Math Problem-Solving

Code	Item	Category
	Whole numbers	Multi-step word problems
	Fractions	
	Decimals	
	Concepts	Multi-step applications
4	Whole numbers	Two-step word problems
4	Fractions	
4	Decimals	
	Concepts	Two-step applications
	Whole numbers	Single-step word problems
	Fractions	
	Decimals	
	Concepts	Single-step applications

*Only codes 2 and 4 have been recorded for ease of reading.

ered on Chuck's learning style preferences and his expressed interest in sports. The "master plan" she generated for Chuck is presented in Figure 8-Q.

When she was ready to teach each of the skills listed on this master plan, Ms. Barth mapped out the specific steps she would follow. Two examples of how she did this are presented in Figure 8-R. The first (A) shows her specification of en route objectives for teaching one of the math skills listed on the master plan. The second example (B) shows her breakdown for teaching a reading skill. Notice that in both cases the en route objectives listed are specific, measurable, and sequentially arranged. Also, they have been broken down into small increments which will permit the learner to progress gradually. Ms. Barth could easily use this information when she updates Chuck's IEP.

When she was ready to prepare her daily teaching plans, Ms. Barth became even more specific in her instructional planning. She knew that to teach each of the en route objectives effectively, a *series* of lessons would have to be prepared. So before initiating any instruction, she outlined a specific teaching sequence for each en route objective.

Student *Chuck*

READING

Objectives	Materials	Mastery Criteria
Phonetic Analysis/Structural Analysis 　1. *consonant blends—bl/br* 　　*fl/fr; cl/cr; all 's' blends* 　2. *consonant digraphs—sh, ph* 　　*ch, ck* 　3. *irregular vowels—oy/oi, ou/ow* 　4. *contractions*	*Point 31—Decoding Skills Book & Tapes* 　　" 　　"	
Sight Vocabulary 　1. *teach unknown Dolch words,* 　　*in groups of 10 (go through* 　　*complete list)* 　2. *teach "survival" sight words* 　　*in groups of 10*		
Comprehension 　1. *inferential—drawing conclusions* 　　*& predicting outcomes* 　2. *inferential—separating fact* 　　*from opinion*	*— Pal Paperbacks— 　Sports Action — Barnell-Loft—Drawing 　Conclusions workbook*	

WRITTEN EXPRESSION

Objectives	Materials	Mastery Criteria
Spelling 　1. *auditory discrimination of* 　　*sounds in words* 　2. *regular phonetic spellings* 　　*(predictable S/S associations)* 　3. *non-phonetic spellings* 　　*(spelling sight words)*	*— Utilize target words dealing 　with sports*	
Conventions of Print 　1. *punctuation—quotation marks;* 　　*exclamation; and commas (words* 　　*in series)* 　2. *capitalization—proper names* 　　*& holidays*		

MATH

Objectives	Materials	Mastery Criteria
Multiplication of whole #'s	*Digiter*	
Measurement—linear liquid		
Division of whole #'s		
Measurement—time		
Money — making change 　　　— simple problem solving 　　　　involving +/- /x/÷		

Figure 8-Q Master Plan of Instructional Objectives for Chuck

A. Objective—Multiplication of Whole Numbers with 90% Accuracy

7. Multiplying 3 digit #'s by 3 digit #'s with regrouping

6. Multiplying 3 digit #'s by 2 digit #'s with regrouping

5. Multiplying 3 digit #'s by 2 digit #'s without regrouping

4. Multiplying 2 digit #'s by 2 digit #'s with regrouping

3. Multiplying 2 digit #'s by 2 digit #'s without regrouping

2. Multiplying 2 digit #'s by 1 digit #'s with regrouping

1. Multiplying 2 digit #'s by 1 digit #'s without regrouping

B. Objective—Decoding Consonant Blends (bl/br; cl/cr; fl/fr) with 90% Accuracy

5. Reading 2 syllable words beginning with target blends

4. Reading long vowel words beginning with target blends

3. Reading short vowel words beginning with target blends

2. Matching target blend sounds with their printed equivalent

1. Auditory discrimination of target blend sounds

Figure 8-R   Teacher's Specification of En Route Objectives for One Math and One Reading Skill

Figure 8-S illustrates one of the teaching sequences she developed. It shows exactly how she intended to teach auditory discrimination of blend sounds. (Referring back to Figure 8-R, we see this is her first step in teaching Chuck to *decode* consonant sounds.) The five activities in this teaching sequence will now be scheduled into Ms. Barth's daily planning book for implementation.

Objective—The student will learn to auditorally discriminate the following sounds—bl, br, fl, fr, cl, cr—with 90% accuracy.

1. Teacher will introduce sounds using "picture cue" chart with blend symbols printed below each picture. Teacher will then say words and student will indicate which blend sound is heard in the word.

2. Teacher will say sets of three words, asking student to indicate which word begins with a particular blend sound.

3. Given pairs of stimulus pictures, the student will identify which picture begins with a blend sound and will record the appropriate sound on tape.

4. Given a set of 25 picture cards which all begin with blends, the student will sort cards according to their blend sound.

5. Given a particular blend sound, the student will say five words beginning with the same sound.

Figure 8-S   Instructional Sequence Developed for Chuck

IMPLEMENTING INSTRUCTION
BASED ON
ASSESSMENT FINDINGS

So far, we have discussed techniques for managing classrooms to gather assessment data, and we have described methods for organizing these data after they are collected. Now we will focus our attention on the final, and in some ways, most critical issue. We will discuss approaches to implementing individualized instruction which is based on the assessment findings. This is an important area of concern in an assessment book, because if instruction cannot be tailored to address students' identified needs, then the assessment served no purpose.

Let us preface our discussion by pointing out that if teachers had complete freedom to pick and choose when they would work with particular students or how many students they would be responsible for at a given time, it would be a relatively simple task to implement individualized programming. Those students with similar needs could be dealt with at one time, and those with unique needs could be seen individually. However, it is rare that a teacher has complete freedom in scheduling students. Usually, a variety of constraints exist. The teacher must work with groups of students whose needs are quite diverse. Given this fact, the task of individualizing instruction becomes somewhat more difficult.

As a first step toward implementing instruction based on assessment findings, the teachers may find it useful to complete an Instructional Grouping Grid like that shown in Figure 8-T. The information placed on this grid comes from the "master plans" already generated for each student (e.g., the information on Chuck came from Figure 8-Q).

On this grid the teacher records his/her immediate instructional priorities for each student. Specific skills are ranged across the top of the form, and space is provided for listing student names down the side. By reading *across the rows*, the teacher can see which skills a particular student will be taught. By reading *down the columns*, the teacher can identify all who need to learn the same skills. Thus, the grid provides the teacher with an overview of the instructional needs of the whole group of students. The Instructional Grouping Grid summarizes unique individual needs as well as overlapping areas. A form of this kind helps the teacher not only to plan instruction, but also to develop instructional groups.

The second step in preparing for instruction based on assessment findings is to gather instructional materials which can be used in independent practice assignments or for review. These materials could be placed in individual work folders prepared for each student. Or, in instances where the instructional materials are too cumbersome to be placed in the folder, they could simply be listed. In gathering together these instructional materials, the teacher should be certain that at least some portion of them reflects students' individual interests. For example, if a student has expressed an interest in dancing, music, and several crafts, his/her folder might contain a few independent reading activities using material on popular recording stars (e.g., Famous People Stories from the Unigraph Co.). There might also be several independent written expression tasks calling for a description of the student's interest in crafts, or for construction of an advertisement to sell some of his/her work. And there might be a math activity which requires that the student compute travel expenses to attend a dance contest in New York City.

Student	Vowels ou/ow	Blends	Multiplication facts (6's)	20 new Dolch words	Rule for (?)	Short vowel discrim.	Comprehension—main idea				Last month's Dolch words	Compound words	Prefixes	Digraphs	Multiplication facts (3's, 4's, 5's)	
	New Objectives										**Review**					
Chuck	X	X	X	X	X						X		X	X		
Anthony		X		X	X		X				X		X	X	X	
John				X	X	X	X				X			X		
Vickie	X		X		X		X				X		X		X	
Ronnie		X		X	X	X					X	X				

Figure 8-T Instructional Grouping Grid

     Other materials and activities placed in the folders would be somewhat more "ordinary" and would not necessarily reflect students' special interests. They would be included because they focus on particular skill needs and provide appropriate practice or drill. To maintain high levels of motivation, the teacher would plan to vary the assignments he/she gives to students, so that the high interest activities are interspersed with the more routine tasks.

     To illustrate how these two steps help the teacher develop and manage a program of instruction based on assessment findings, we will return to Ms. Barth's resource room and Mr. Sellers' self-contained class. This illustration will show how they utilized Instructional Grouping Grids and collections of independent tasks to help in their planning. It will also demonstrate how the management systems initiated to gather assessment data were maintained and adapted when they moved from a focus on assessment to a focus on instruction. Finally, the method the teachers used to incorporate data on *how* to teach students in their instructional plans will be illustrated.

     Illustration: Resource Room—First Period Class. Ms. Barth, the resource room teacher, completed an Instructional Grouping Grid for her first period class and developed folders for each student, with an appropriate mix of "interesting" and "routine" independent work assignments. Then she began to schedule her daily routine by blocking out her own time to work with individual students or small groups. This pattern was consistent with the method she used when she planned assessment activities. During these teacher-directed one-to-one or small group sessions, she planned to introduce new skills to the students and to monitor their practice closely. The Instructional Grouping Grids helped her to identify students who could be scheduled together for instruction and students who needed to be taught one-to-one.

Next, she planned a schedule of independent assignments for the students to complete when they were not working with her. They involved some learning center activities which she developed for *all* her students to complete (e.g., a reading center tape unit on survival sight words) and some assignments that were unique for each student.

Ms. Barth took several precautions to insure that her class would operate smoothly when she put her plans into action. She did four critical things which would help her management system to work:

1. She gave each student a schedule that told him/her what to do during the class period. It was the same type of schedule she had used when gathering her assessment data (see Figure 8-H). However, now instructional activities, rather than assessment tasks, were scheduled.

2. She employed a reinforcement system which she hoped would help keep students on-task when they were working independently. The contingencies she used were varied, and reflected students' individual preferences as much as possible. Her assessment data on *how* to teach was particularly useful to her in developing the reinforcement system.

3. She taught her students a *specific procedure* for getting help when they were working independently and had a problem. They were to raise a hand to get the teacher's attention. Once she acknowledged them, they were to continue work on other items, if possible, until she came to offer help. If they could not continue with their assignment, they were to read silently from the independent reader which they always kept with them.

4. She frequently made a "management pass" of the classroom. That is, at timely intervals, between small group or one-to-one instructional sessions, she moved around the class, answering questions and monitoring students' work. She took care to do this often, so that students working independently received sufficient corrective feedback.

Ms. Barth scheduled her time to work with the entire group when her Instructional Grouping Grid indicated that everyone needed to learn the same skill. During these times, she kept the learning style data in mind, and prepared herself to give additional direction and support to those who needed it. For example, she remembered that John usually required a lot of teacher direction. So, in group lessons, she made sure to call on him frequently, and to provide him with considerable corrective feedback. She prompted him and provided numerous cues to lead him to correct responses. Also, when she assigned follow-up work after a large group lesson, she went over the first few items with John at his work station, to make certain he was on the "right track."

Within the same large-group lesson, she accommodated Vickie and Ron (who had demonstrated poor listening skills on her assessment of learning style) by frequently asking them to restate information or directions. Visual cues and supports were provided to help them organize and remember. (Of course, Ms. Barth was equally sensitive to her students' learning style in conducting her small group and her one-to-one instructional sessions.)

Figure 8-U Daily Planning Book: Three Days of Teaching Plans

Period ___1—9-9:45___   Week of: _____

Monday

Chuck— [Tchr.] —Intro. vowels ou/ow; (Folder) — new vowel activity, p. 102; choice of math page

Anthony & John— (Folder) —Red Racer story; answer main idea questions; [Tchr.] —new blends

Vickie— [Tchr.] intro. vowels ou/ow; (Folder) — new vowel activity, p. 102; choice of math page

Ronnie—Language Master—Activity #1; new Dolch words; [Tchr.] —new blends

Tuesday

Chuck— (Folder) —choice of math activity; Tchr. —new vowel review; Reader, pp. 68-72

Anthony & John—Reading Center—blend activity tapes 1 and 2; (Folder) —choice of 1 review activity

Vickie—Language Master—Activity #1; new Dolch words; [Tchr.] —new vowel review; Reader, pp. 68-72

Ronnie— [Tchr.] —new Dolch words; Language Master—Dolch Activity #2; (Folder) — blends work sheet

Wednesday

Chuck
Anthony
John
Vickie
Ronnie

group lesson—
— rule for question marks
— practice working/writing questions
— seat assignment———→ turn statements into Q's

Thursday

Friday

Finish Next Week:

Figure 8-U shows Ms. Barth's lesson plans for three typical days of instruction for her first period class. The students' individual schedules, which she would also prepare, would reflect this information. Chuck's schedule for that same three-day period is shown in Figure 8-V.

Figure 8-V Assignment Schedule for Chuck

Period _Chuck_   Week of: _10/14_

Monday

☐ _T_   _New vowels: ou/ow_
⬭_Folder_—_new vowels, p. 102_
         —pick any math page

Tuesday

⬭_Folder_—_pick any math page_

☐ _T_   _—new vowels: ou/ow_
            —Reader, pp. 68-72

Wednesday

Group work with   ☐ _T_

Thursday

Friday

Finish Next Week:

Illustration: Self-Contained Class.   The teacher in the self-contained classroom, Mr. Sellers, used a slightly different method for planning and implementing instruction based on assessment findings. Because his students spend most of their day with him, he developed general class schedules for each day of the week. One of these is posted each morning to show students how *they* (not the teacher) will be spending their time over the course of the day.

Mornings were usually devoted to reading and language arts activities. Afternoons usually began with math and then included other subjects such as science, social studies, or current events. A copy of the weekly class schedule for *students* is shown in Figure 8-W.

Mr. Sellers generated *his own* schedule by concentrating on how *he* would spend his time. Since he was required by the school district to use a designated reading and math series, he used the information on his Instructional Grouping Grids to form instructional groups for these two areas. Then his first step in daily planning was to decide what he would do with each of his reading and math groups when he met them for small-group instruction. He also planned follow-up assignments which would be given.

Next, he planned activities for the other subjects. Although these were generally planned as group lessons, he indicated particular techniques and accommodations which he would use with certain students, based on his assessments of *how* to teach.

All of his information was recorded in his planning book, using the format presented in Figure 8-X.

Finally, he selected independent assignments for students from the work folders he had already prepared. These assignments were stacked on each student's desk, along with the reading and/or math follow-up assignments he had selected. They were stacked in the order that they should be completed by the students. (Assignments were ordered to reflect the daily class schedule, so that everyone worked on spelling assignments first, reading assignments second, and so forth.)

To implement his plans, Mr. Sellers began each morning by going over the

MONDAY	TUESDAY	WEDNESDAY	THURSDAY	FRIDAY
Spelling	Spelling	Spelling	Spelling	Spelling
Reading	Reading	Reading	Reading	Reading
Language	Library	Language	Gym	Language
-Lunch-	-Lunch-	-Lunch-	-Lunch-	-Lunch-
Gym	Math	Art	Math	Math
Math	Social Studies	Math	Current Events	Music
Science	Following Directions	Science		Activity Pd.
Following Directions				

Figure 8-W Students' Weekly Class Schedule (Self-Contained Class)

MONDAY

Class Schedule	Teacher's Plan
•Spelling (9-9:30)	Reading Group #1 (9-9:30) Work on: _____ _____ _____
•Reading (9:30-10:15)	MGMT (9:30-9:45) Reading Group #2 (9:45-10:15) Work on: _____ _____ _____
•Language Development (10:15-10:45)	Reading Group #3 (10:15-10:45) Work on: _____ _____ _____
•Clean-up & Corrections Restrooms (10:45-11:15)	MGMT (10:45-11:15)

————LUNCH————

•Gym (12-12:30)	Planning (12-12:30)
•Math (12:45-1:45)	Math Group #1 (12:45-1:10) Work on: _____ _____ _____ MGMT (1:10-1:20) Math Group #2 (1:20-1:45) Work on: _____ _____ _____
•Science (1:45-2:15)	Science--group lesson (1:45-2:15) Topic: _____

——————FREE TIME——————

•Following Directions (2:30-3)	Following Directions--group lesson (2:30-3) Activities: _____

Figure 8-X Daily Planning Book (Self-Contained Class)

general schedule for the day. He then explained directions for completing the independent assignments he had placed on students' desks. As students began working, Mr. Sellers passed among them to make sure everyone knew what to do on the independent reading, spelling, and language assignments. He then called his first reading group and worked with them.

At the end of the small-group session, Mr. Sellers made a second "management pass," giving corrective feedback and repeating the directions for seatwork activities as necessary. He then called his next reading group.

This same procedure was followed for the remainder of the morning and for the math portion of the afternoon. The day generally ended with one or two large-group activities.

Like Ms. Barth, Mr. Sellers took steps to insure that his system operated smoothly. He posted a schedule so that his students would know what they should be doing throughout the day. He used a point system to reinforce students' on-task behavior and, during the Friday activity period, he permitted students to exchange points for a range of rewards based on their individual preferences. He also instituted a procedure for students to get help from the teacher. When a student needed assistance, he/she took a number from a small box on the teacher's desk. Mr. Sellers then dealt with students' problems in numerical order as he made each "management pass" of the classroom between instructional groups.

Although both Ms. Barth and Mr. Sellers utilized different methods for planning and implementing instruction, their approaches can be summarized as follows:

1. They completed Instructional Grouping Grids based on their assessment data to identify instructional groups.
2. They gathered together instructional materials which could be given as independent activities, taking care to include some high interest tasks.
3. They developed daily plans by considering how *their* time with students would be spent, and how students would spend "non-teacher" time.
4. They had a method for letting students know what they should be working on at any given time.
5. They took precautions to insure that things would operate smoothly.
6. As instruction continued, both teachers updated the individual folders they prepared for students. Independent work assignments, which provided follow-up practice for skills introduced in the teacher-directed sessions, were added, as were additional review activities, where appropriate.

SUMMARY

In this chapter we have presented techniques and suggestions to enable teachers to both organize and manage the assessment process.

We recognize that assessment for instructional planning makes a variety of demands on the teacher, and may seem cumbersome and complicated, particularly for an inexperienced teacher. The material presented in this chapter was created to enable teachers to accomplish the assessment in a smooth fashion.

We suggested that planning for assessment has three elements: summarizing student assessment needs, scheduling teacher and student time and structuring classroom space. Both a resource room and a self-contained classroom were used to illustrate the implementation of these three elements in the assessment procedure.

Finally, we demonstrated how the assessment plan flows naturally into the instructional plan, as the teacher shifts his/her emphasis from assessment to instruction.

9

Concluding Comments

The task of a remedial or special education teacher is enormous. She/he must help students learn what they cannot learn on their own, so that they can become literate and productive members of society. The strategies that we have presented in this text do not simplify that task. They are time consuming in their planning and implementation. But they do make the goal of the remedial teacher more attainable. They help the teacher to discover what and how to teach each student, so that more targeted and productive instruction can be planned.

The 12-step procedure for the assessment for instructional planning introduced in Chapter 3 and reiterated throughout the text will be reviewed here one last time. Then we will offer some suggestions for the use of the strategy beyond the assessment of basic skills and some concluding comments about assessment in general. But first we will review briefly the principles outlined in Chapter 1 which guided the development of the 12-step procedure.

PRINCIPLES WHICH GUIDE THE ASSESSMENT FOR INSTRUCTIONAL PLANNING

Principle 1. The remedial or special education teacher has flexibility in planning what to teach and how to teach it. This flexibility carries with it the responsibility to understand the unique needs of each individual student. It frees the teacher from the requirement of covering a prescribed curriculum at a prescribed pace, but adds the burden of curriculum planning to the teacher's job. It creates the need for assessments on which to base curricular decisions.

Principle 2.   The initial assessment will not be exhaustive. It need only provide the teacher with some information on where to begin teaching each student. To do otherwise would take far too much time away from the teacher's main concern, which is instruction. The assessment for instructional planning is intended to get the student and the teacher started on the right track, and to provide a framework within which more information and more detailed data, forthcoming in the course of teaching, can be fit.

Principle 3.   It is efficient to begin by collecting survey information (an overview of skill development) and to probe for more specific or more detailed information only as needed.

Teachers need specific information about student skill performances in order to know what to do instructionally for a student. But there are hundreds of individual skills which could be assessed in a school-age child. For efficiency in testing, the assessment should begin with a sampling of skills in each domain of interest—an overview of student performance in representative skills. If the student makes no errors, he/she is assumed to be competent. If errors are made, more detailed information can be sought through probes or interviews.

Principle 4.   It is appropriate and efficient to "test down" rather than "test up." When skill, language, or response hierarchies are developed as guides to the assessment process, the teacher must estimate the highest level at which reasonable performance (neither error-free nor "error-full") can be expected. The assessment would begin at that level. The teacher would then "test down" the hierarchy to a level at which the students perform well (virtually error-free). Once that level has been identified, all skills lower on the hierarchy (presumed to be prerequisite to performance at that level) are assumed to have been mastered and are not tested. The only time the teacher might "test up" would be if the initial estimate of the starting point was too low, i.e., the student performed too well on the survey task, and no useful error analysis could be accomplished.

This "test down" procedure has several advantages. It terminates testing on a positive, successful note. It also dissuades the teacher from focusing attention on poor performance on a prerequisite skill in a student who performs adequately at a higher level.

Principle 5.   Each assessment task must elicit the student's best performance. The teacher is responsible for structuring the environment so that during surveys and probes the student is comfortable, at ease, and motivated to perform. When these conditions prevail, errors can more readily be interpreted to reflect poor skill development and to indicate instructional needs.

Principle 6.   The teacher should select appropriate vehicles for obtaining assessment information. Testing, observing, and interviewing are three methods for collecting data useful for instructional planning. The teacher must have a clear picture of what kind of information is being sought and which method of data collection will produce the most satisfying results. Most often, information on *what* to teach will be obtained through testing, while information on *how* to teach will come from observation and interviews. But this will not always be the case.

Principle 7. If tests are used to collect information, they should be technically sound. The emphasis in our approach to assessment for instructional planning is on the use of informal rather than standardized, formal tests, and on the interpretation of performance patterns and error analyses, rather than on the reporting of scores. Therefore, our primary concern is with test validity—making certain that a test measures what we intend it to measure, in the manner we intended as well.

If scores are to be reported for any reason, teachers must be concerned with test reliability. They must recognize that many tests developed for use with underachieving students provide inadequate reliability data, making *scores* derived from these tests of questionable value.

THE 12-STEP STRATEGY FOR ASSESSMENT FOR INSTRUCTIONAL PLANNING

Using these principles, a 12-step strategy for assessment for instructional planning was developed and introduced in Chapter 3. The twelve steps, presented one last time in Table 9-1, carry the teacher from the initial decisions to test, to the instruction that is planned on the basis of the data collected. In subsequent chapters, the 12-step procedure formed the basis for descriptions of assessment procedures in reading (for functional and beginning readers), in written expression (for functional and

Table 9-1 Twelve-Step Strategy for Assessment for Instructional Planning

1. Decide what to assess.
2. Select or develop a skill hierarchy.
3. Decide where to begin.
4. Select or develop survey instrument.
5. Get ready to test.
6. Administer the survey.
7. Note errors and performance style.
8. Analyze findings and summarize outcomes.
9. Hypothesize reasons for errors and determine areas to probe.
10. Probe.
11. Complete recordkeeping forms and generate teaching objectives.
12. Start teaching; update assessment information.

beginning writers), and in mathematics, as well as in learning style, interest, and motivators. Only minor modifications in the 12-step procedure were introduced to emphasize the orderliness and utility of the strategy, and the importance of following the procedures until they become second nature.

Once a teacher is familiar with the 12-step strategy and has a clear view of the assessment information being sought and of the recordkeeping forms onto which the data will be summarized, it may be natural to make some changes in the assessment strategy. Steps may be reordered. Certain steps may be eliminated or combined to shorten the procedure. Recordkeeping forms may be altered, and certain ones discarded altogether. Such changes are acceptable so long as they do not jeopardize the outcome of the assessment. The teacher must still arrive at a clear, student-specific picture of which skills have been mastered, which need to be taught, and which must be probed further in the course of instruction. The only unacceptable adaptation to the assessment strategy is the development of a standard battery of formal tests to be administered to all students as the school year begins. The practice of administering such tests is antithetical to the proposal of an individually planned, informal assessment for instructional planning which we have described.

APPLICATION OF THE STRATEGY TO OTHER AREAS OF ASSESSMENT

Throughout this text, we have concentrated on assessment of basic skill areas in the school-age student because it is in the areas of reading, written expression, and mathematics that remedial and special education teachers concentrate their energies. But the strategy for informal assessment introduced in this text has much wider applicability. The same 12-step procedure could be used to assess learning needs in any subject area: oral language proficiency or fine and gross motor skill development in the preschooler; vocational skills in the adolescent or young adult; subject content knowledge (science or social studies) in the school-age student, etc.

In each case the assessment would begin by establishing who is to be tested. Then the teacher would set out the series of skills (hierarchy) which constitute that domain. As in the case of the basic skill areas, this may mean an ordering of curriculum objectives or a selection of an already developed skill hierarchy from a reputable source. With skill hierarchy in hand, the teacher would decide where to begin testing each student who is to be assessed. The "test down" principle would apply, and the teacher would estimate the highest level at which the student could conceivably perform. An appropriate survey instrument could be selected or developed to measure knowledge (skill development) at that level, and recordkeeping forms would need to be created or adapted for use in summarizing the survey information. As before, the teacher would prepare to test oral language, motor skills, vocational skills or knowledge of science or social studies by gathering the necessary materials and constructing an environment that would ensure maximum student performance. After administration of the survey, findings would be analyzed to determine reasons for errors. Follow-up probes would be used to obtain more detailed and specific information, and summary recordkeeping forms, based on the skill hierarchy set out at the start of the assessment, would be completed.

By following the 12-step procedure for the assessment of knowledge or skill, the teacher would be directed to the first several teaching objectives appropriate for each individual student. Regardless of the age of the students or the subject area in which teaching is to take place, the 12-step procedure can be applied or adapted to provide valuable information on what needs to be taught.

ASSESSMENT AND INSTRUCTION

Repeated application of the assessment strategy for each student in each domain of interest may seem very tiresome and a waste of teacher and student time. Some may even feel that our commitment to the 12-step strategy is overzealous. After all, we ourselves said in Chapter 1 that the important activity for a teacher to engage in is teaching, not testing. However, in the race to achieve literacy and competence in underachieving students before they leave school, our assessment strategy will save time and effort, not waste it. Assessment for Instructional Planning is the means by which teachers can develop valid, data-based programming decisions for their students. It is the key to appropriate treatments and suitable lessons for all students who have learning problems. The 12-step assessment strategy is actually the first step towards real understanding of the learning needs of special students. But, of course, it is *only* the beginning. Assessment is a means to an end, not an end in itself. It is the *link* to effective instruction. Instruction must follow from it, or both assessment and instruction are likely to be worthless activities.

We recognize that it is difficult for some teachers to carry out assessment in systematic and useful ways. Testing and teaching are very different sorts of activities. Teaching permits a variety of activities on the part of the teacher to assist and facilitate student performance. The teacher may be spontaneous, creative, and flexible in carrying out such plans. In testing, even in the informal teacher-designed testing such as we have described in the assessment for instructional planning, standards of teacher behavior are more formal. Teacher behavior must be more constrained. Students are expected to respond on their own to tasks administered under particular sets of conditions. Teachers must maintain a certain level of precision in the development and selection of these tasks and in their observations of test conditions, student behaviors, and their own behaviors in administering the tests. They must also be precise in taking notes, scoring responses, and transferring data to recordkeeping forms. These may not be comfortable, natural behaviors for some teachers, but they are essential for accuracy in the interpretation of assessment findings and in program planning.

CONCLUDING COMMENTS

Our goal in writing this text was to help teachers teach well. Our emphasis was on assessment as the vehicle by which teachers can discover *what* and *how* to teach each student. To carry out the assessment and the instruction which follows from it, teachers must have a strong commitment to their work, and must be *organized*. The importance of being organized cannot be overstated. Organization, a concept that is implicit throughout the book and discussed explicitly in Chapter 8, is crucial to the smooth running of both the assessment and teaching phases of any classroom in which individualized programs are to be carried out. Organization applies to information management (on forms), environmental management (of the physical space and instructional materials), self-management (in specifying goals, allotting teacher time) and student management (having students know what to do, how, when, and where to do it, and what consequences to expect if it does or does not get done). To the extent that the teacher can develop an organizational plan for information, environmental, self, and student management, it will be easier to carry out the complex task of teaching each student well. Teaching well is hard work. Getting organized is hard work. Designing and implementing assessments for instructional planning is hard work. But in our experience, the satisfactions in student progress are well worth the effort.

References

Alexander, J. E. (Ed.), *Teaching reading.* Boston: Little, Brown & Company, 1979.

Ashlock, R. B. *Error patterns in computation* (2nd ed.). Columbus, Ohio: Charles E. Merrill Publishing Company, 1976.

Betts, E. *Foundations of reading instruction.* New York: American Book Company, 1950.

Charles, C. M. *Individualized instruction* (2nd ed.). St. Louis: The C. V. Mosby Company, 1980.

Chase, C. I. *Measurement for educational evaluation* (2nd ed.). Reading, Mass.: Addison-Wesley Publishing Company, 1978.

Crown, W. *Diagnostic arithmetic interview,* mimeograph. New Brunswick, N.J.: Rutgers College, 1980.

Dunn, R. and Dunn, K. *Educator's self-teaching guide to individualizing instructional programs.* Reston, Va.: Parker Publishing Company, Inc., 1975.

Fry, E. *Elementary reading instruction.* New York: McGraw-Hill Book Company, 1977.

Hammill, D. D. and Bartel, N. R. *Teaching children with learning and behavior problems* (2nd ed.). Boston: Allyn & Bacon, Inc., 1978.

Howards, M. *Reading diagnosis and instruction.* Reston, Va.: Reston Publishing Company, Inc., 1980.

Howell, K. W., Kaplan, J. S., and O'Connell, C. Y. *Evaluating exceptional children: A task analysis approach.* Columbus, Ohio: Charles E. Merrill Publishing Company, 1979.

Ingram, C. F. *Fundamentals of educational assessment.* New York: D. Van Nostrand Company, 1980.

LaPray, M. H. *On the spot reading diagnosis file.* W. Nyack, N.Y.: The Center for Applied Research in Education, Inc., 1978.

Perfetti, C. A. and Hogaboam, T. The relationship between single word decoding and reading comprehension skills. *Journal of Educational Psychology,* 1975, *67,* 461-469.

Richardson, M. W. and Kuder, G. F. The calculation of test reliability coefficients based upon the method of rational equivalence. *Journal of Educational Psychology,* 1939, *30,* 681-687.

Roberts, G. H. The failure strategies of third grade arithmetic pupils. *The Arithmetic Teacher,* 1968, *15,* 442-446.

Salvia, J. and Ysseldyke, J. E. *Assessment in special and remedial education* (2nd ed.). Boston: Houghton Mifflin Company, 1981.

Smith, N. B. and Robinson, H. A. *Reading instruction for today's children* (2nd ed.). Englewood Cliffs, N.J.: Prentice-Hall, Inc., 1980.

Turnbull, A., Strickland, B., and Brantley, J. *Developing and implementing individualized educational programs.* Columbus, Ohio: Charles E. Merrill Publishing Company, 1978.

Underhill, B., Uprichard, E., and Heddens, J. *Diagnosing mathematical difficulties.* Columbus, Ohio: Charles E. Merrill Publishing Company, 1980.

Wallace, G. and Larsen, S. C. *Educational assessment of learning problems: Testing for teaching.* Boston: Allyn & Bacon, Inc., 1978.

Wilson, R. M. *Diagnostic and remedial reading for classroom and clinic* (3rd ed.). Columbus, Ohio: Charles E. Merrill Publishing Company, 1977.

Appendices

APPENDIX A: SOURCES FOR ASSESSMENT TASKS

Published Tests

This appendix provides a listing of achievement, diagnostic, and criterion-referenced measures commonly used in assessing children with special needs. It includes tests mentioned throughout the book as well as others. (Publisher's addresses are presented at the end of the appendix.)

Adequate reliability information has been reported for those tests marked with an asterisk. Tests which are not marked in this fashion are recommended for use for performance data only. Reliability information is either inadequate or unreported. A more detailed description of these tests can be obtained from the *Mental Measurements Yearbooks* (O. K. Buros, Editor), which are generally available in reference libraries.

Advanced Reading Inventory; William C. Brown, Co., Publishers

Analytical Reading Inventory; Charles E. Merrill Publishing Company

Assessment of Children's Language Comprehension; Consulting Psychologists Press

Basic Educational Skills Inventory: Math; Brad Winch & Associates

Boehm Test of Basic Concepts; Psychological Corporation

Botel Reading Inventory; Follett Educational Corporation

Brigance Inventory of Basic Skills; Curriculum Associates, Inc.

Brigance Inventory of Essential Skills; Curriculum Associates Inc.

*California Achievement Tests; California Test Bureau

*California Test of Basic Skills; McGraw-Hill Book Company

*Carrow Elicited Language Inventory; Learning Concepts, Inc.

*Carrow Test for Auditory Comprehension of Language; Learning Concepts, Inc.

Classroom Reading Inventory; William C. Brown, Co., Publishers

*Clinical Evaluation of Language Functions; Charles E. Merrill Publishing Company

Criterion Test of Basic Skills; Academic Therapy Publications

Diagnostic Achievement Test in Spelling; Barnell-Loft, Ltd.

Diagnostic Tests and Self-Helps in Arithmetic; California Test Bureau

*Doren Diagnostic Reading Test of Word Recognition Skills; American Guidance Services

Durrell Analysis of Reading Difficulty; Harcourt Brace Jovanovich, Inc.

*Gates-MacGinitie Reading Tests; Teachers College Press

Gates-McKillop Reading Diagnostic Tests; Teachers College Press

Gates-Russell Spelling Diagnosis Test; Teachers College Press

Gilmore Oral Reading Test; Harcourt Brace Jovanovich, Inc.

Gray Oral Reading Tests; The Bobbs-Merrill Co., Inc.

IEP Educational Diagnostic Inventories; National Center for Learning Disabilities

Individual Pupil Monitoring Systems: Mathematics; Houghton Mifflin Company

Individual Reading Placement Inventory; Follett Educational Group

Individualized Computation Skills Series; Holt, Rinehart and Winston

Individualized Math Drill and Practice Kits (includes criterion-referenced tests); Random House-Singer

Informal Reading Diagnosis; Prentice-Hall, Inc.

*Iowa Test of Basic Skills; Houghton Mifflin Company

*Key Math Diagnostic Arithmetic Test; American Guidance Services

Kottmeyer Diagnostic Spelling Test; Webster Publishing Company

Kraner Tests of Mathematics; C. C. Publications, Inc.

*Larsen-Hammill Test of Written Spelling; Pro-Ed

Lincoln Diagnostic Spelling Tests; The Bobbs-Merrill Co., Inc.

Mann-Suiter Development Reading Diagnosis; Allyn & Bacon, Inc.

*McCullough Word Analysis Tests; Ginn & Company

*Metropolitan Achievement Tests; Harcourt Brace Jovanovich, Inc.

Northwestern Syntax Screening Test; Northwestern University Press

On the Spot Reading Diagnosis File; Center for Applied Research in Education

*Peabody Individual Achievement Test; American Guidance Services

Peabody Picture Vocabulary Test; American Guidance Services

Picture Story Language Test; Grune & Stratton, Inc.

Reading Miscue Inventory; Macmillan, Inc.

Roswell-Chall Diagnostic Reading Test of Word Analysis Skills; Essay Press

Screening Test for Identifying Specific Language Disabilities; Educators Publishing Services

*Sequential Test of Educational Progress; Educational Testing Service

Skills for Arithmetic; The Ohio State Univeristy

Spache Diagnostic Reading Scales; California Test Bureau

*SRA Achievement Scales; Science Research Associates

SRA Diagnosis Kit; Science Research Associates

*Stanford Achievement Test; Harcourt Brace Jovanovich, Inc.

*Stanford Diagnostic Arithmetic Test; Harcourt Brace Jovanovich, Inc.

*Stanford Diagnostic Reading Test; Harcourt Brace Jovanovich, Inc.

Sucher-Allfred Reading Placement Inventory; The Economy Company

*Test of Adolescent Language (TOAL); Pro-Ed

*Test of Early Reading Ability (TERA); Pro-Ed

*Test of Language Development (TOLD); Pro-Ed

*Test of Reading Comprehension (TORC); Pro-Ed

*Test of Written Language; Pro-Ed

*Test of Written Spelling; Pro-Ed

Utah Test of Language Development; Communication Research Associates

*Wechsler Intelligence Scale for Children; Psychological Corporation

*Wide Range Achievement Test; Guidance Associates

*Wisconsin Tests of Reading Skill Development; National Computer Systems

*Woodcock-Johnson Psycho-Educational Battery; Teaching Resources

*Woodcock Reading Mastery Tests; American Guidance Services

Zaner-Bloser Evaluation Scales; Zaner-Bloser Co.

Addresses of Publishers

Academic Therapy Publications, 20 Commercial Boulevard, Navato, California 94947

Adston Educational Enterprises, 945 East River Oaks Drive, Baton Rouge, Louisiana 70875

Allyn & Bacon, Inc., 470 Atlantic Avenue, Boston, Massachusetts 02210

American Guidance Services, Inc., Publishers' Building, Circle Pines, Minnesota 55014

Barnell-Loft, Ltd., 958 Church Street, Baldwin, New York 11510

The Bobbs-Merrill Co., Inc., 4300 West 62 Street, Indianapolis, Indiana 46205

Brad Winch & Associates, Torrance, California 90505

C. C. Publications, Inc., Post Office Box 23699, Tigard, Oregon 97223

California Test Bureau, A Division of McGraw-Hill, Del Monte Research Park, Monterey, California 93940

The Center for Applied Research, Inc., West Nyack, New York 10994

Charles E. Merrill Publishing Company, 1300 Alum Creek Drive, Columbus, Ohio 43216

Consulting Psychologists Press, Palo Alto, California

Communication Research Associates, Post Office Box 110012, Salt Lake City, Utah

Curriculum Associates, Inc., 5 Esquire Road, North Billerica, Massachusetts, 01862

The Economy Company, 1901 North Walnut Avenue, Oklahoma City, Oklahoma, 74103

Educators Publishing Service, 75 Moulton Street, Cambridge, Massachusetts, 02138

Educational Testing Service, Princeton, New Jersey 08540

Essay Press, Box 5, Planetarium Station, New York, New York, 10024

Follett Educational Corporation, 1010 West Washington Boulevard, Chicago, Illinois 60607

Ginn & Company, 191 Spring Street, Lexington, Massachusetts 02173

Grune & Stratton, Inc., 111 Fifth Avenue, New York, New York 10003

Guidance Associates, 1526 Gilpin Avenue, Wilmington, Delaware 19800

Harcourt Brace Jovanovich, Inc., 757 Third Avenue, New York, New York 10022

Holt, Rinehart and Winston, 383 Madison Avenue, New York, New York 10017

Houghton Mifflin Company, One Beacon Street, Boston, Massachusetts, 02107

Learning Concepts, Inc., 2501 N. Lamar, Austin, Texas 78705

Macmillan, Inc., 866 Third Avenue, New York, New York 10022

McGraw-Hill Book Company, 1221 Avenue of the Americas, New York, New York 10022

National Computer Systems, Inc., Minneapolis, Minnesota

Northwestern University Press, 1735 Benson Avenue, Evanston, Illinois 60201

The Ohio State University, 356 Arps, Columbus, Ohio 43210

Prentice-Hall, Inc., Englewood Cliffs, New Jersey 07632

Pro-Ed, 33 Perry Brook Building, Austin, Texas 78751

Psychological Corporation, 304 E. 45 Street, New York, New York 10017

Random House-Singer, 201 E. 50 Street, New York, New York 10022

Science Research Associates, 259 E. Erie Street, Chicago, Illinois 60611

Select-Ed, Olathe, Kansas 66061

Teachers College Press, Teachers College, Columbia University, 1234 Amsterdam Avenue, New York, New York 10027

Teaching Resources Corp., 100 Boylston Street, Boston, Massachusetts 02116

Webster Publishing Company, Manchester, Missouri

William C. Brown Co., Publishers, 2460 Kerper Boulevard, Dubuque, Iowa 52001

Zanner-Bloser Co., 612 North Park Street, Columbus, Ohio 43215

APPENDIX B: GRAPH FOR ESTIMATING READABILITY*

Directions for Using the Readability Graph

1. Select three one-hundred-word passages from near the beginning, middle, and end of the book. Skip all proper nouns.

2. Count the total number of sentences in each hundred-word passage (estimating to nearest tenth of a sentence). Average these three numbers.

3. Count the total number of syllables in each hundred-word sample. There is a syllable for each vowel sound; for example: *cat* (1), *blackbird* (2), *continental* (4). Don't be fooled by word size; for example: *polio* (3), *through* (1). Endings such as *-y, -ed, -el,* or *-le* usually make a syllable, for example: *ready* (2), *bottle* (2). It may be convenient to count every syllable over one in each word and add 100. Average the total number of syllables for the three samples.

4. Plot on the graph the average number of sentences per hundred words and the average number of syllables per hundred words. Most plot points fall near the heavy curved line. Diagonal lines mark off approximate grade-level areas.

If great variability is encountered either in sentence length or in the syllable count for the three selections, then randomly select several more passages and average them in before plotting.

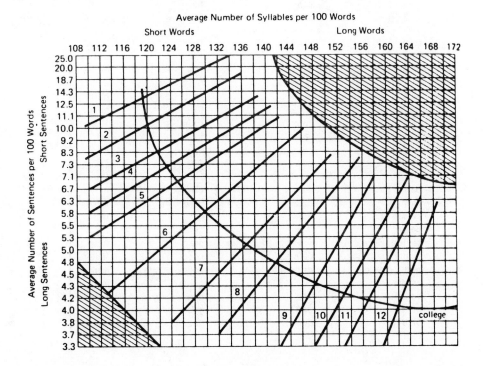

*Reprinted from: Fry, E., *Elementary Reading Instruction.* New York: McGraw-Hill Book Co., 1977, pp. 216-217.

APPENDIX C: HIGH FREQUENCY WORD LIST*

Phonetically Predictable

a	birthday	draw	green	land
about	black	dress	grow	large
after	blue	drink	had	last
airplane	boat	drop	hair	left
all	book	duck	hand	leg
almost	both	each	happy	let
along	box	eat	hard	letter
also	boy	end	has	life
always	bring	even	hat	like
am	brown	ever	he	line
an	bus	every	hear	little
and	but	fall	hello*	live
animals	buy	family	help	long
another	by	far	hen	lost
any	cage	farm	her	made
anything	cake	fast	here	make
are	call	fat	hill	man
around	called	father	him	may
as	came	feet	his	maybe
ask	can	few	hold	me
at	can't	find	home	men
ate	car	fire	hop	met
away	carry	first	horse	miss
baby	cat	fish	hot	more
back	catch	five	house	morning
bag	children	fly	how	mother
ball	city	food	hurry	much
balloon	clean	for	hurt	must
bark	coat	found	I	my
barn	cold	fox	ice	myself
bear	colds	full	if	name
because	cow	fun	I'll	need
bed	cry	funny	I'm	never
be	cut	game	in	new
bee	daddy	gave	into	next
before	dark	get	is	no
began	day	girl	it	not
behind	did	go	its	nothing
below	didn't	goat	it's	now
best	different	goes	jump	number
better	do	going	just	of
between	dog	good	keep	off
big	don't	good-by	kitten	often
bike	door	got	knew	old
bird	down	grass	know	on

*From *Direct Instruction Reading* by Carnine, D. and Silbert J., Columbus Ohio: Charles E. Merrill, 1979, pp. 520-521, Copyright © 1979 by Bell & Howell Company.

Phonetically Predictable (cont.)

only	rain	so	thing	wagon
open	ran	soon	things	want
or	read	sound	think	was
other	red	small	this	wash
our	ride	start	those	water
out	road	stay	three	way
over	rocket	step	time	we
own	room	still	to	well
paint	round	stop	today	went
pan	run	stopped	together	when
part	same	store	told	which
party	sang	story	too	while
peanut	sat	street	town	white
penny	saw	such	toy	why
pet	say	sun	train	will
pick	see	surprise	tree	window
pig	seen	table	truck	wish
picnic	set	take	try	with
place	seven	tell	turtle	word
play	shall	ten	TV	words
please	she	than	under	work
pocket	show	that	until	world
pony	side	the	up	write
pretty	sing	their	upon	year
prize	sister	them	us	yellow
pull	sit	then	use	you
rabbit	six	these	used	yes
race	sleep	they	very	zoo

Phonetically Irregular

again	from	looked	right	tomorrow
been	give	many	said	took
brought	gone	might	school	two
build	great	money	shoe	walk
come	guess	most	should	warm
could	half	night	some	were
does	have	oh	something	what
done	head	once	sure	where
eight	heard	one	talk	who
enough	kind	people	thank	won't
fight	laugh	picture	there	would
four	light	put	thought	your
friend	look	ready	through	

APPENDIX D: COMMON PHONICS GENERALIZATIONS*

1. When a one-syllable word contains two or more vowels, the first usually stands for a long vowel sound. All other vowels in the word are silent.

2. When a one-syllable word contains only one vowel, it usually represents a short vowel sound unless it is at the end of the word.

3. The letters *e, o,* or *y* stand for long vowel sounds when they occur at the end of a word and are the only letters which could represent vowel sounds in the word.

4. If the vowel *o* immediately precedes two consonant letters at the end of a one-syllable word, it usually represents /ŏ/ or /ô/.

5. When *a* immediately precedes *lk* or *ll,* it usually represents /ô/.

6. When *a* immediately follows *w* and is the only vowel in a monosyllable or syllable, it usually represents /ŏ/ or /ô/.

7. The letter *e* is usually silent when it occurs at the end of a word.

8. The letters *ey* usually stand for /ā/ when they occur at the end of a monosyllable.

9. The letter *i* usually represents /ī/ when it immediately precedes *ld* or *nd* at the end of a monosyllable.

10. The letters *au* and *aw* usually represent /ô/.

11. The letters *ay* usually stand for /ā/ when they occur at the end of a word or syllable.

12. The letters *er, ir,* and *ur* usually represent /ûr/ unless they are immediately followed by or come at the end of a plurisyllable word.

13. When the letters *ar, or, er,* or *ir* are immediately followed by another *r,* the vowel usually represents its short sound.

14. The spellings *oi* and *oy* represent the diphthong /oi/.

15. The spellings *ou* and *ow* usually represent the diphthong /ou/.

16. The consonant letters *b, f, h, j, k, l, m, p, q, r, v,* and *w* represent only one sound.

17. The consonant letter *c* usually represents /k/ unless it is followed by *e, i, y,* or *h.*

18. When the consonant letter *c* is followed by *e, i,* or *y,* it usually represents /*s*/.

19. The consonant letter *g* usually represents /*g*/ unless it precedes *e, i, y,* or *n.*

20. When the consonant letter *g* is followed by *e, i,* or *y,* it usually represents /*j*/.

APPENDIX E: DIAGNOSTIC ARITHMETIC INTERVIEW*
(Revised, 1980 Clinician's Script)

(Note: Individual items should be shown to the child on 3 × 5 cards.)

I. **Counting, Place Value, and Number System**

A. Can you tell me what comes next in these strings of numbers?

1) 1, 2, 3, 4, 5, _____   5) 407, 408, 409, _____

2) 2, 4, 6, 8, _____   6) 100, 200, 300, _____

3) 1, 5, 9, 13, _____   7) 1097, 1098, 1099, _____

4) 84, 86, 88, _____   8) 197, 196, 195, _____

B. 1) How old are you? _____

2) How old will you be in ten years? _____

3) How old were you five years ago? _____

(Note strategies—finger counting, fact recall, etc.)

C. 1) Count by tens starting with 10.

_____ _____ _____ _____

2) Count by tens starting with 13

_____ _____ _____ _____

---

*Crown, W. *Diagnostic arithmetic interview*, mimeograph. New Brunswick, N.J.: Rutgers College, 1980. Reprinted with permission.

(Is the student adding ten ones on each step or one ten?)

    D. Write these numbers

        1) Fifty-four_____   3) Four hundred ninety-eight_____

        2) Three hundred _____   4) Two hundred three _____

                 5) Five hundred fifty _____

    E. Tell me what these numbers are:
       (Record the language used precisely)

        1) 13_____

        2) 60_____

        3) 400_____

        4) 207_____

        5) 230_____

    F. Use these groups of sticks to show me these numbers:

       1) 37   2) 90   3) 7   4) 102   5) 240

II. Addition

Do you know what addition is? What is it?

What do you do when you add?

Can you tell me sometime outside of school when somebody might add?

Can you do these problems? *Tell me what you're doing as you do them.*

<table>
<tr><td colspan="2" align="center">*Basic facts
below ten*</td><td colspan="2" align="center">*Basic facts
above ten*</td></tr>
<tr><td align="center">4
+3</td><td align="center">5
+4</td><td align="center">6
+7</td><td align="center">8
+4</td></tr>
</table>

(Note strategies—finger counting, head counting, memory, etc.)

If you didn't remember any of these answers, how could you have found them?

Can you do those same problems with these poker chips or popsicle sticks? Show me how you would do them.

How about these? Remember, you should be describing to me what it is that you're doing.

<table>
<tr><td colspan="2" align="center">*2-digit,
no regrouping*</td><td colspan="2" align="center">*2-digit,
regrouping*</td><td colspan="2" align="center">*2- and 3-digit,
two regroupings*</td></tr>
<tr><td align="center">13
+24</td><td align="center">25
+42</td><td align="center">37
+24</td><td align="center">46
+37</td><td align="center">65
+89</td><td align="center">327
+593</td></tr>
</table>

What does carrying mean? (or regrouping, or renaming)

When do you have to carry?

III. Subtraction

Do you know what subtraction is?

What do you do when you subtract?

Do you know some other way to say "subtract"?

Can you tell me a situation where someone outside of school might need to subtract?

Can you do these problems? *(Note strategies.)*

Basic facts below ten			*Basic facts above ten*		
9 −5	8 −1	4 −2	13 − 6	12 − 4	16 − 9

If you didn't remember those answers, do you know any way that you could have figured them out?

Can you do them with these popsicle sticks or poker chips? Show me how? *(Note: Take-away or comparison?)*

Can you do these? Tell me what you're doing as you do them.

2-digit, no regrouping		*2-digit, regrouping*	
24 −13	37 −21	42 −27	65 −48

2- and 3-digit, regrouping, zero

126 − 59	407 −392	200 −166

What does borrowing mean? (or regrouping, or renaming)

When do you have to borrow?

IV. Number Order

I'm thinking of a number between 1 and 100 and I want you to try to guess it. Every time you make a guess I'll tell you whether it's too high or too low and I'll write it down on this chart. See how fast you can guess it. (Pick 63)

Too Low	*Too High*

APPENDIX

Teacher-Made
Surveys
and Probes

PROBE—CONVENTIONS OF PRINT

Name _____ **Date** _____

Part I - Knowledge of Punctuation and Capitalization Conventions

(Teacher reads directions and/or sentences to the student)

These sentences were written without any punctuation or capital letters.
Please rewrite each sentence using correct punctuation and capitalization.

1. the book is red _____

    _____

    _____

2. im sure his name is mr smith _____

    _____

    _____

3. my sister goes to washington high school _____

    _____

    _____

4. we re meeting with the boy scouts 4 30 p m _____

    _____

    _____

5. yes john did sail on the pacific ocean _____

    _____

    _____

PROBE—CONVENTIONS OF PRINT (CONT.)

6. shell bring the following people john sally mary and bill _____

    _____

    _____

7. you run fast but the russian was the fastest runner of them all

    _____

    _____

    _____

8. oh lauras mother said in surprise _____

    _____

    _____

Part II - Knowledge of Word Usage Conventions

These sentences have one word missing. Please write in the missing word.

1. Jim is very tall. Jim has _____ three inches since I
    last saw him.

2. John is a good player. Bill is a better player. But Ann is the
    _____ player of them all.

3. It is autumn. The _____ on the trees are turning brown.

4. What time does the sun _____ in the morning?

5. One woman was talking to another woman. The two _____
    were talking to each other.

6. One deer is by the barn. Two other _____ are by the trees.

7. I wish I _____ seen the movie.

8. Joe throws a ball every day. Yesterday, he _____ a ball.

PROBE—CONVENTIONS OF PRINT (CONT.)

Part III - Knowledge of Sentence Structure Conventions

Some of these groups of words make a complete sentence and some of them
do not. Some of them are really <u>more</u> <u>than</u> <u>one</u> sentence.

If the group of words is one complete sentence, put a <u>✓</u> in the box.

If the group of words is an incomplete sentence, put an <u>X</u> in the box.

If the group of words is really more than one sentence, show how to
write them correctly.

1. A strange spaceship landed. ☐

_____

_____

2. Since it was in the field. ☐

_____

_____

3. She was too afraid to run so she just stood there shaking. ☐

_____

_____

③

PROBE—CONVENTIONS OF PRINT (CONT.)

4. A clam can weigh over 225 kilograms they live in the ocean. ☐

_____

_____

5. When mother found out what the children were doing. ☐

_____

_____

6. He will take a trip before he starts his new job. ☐

_____

_____

7. We are going to my Grandmother's and she lives on a farm and we will have lots of fun. ☐

_____

_____

8. The game was tied until the last inning our team scored a run. ☐

_____

_____

④

COMPUTATIONS AND CONCEPTS SURVEY (EARLY 3rd GRADE)

Name _____**Date** _____

```
        61¢           46           638           394            36
(1)    +38¢    (2)    +75   (3)    +294   (4)    +576   (5)    -14
```

```
        74           825         $6.19           854         $9.81
(6)    -38    (7)   -163   (8)   -2.63   (9)    -626   (10)   -3.04
```

```
         2            4            5            0            8            6
(11)    x9    (12)    x1   (13)    x3   (14)    x7   (15)    x2   (16)    x3
```

(17) What does this sign ÷ mean? _____

(18) What happens when you divide? (What does it mean to divide?) _____

Write the name for the shaded part:

(19) 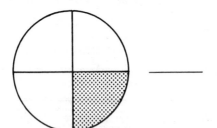 _____

(20) 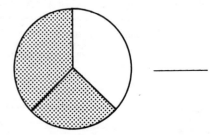 _____

(21)  = _____   (22)  = _____

COMPUTATIONS AND CONCEPTS SURVEY (EARLY 3rd GRADE) (CONT.)

(23) What time does this clock say?   (24) Show this time on the clock - 7:18

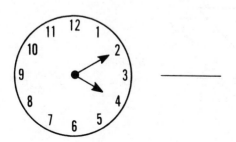

————

(25) Write the number
      3 hundreds, 5 tens, 0 ones   _____

(26) In this number, 56,493

         what number is in the thousands place   _____

                              tens place   _____

                              hundreds place   _____

                              ones place   _____

                              ten thousands place_____

(27) How many 10s are in 4378   _____

     how many 100s are in 68042   _____

     how many 1000s are in 903,148 _____

     how many ones are in 627   _____

(28) Mark the angles:

COMPUTATIONS AND CONCEPTS SURVEY (EARLY 3rd GRADE) (CONT.)

(29) Match the shape to its name:

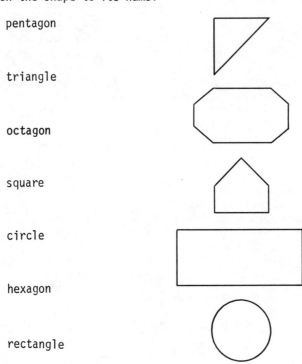

pentagon

triangle

octagon

square

circle

hexagon

rectangle

(30) How many:

feet in a yard? _____

meters in a kilometer? _____

pints in a quart? _____

(31) Which is larger?

gram or kilogram?

foot or yard?

quart or cup?

(3)

COMPUTATIONS AND CONCEPTS SURVEY (END OF 4th GRADE)

Name _____**Date** _____

(1) 487
   +368

(2) 8693
   +4748

(3) 902
   -367

(4) 4162
   -1864

(5) 26
   x46

(6) 49
   x62

(7) $5\overline{)768}$

(8) $23\overline{)917}$

(9) Work this problem: 4.2 + 3.37 + .61

(10) Work this problem: 3.7 - .16

(11) $\dfrac{3}{8}$

   $+\dfrac{2}{8}$

(12) $\dfrac{2}{3}$

   $+\dfrac{2}{3}$

(13) $\dfrac{6}{10}$

   $-\dfrac{2}{10}$

(14) $\dfrac{4}{5}$

   $-\dfrac{1}{5}$

(15) Show these fractions another way:

$\dfrac{7}{5} =$ $\dfrac{6}{2} =$ $\dfrac{4}{4} =$

(1)

COMPUTATIONS AND CONCEPTS SURVEY (END OF 4th GRADE) (CONT.)

(16) Reduce these fractions:

$$\frac{2}{4} =$$ $$\frac{5}{15} =$$ $$\frac{4}{12} =$$

(17) What time do these clocks say?

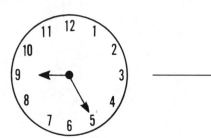 _____

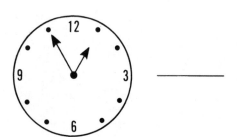 _____

(18) 11 cm = ___ dm ___ cm

23 cm = ___ dm ___ cm

Each ☐ is 1 square foot. Write the area in square feet.

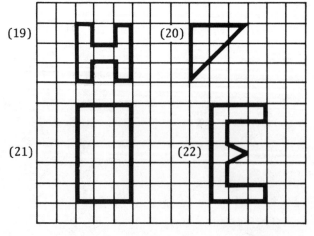

(19) _____

(20) _____

(21) _____

(22) _____

COMPUTATIONS AND CONCEPTS SURVEY (END OF 4th GRADE) (CONT.)

(23) Given one dollar, tell me how much change you would receive if you
bought something for 33¢?   _____

Given one dollar, tell me how much change you would receive if you
bought something for 52¢?   _____

Given five dollars, tell me how much change you would receive if you
bought something for $1.39?   _____

Given five dollars, tell me how much change you would receive if you
bought something for $3.75?   _____

In the picture find two:

(24) rays _____   _____

(25) right angles _____   _____

(26) angles that are not right angles _____   _____

(27) lines that are parallel _____   _____

(28) lines that are perpendicular

_____   _____

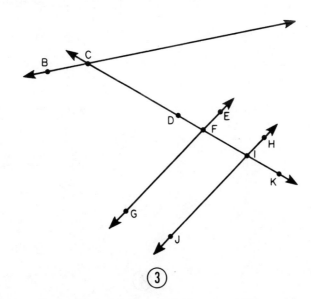

③

COMPUTATIONS AND CONCEPTS SURVEY (END OF 4th GRADE) (CONT.)

(29)   Round these numbers to the nearest ten:

    67 = _____

    45 = _____

    311 = _____

(30)   Round these numbers to the nearest hundred:

    421 = _____

    838 = _____

    1471 = _____

(31)   Round these numbers to the nearest thousand:

    1099 = _____

    57502 = _____

PROBLEM-SOLVING AND APPLICATIONS SURVEY

Name _____**Date** _____

Work these problems. Show your work.

1. A school has 173 students in ninth grade, 166 in tenth grade, 94 in eleventh grade, and 85 in 12th grade. How many students are in the school?   _____

2. In question 1, how many more students are in the 9th grade than in the 12th grade?
                                                       _____

3. Judy, Ed, and Terry are going to share a piece of cheese which weighs 71 ounces. How many ounces will each of them get?
                                                       _____

4. Karen is painting the steps. If it takes her 21 minutes to paint the first step, how long will it take her to paint 4 steps?
                                          _____ hr. _____ min.

5. Jim spent $17.45 and bought a sweater, a belt, and a tie. The sweater cost $9.95 and the belt cost $5.25. How much did the tie cost?   _____

PROBLEM-SOLVING AND APPLICATIONS SURVEY (CONT.)

6. Kevin and Larry had the following recipe for a milkshake:

> Banana-Strawberry Milkshake
>
> serves 1
>
> 1 cup milk
> 2 scoops strawberry ice cream
> 1 banana, cut into pieces
> 6 strawberries, cut in half
>
> Put all the ingredients into a blender and blend
> on high speed until smooth.

Rewrite the recipe to show how it would read to make 4 milkshakes.

7.   TRAIN SCHEDULE   Philadelphia - New York

Train number	#121	#131	#141	#151	#161	#171	#181	#191	#201
	a.m.	a.m.	a.m.	a.m.	p.m.	p.m.	p.m.	p.m.	p.m.
Philadelphia	6:00	7:05	8:20	10:00	12:20	2:52	4:09	5:00	6:01
Trenton	6:25	7:39	8:53	10:28	1:30	3:20		5:28	6:34
Princeton	6:36	7:49	9:02		1:40			5:36	
New Brunswick	6:58	8:07			1:55	3:50		5:49	
Newark	7:07	8:32	9:38	11:05	2:25	4:00	5:25	6:08	7:20
New York (ar)	7:21	8:47	9:54	11:17	2:42	4:17	5:41	6:22	7:37

a. What time would you leave Philadelphia to arrive in New York
    at 11:17 a.m.? _____

b. Which trains do not stop in either Princeton or New Brunswick? _____

c. Which train takes the shortest time to travel between Philadelphia
    and New York? _____   the longest time? _____

d. If I took #171, how long would it take me to travel between
    New Brunswick and New York? _____

e. If I live in New Brunswick and want to be home from Philadelphia
    by 5:00 p.m., what train should I take? _____

②

SURVEY OF FREE-TIME INTERESTS

Name _____**Date** _____

Check the things you like to do during free time.

____1. Play games   ____Scrabble   ____Battleship

                        ____checkers   ____Othello

                        ____chess   ____Backgammon

____2. Read books   ____animal stories   ____space/sci-fi

                        ____sports stories

                        ____adventure stories

____3. Read magazines ____sports   ____Mad

                        ____cars   ____TV/movie

                        ____comic books   ____news

____4. Use AV equip-
        ment   ____tapes   ____record player

                        ____filmstrips   ____typewriter

____5. Make things   ____puzzles   ____erector set

                        ____lego   ____models

                        ____lincoln logs   ____art projects

____6. Help the
        teacher   ____clean boards   ____run dittos

                        ____water plants   ____clean fish bowl

____7. List other things you would like to do during free time.

        _____   _____   _____

        _____   _____   _____

        _____   _____   _____

(1)

INTEREST INVENTORY

Name _____ **Date** _____

1. If I could do anything I wanted, I would _____

    _____

2. When I grow up I would like to _____

    _____

3. My favorite movies are _____

    _____

4. My favorite TV shows are _____

    _____

5. The books I like to read are about _____

    _____

6. I think the most interesting job is _____

    _____

7. If I had $100.00 I would spend it on _____

    _____

8. When I am with my friends I like to _____

    _____

9. When I am with my family I like to _____

    _____

10. When I am alone I like to _____

    _____

11. Put a check ( ) beside the things that interest you.

    ___cars   ___music   ___radio   ___puzzles   ___fashion

    ___sports   ___movies   ___acting   ___food/cooking ___CB

    ___animals   ___TV   ___books   ___news   ___body building

    others _____

_____

①

Indexes

AUTHOR INDEX